PO/08

DRAMACON

Created by
Svetlana Chmakova

HAMBURG // LONDON // LOS ANGELES // TOKYO

Dramacon Vol. 1
Created by Svetlana Chmakova

Digital Toning Assistants - Alexis Tyrala and J. Dee DuPuy
Lettering - Jason Milligan
Production Artist - Jason Milligan
Cover Design - Seth Cable

Editor - Lillian Diaz-Przybyl
Digital Imaging Manager - Chris Buford
Production Managers - Jennifer Miller and Mutsumi Miyazaki
Managing Editor - Lindsey Johnston
Editorial Director - Jeremy Ross
VP of Production - Ron Klamert
Publisher and E.I.C. - Mike Kiley
President and C.O.O. - John Parker
C.E.O. - Stuart Levy

A  Manga

TOKYOPOP Inc.
5900 Wilshire Blvd. Suite 2000
Los Angeles, CA 90036

E-mail: info@TOKYOPOP.com
Come visit us online at www.TOKYOPOP.com

ISBN: 1-59816-129-6

First TOKYOPOP printing: October 2005
10 9 8 7 6 5 4
Printed in the USA

GRAPH
CHMA
KOVA
v.1

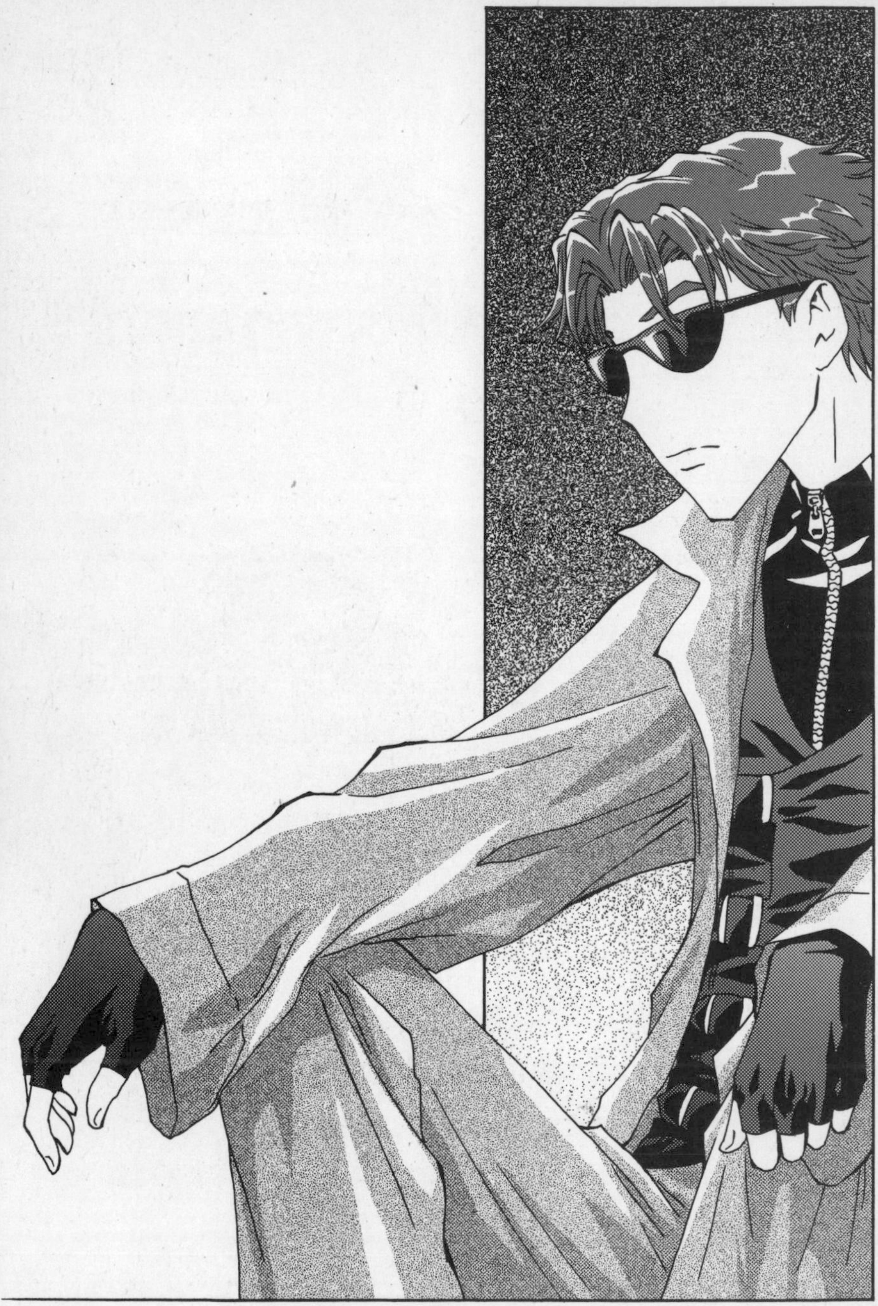

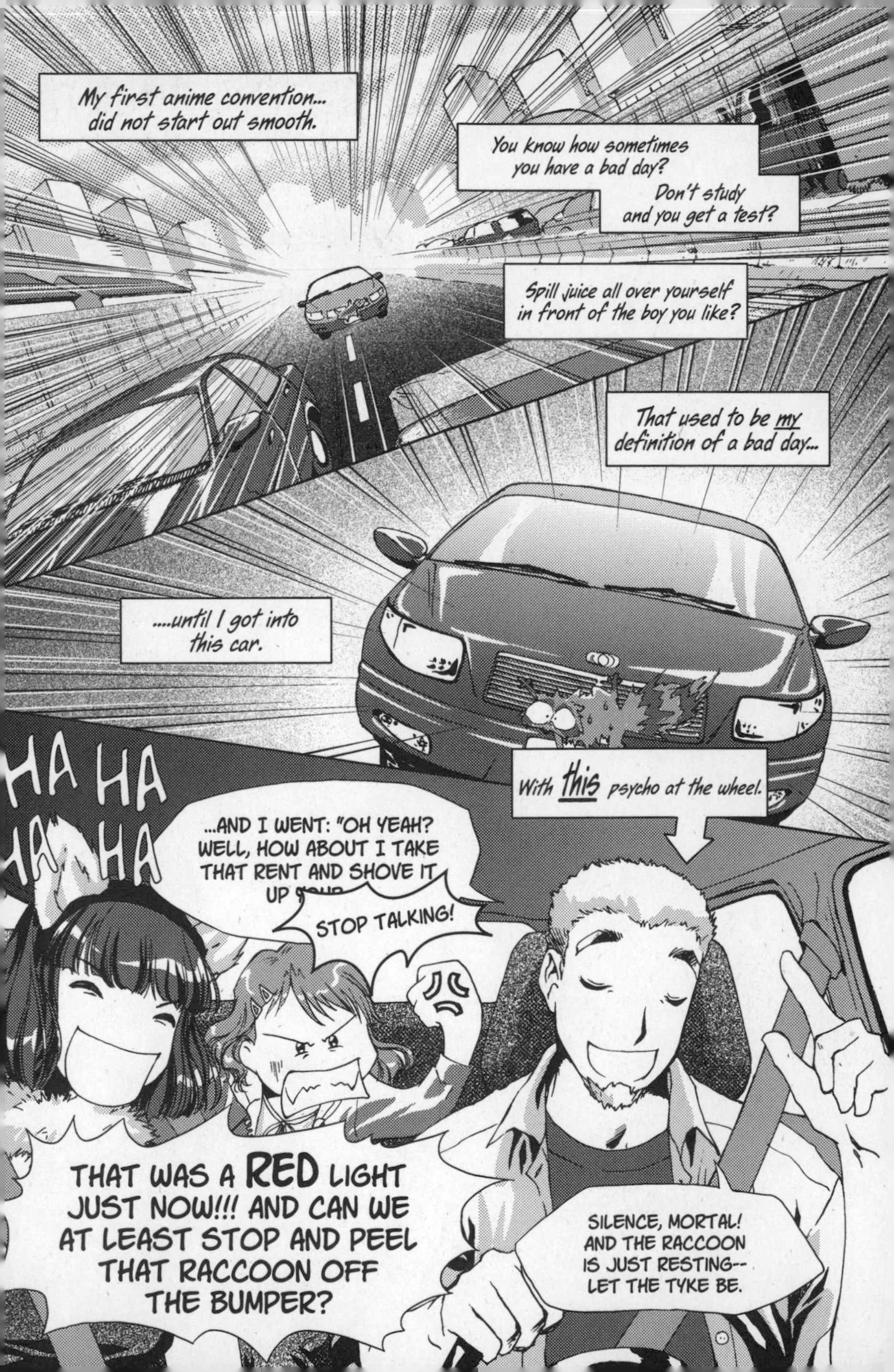
My first anime convention... did not start out smooth.
You know how sometimes you have a bad day?
Don't study and you get a test?
Spill juice all over yourself in front of the boy you like?
That used to be my definition of a bad day...
....until I got into this car.
With this psycho at the wheel.
HA HA HA HA
...AND I WENT: "OH YEAH? WELL, HOW ABOUT I TAKE THAT RENT AND SHOVE IT UP
STOP TALKING!
THAT WAS A RED LIGHT JUST NOW!!! AND CAN WE AT LEAST STOP AND PEEL THAT RACCOON OFF THE BUMPER?
SILENCE, MORTAL! AND THE RACCOON IS JUST RESTING-- LET THE TYKE BE.

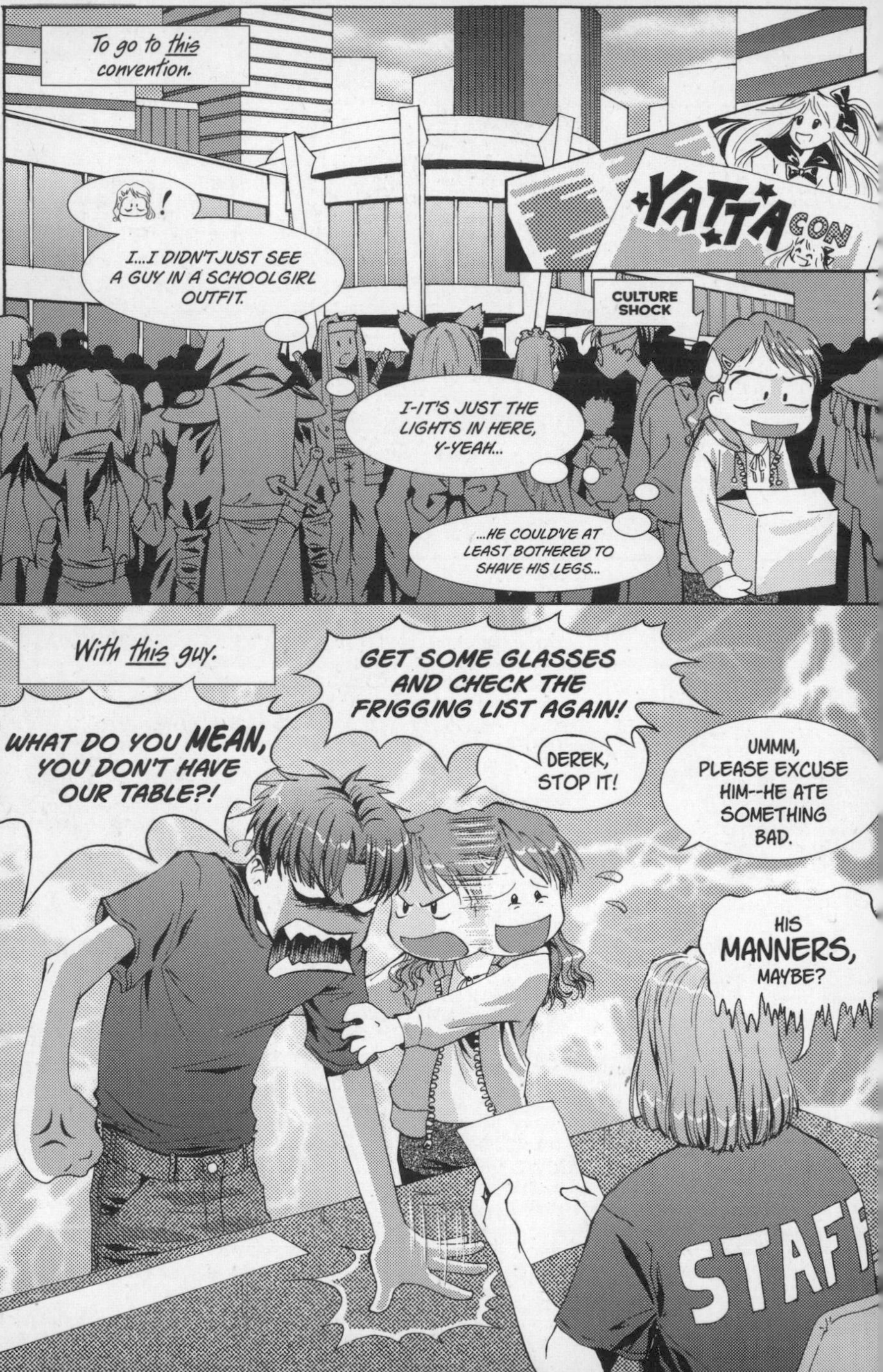
To go to this convention.
!
I...I DIDN'T JUST SEE A GUY IN A SCHOOLGIRL OUTFIT.
YATTA CON
CULTURE SHOCK
I-IT'S JUST THE LIGHTS IN HERE, Y-YEAH...
...HE COULD'VE AT LEAST BOTHERED TO SHAVE HIS LEGS...
With this guy.
GET SOME GLASSES AND CHECK THE FRIGGING LIST AGAIN!
WHAT DO YOU MEAN, YOU DON'T HAVE OUR TABLE?!
DEREK, STOP IT!
UMMM, PLEASE EXCUSE HIM--HE ATE SOMETHING BAD.
HIS MANNERS, MAYBE?
STAFF

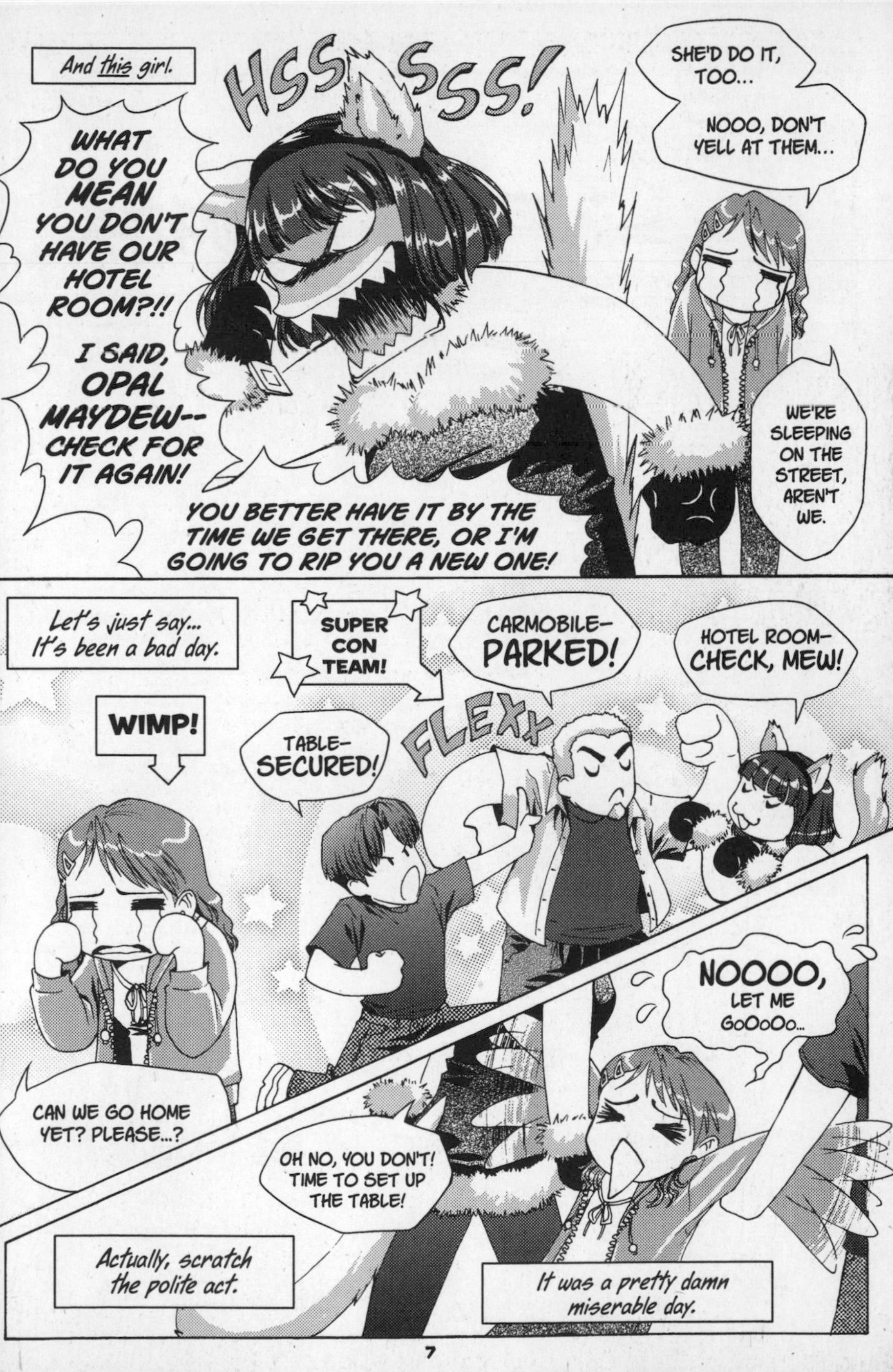
And this girl.
HSS SSS!
WHAT DO YOU MEAN YOU DON'T HAVE OUR HOTEL ROOM?!! I SAID, OPAL MAYDEW-- CHECK FOR IT AGAIN!
YOU BETTER HAVE IT BY THE TIME WE GET THERE, OR I'M GOING TO RIP YOU A NEW ONE!
SHE'D DO IT, TOO...
NOOO, DON'T YELL AT THEM...
WE'RE SLEEPING ON THE STREET, AREN'T WE.
Let's just say... It's been a bad day.
SUPER CON TEAM!
CARMOBILE- PARKED!
HOTEL ROOM- CHECK, MEW!
WIMP!
TABLE- SECURED!
FLEXX
CAN WE GO HOME YET? PLEASE...?
NOOOO, LET ME GoOoOo...
OH NO, YOU DON'T! TIME TO SET UP THE TABLE!
Actually, scratch the polite act.
It was a pretty damn miserable day.

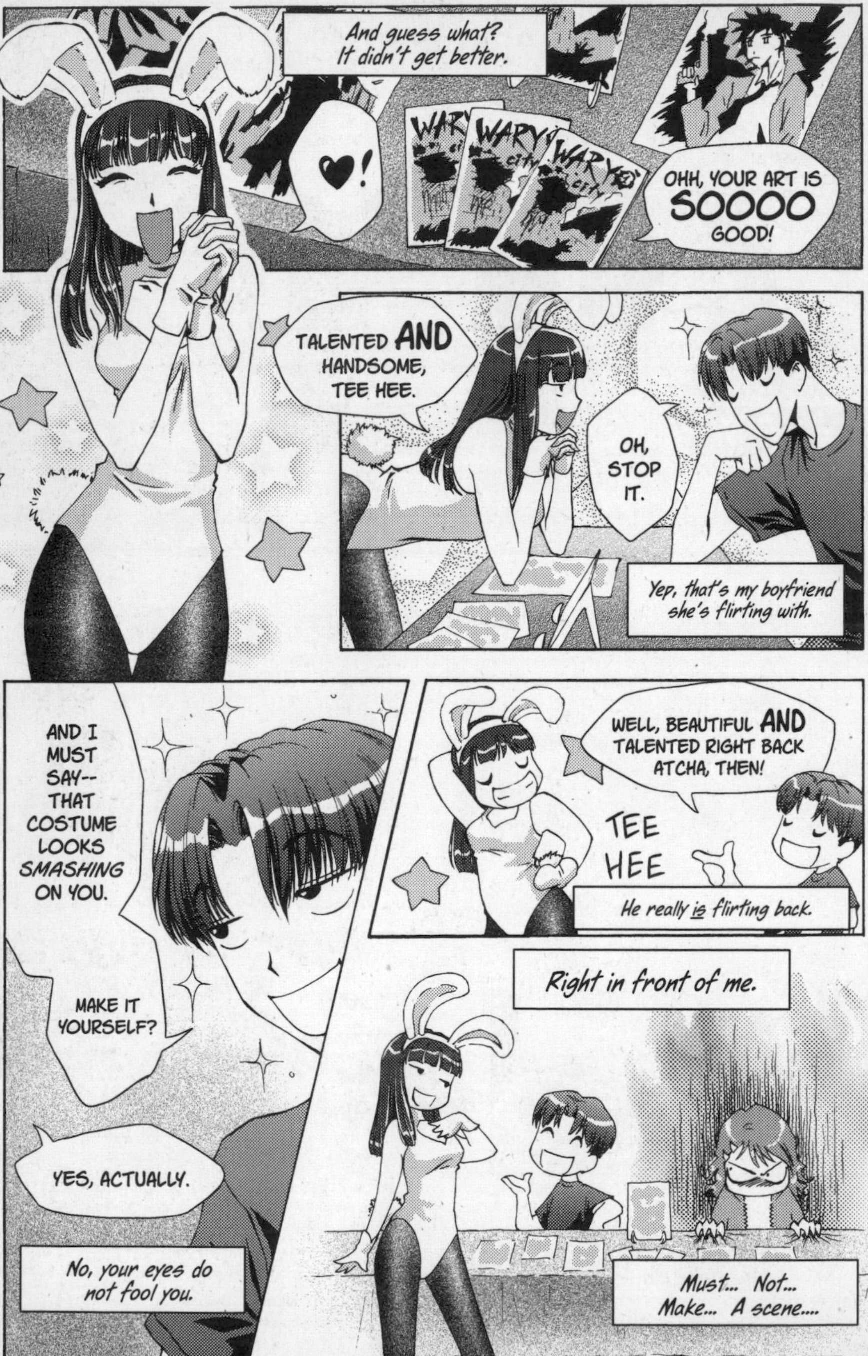

And guess what? It didn't get better.
♥!
OHH, YOUR ART IS SOOOO GOOD!
TALENTED AND HANDSOME, TEE HEE.
OH, STOP IT.
Yep, that's my boyfriend she's flirting with.
AND I MUST SAY-- THAT COSTUME LOOKS SMASHING ON YOU.
MAKE IT YOURSELF?
YES, ACTUALLY.
No, your eyes do not fool you.
WELL, BEAUTIFUL AND TALENTED RIGHT BACK ATCHA, THEN!
TEE HEE
He really is flirting back.
Right in front of me.
Must... Not... Make... A scene....

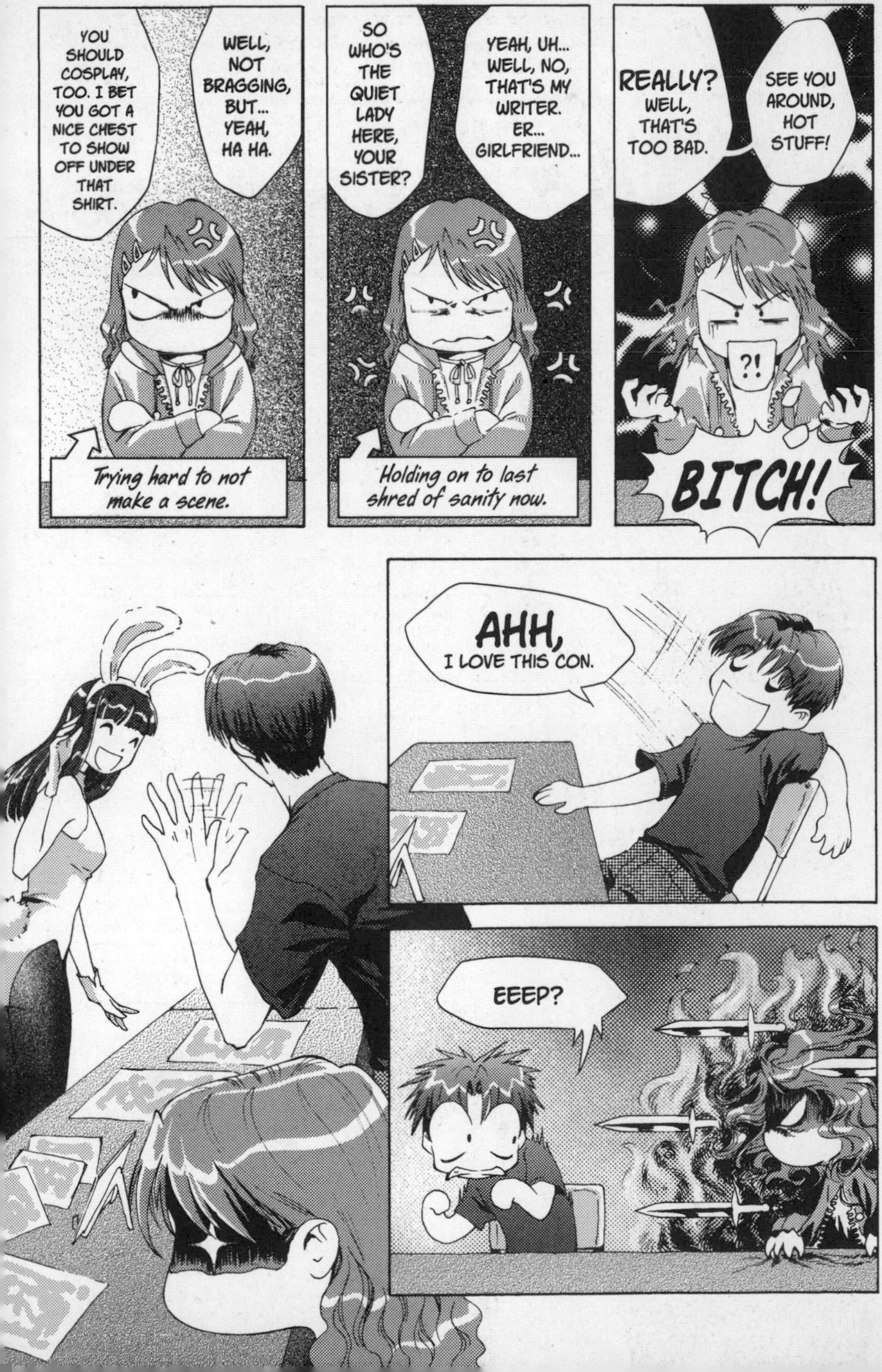
YOU SHOULD COSPLAY, TOO. I BET YOU GOT A NICE CHEST TO SHOW OFF UNDER THAT SHIRT.
WELL, NOT BRAGGING, BUT... YEAH, HA HA.
Trying hard to not make a scene.
SO WHO'S THE QUIET LADY HERE, YOUR SISTER?
YEAH, UH... WELL, NO, THAT'S MY WRITER. ER... GIRLFRIEND...
Holding on to last shred of sanity now.
REALLY? WELL, THAT'S TOO BAD.
SEE YOU AROUND, HOT STUFF!
?!
BITCH!
AHH, I LOVE THIS CON.
EEEP?

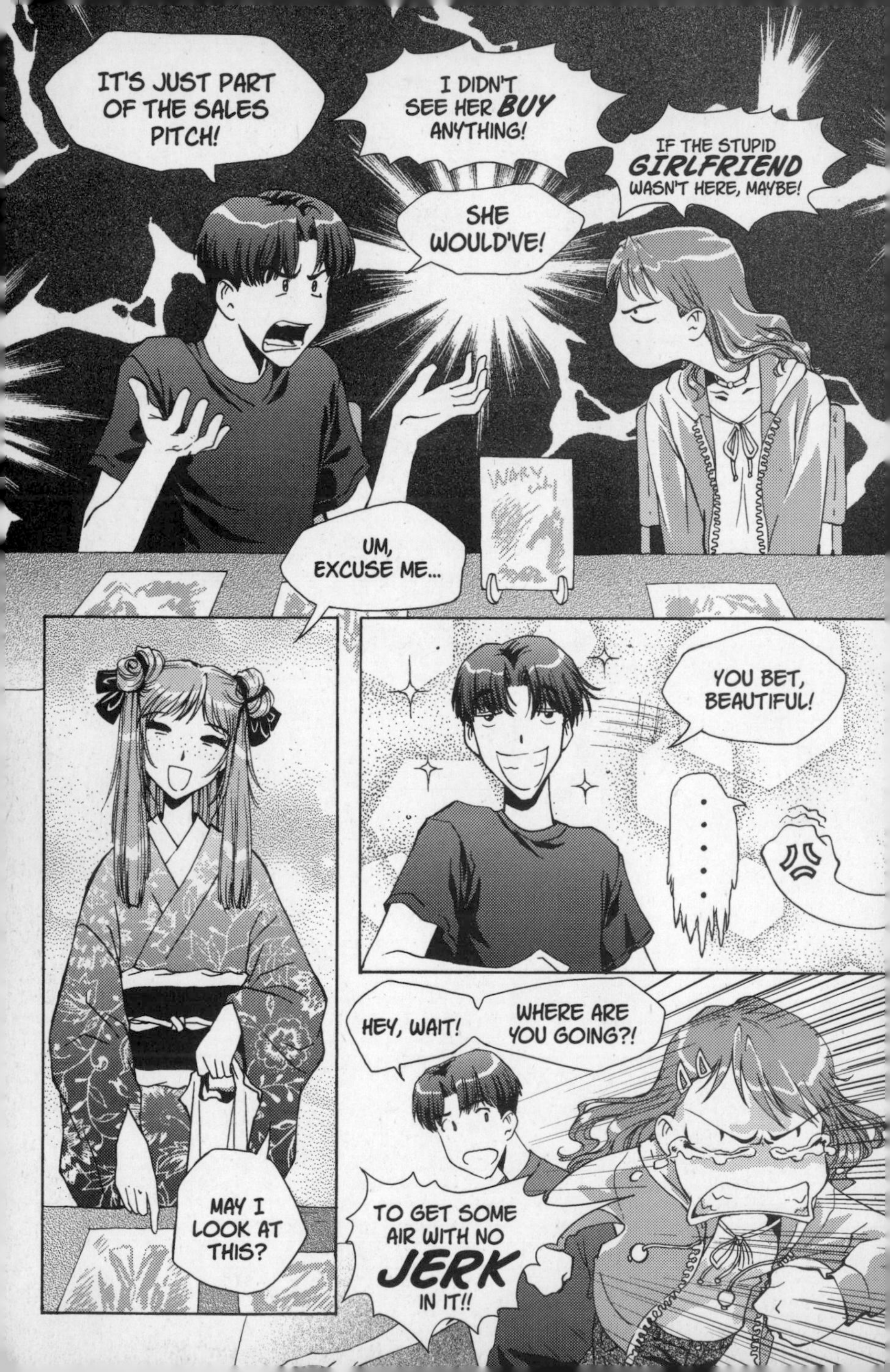
IT'S JUST PART OF THE SALES PITCH!
I DIDN'T SEE HER BUY ANYTHING!
SHE WOULD'VE!
IF THE STUPID GIRLFRIEND WASN'T HERE, MAYBE!
UM, EXCUSE ME...
MAY I LOOK AT THIS?
YOU BET, BEAUTIFUL!
.....
HEY, WAIT!
WHERE ARE YOU GOING?!
TO GET SOME AIR WITH NO JERK IN IT!!

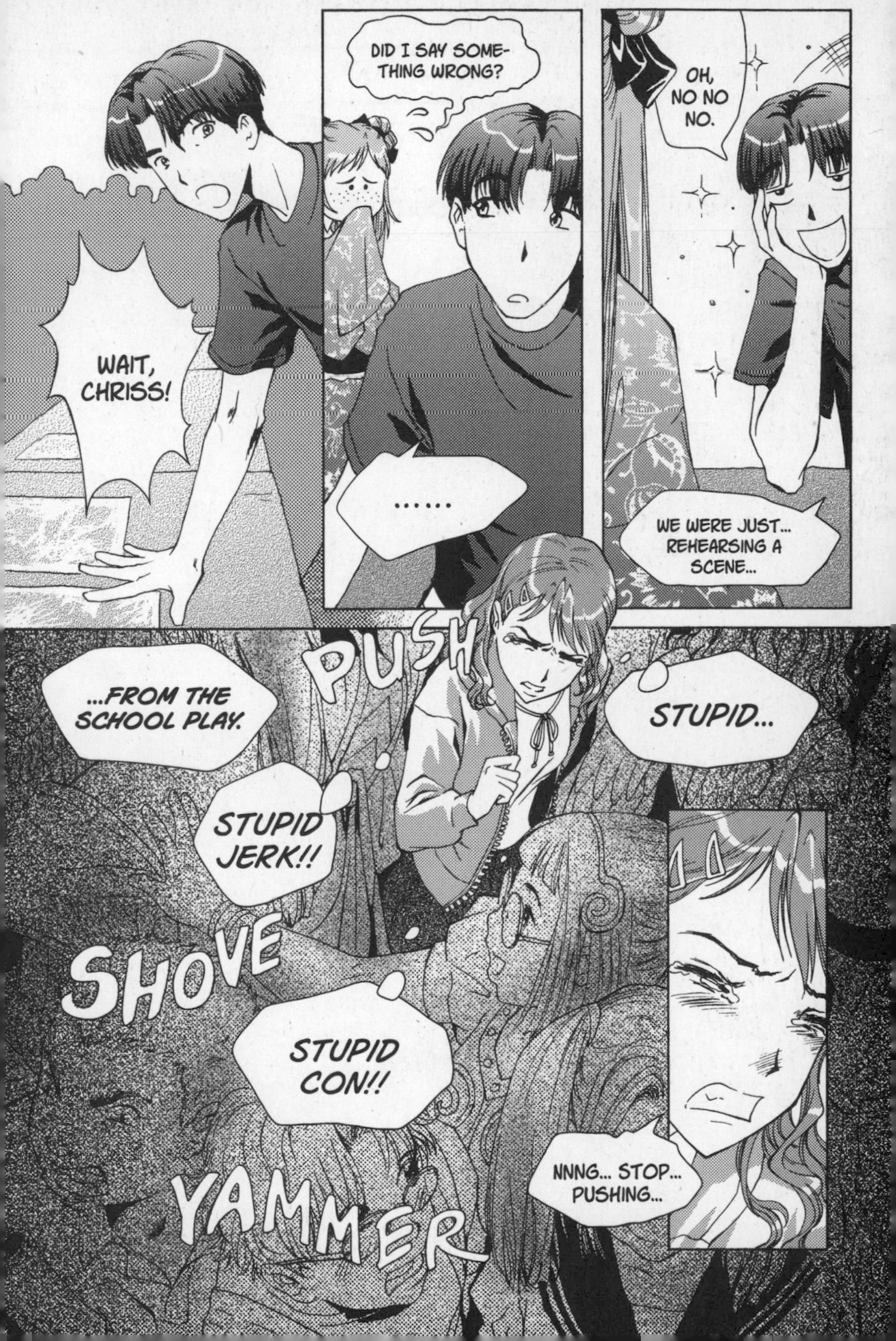
WAIT, CHRISS!
DID I SAY SOME-THING WRONG?
......
OH, NO NO NO.
WE WERE JUST... REHEARSING A SCENE...
...FROM THE SCHOOL PLAY.
PUSH
STUPID...
STUPID JERK!!
SHOVE
STUPID CON!!
YAMMER
NNNG... STOP... PUSHING...

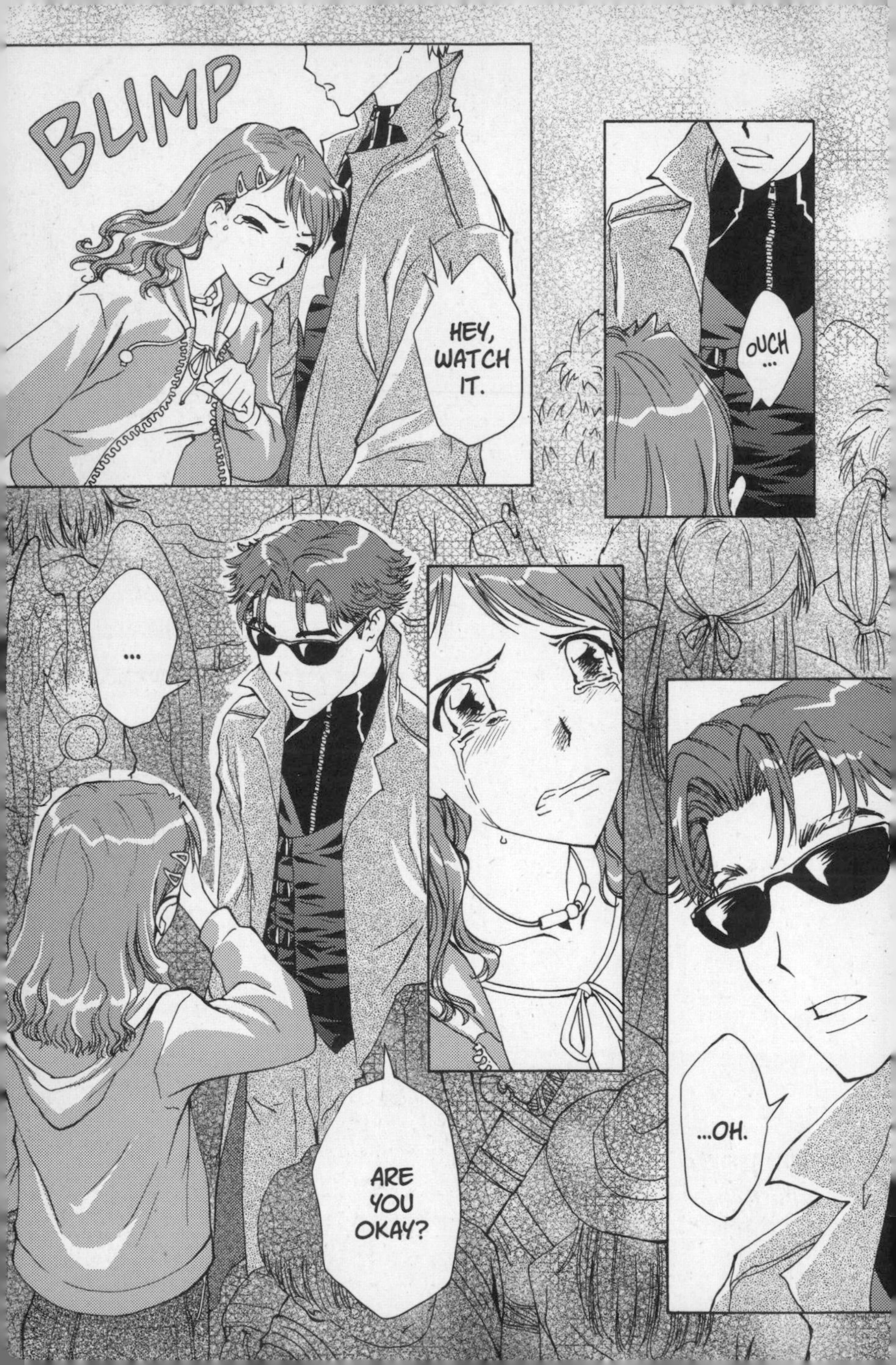
BUMP
HEY, WATCH IT.
OUCH ...
...
ARE YOU OKAY?
...OH.

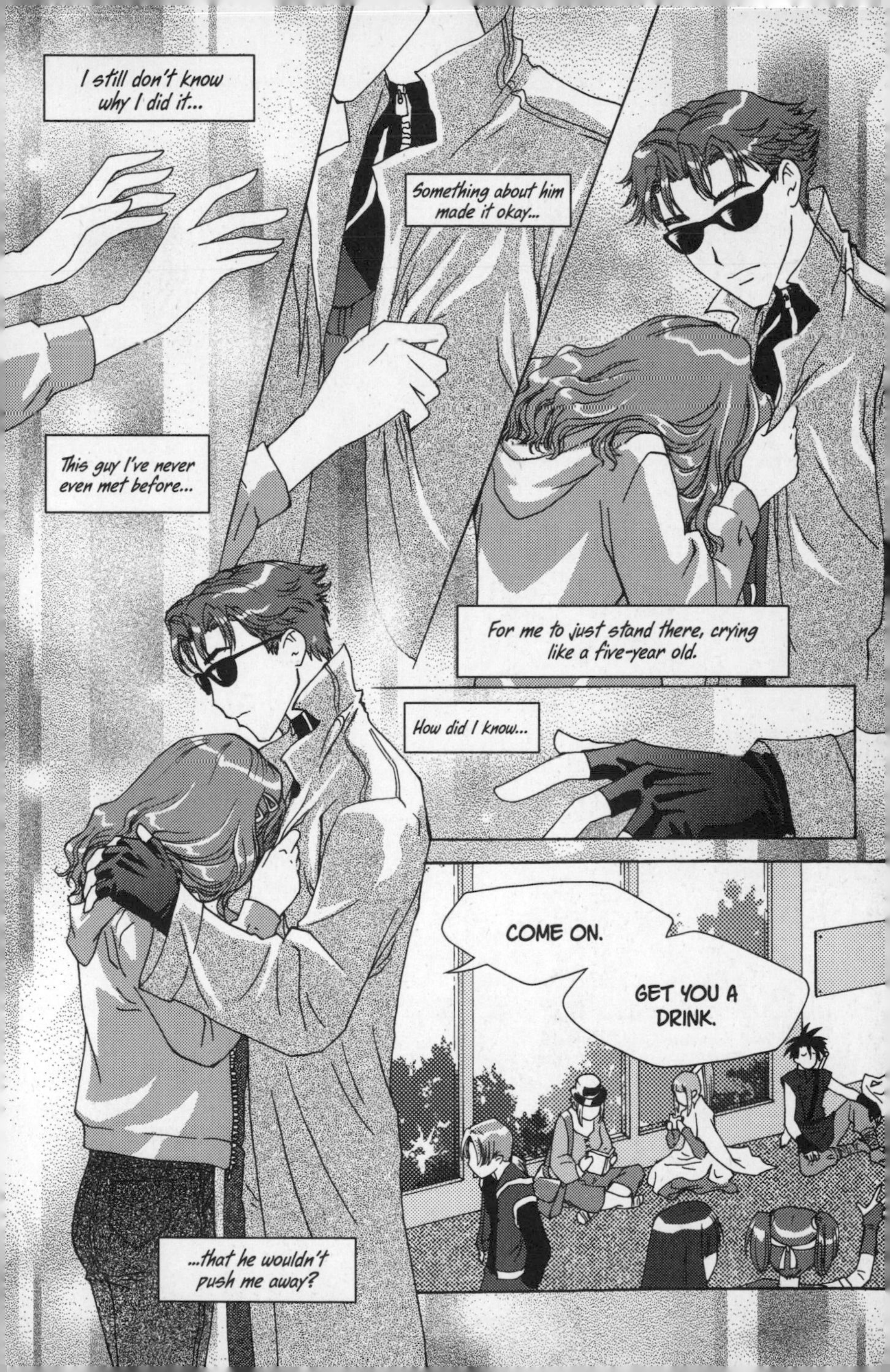
I still don't know why I did it...
Something about him made it okay...
This guy I've never even met before...
For me to just stand there, crying like a five-year old.
How did I know...
...that he wouldn't push me away?
COME ON.
GET YOU A DRINK.

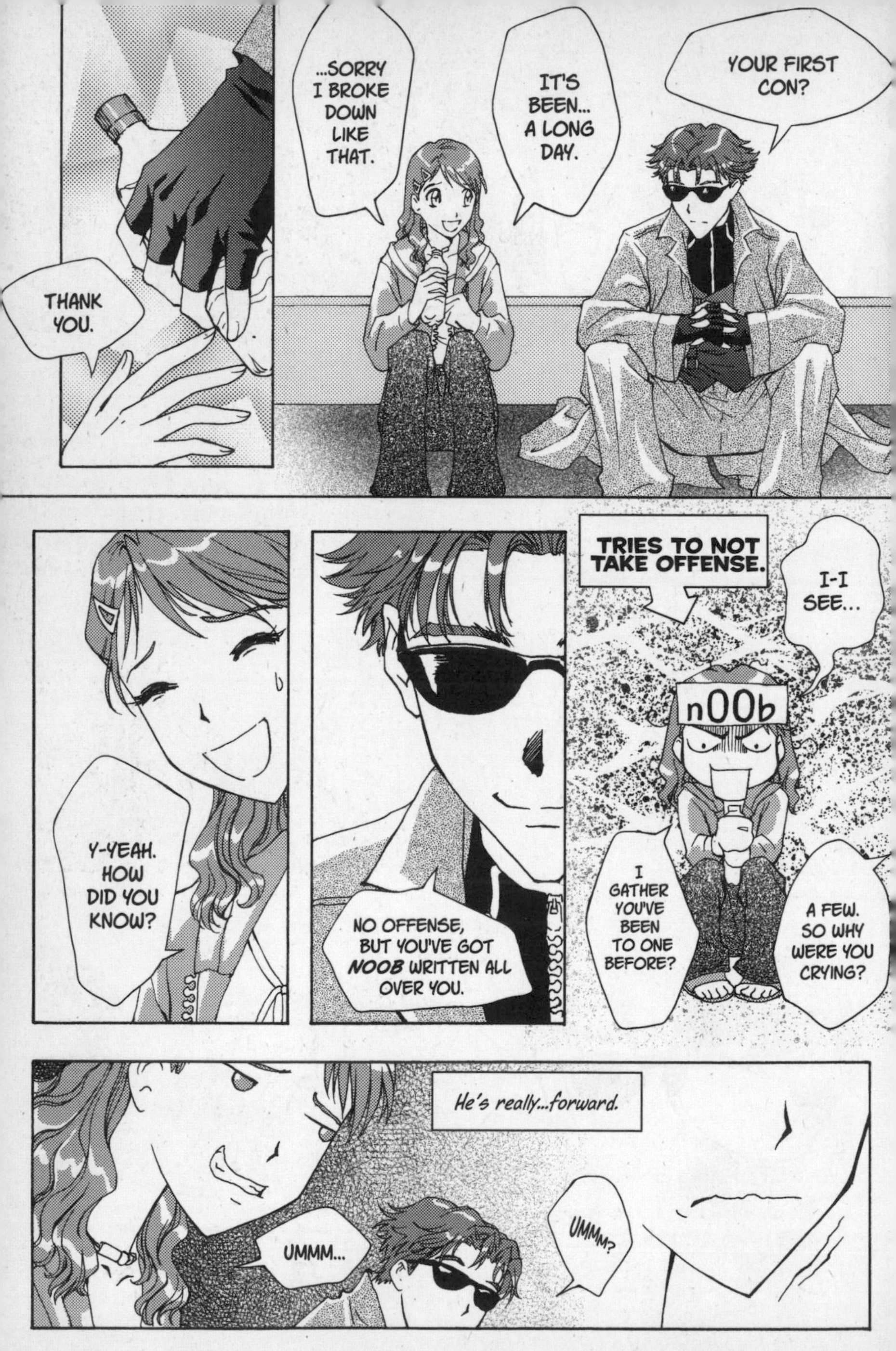
THANK YOU.
...SORRY I BROKE DOWN LIKE THAT.
IT'S BEEN... A LONG DAY.
YOUR FIRST CON?
Y-YEAH. HOW DID YOU KNOW?
NO OFFENSE, BUT YOU'VE GOT *NOOB* WRITTEN ALL OVER YOU.
TRIES TO NOT TAKE OFFENSE.
I-I SEE...
n00b
I GATHER YOU'VE BEEN TO ONE BEFORE?
A FEW. SO WHY WERE YOU CRYING?
He's really...forward.
UMMM...
UMMm?

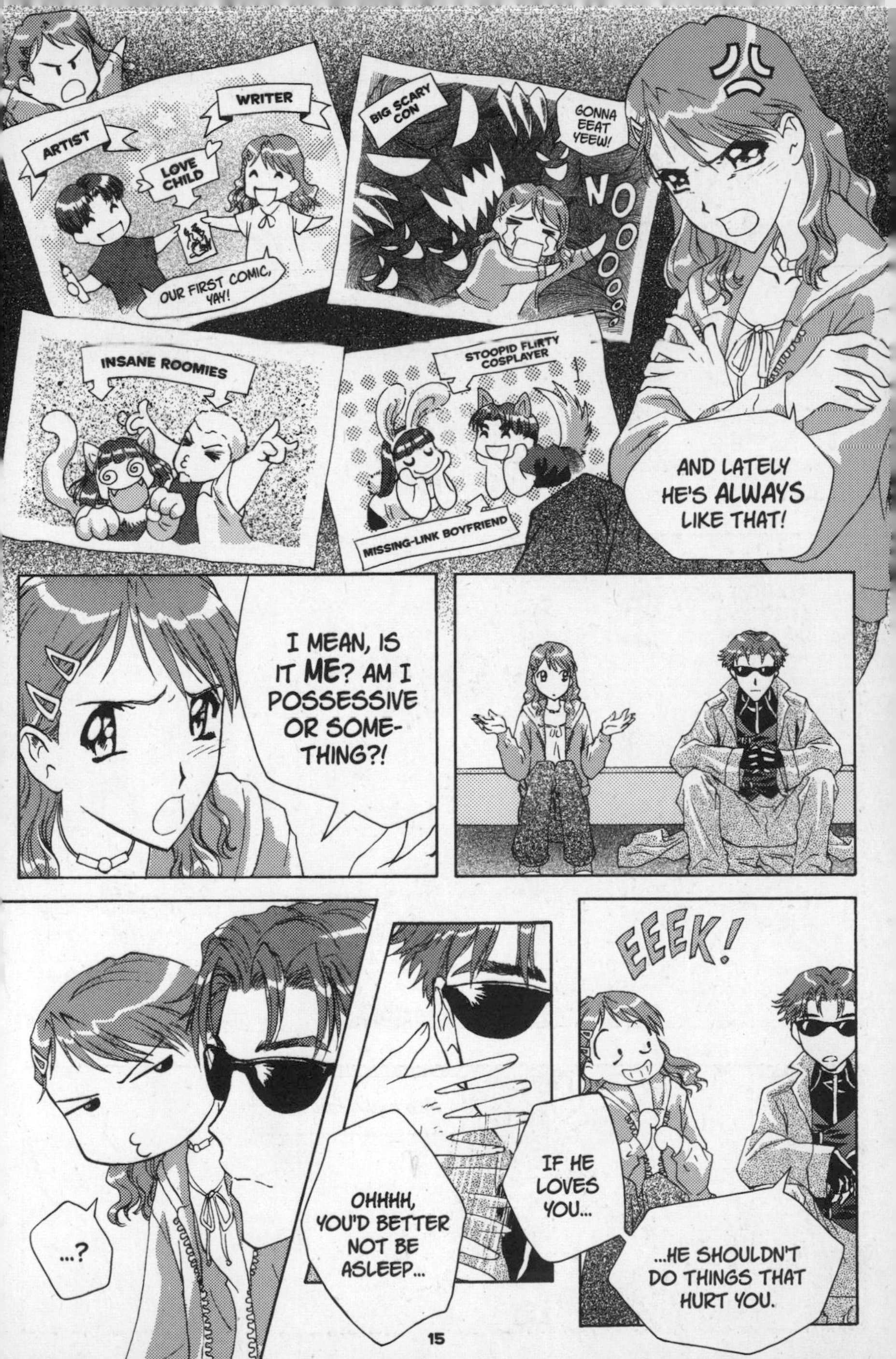
ARTIST
WRITER
LOVE CHILD
OUR FIRST COMIC, YAY!
BIG SCARY CON
GONNA EEAT YEEW!
NOOOOOOOO
INSANE ROOMIES
STOOPID FLIRTY COSPLAYER
MISSING-LINK BOYFRIEND
AND LATELY HE'S ALWAYS LIKE THAT!
I MEAN, IS IT ME? AM I POSSESSIVE OR SOME-THING?!
...?
OHHHH, YOU'D BETTER NOT BE ASLEEP...
EEEK!
IF HE LOVES YOU...
...HE SHOULDN'T DO THINGS THAT HURT YOU.

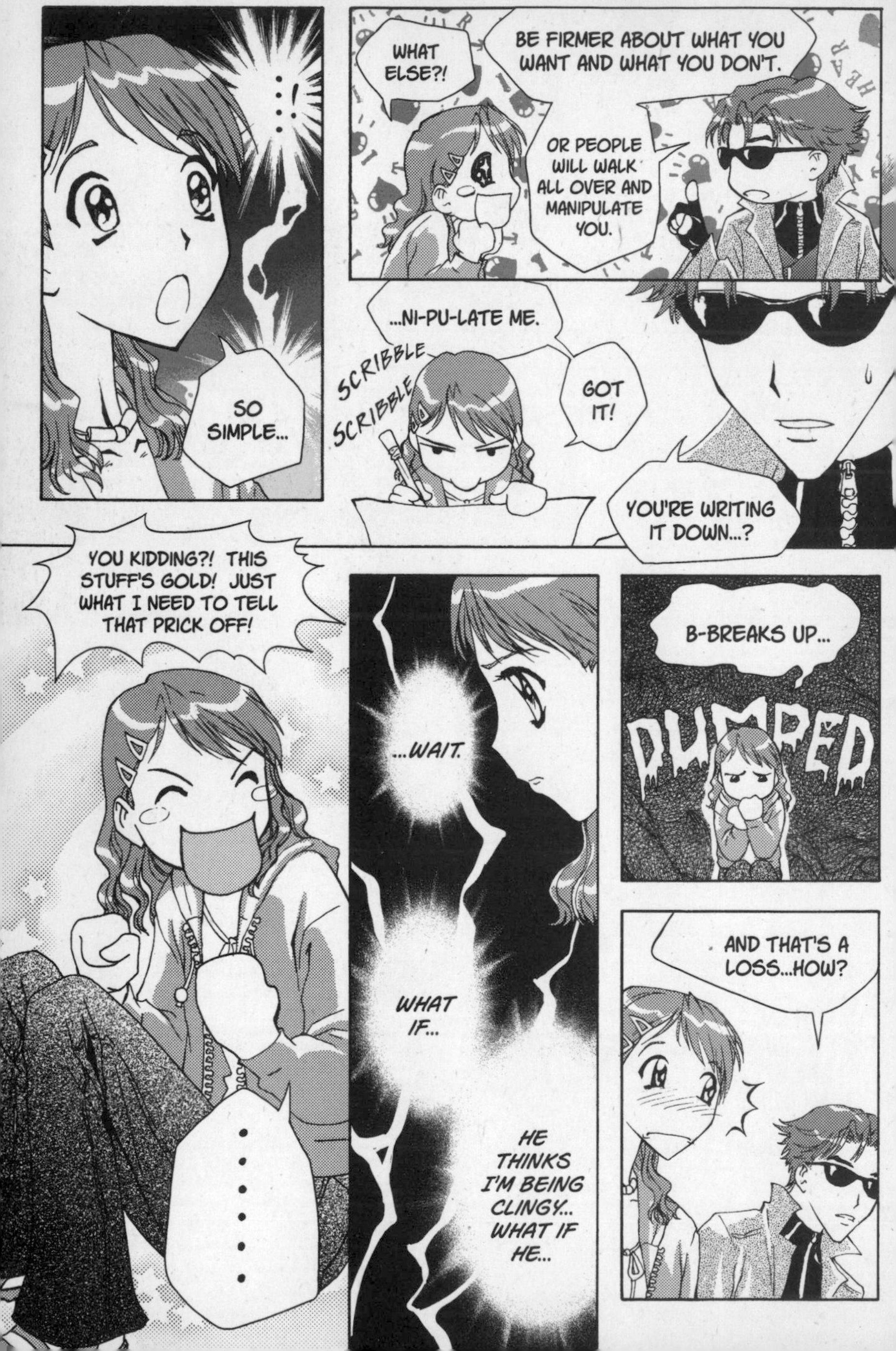
...!
SO SIMPLE...
WHAT ELSE?!
BE FIRMER ABOUT WHAT YOU WANT AND WHAT YOU DON'T.
OR PEOPLE WILL WALK ALL OVER AND MANIPULATE YOU.
...NI-PU-LATE ME.
SCRIBBLE
SCRIBBLE
GOT IT!
YOU'RE WRITING IT DOWN...?
YOU KIDDING?! THIS STUFF'S GOLD! JUST WHAT I NEED TO TELL THAT PRICK OFF!
......
...WAIT.
WHAT IF...
HE THINKS I'M BEING CLINGY... WHAT IF HE...
B-BREAKS UP...
DUMPED
AND THAT'S A LOSS...HOW?

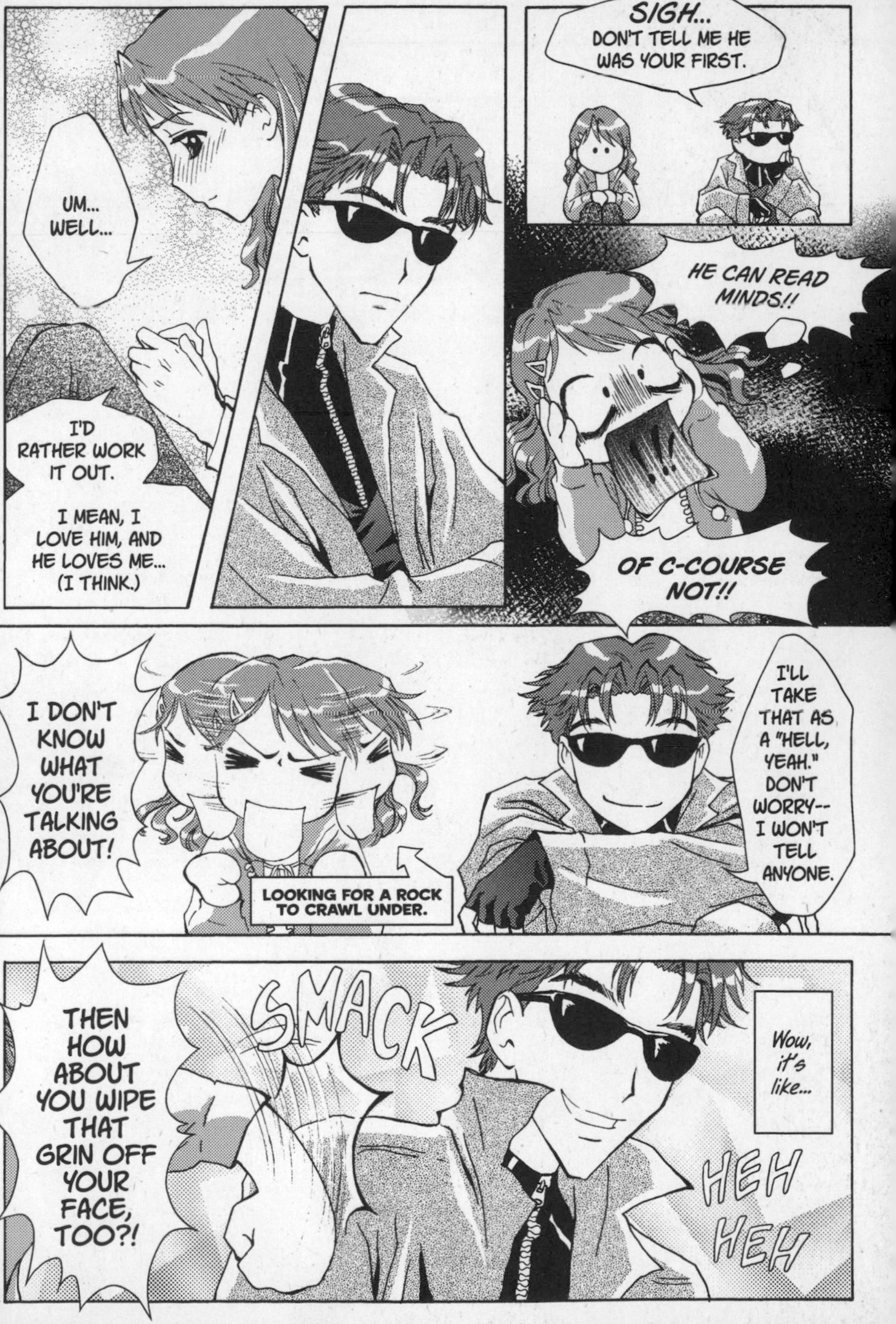
UM... WELL...
I'D RATHER WORK IT OUT.
I MEAN, I LOVE HIM, AND HE LOVES ME... (I THINK.)
SIGH... DON'T TELL ME HE WAS YOUR FIRST.
HE CAN READ MINDS!!
OF C-COURSE NOT!!
I DON'T KNOW WHAT YOU'RE TALKING ABOUT!
LOOKING FOR A ROCK TO CRAWL UNDER.
I'LL TAKE THAT AS A "HELL, YEAH." DON'T WORRY-- I WON'T TELL ANYONE.
THEN HOW ABOUT YOU WIPE THAT GRIN OFF YOUR FACE, TOO?!
SMACK
Wow, it's like...
HEH HEH

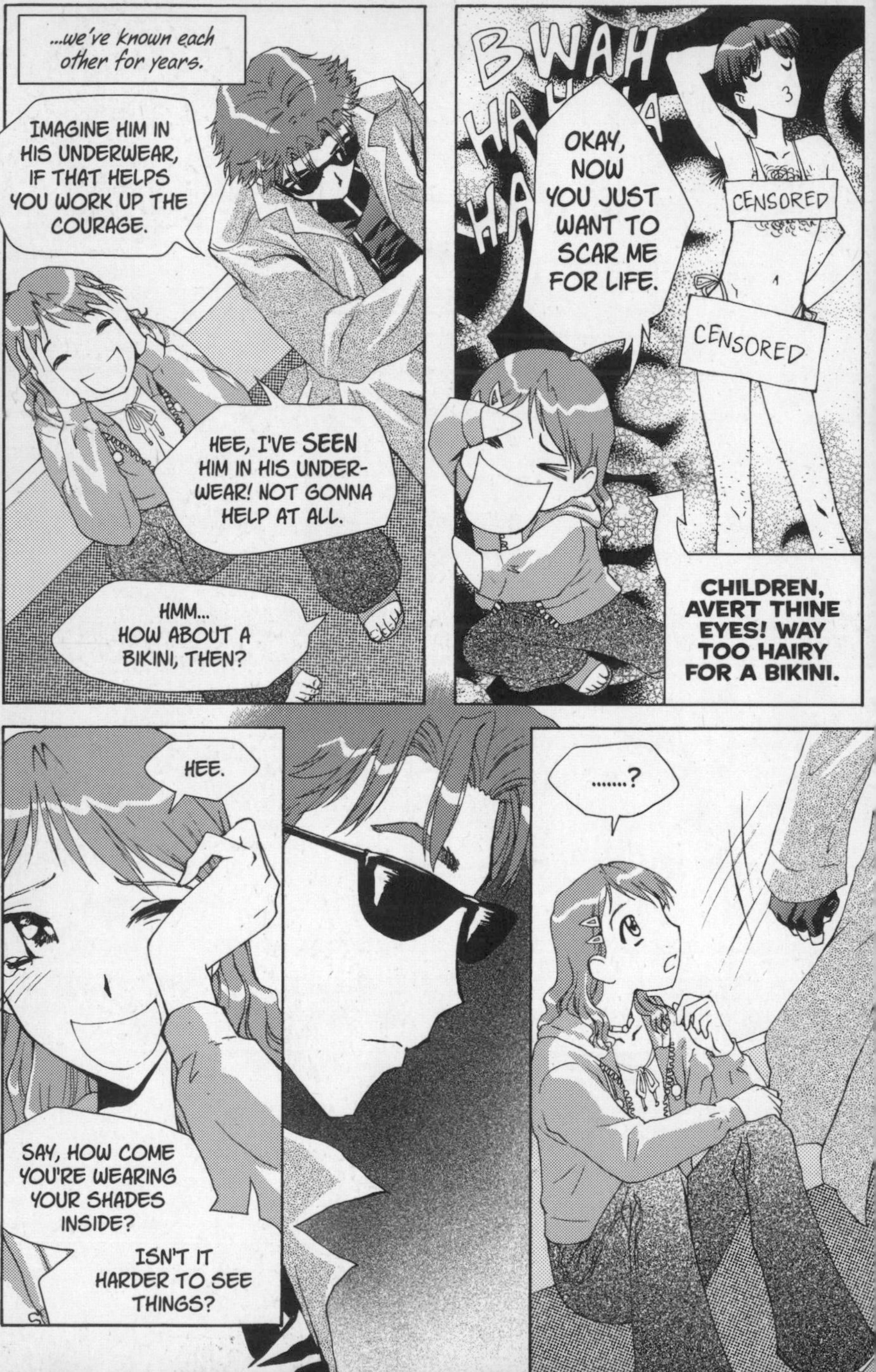
...we've known each other for years.
IMAGINE HIM IN HIS UNDERWEAR, IF THAT HELPS YOU WORK UP THE COURAGE.
HEE, I'VE SEEN HIM IN HIS UNDER-WEAR! NOT GONNA HELP AT ALL.
HMM... HOW ABOUT A BIKINI, THEN?
BWAH
OKAY, NOW YOU JUST WANT TO SCAR ME FOR LIFE.
CENSORED
CENSORED
CHILDREN, AVERT THINE EYES! WAY TOO HAIRY FOR A BIKINI.
HEE.
SAY, HOW COME YOU'RE WEARING YOUR SHADES INSIDE?
ISN'T IT HARDER TO SEE THINGS?
.......?

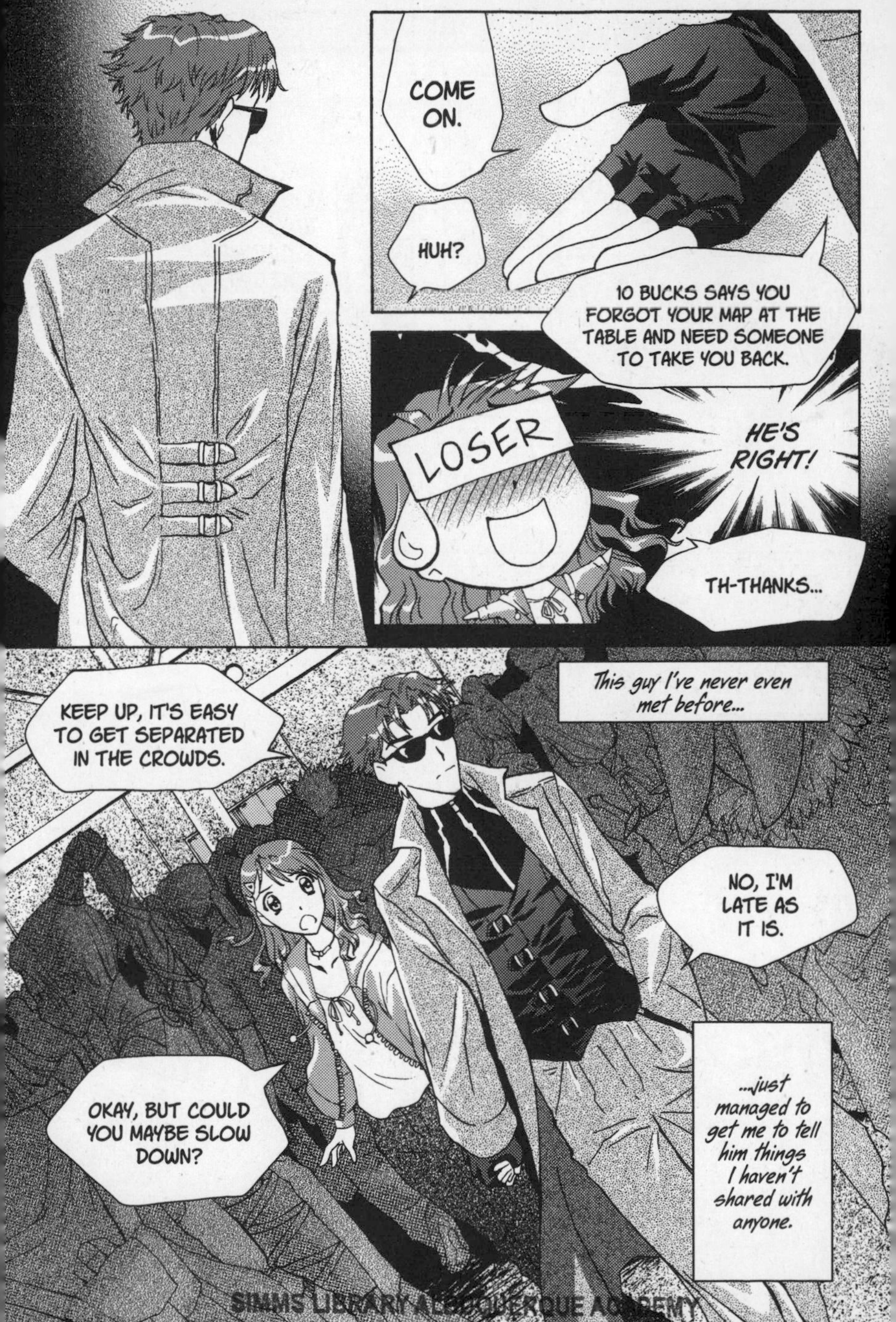
COME ON.
HUH?
10 BUCKS SAYS YOU FORGOT YOUR MAP AT THE TABLE AND NEED SOMEONE TO TAKE YOU BACK.
LOSER
HE'S RIGHT!
TH-THANKS...
KEEP UP, IT'S EASY TO GET SEPARATED IN THE CROWDS.
This guy I've never even met before...
NO, I'M LATE AS IT IS.
OKAY, BUT COULD YOU MAYBE SLOW DOWN?
...just managed to get me to tell him things I haven't shared with anyone.

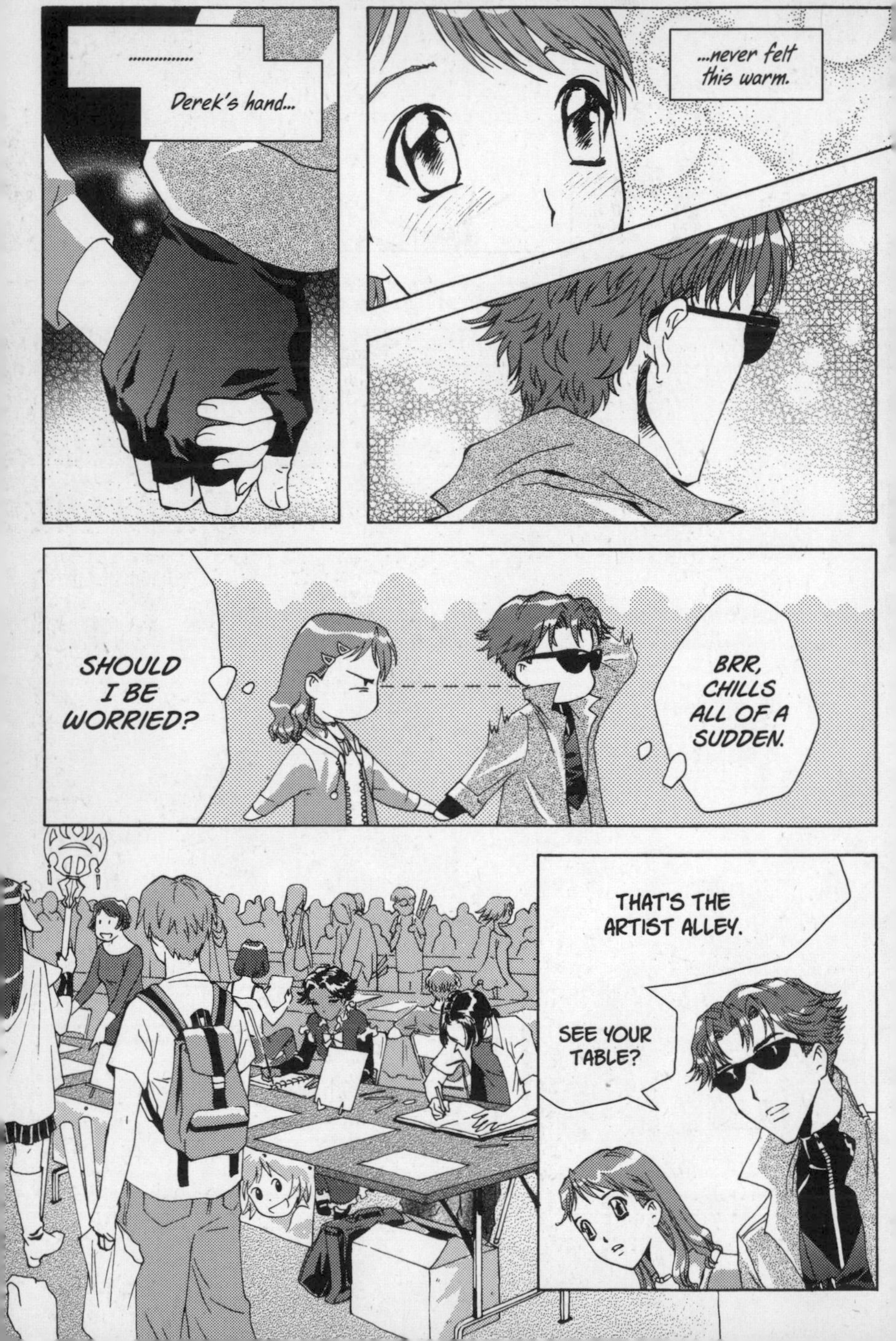
....
Derek's hand...
...never felt this warm.
SHOULD I BE WORRIED?
BRR, CHILLS ALL OF A SUDDEN.
THAT'S THE ARTIST ALLEY.
SEE YOUR TABLE?

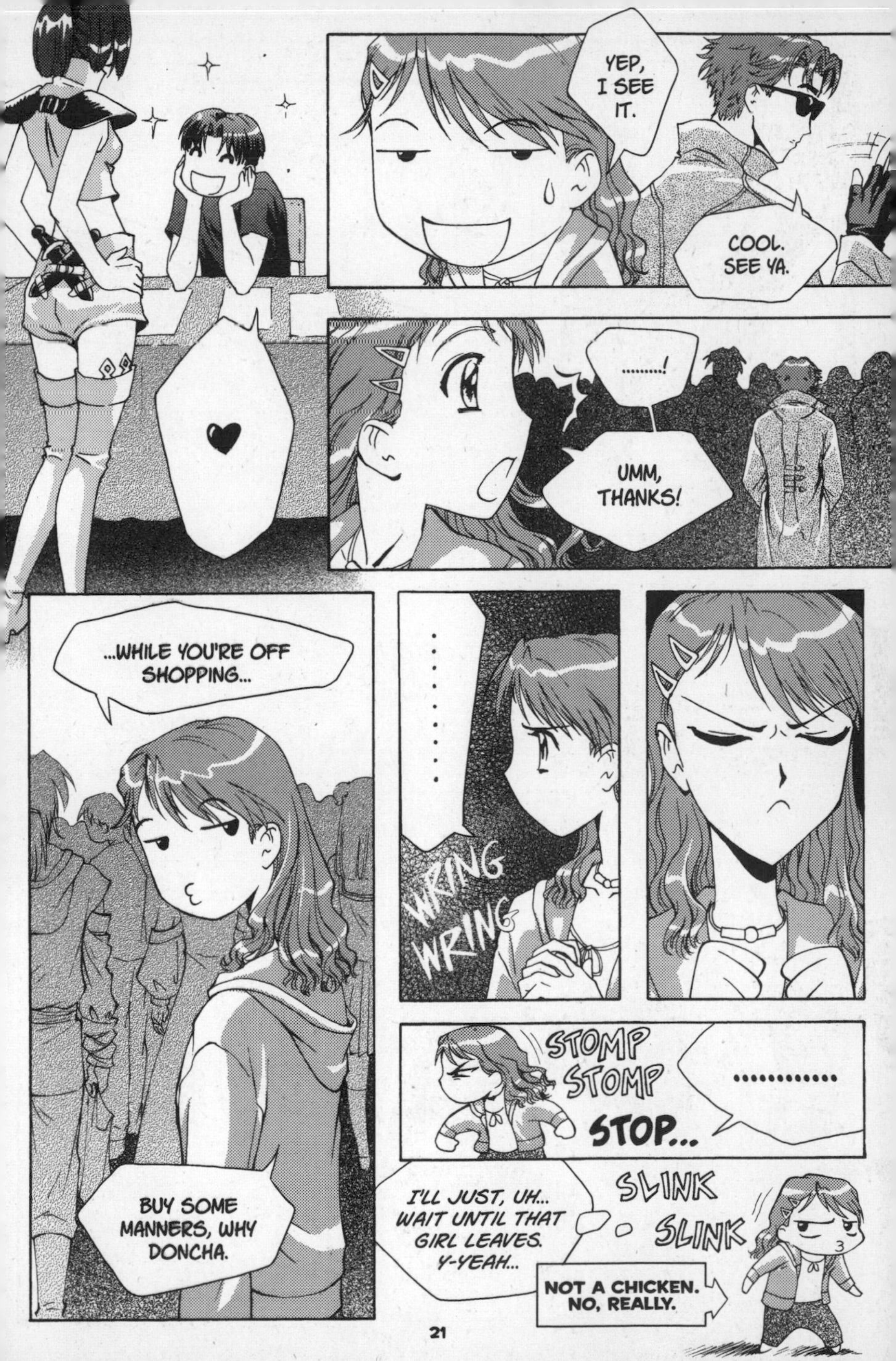

YEP, I SEE IT.
COOL. SEE YA.
.........!
UMM, THANKS!
...WHILE YOU'RE OFF SHOPPING...
BUY SOME MANNERS, WHY DONCHA.
....
WRING WRING
STOMP STOMP STOP...
....
I'LL JUST, UH... WAIT UNTIL THAT GIRL LEAVES. Y-YEAH...
SLINK SLINK
NOT A CHICKEN. NO, REALLY.

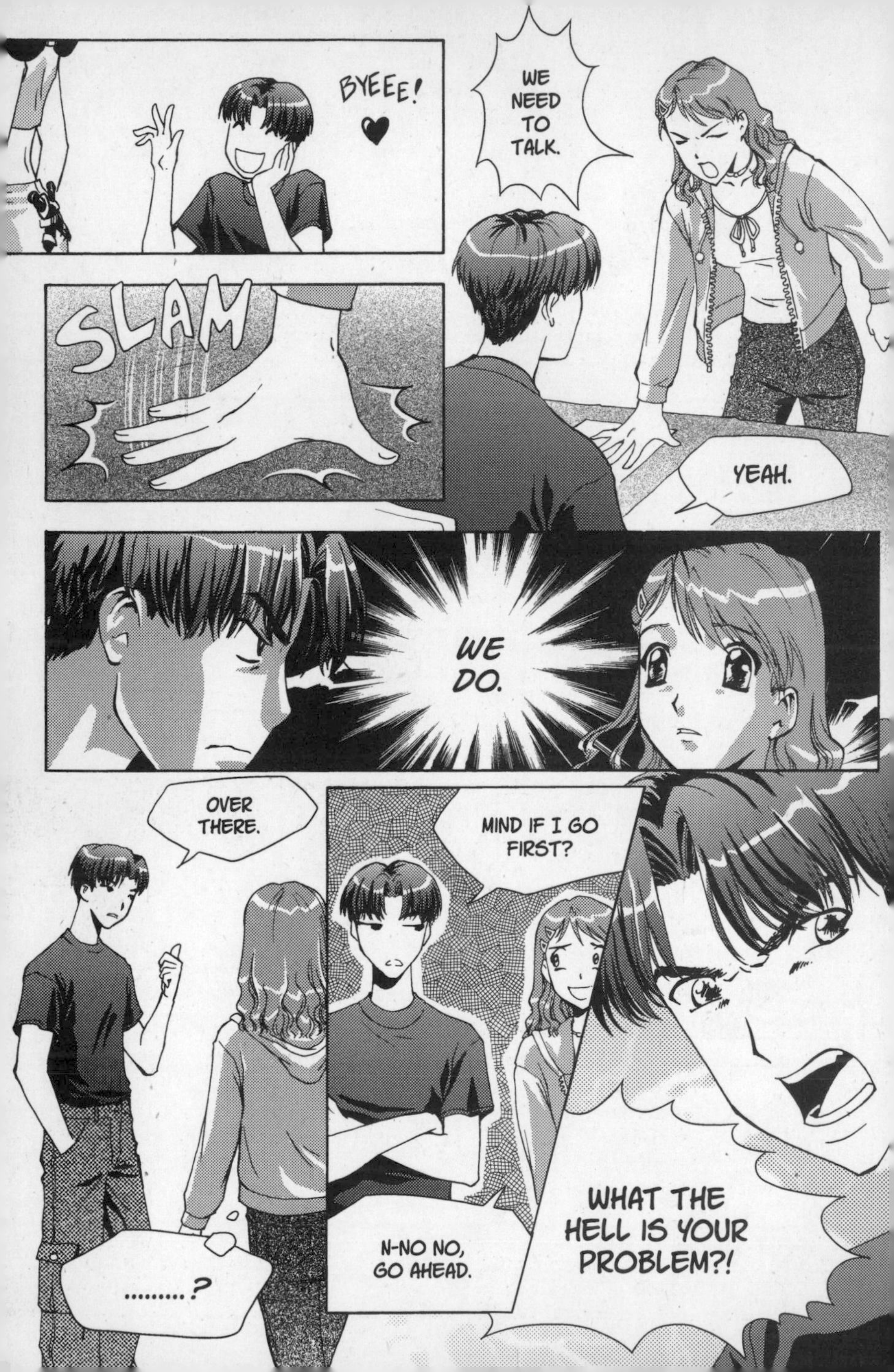
BYEEEE!
SLAM
WE NEED TO TALK.
YEAH.
WE DO.
OVER THERE.
.........?
MIND IF I GO FIRST?
N-NO NO, GO AHEAD.
WHAT THE HELL IS YOUR PROBLEM?!

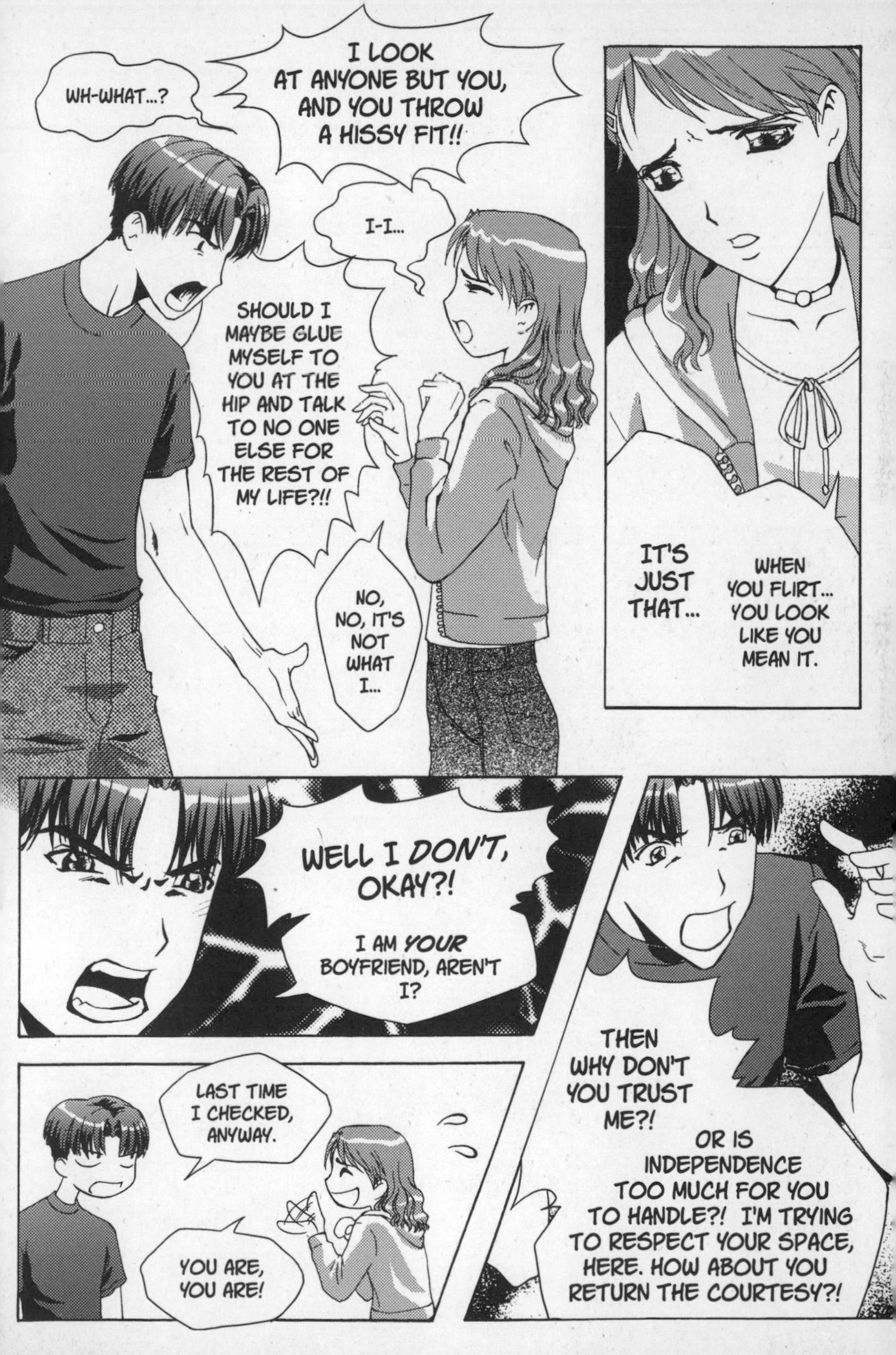
WH-WHAT...?
I LOOK AT ANYONE BUT YOU, AND YOU THROW A HISSY FIT!!
I-I...
SHOULD I MAYBE GLUE MYSELF TO YOU AT THE HIP AND TALK TO NO ONE ELSE FOR THE REST OF MY LIFE?!!
NO, NO, IT'S NOT WHAT I...
IT'S JUST THAT...
WHEN YOU FLIRT... YOU LOOK LIKE YOU MEAN IT.
WELL I *DON'T*, OKAY?!
I AM *YOUR* BOYFRIEND, AREN'T I?
LAST TIME I CHECKED, ANYWAY.
YOU ARE, YOU ARE!
THEN WHY DON'T YOU TRUST ME?!
OR IS INDEPENDENCE TOO MUCH FOR YOU TO HANDLE?! I'M TRYING TO RESPECT YOUR SPACE, HERE. HOW ABOUT YOU RETURN THE COURTESY?!

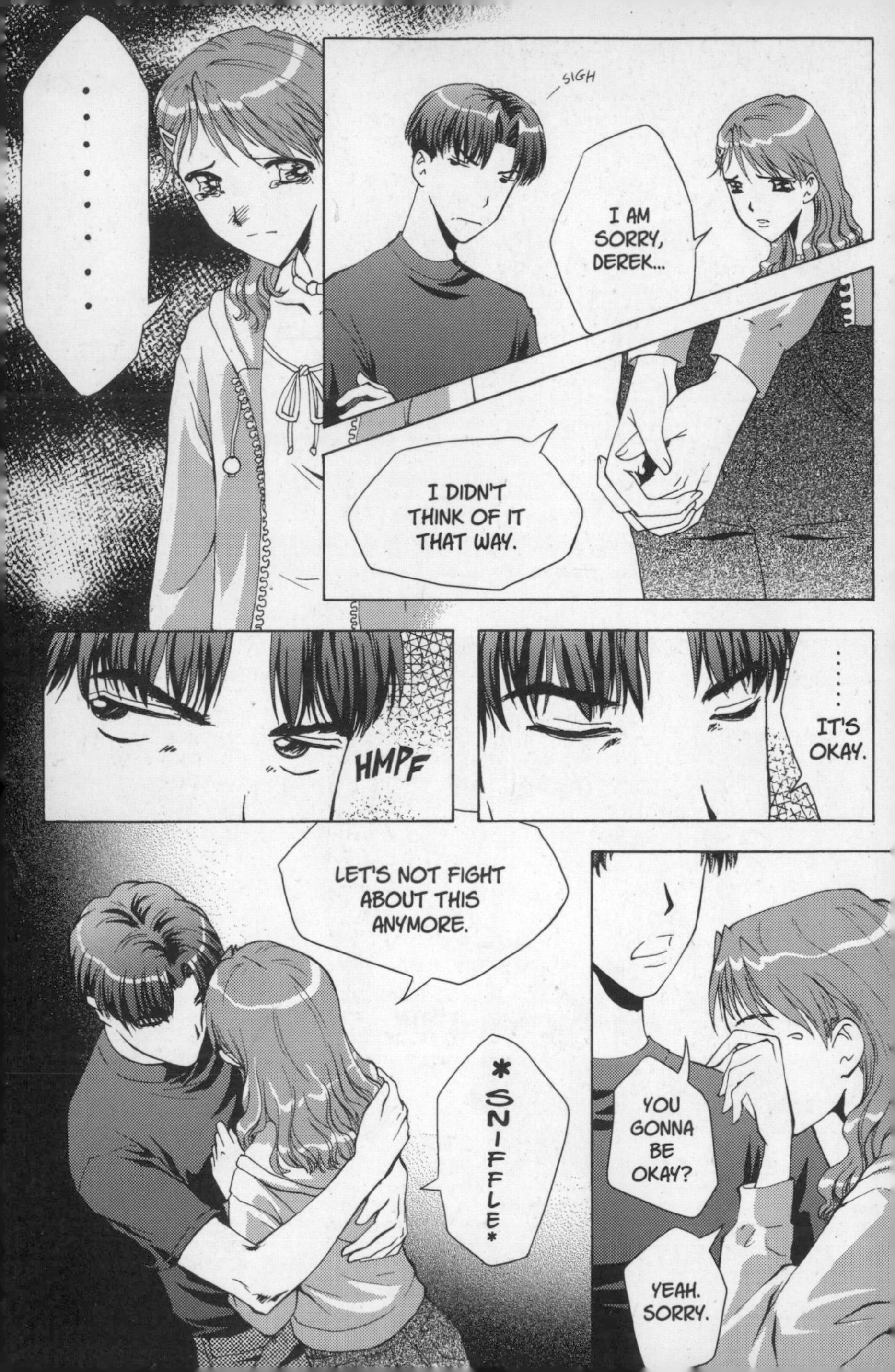
......
SIGH
I AM SORRY, DEREK...
I DIDN'T THINK OF IT THAT WAY.
HMPF
...... IT'S OKAY.
LET'S NOT FIGHT ABOUT THIS ANYMORE.
SNIFFLE
YOU GONNA BE OKAY?
YEAH. SORRY.

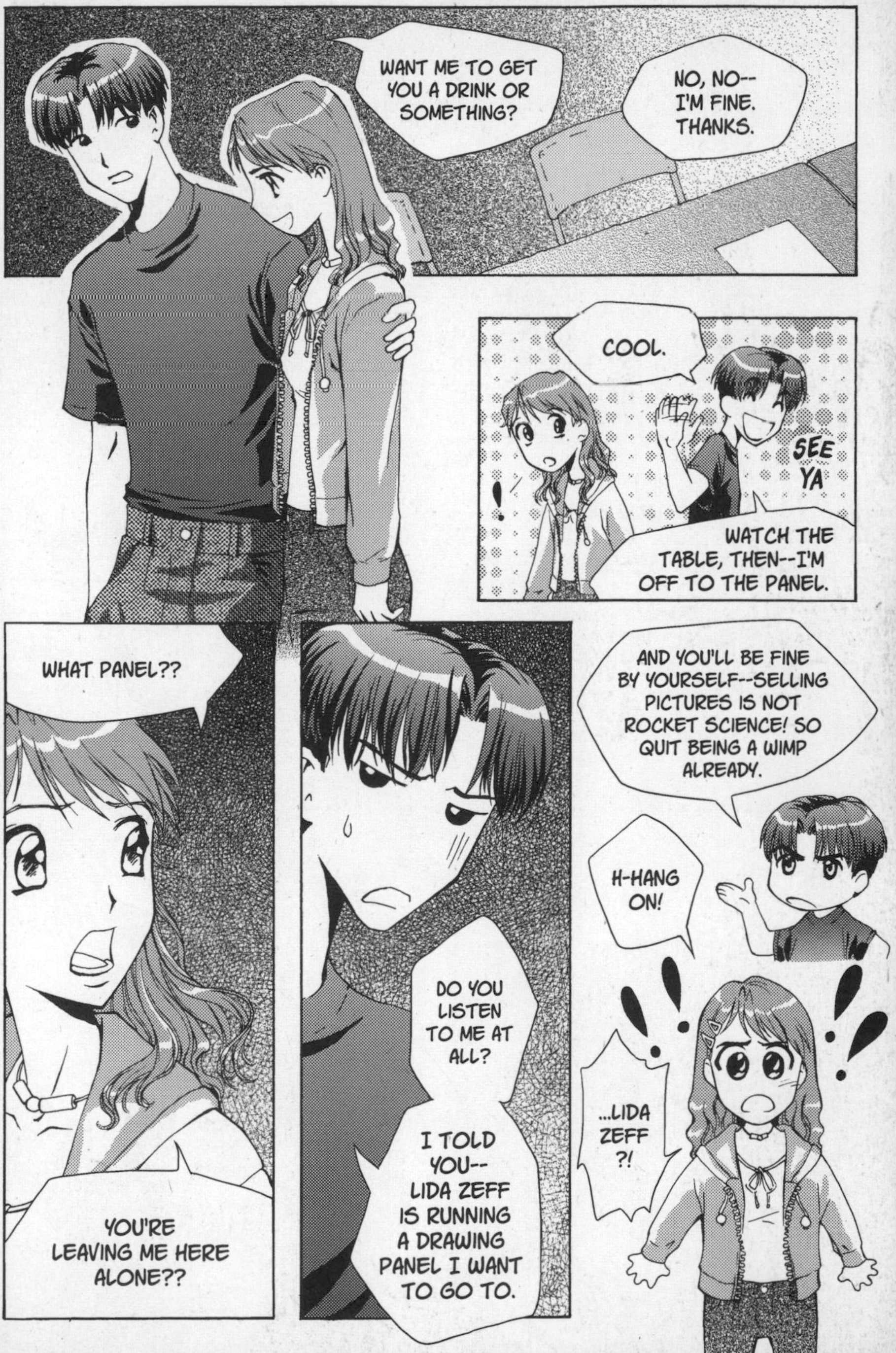
WANT ME TO GET YOU A DRINK OR SOMETHING?
NO, NO-- I'M FINE. THANKS.
COOL.
SEE YA
WATCH THE TABLE, THEN--I'M OFF TO THE PANEL.
WHAT PANEL??
YOU'RE LEAVING ME HERE ALONE??
DO YOU LISTEN TO ME AT ALL?
I TOLD YOU-- LIDA ZEFF IS RUNNING A DRAWING PANEL I WANT TO GO TO.
AND YOU'LL BE FINE BY YOURSELF--SELLING PICTURES IS NOT ROCKET SCIENCE! SO QUIT BEING A WIMP ALREADY.
H-HANG ON!
...LIDA ZEFF ?!

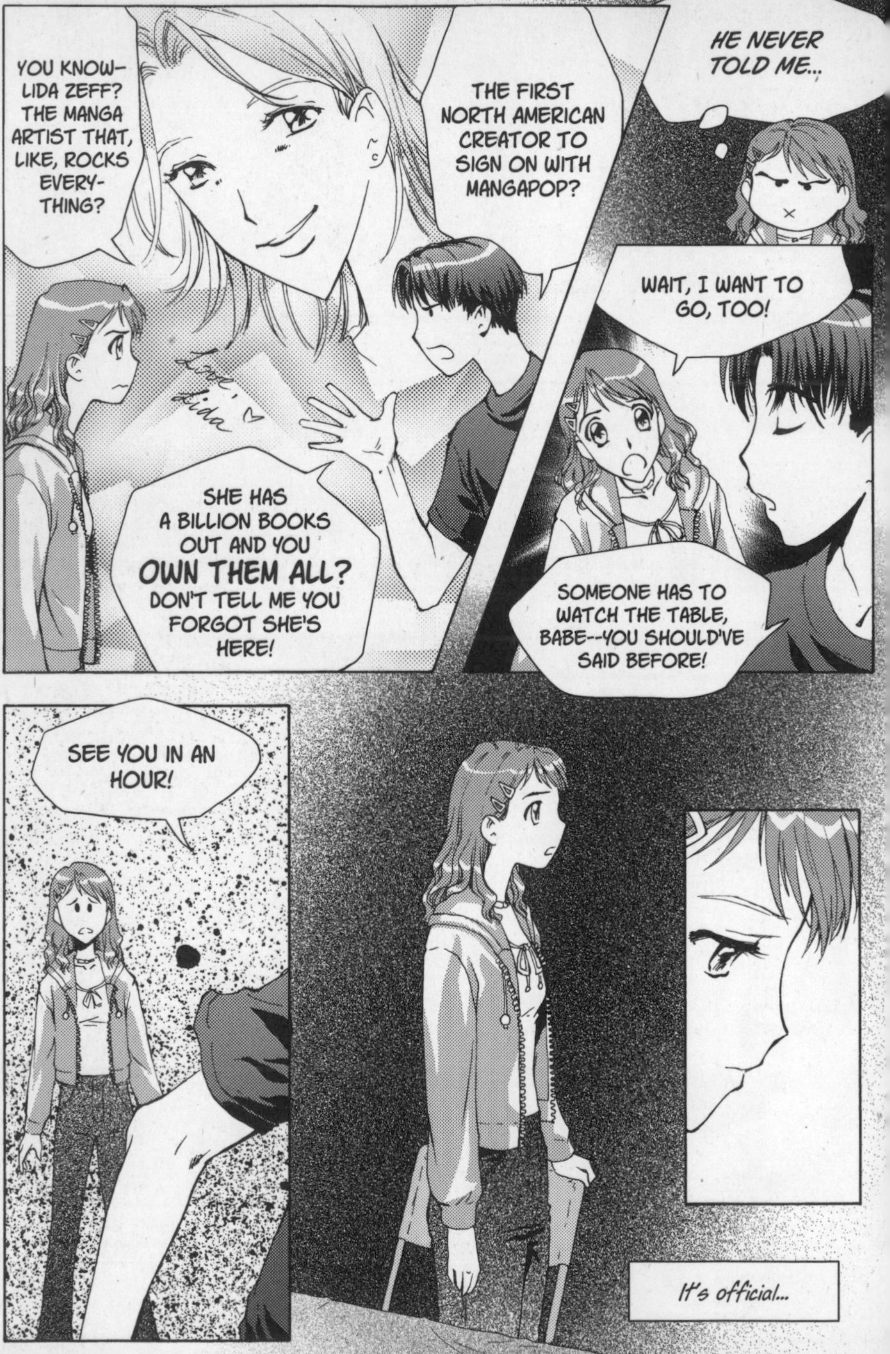
YOU KNOW—LIDA ZEFF? THE MANGA ARTIST THAT, LIKE, ROCKS EVERYTHING?
THE FIRST NORTH AMERICAN CREATOR TO SIGN ON WITH MANGAPOP?
Love, Lida
SHE HAS A BILLION BOOKS OUT AND YOU **OWN THEM ALL?** DON'T TELL ME YOU FORGOT SHE'S HERE!
HE NEVER TOLD ME...
WAIT, I WANT TO GO, TOO!
SOMEONE HAS TO WATCH THE TABLE, BABE--YOU SHOULD'VE SAID BEFORE!
SEE YOU IN AN HOUR!
It's official...

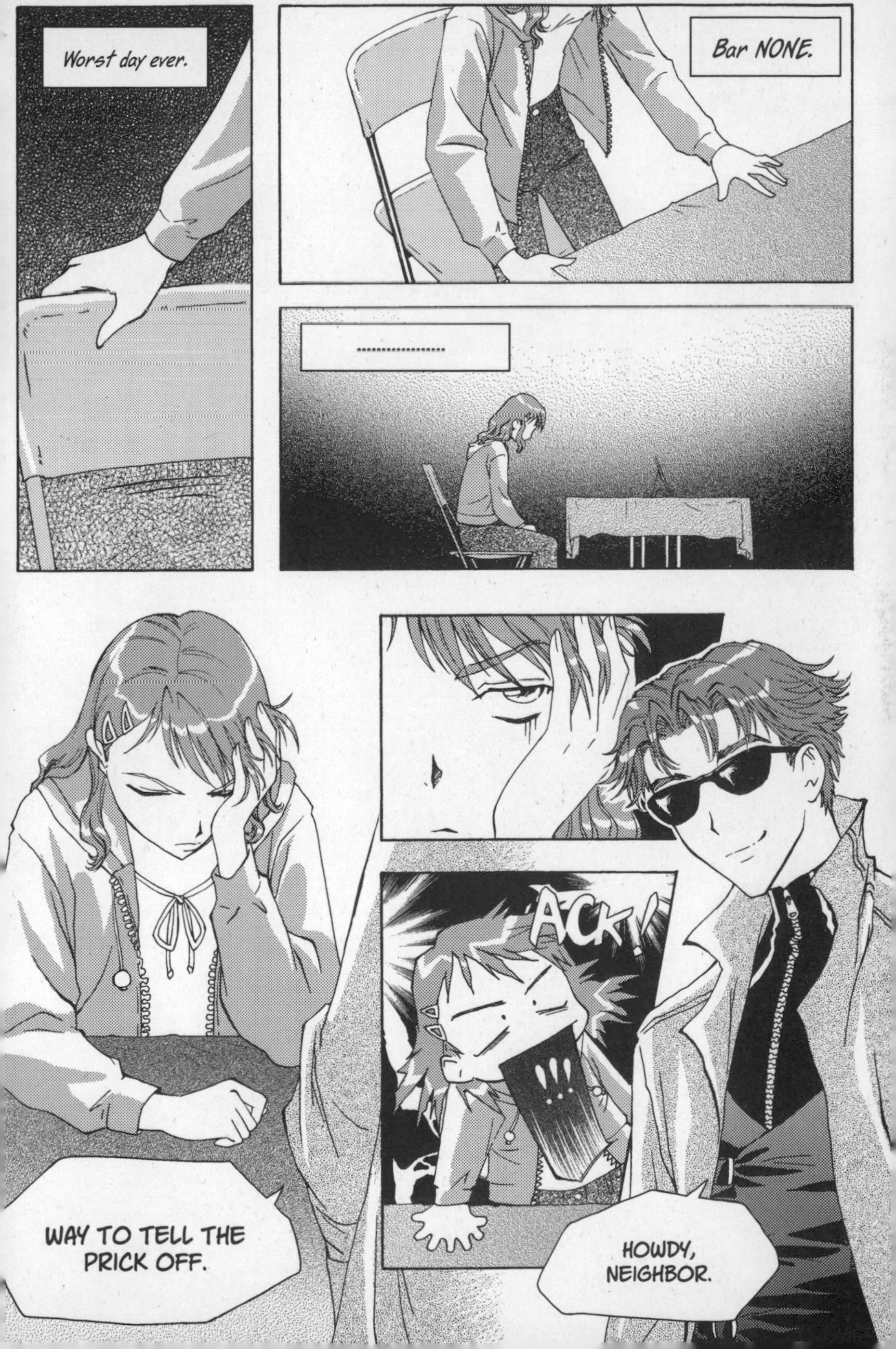
Worst day ever.
Bar NONE.
....
WAY TO TELL THE PRICK OFF.
ACK!
!!!
HOWDY, NEIGHBOR.

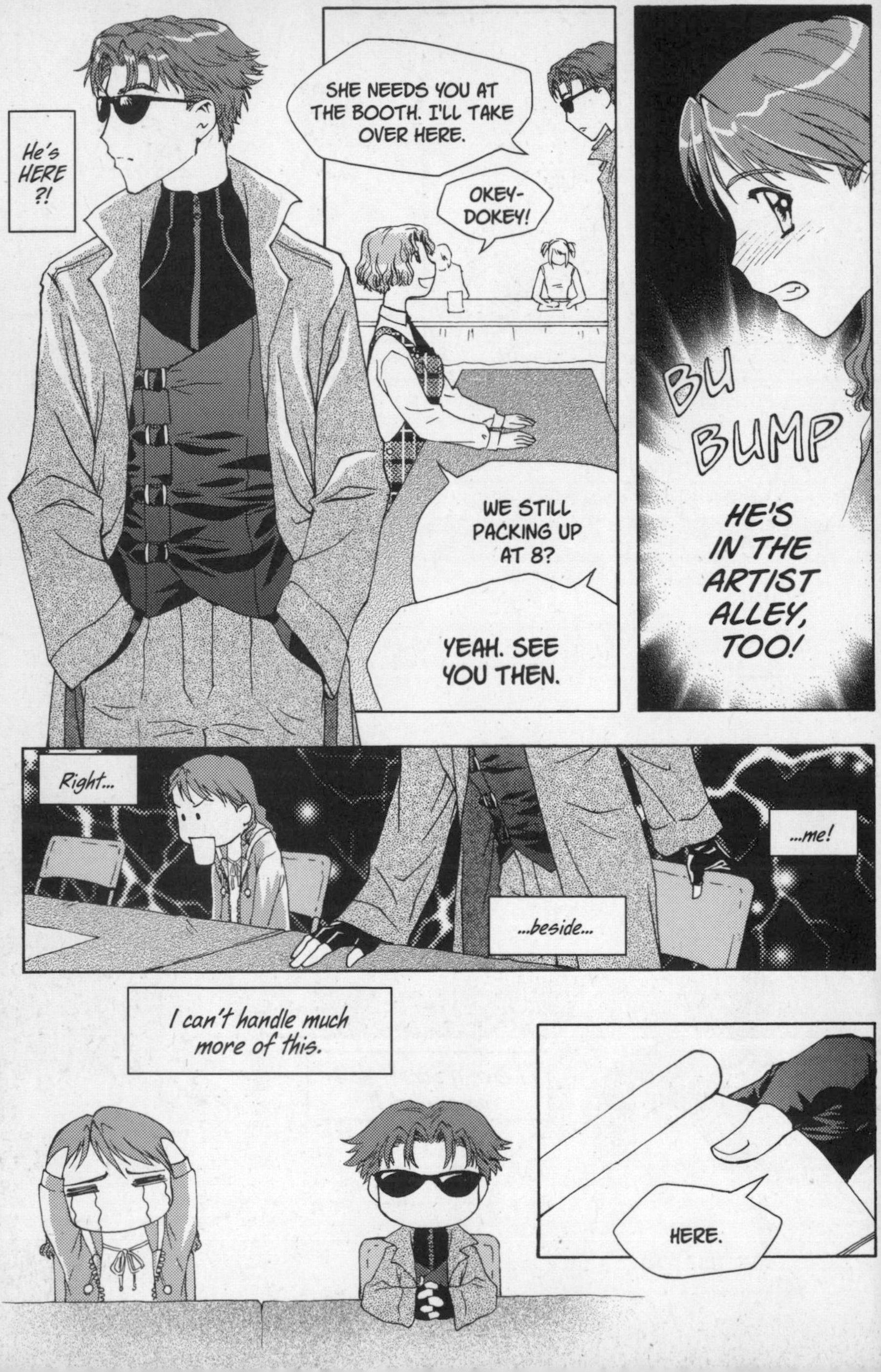
He's HERE ?!
SHE NEEDS YOU AT THE BOOTH. I'LL TAKE OVER HERE.
OKEY-DOKEY!
WE STILL PACKING UP AT 8?
YEAH. SEE YOU THEN.
BU BUMP
HE'S IN THE ARTIST ALLEY, TOO!
Right...
...beside...
...me!
I can't handle much more of this.
HERE.

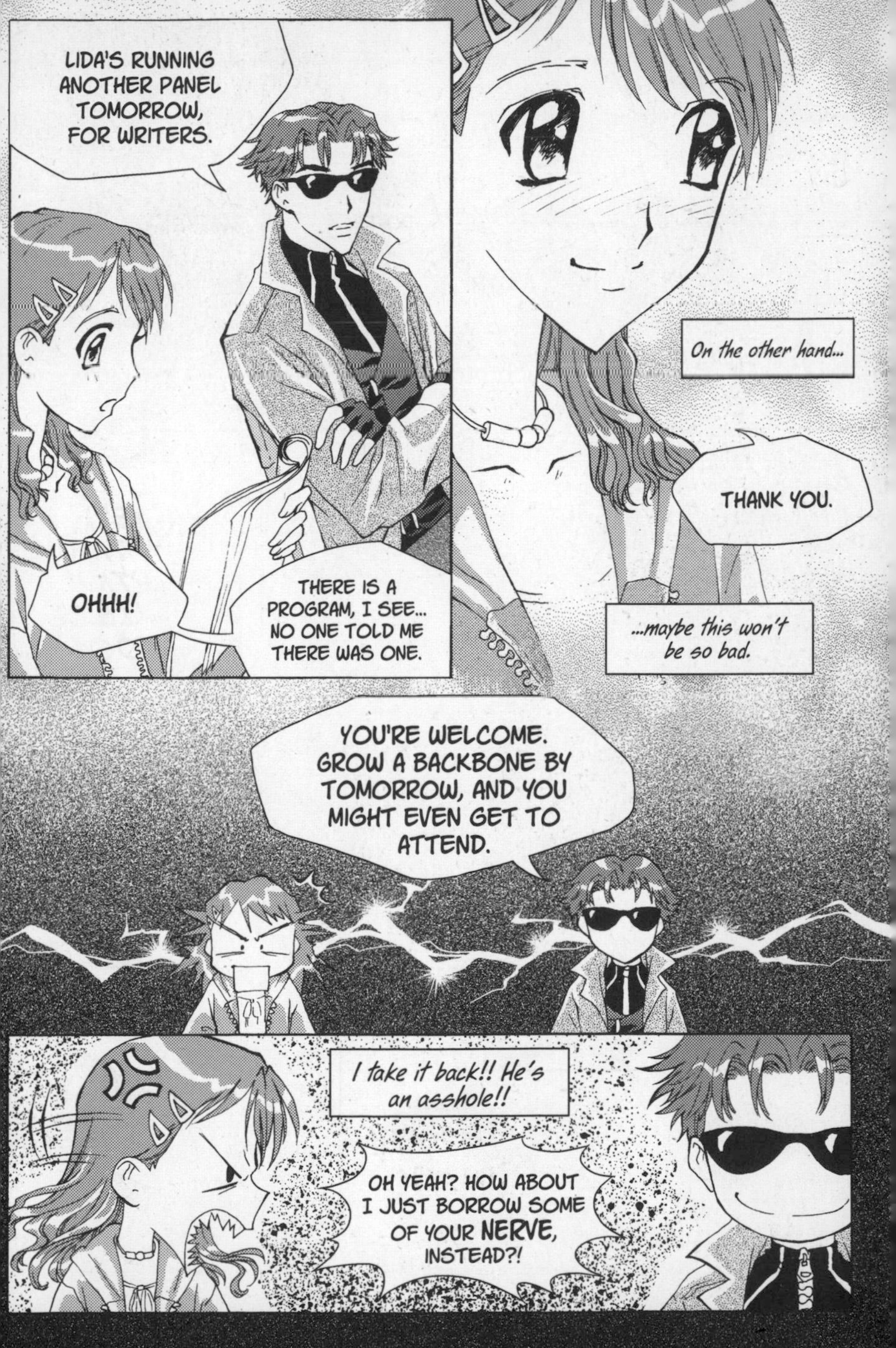
LIDA'S RUNNING ANOTHER PANEL TOMORROW, FOR WRITERS.
OHHH!
THERE IS A PROGRAM, I SEE... NO ONE TOLD ME THERE WAS ONE.
On the other hand...
THANK YOU.
...maybe this won't be so bad.
YOU'RE WELCOME. GROW A BACKBONE BY TOMORROW, AND YOU MIGHT EVEN GET TO ATTEND.
I take it back!! He's an asshole!!
OH YEAH? HOW ABOUT I JUST BORROW SOME OF YOUR NERVE, INSTEAD?!

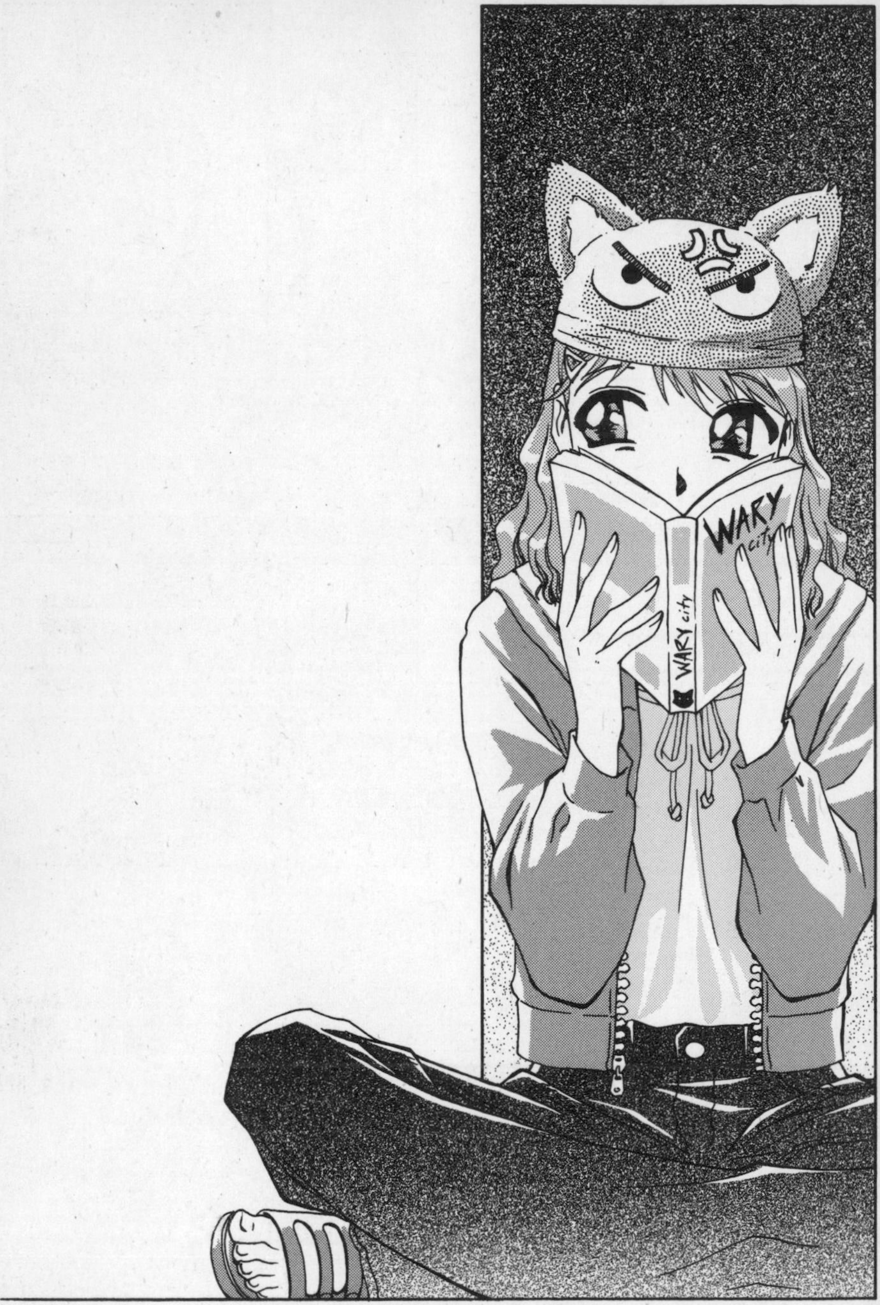
WARY city
WARY city

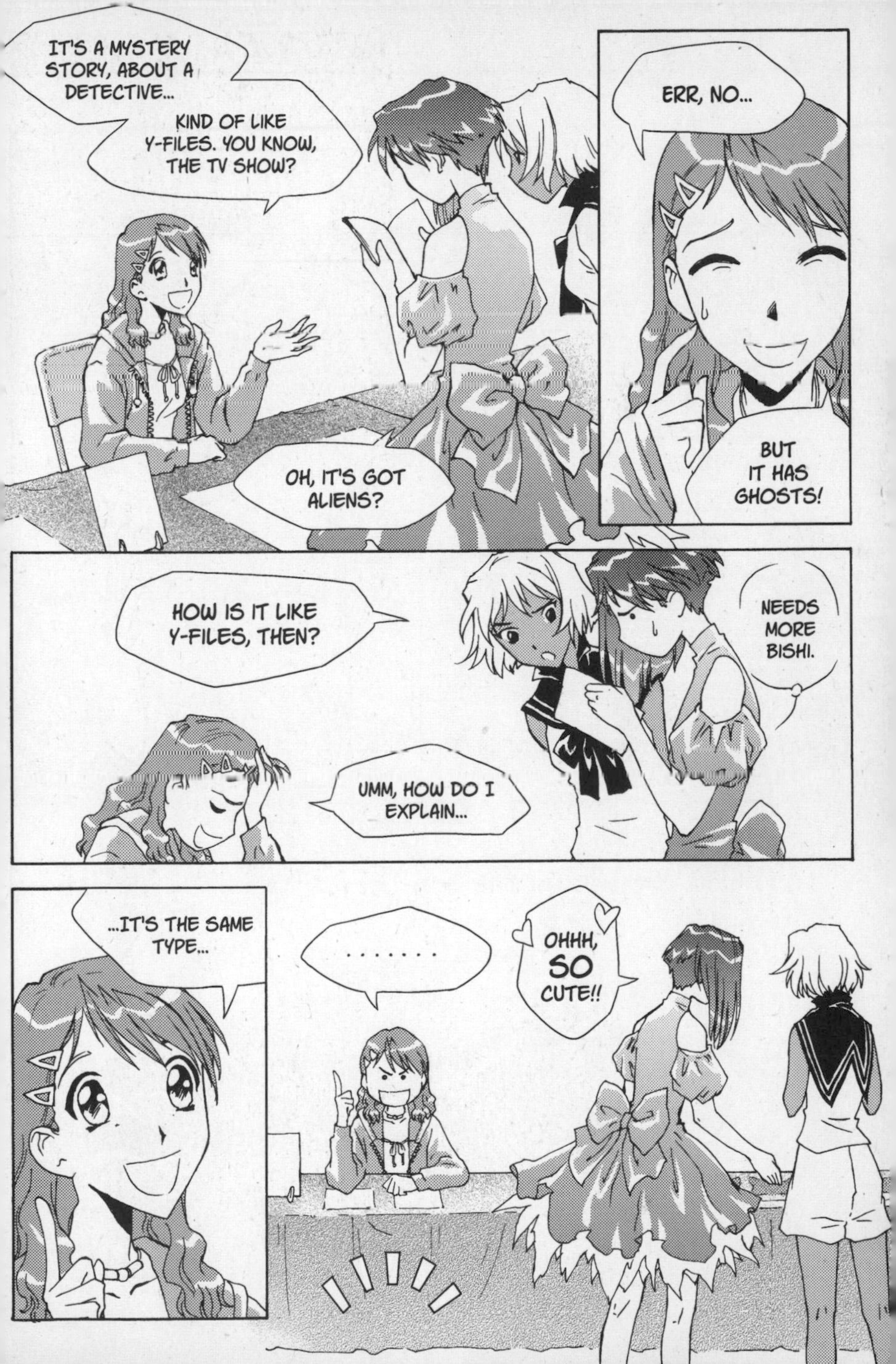
IT'S A MYSTERY STORY, ABOUT A DETECTIVE...
KIND OF LIKE Y-FILES. YOU KNOW, THE TV SHOW?
OH, IT'S GOT ALIENS?
ERR, NO...
BUT IT HAS GHOSTS!
HOW IS IT LIKE Y-FILES, THEN?
NEEDS MORE BISHI.
UMM, HOW DO I EXPLAIN...
...IT'S THE SAME TYPE...
....
OHHH, SO CUTE!!

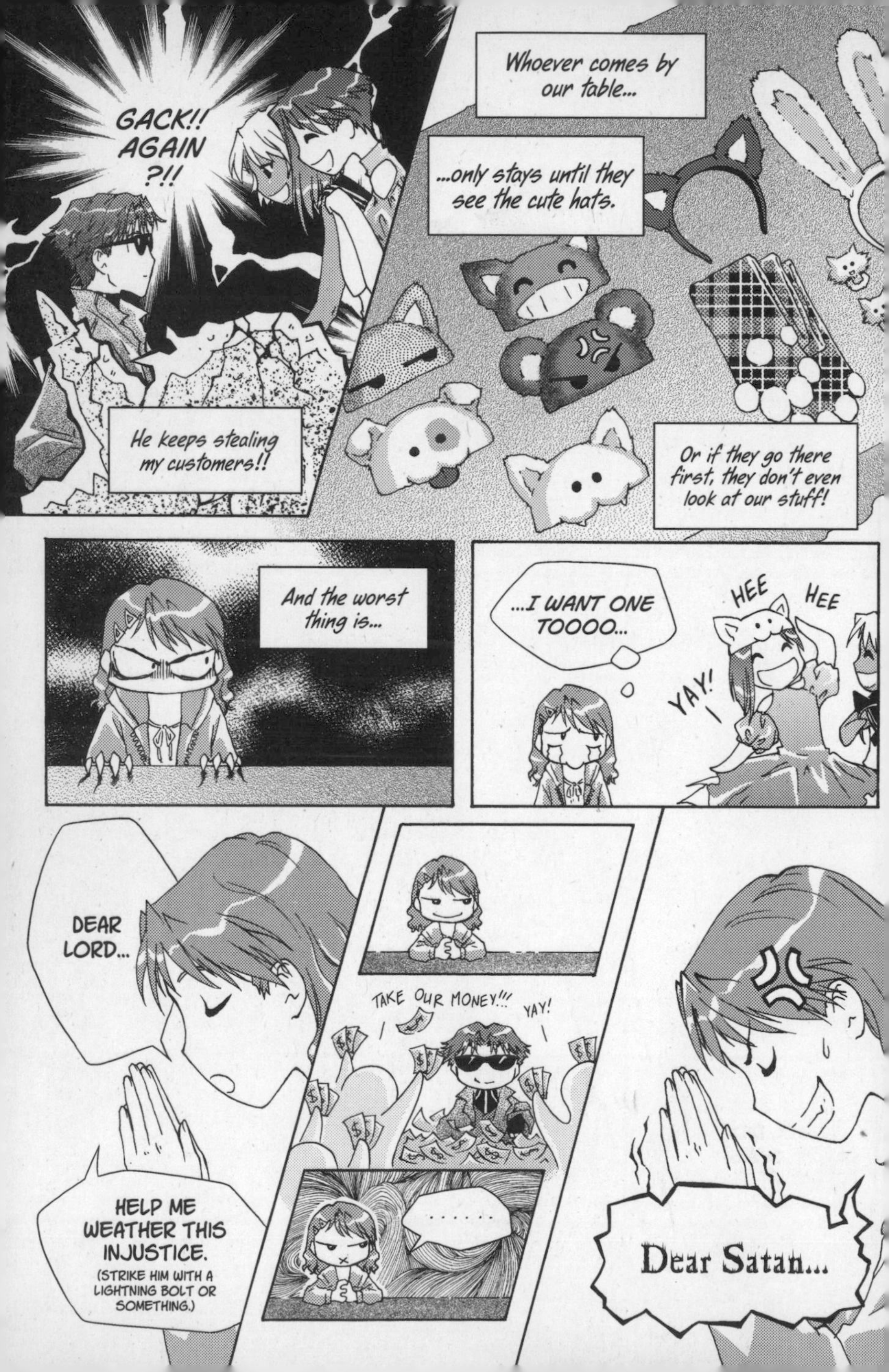
GACK!! AGAIN ?!!
He keeps stealing my customers!!
Whoever comes by our table...
...only stays until they see the cute hats.
Or if they go there first, they don't even look at our stuff!
And the worst thing is...
...I WANT ONE TOOOO...
HEE
HEE
YAY!
DEAR LORD...
HELP ME WEATHER THIS INJUSTICE.
(STRIKE HIM WITH A LIGHTNING BOLT OR SOMETHING.)
TAKE OUR MONEY!!!
YAY!
......
Dear Satan...

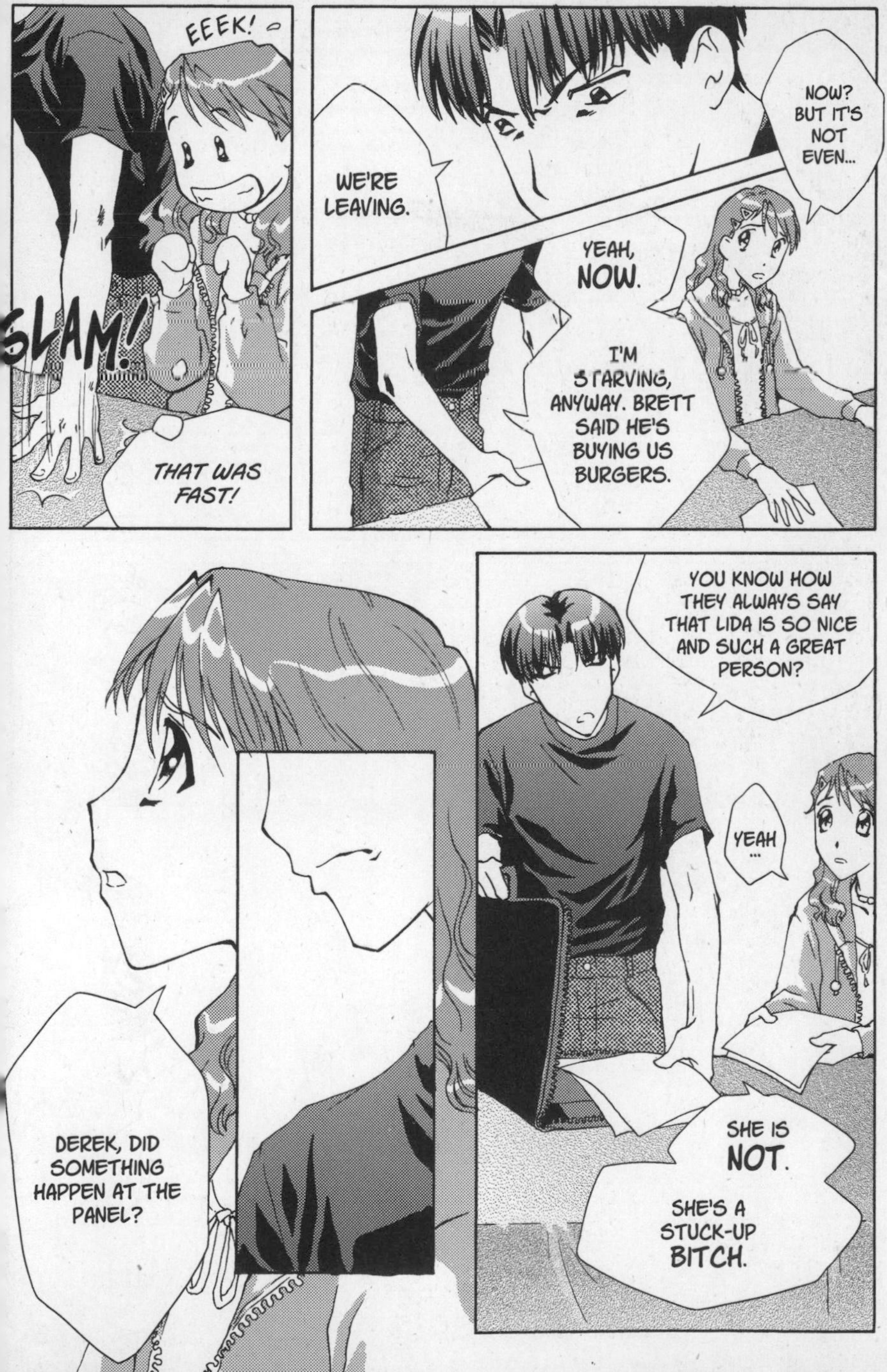
EEEK!
SLAM!
THAT WAS FAST!
WE'RE LEAVING.
NOW? BUT IT'S NOT EVEN...
YEAH, NOW.
I'M STARVING, ANYWAY. BRETT SAID HE'S BUYING US BURGERS.
DEREK, DID SOMETHING HAPPEN AT THE PANEL?
YOU KNOW HOW THEY ALWAYS SAY THAT LIDA IS SO NICE AND SUCH A GREAT PERSON?
YEAH ...
SHE IS NOT.
SHE'S A STUCK-UP BITCH.

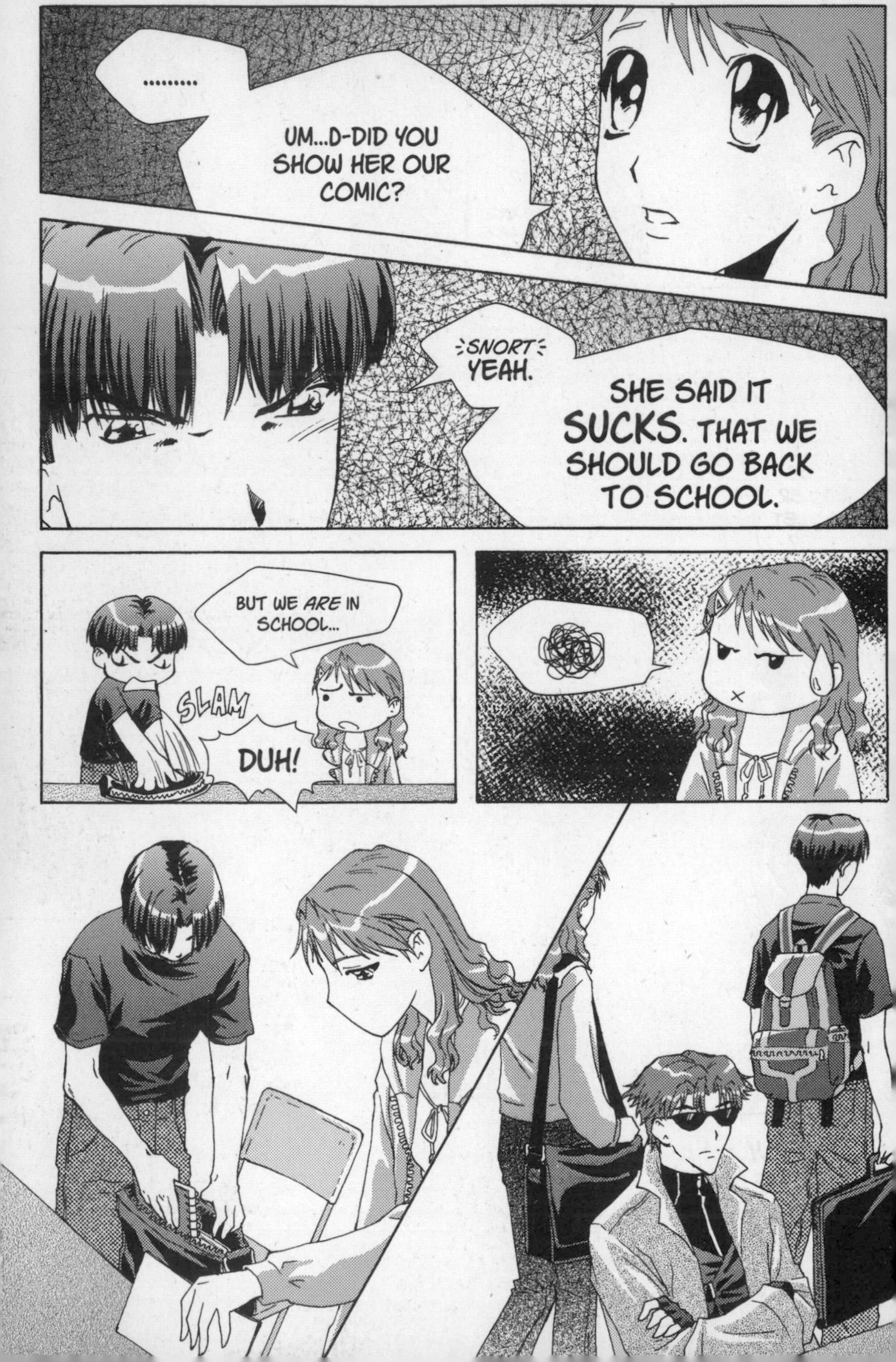
....
UM...D-DID YOU SHOW HER OUR COMIC?
SNORT YEAH.
SHE SAID IT SUCKS. THAT WE SHOULD GO BACK TO SCHOOL.
BUT WE ARE IN SCHOOL...
SLAM
DUH!

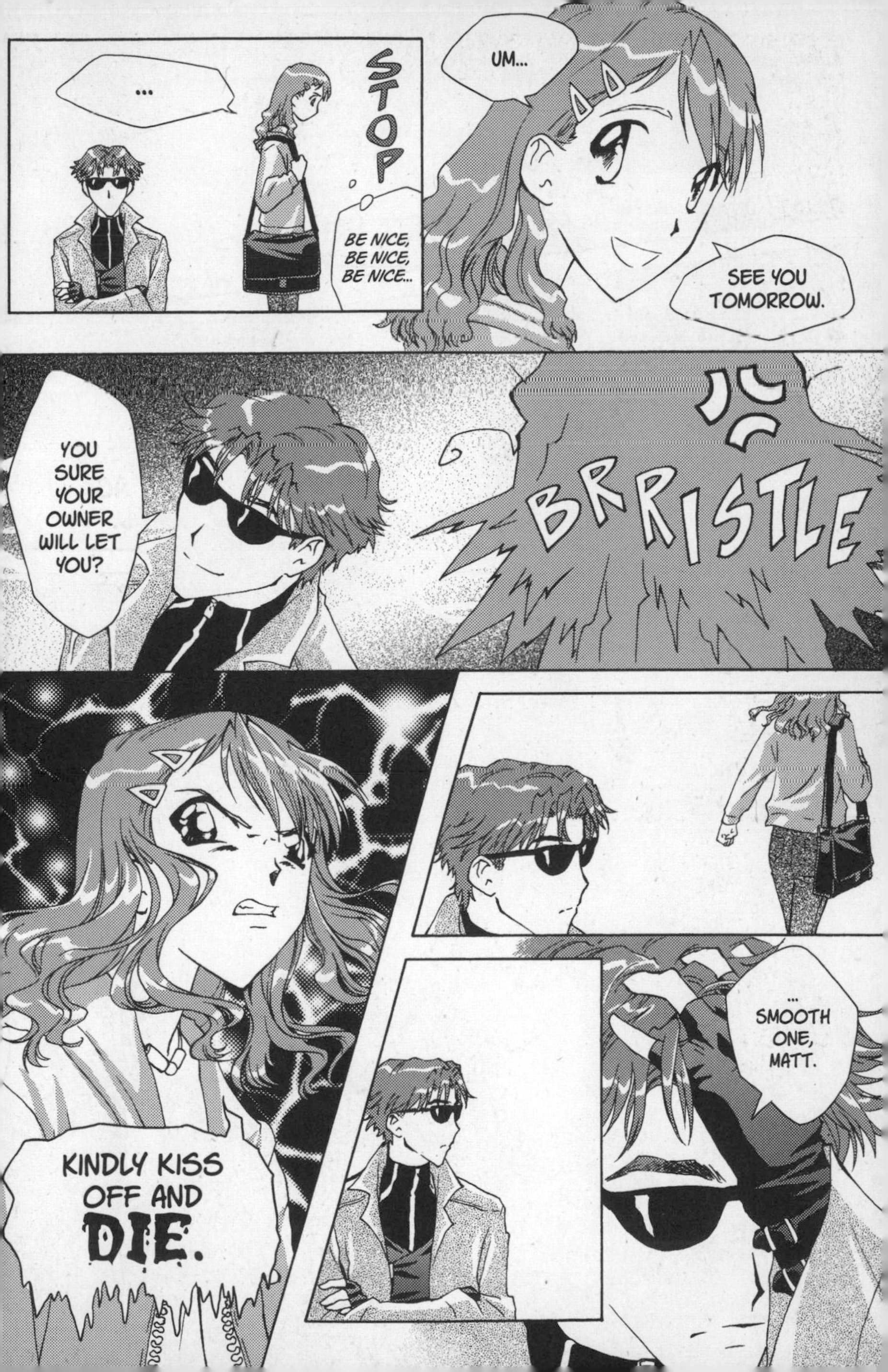
...
STOP
BE NICE, BE NICE, BE NICE...
UM...
SEE YOU TOMORROW.
YOU SURE YOUR OWNER WILL LET YOU?
BRRISTLE
KINDLY KISS OFF AND DIE.
... SMOOTH ONE, MATT.

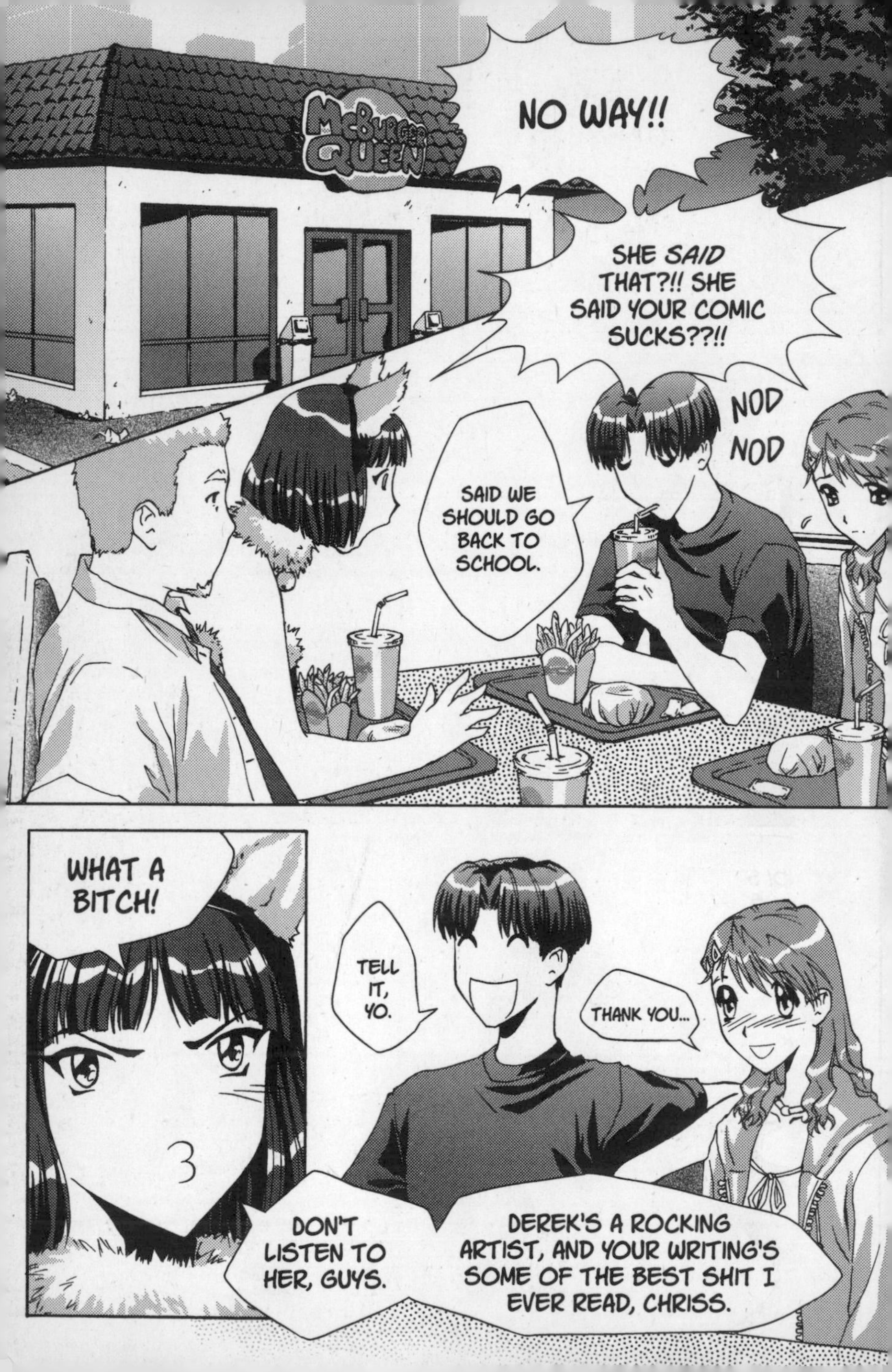
McBURGER QUEEN
NO WAY!!
SHE SAID THAT?!! SHE SAID YOUR COMIC SUCKS??!!
NOD NOD
SAID WE SHOULD GO BACK TO SCHOOL.
WHAT A BITCH!
TELL IT, YO.
THANK YOU...
DON'T LISTEN TO HER, GUYS.
DEREK'S A ROCKING ARTIST, AND YOUR WRITING'S SOME OF THE BEST SHIT I EVER READ, CHRISS.

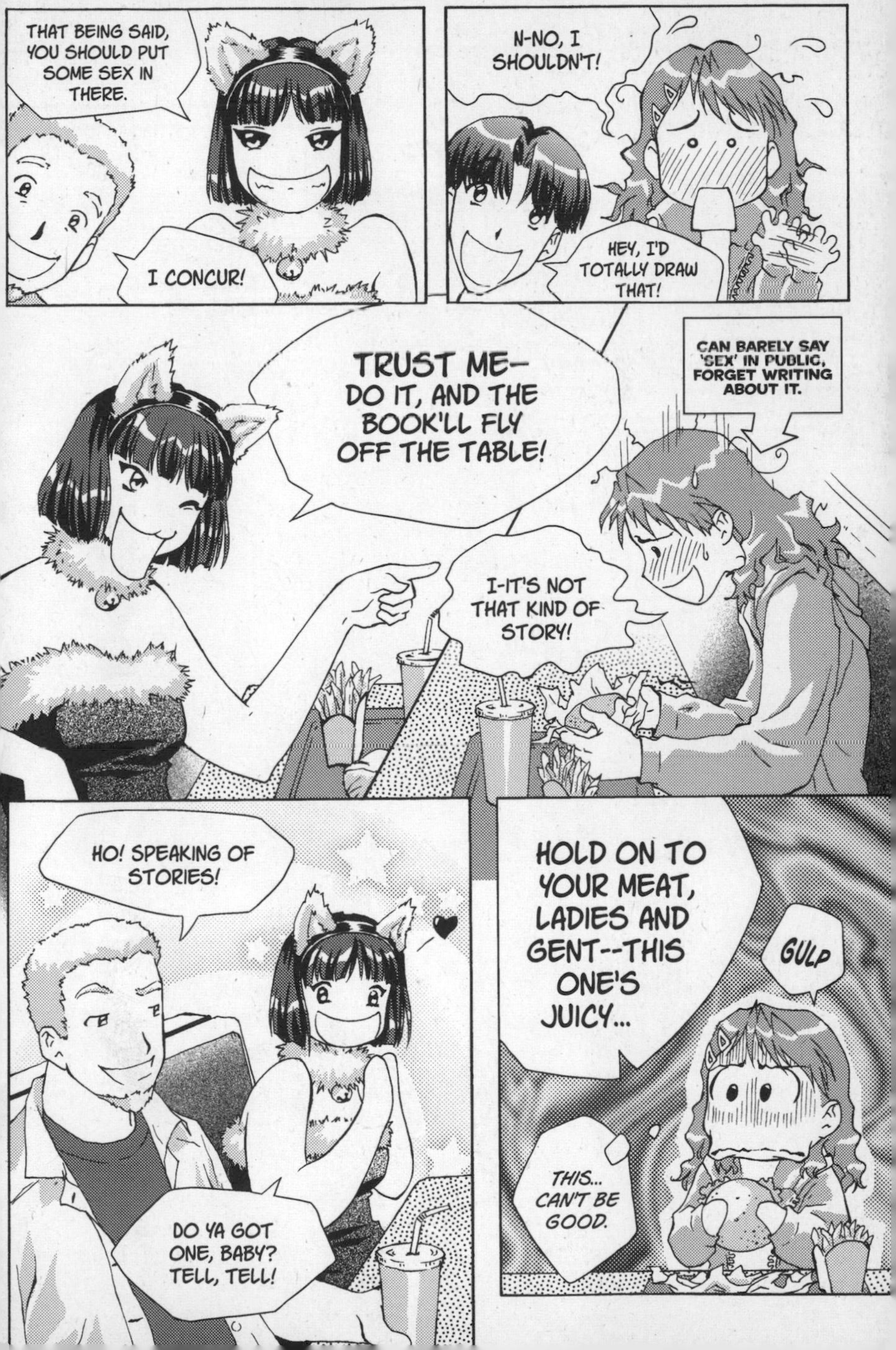
THAT BEING SAID, YOU SHOULD PUT SOME SEX IN THERE.
I CONCUR!
N-NO, I SHOULDN'T!
HEY, I'D TOTALLY DRAW THAT!
TRUST ME-- DO IT, AND THE BOOK'LL FLY OFF THE TABLE!
CAN BARELY SAY 'SEX' IN PUBLIC, FORGET WRITING ABOUT IT.
I-IT'S NOT THAT KIND OF STORY!
HO! SPEAKING OF STORIES!
DO YA GOT ONE, BABY? TELL, TELL!
HOLD ON TO YOUR MEAT, LADIES AND GENT--THIS ONE'S JUICY...
GULP
THIS... CAN'T BE GOOD.

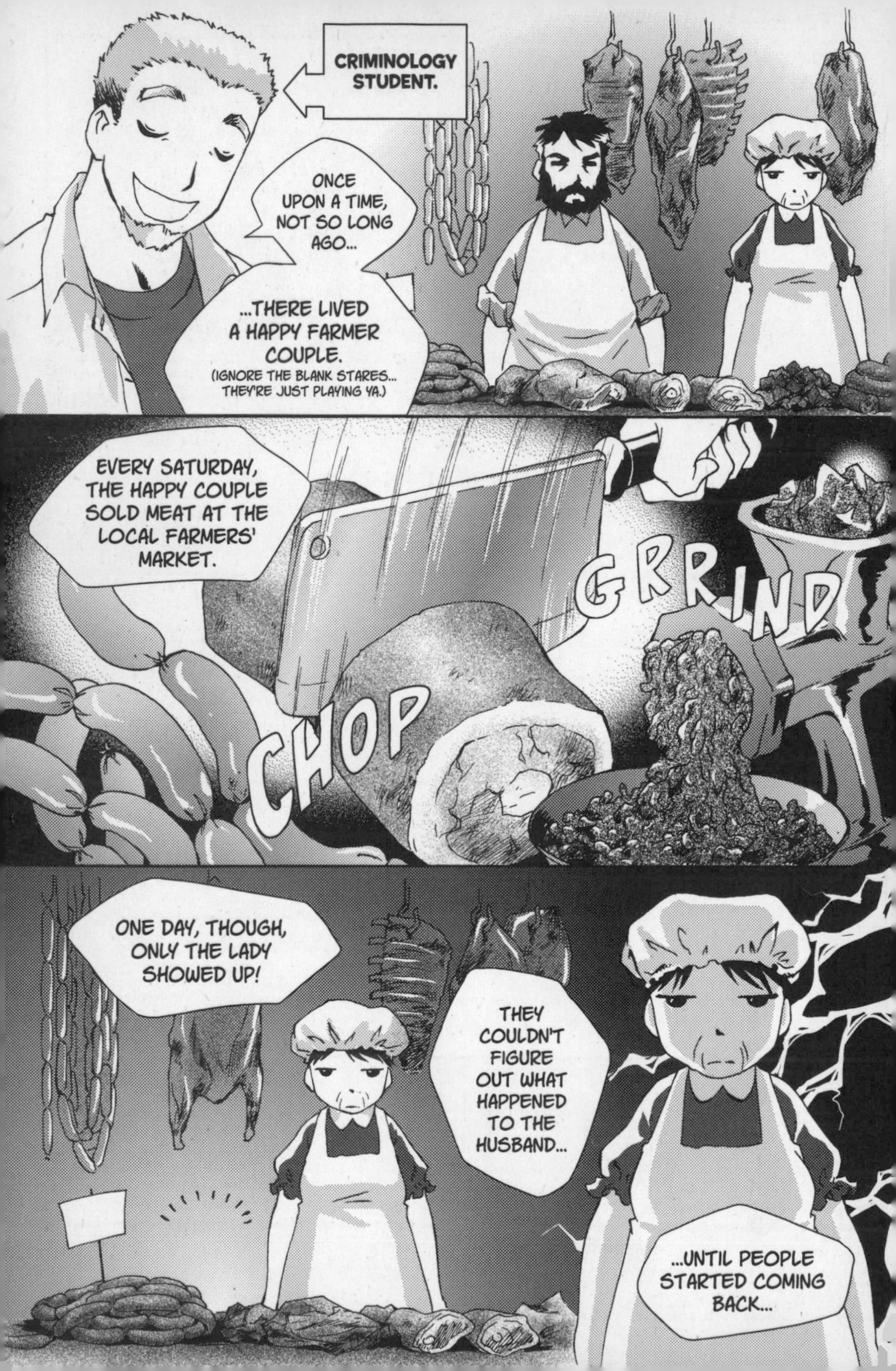
CRIMINOLOGY STUDENT.
ONCE UPON A TIME, NOT SO LONG AGO...
...THERE LIVED A HAPPY FARMER COUPLE.
(IGNORE THE BLANK STARES... THEY'RE JUST PLAYING YA.)
EVERY SATURDAY, THE HAPPY COUPLE SOLD MEAT AT THE LOCAL FARMERS' MARKET.
CHOP
GRRIND
ONE DAY, THOUGH, ONLY THE LADY SHOWED UP!
THEY COULDN'T FIGURE OUT WHAT HAPPENED TO THE HUSBAND...
...UNTIL PEOPLE STARTED COMING BACK...

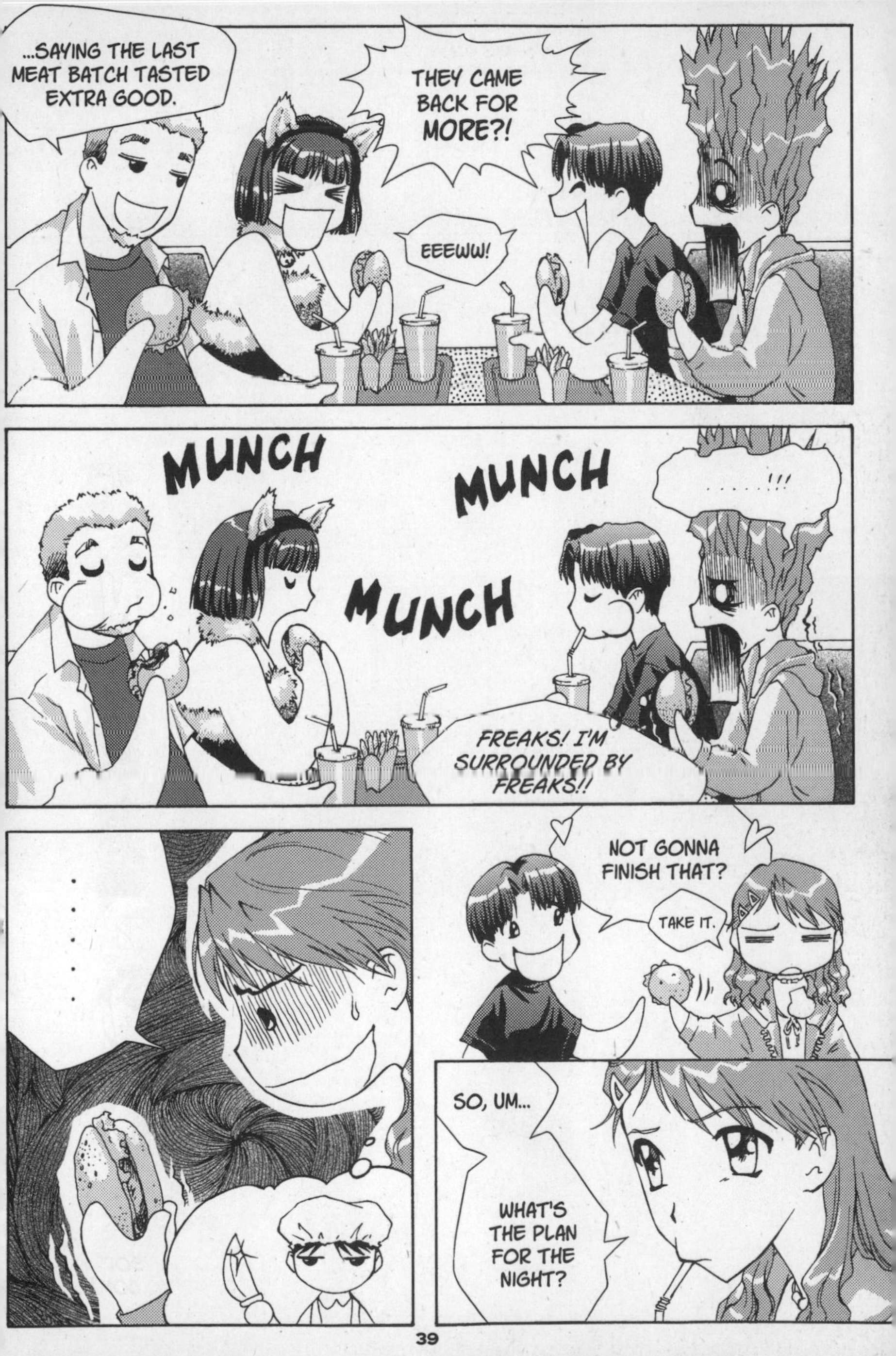
...SAYING THE LAST MEAT BATCH TASTED EXTRA GOOD.
THEY CAME BACK FOR MORE?!
EEEWW!
MUNCH
MUNCH
MUNCH
......!!!
FREAKS! I'M SURROUNDED BY FREAKS!!
.....
NOT GONNA FINISH THAT?
TAKE IT.
SO, UM...
WHAT'S THE PLAN FOR THE NIGHT?

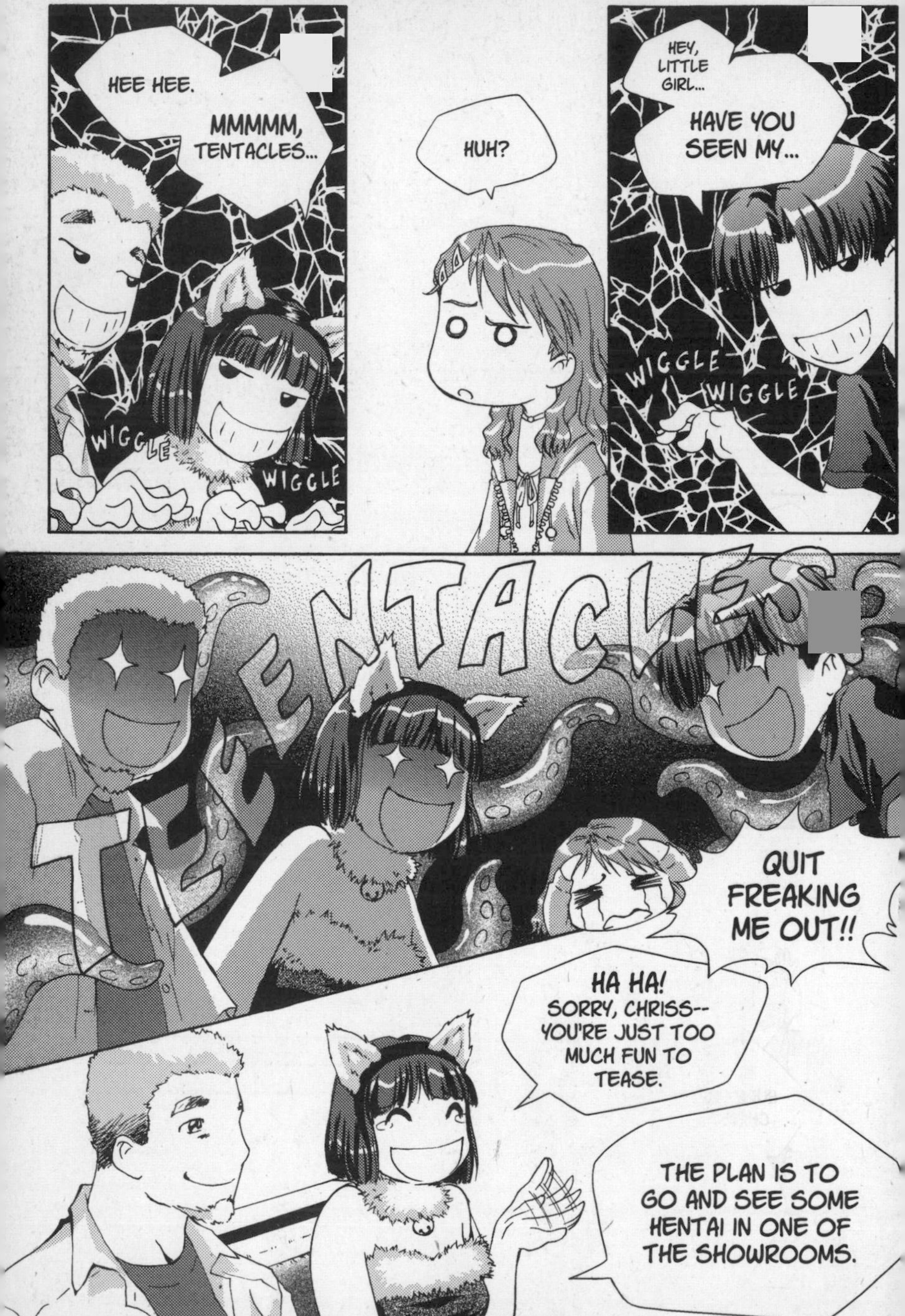
HEE HEE.
MMMMM, TENTACLES...
WIGGLE
WIGGLE
HUH?
HEY, LITTLE GIRL...
HAVE YOU SEEN MY...
WIGGLE
WIGGLE
TENTACLES
QUIT FREAKING ME OUT!!
HA HA! SORRY, CHRISS-- YOU'RE JUST TOO MUCH FUN TO TEASE.
THE PLAN IS TO GO AND SEE SOME HENTAI IN ONE OF THE SHOWROOMS.

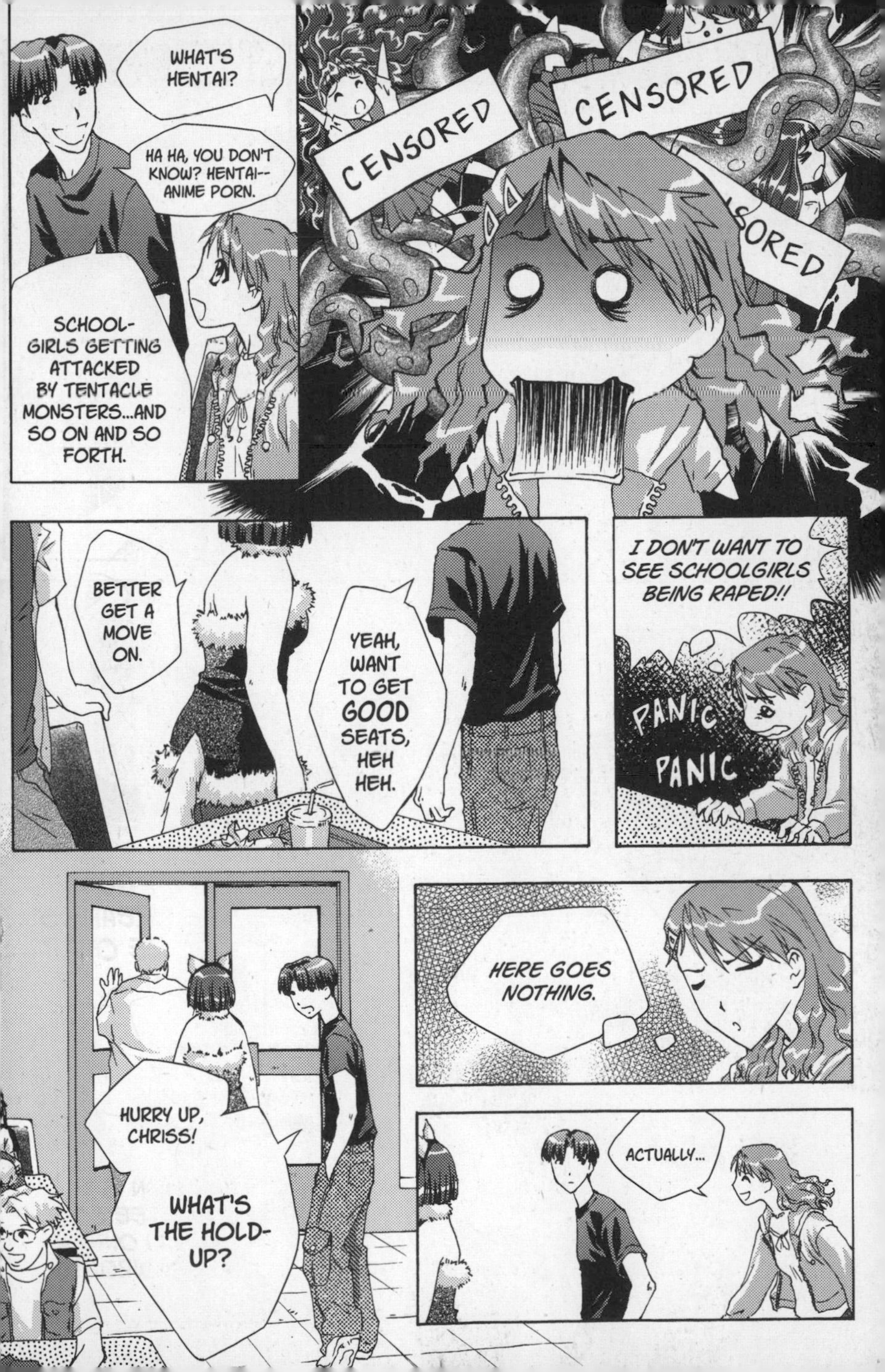
WHAT'S HENTAI?
HA HA, YOU DON'T KNOW? HENTAI--ANIME PORN.
SCHOOL-GIRLS GETTING ATTACKED BY TENTACLE MONSTERS...AND SO ON AND SO FORTH.
CENSORED
CENSORED
SORED
BETTER GET A MOVE ON.
YEAH, WANT TO GET GOOD SEATS, HEH HEH.
I DON'T WANT TO SEE SCHOOLGIRLS BEING RAPED!!
PANIC
PANIC
HURRY UP, CHRISS!
WHAT'S THE HOLD-UP?
HERE GOES NOTHING.
ACTUALLY...

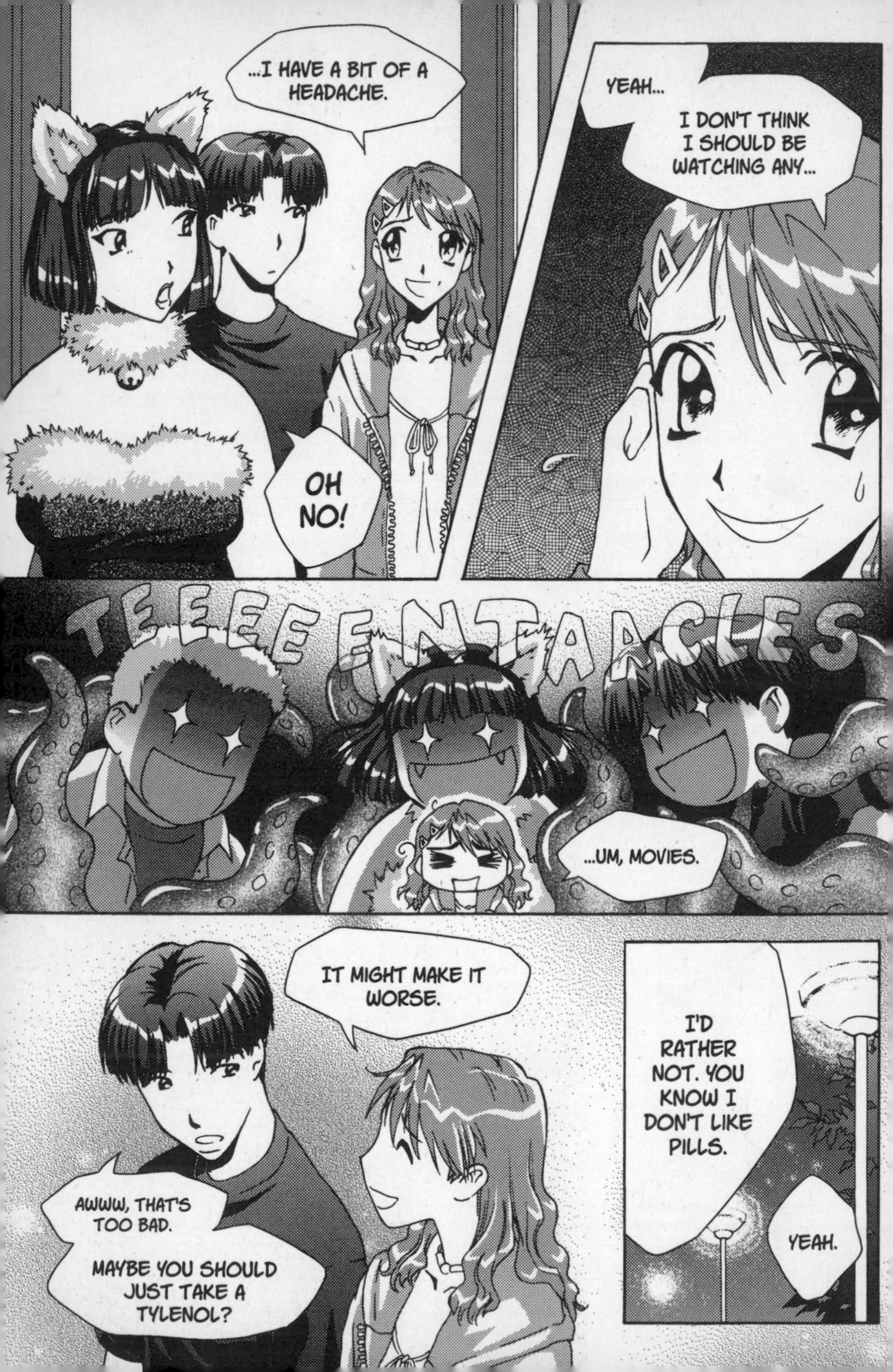
...I HAVE A BIT OF A HEADACHE.
OH NO!
YEAH...
I DON'T THINK I SHOULD BE WATCHING ANY...
TEEEENTACLES
...UM, MOVIES.
IT MIGHT MAKE IT WORSE.
AWWW, THAT'S TOO BAD.
MAYBE YOU SHOULD JUST TAKE A TYLENOL?
I'D RATHER NOT. YOU KNOW I DON'T LIKE PILLS.
YEAH.

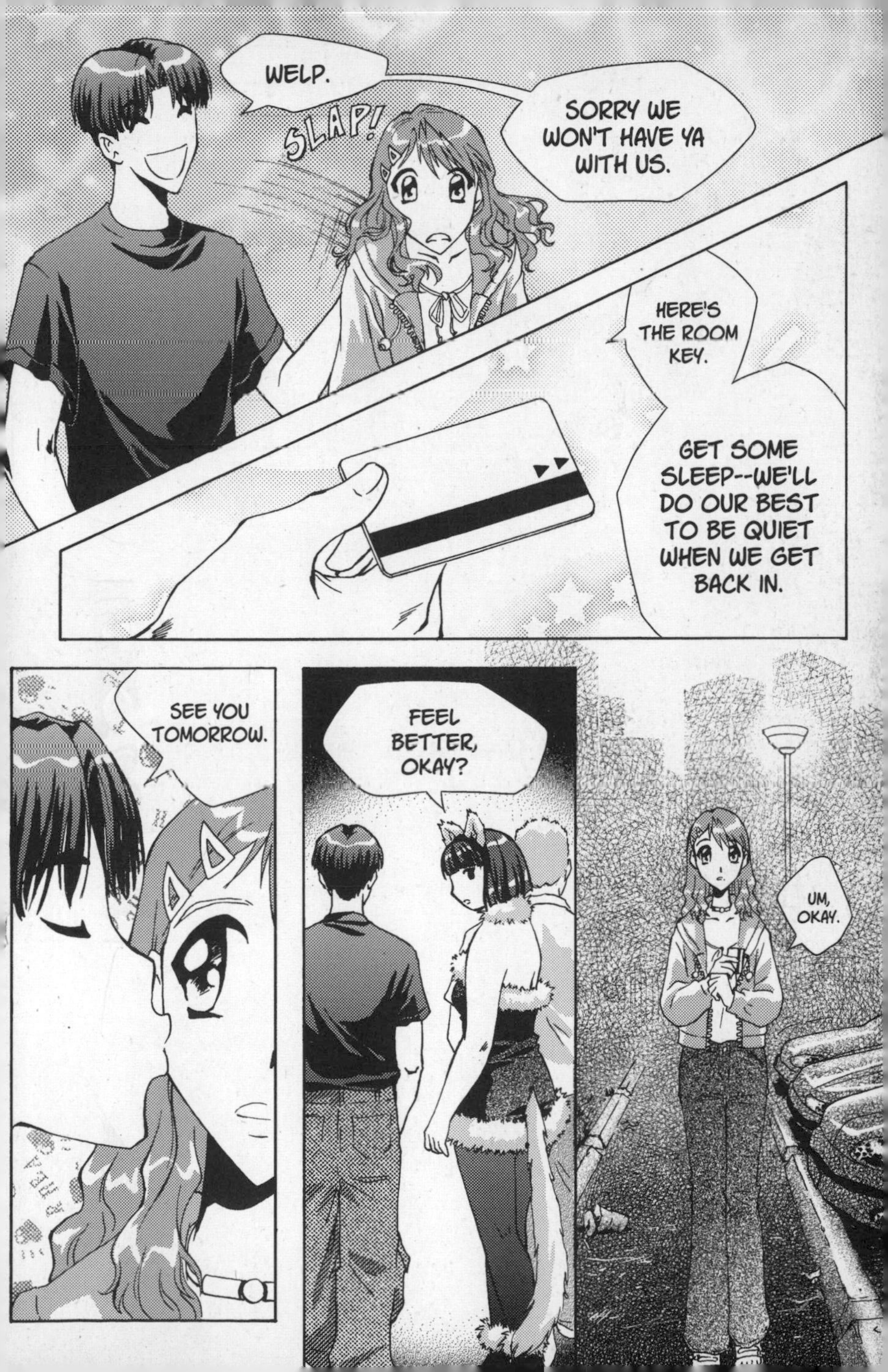
WELP.
SLAP!
SORRY WE WON'T HAVE YA WITH US.
HERE'S THE ROOM KEY.
GET SOME SLEEP--WE'LL DO OUR BEST TO BE QUIET WHEN WE GET BACK IN.
SEE YOU TOMORROW.
FEEL BETTER, OKAY?
UM, OKAY.

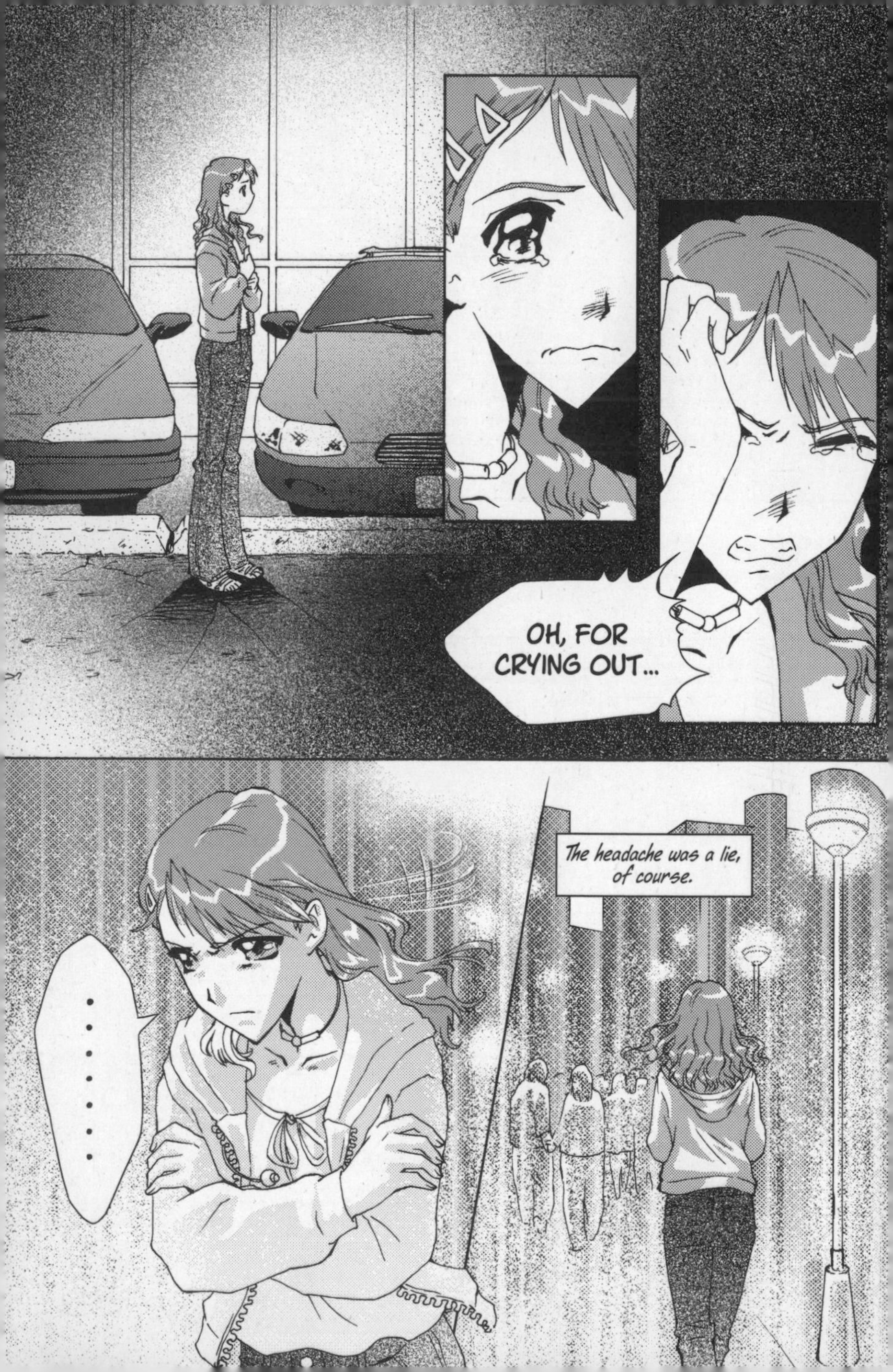
OH, FOR CRYING OUT...
. . . .
The headache was a lie, of course.

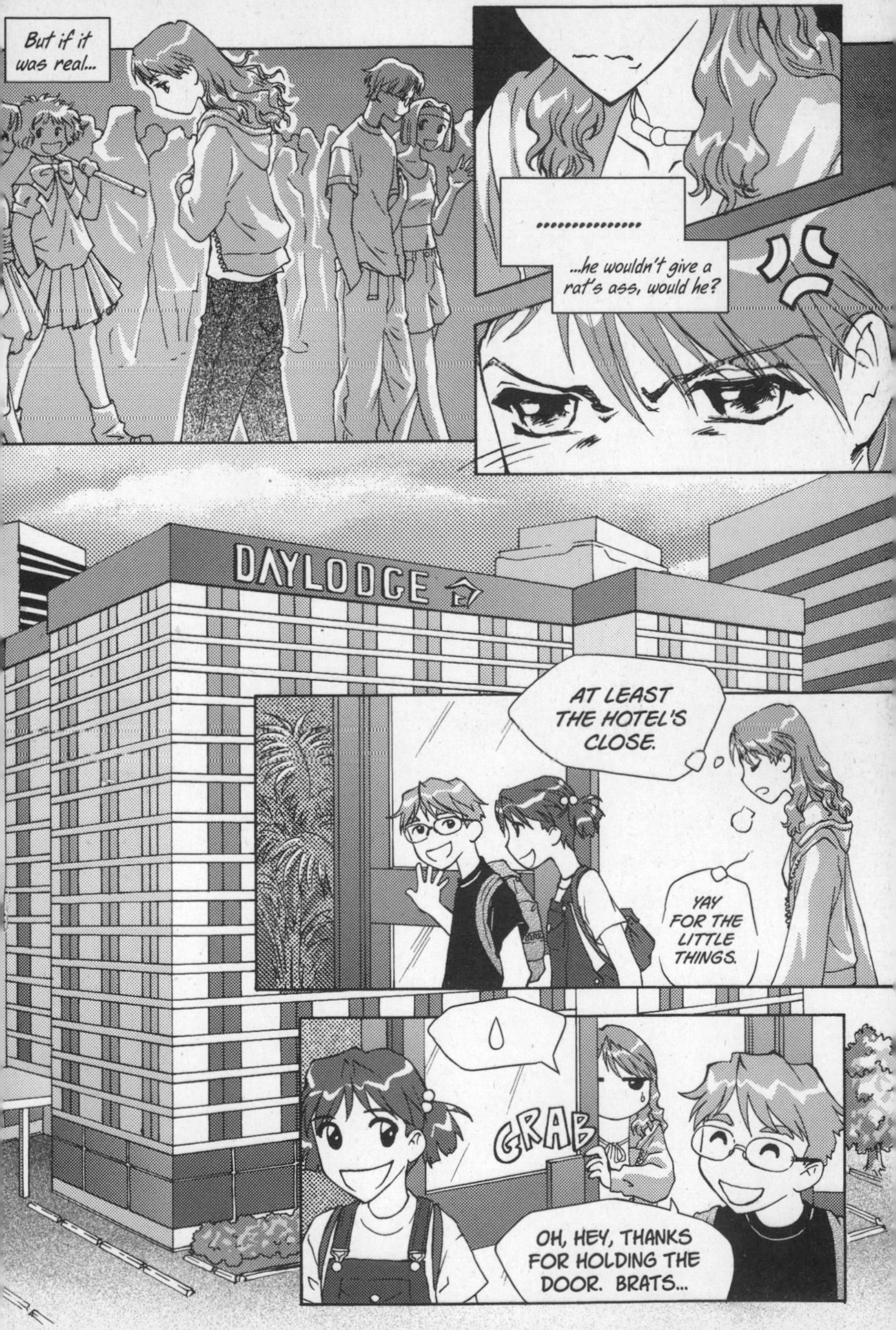
But if it was real...
....
...he wouldn't give a rat's ass, would he?
DAYLODGE
AT LEAST THE HOTEL'S CLOSE.
YAY FOR THE LITTLE THINGS.
GRAB
OH, HEY, THANKS FOR HOLDING THE DOOR. BRATS...

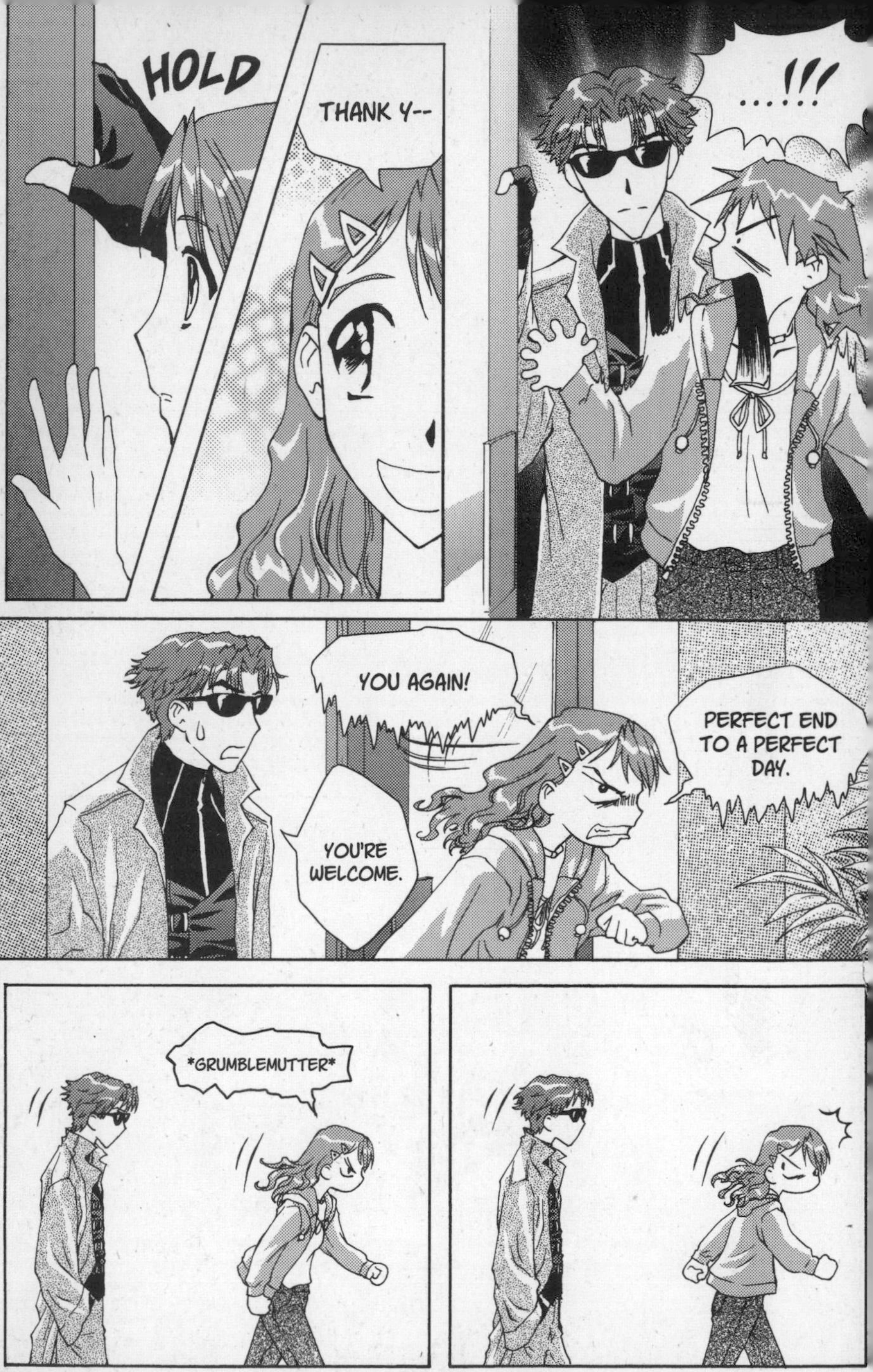
HOLD
THANK Y--
...!!!
YOU AGAIN!
YOU'RE WELCOME.
PERFECT END TO A PERFECT DAY.
GRUMBLEMUTTER

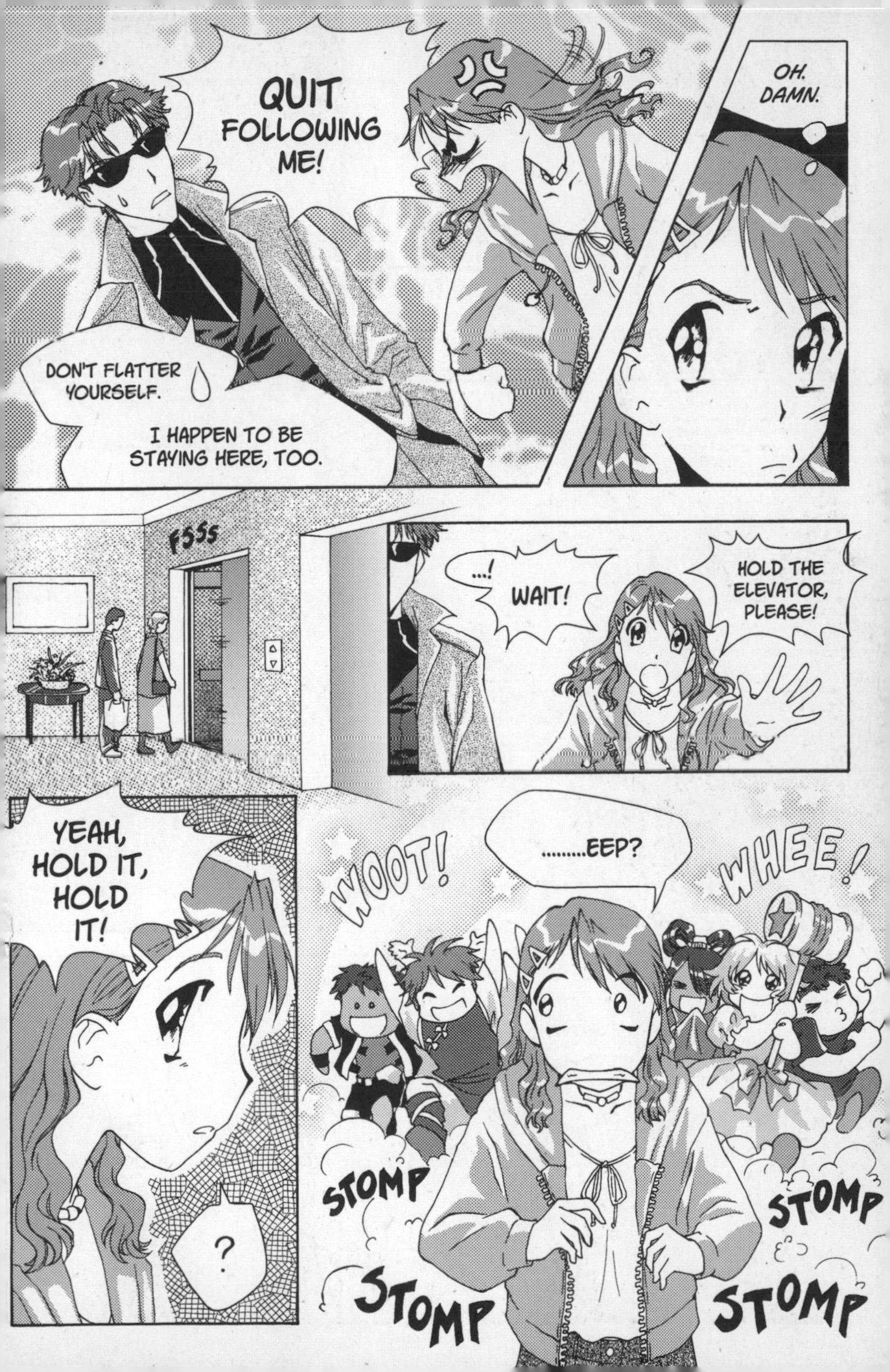
QUIT FOLLOWING ME!
DON'T FLATTER YOURSELF.
I HAPPEN TO BE STAYING HERE, TOO.
OH. DAMN.
FSSS
...!
WAIT!
HOLD THE ELEVATOR, PLEASE!
YEAH, HOLD IT, HOLD IT!
?
WOOT!
.........EEP?
WHEE!
STOMP
STOMP
STOMP
STOMP

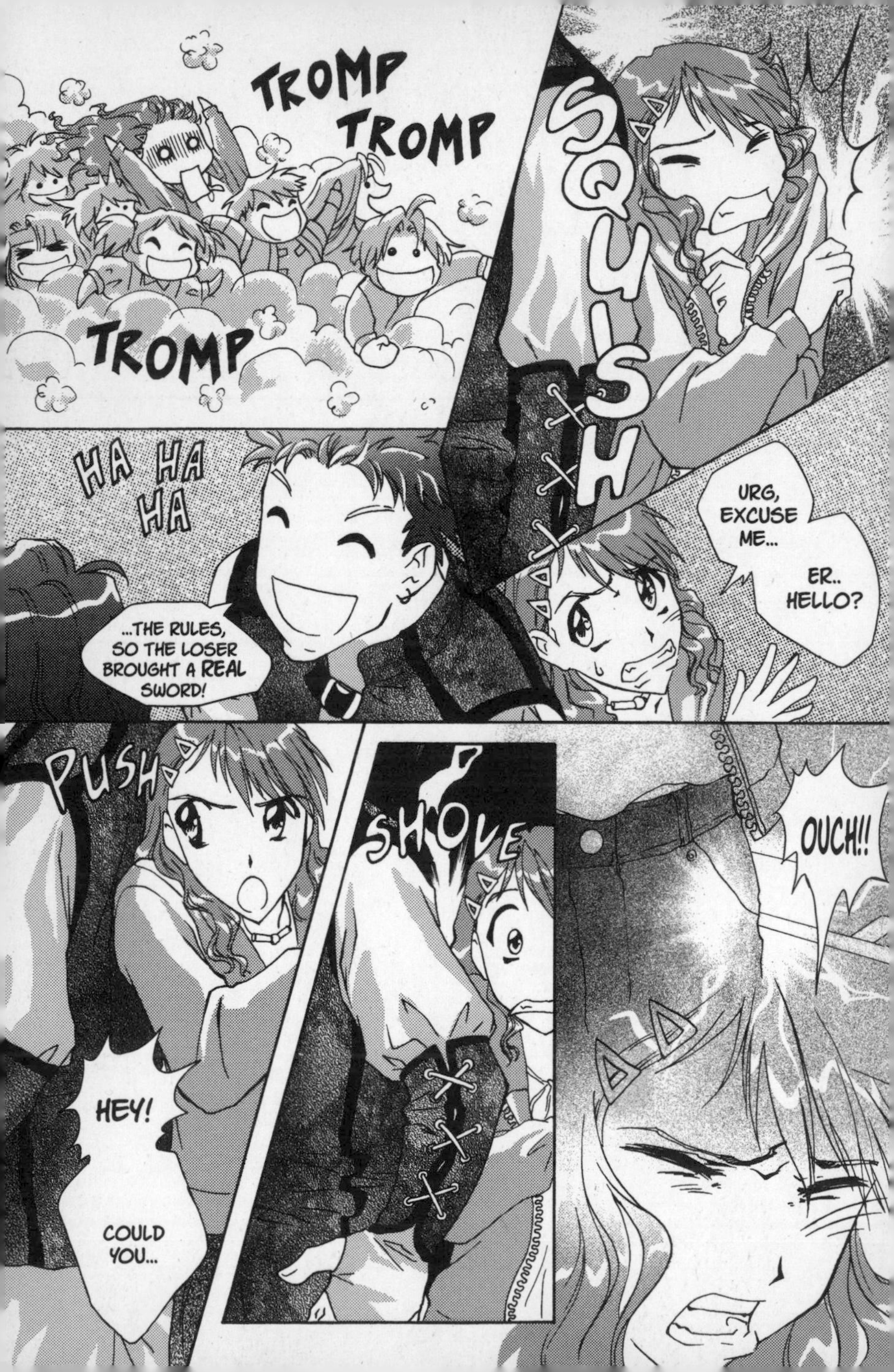
TROMP
TROMP
TROMP
SQUISH
HA HA HA
...THE RULES, SO THE LOSER BROUGHT A REAL SWORD!
URG, EXCUSE ME...
ER.. HELLO?
PUSH
HEY!
COULD YOU...
SHOVE
OUCH!!

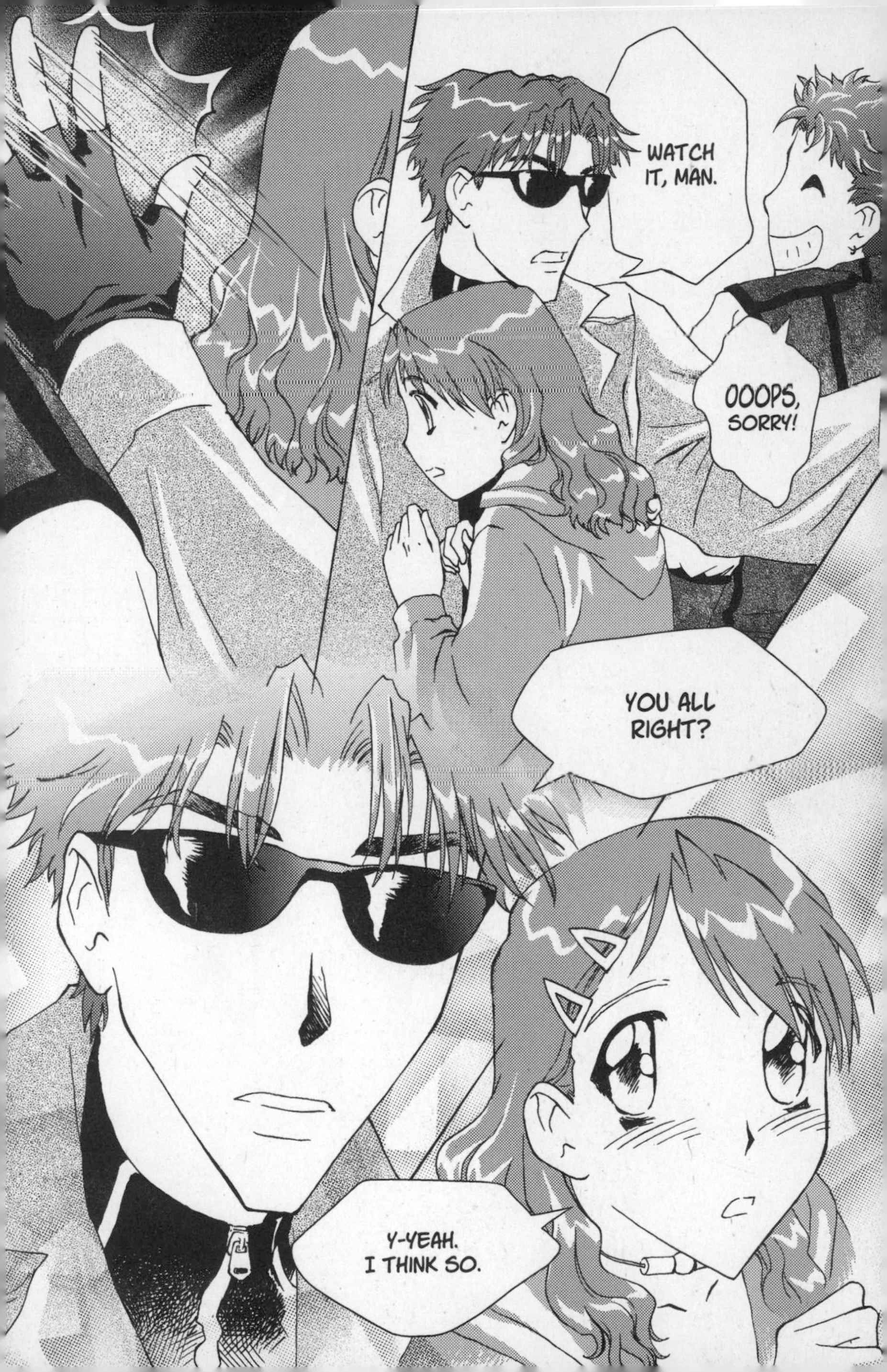
WATCH IT, MAN.
OOOPS, SORRY!
YOU ALL RIGHT?
Y-YEAH. I THINK SO.

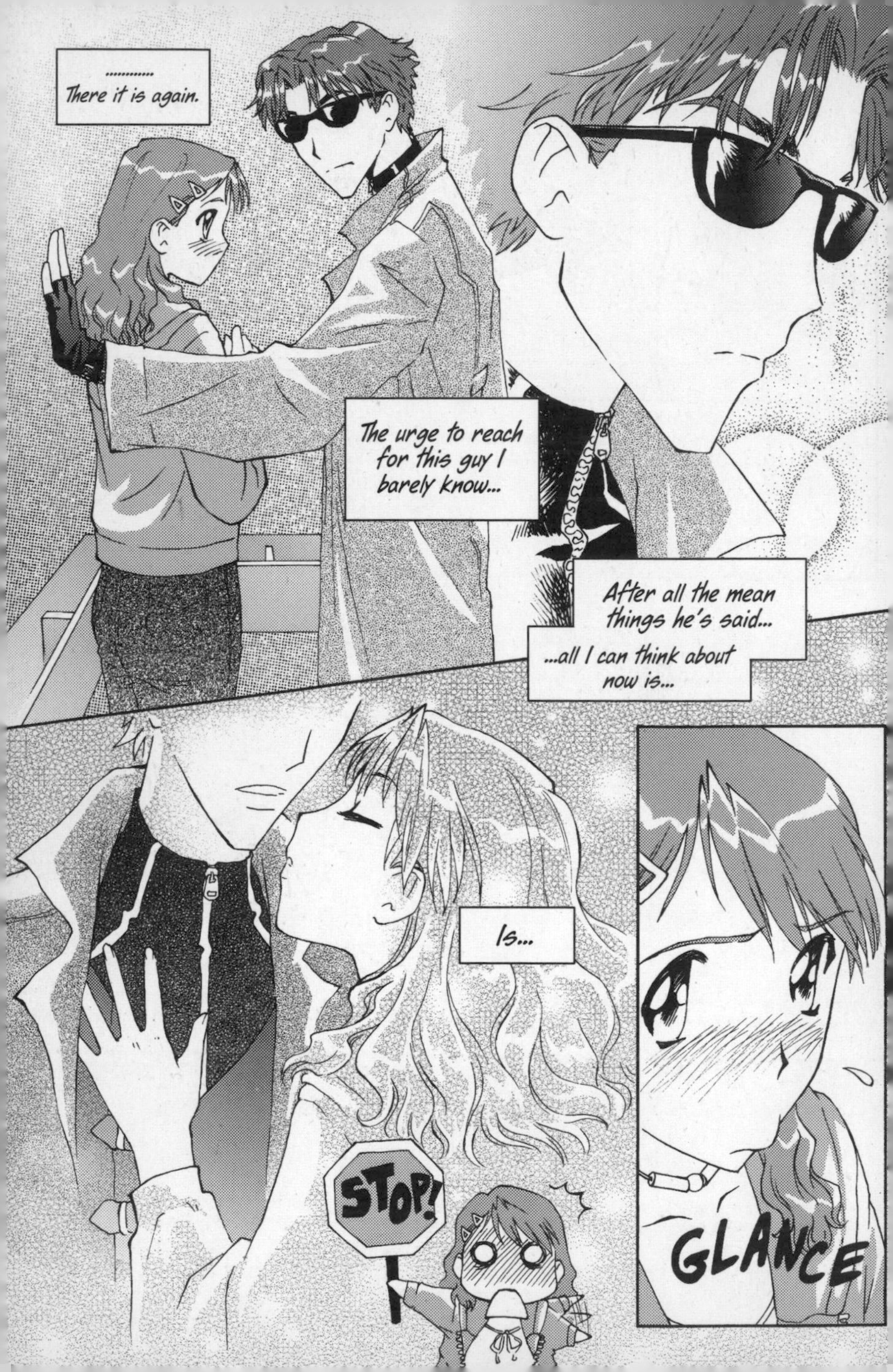

....
There it is again.
The urge to reach for this guy I barely know...
After all the mean things he's said...
...all I can think about now is...
Is...
STOP!
GLANCE

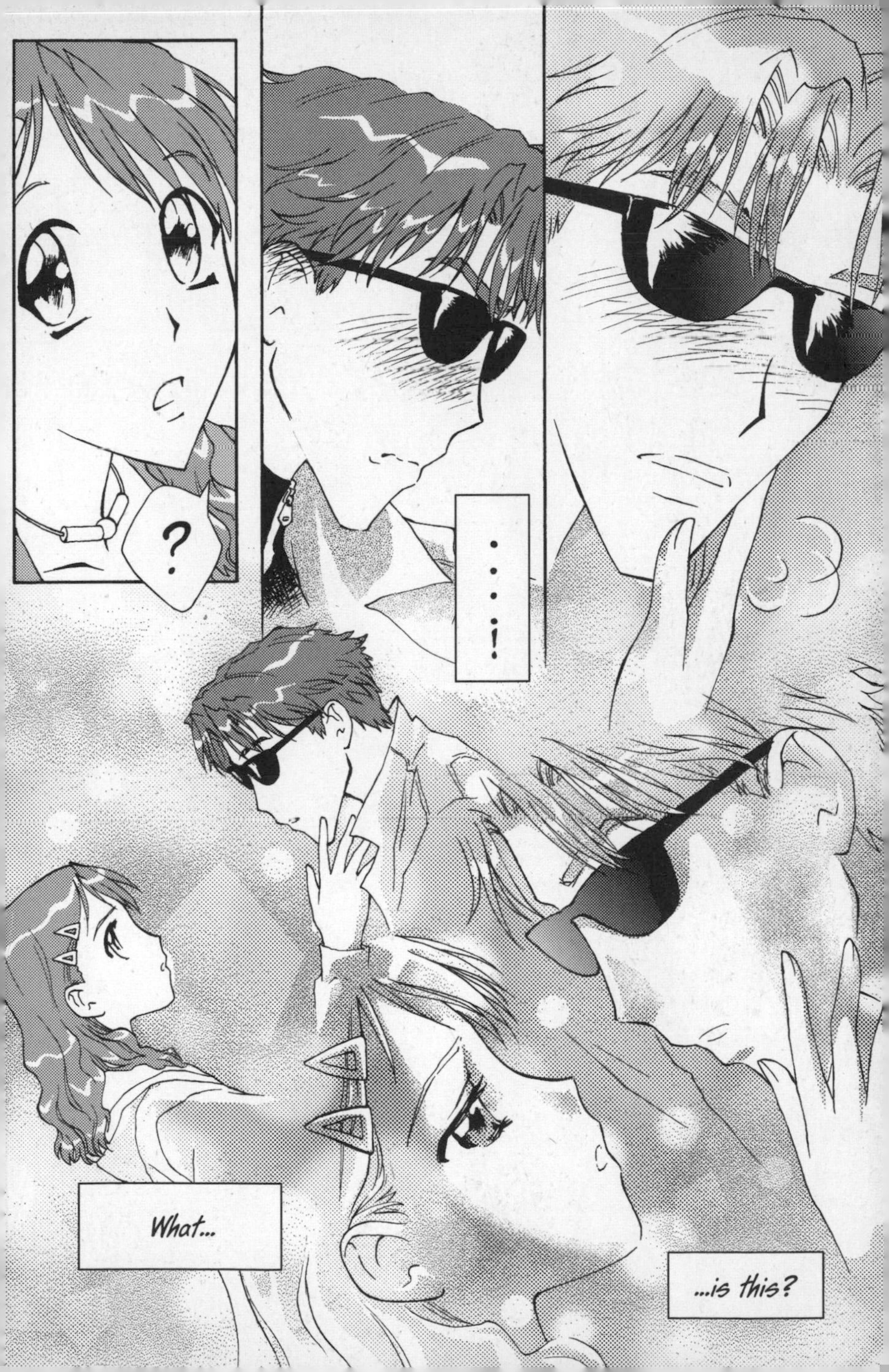
?
. . . !
What...
...is this?

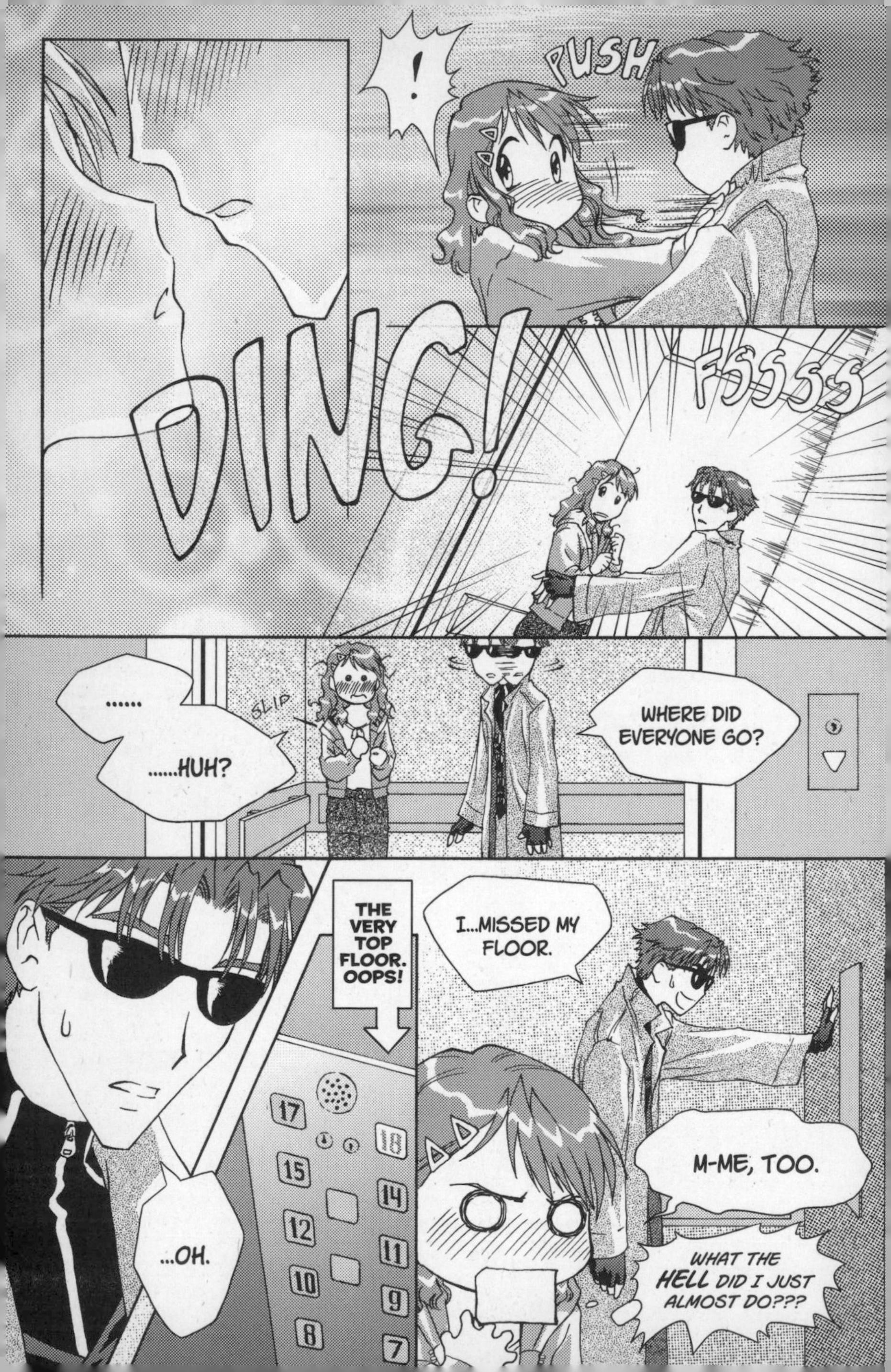

DING!
!
PUSH
FSSSS
......
......HUH?
SLIP
WHERE DID EVERYONE GO?
...OH.
THE VERY TOP FLOOR. OOPS!
17 18 15 14 12 11 10 9 8 7
I...MISSED MY FLOOR.
M-ME, TOO.
WHAT THE HELL DID I JUST ALMOST DO???

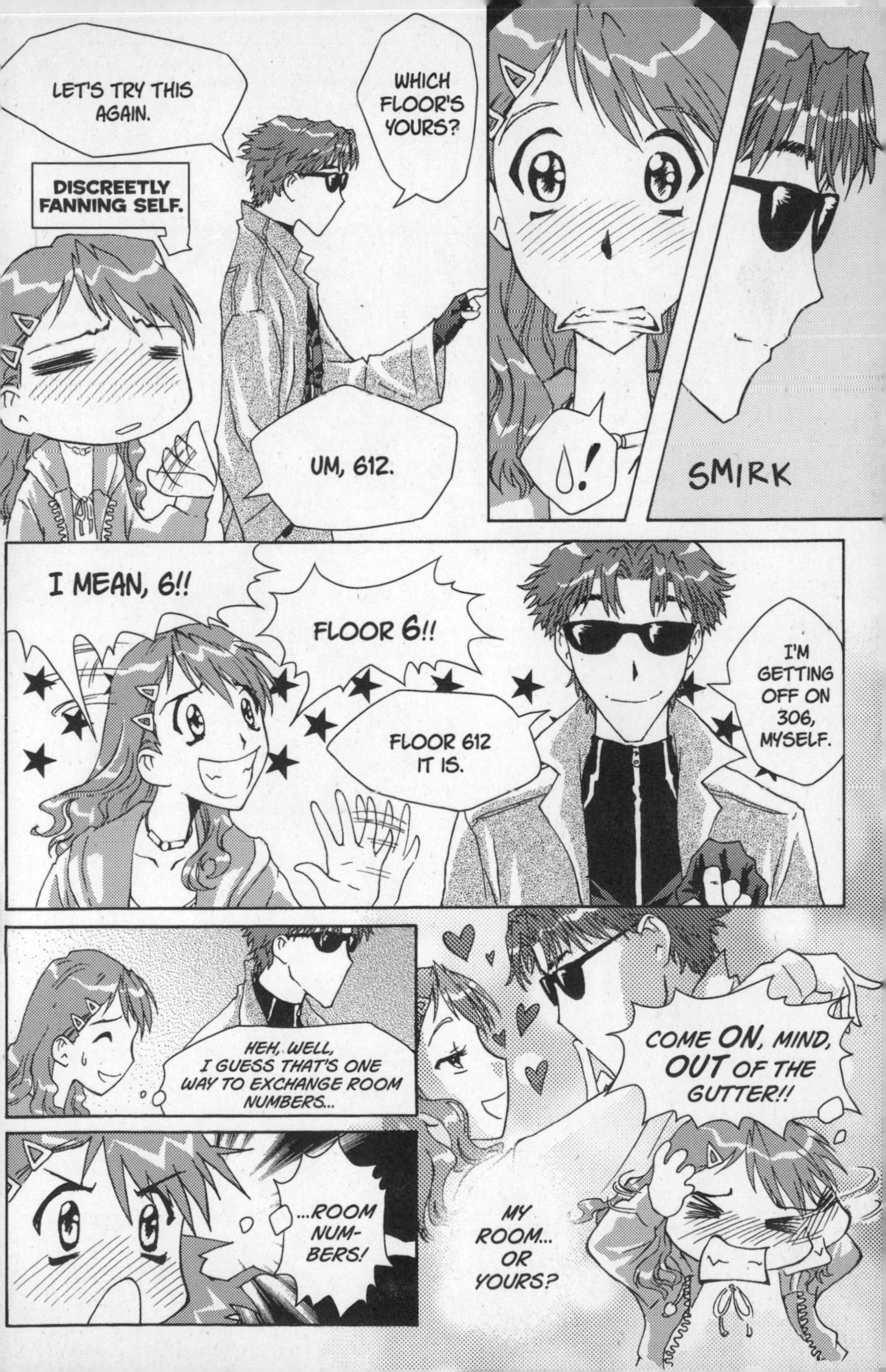
LET'S TRY THIS AGAIN.
WHICH FLOOR'S YOURS?
DISCREETLY FANNING SELF.
UM, 612.
!
SMIRK
I MEAN, 6!!
FLOOR 6!!
FLOOR 612 IT IS.
I'M GETTING OFF ON 306, MYSELF.
HEH, WELL, I GUESS THAT'S ONE WAY TO EXCHANGE ROOM NUMBERS...
...ROOM NUM-BERS!
MY ROOM... OR YOURS?
COME ON, MIND, OUT OF THE GUTTER!!

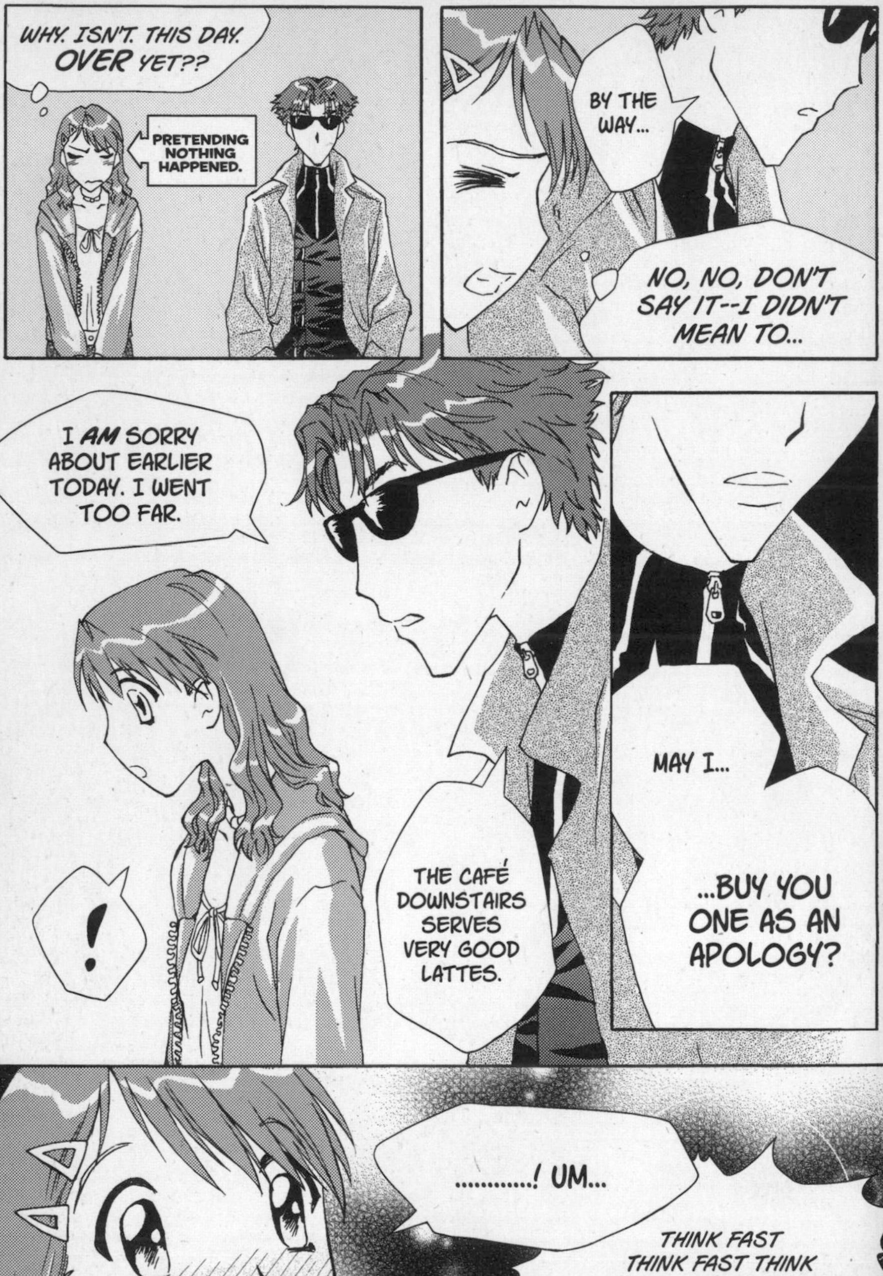
WHY. ISN'T. THIS DAY. OVER YET??
PRETENDING NOTHING HAPPENED.
BY THE WAY...
NO, NO, DON'T SAY IT--I DIDN'T MEAN TO...
I **AM** SORRY ABOUT EARLIER TODAY. I WENT TOO FAR.
!
THE CAFÉ DOWNSTAIRS SERVES VERY GOOD LATTES.
MAY I...
...BUY YOU ONE AS AN APOLOGY?
............! UM...
THINK FAST THINK FAST THINK FAST THINK FAST THINK FAST...

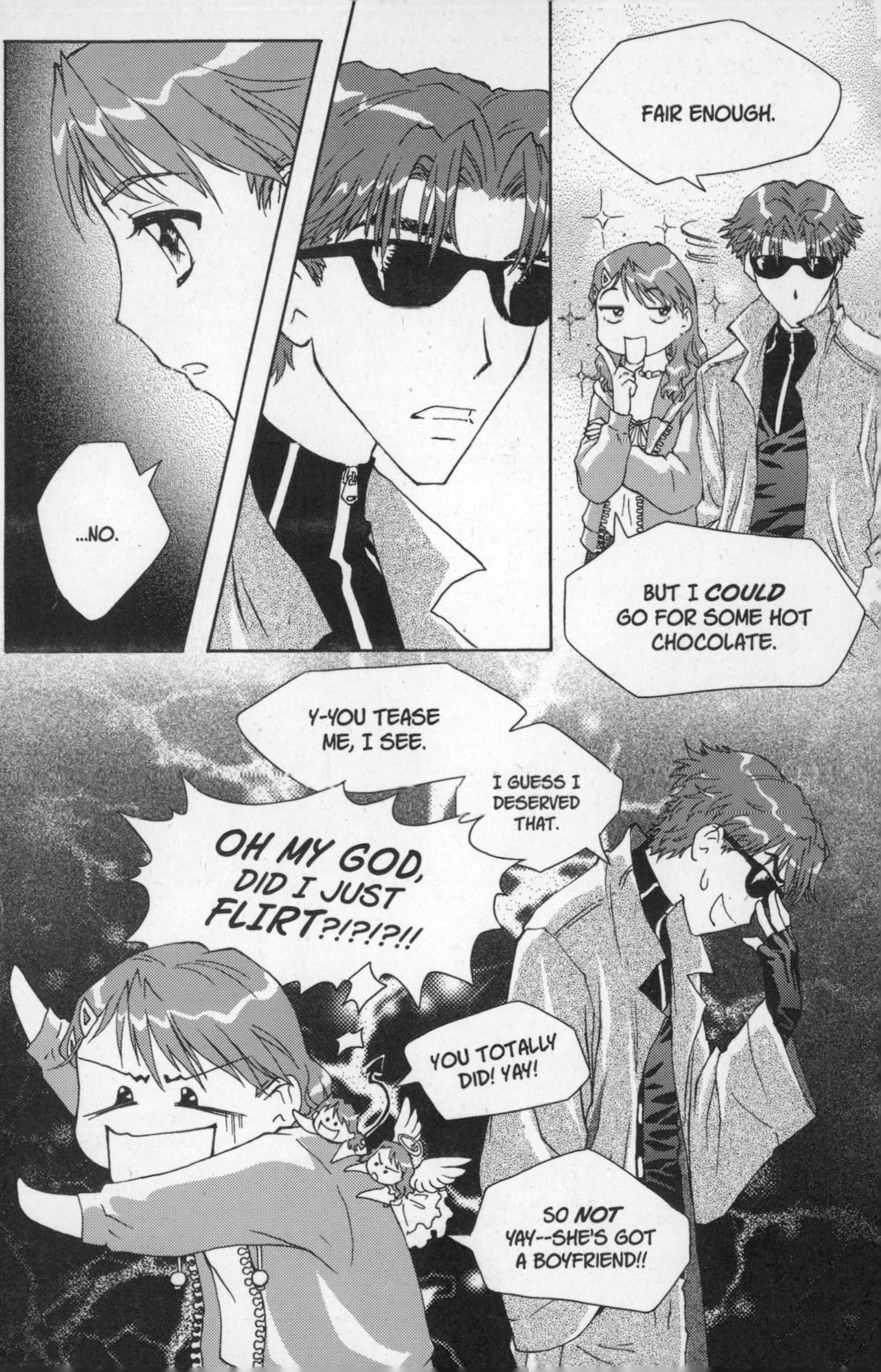
...NO.
FAIR ENOUGH.
BUT I *COULD* GO FOR SOME HOT CHOCOLATE.
Y-YOU TEASE ME, I SEE.
I GUESS I DESERVED THAT.
OH MY GOD, DID I JUST FLIRT?!?!?!!
YOU TOTALLY DID! YAY!
SO *NOT* YAY--SHE'S GOT A BOYFRIEND!!

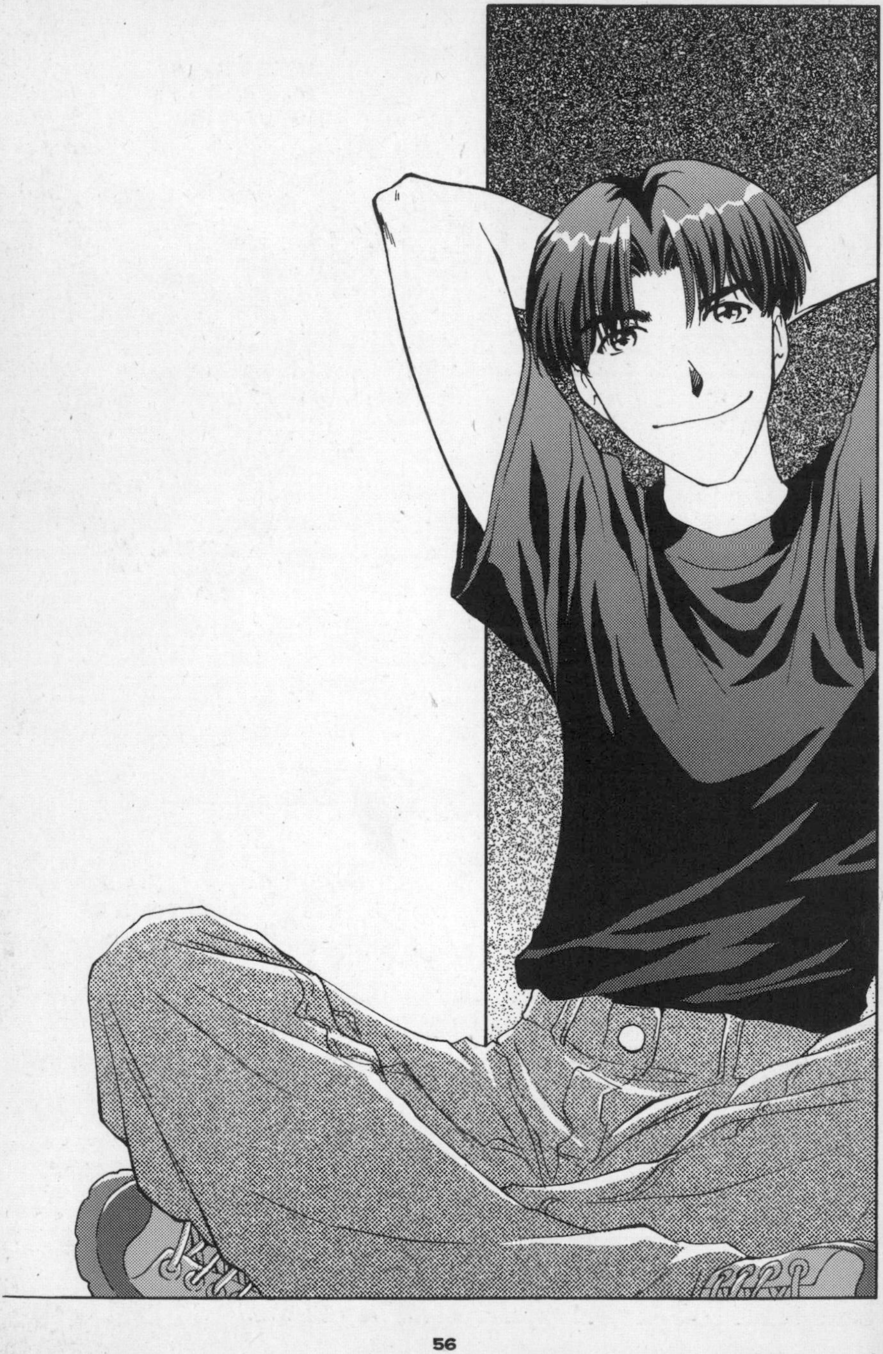

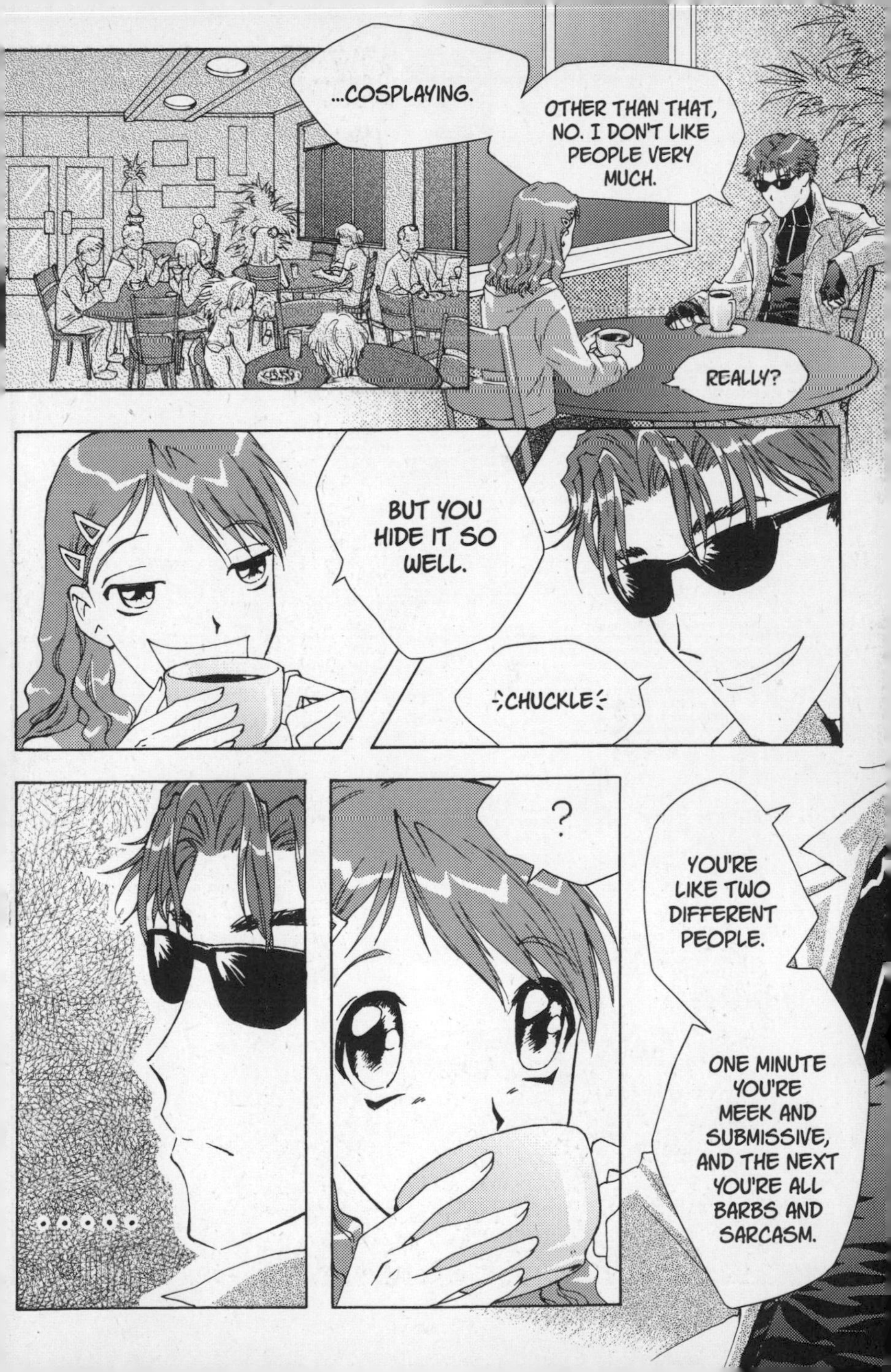
...COSPLAYING.
OTHER THAN THAT, NO. I DON'T LIKE PEOPLE VERY MUCH.
REALLY?
BUT YOU HIDE IT SO WELL.
CHUCKLE
.....
?
YOU'RE LIKE TWO DIFFERENT PEOPLE.
ONE MINUTE YOU'RE MEEK AND SUBMISSIVE, AND THE NEXT YOU'RE ALL BARBS AND SARCASM.

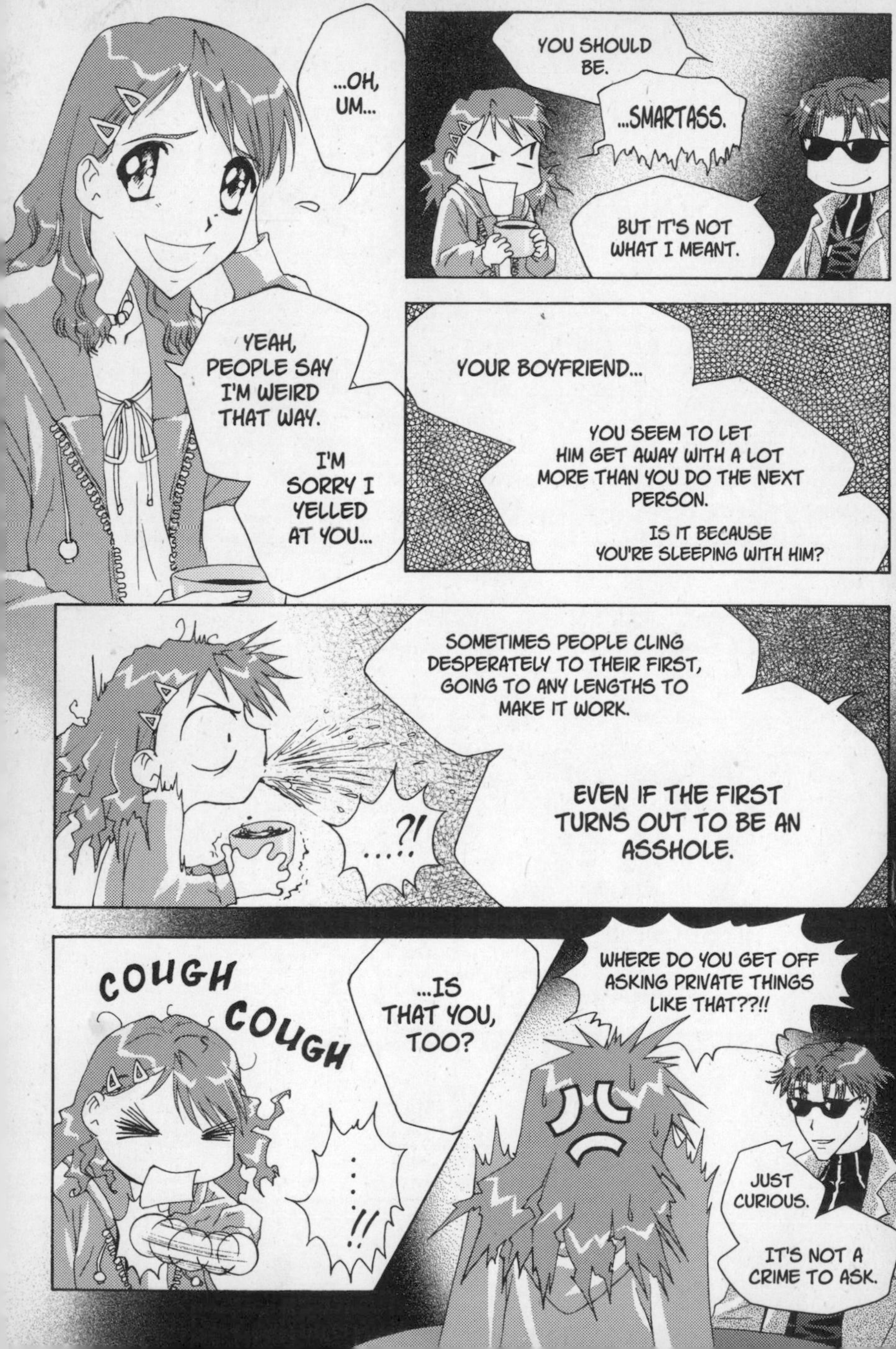
YOU SHOULD BE.
...SMARTASS.
BUT IT'S NOT WHAT I MEANT.
...OH, UM...
YEAH, PEOPLE SAY I'M WEIRD THAT WAY.
I'M SORRY I YELLED AT YOU...
YOUR BOYFRIEND...
YOU SEEM TO LET HIM GET AWAY WITH A LOT MORE THAN YOU DO THE NEXT PERSON.
IS IT BECAUSE YOU'RE SLEEPING WITH HIM?
SOMETIMES PEOPLE CLING DESPERATELY TO THEIR FIRST, GOING TO ANY LENGTHS TO MAKE IT WORK.
EVEN IF THE FIRST TURNS OUT TO BE AN ASSHOLE.
...?!
WHERE DO YOU GET OFF ASKING PRIVATE THINGS LIKE THAT??!!
JUST CURIOUS.
IT'S NOT A CRIME TO ASK.
...IS THAT YOU, TOO?
...!!
COUGH
COUGH

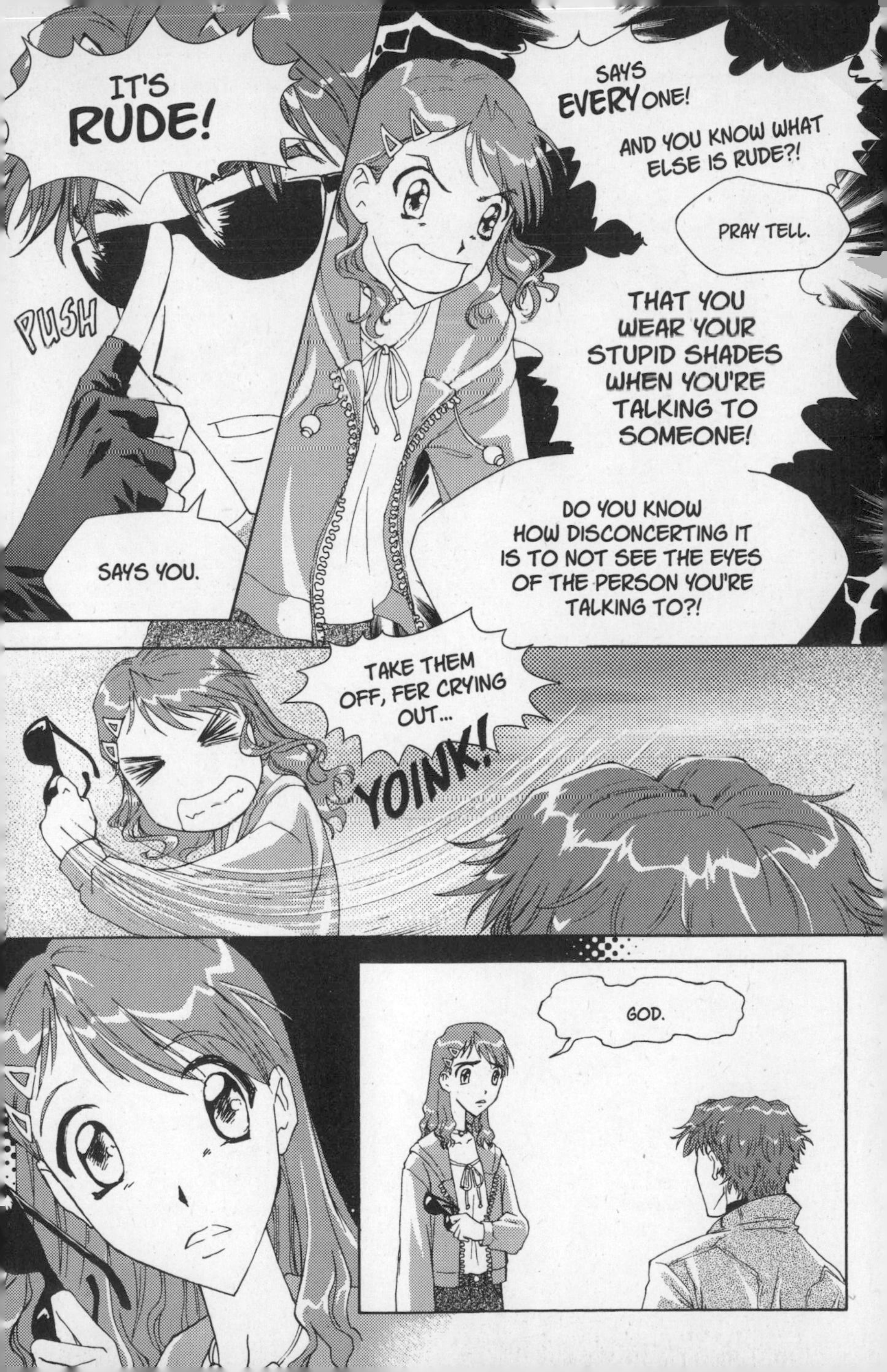

IT'S RUDE!
PUSH
SAYS YOU.
SAYS EVERYONE!
AND YOU KNOW WHAT ELSE IS RUDE?!
PRAY TELL.
THAT YOU WEAR YOUR STUPID SHADES WHEN YOU'RE TALKING TO SOMEONE!
DO YOU KNOW HOW DISCONCERTING IT IS TO NOT SEE THE EYES OF THE PERSON YOU'RE TALKING TO?!
TAKE THEM OFF, FER CRYING OUT...
YOINK!
GOD.

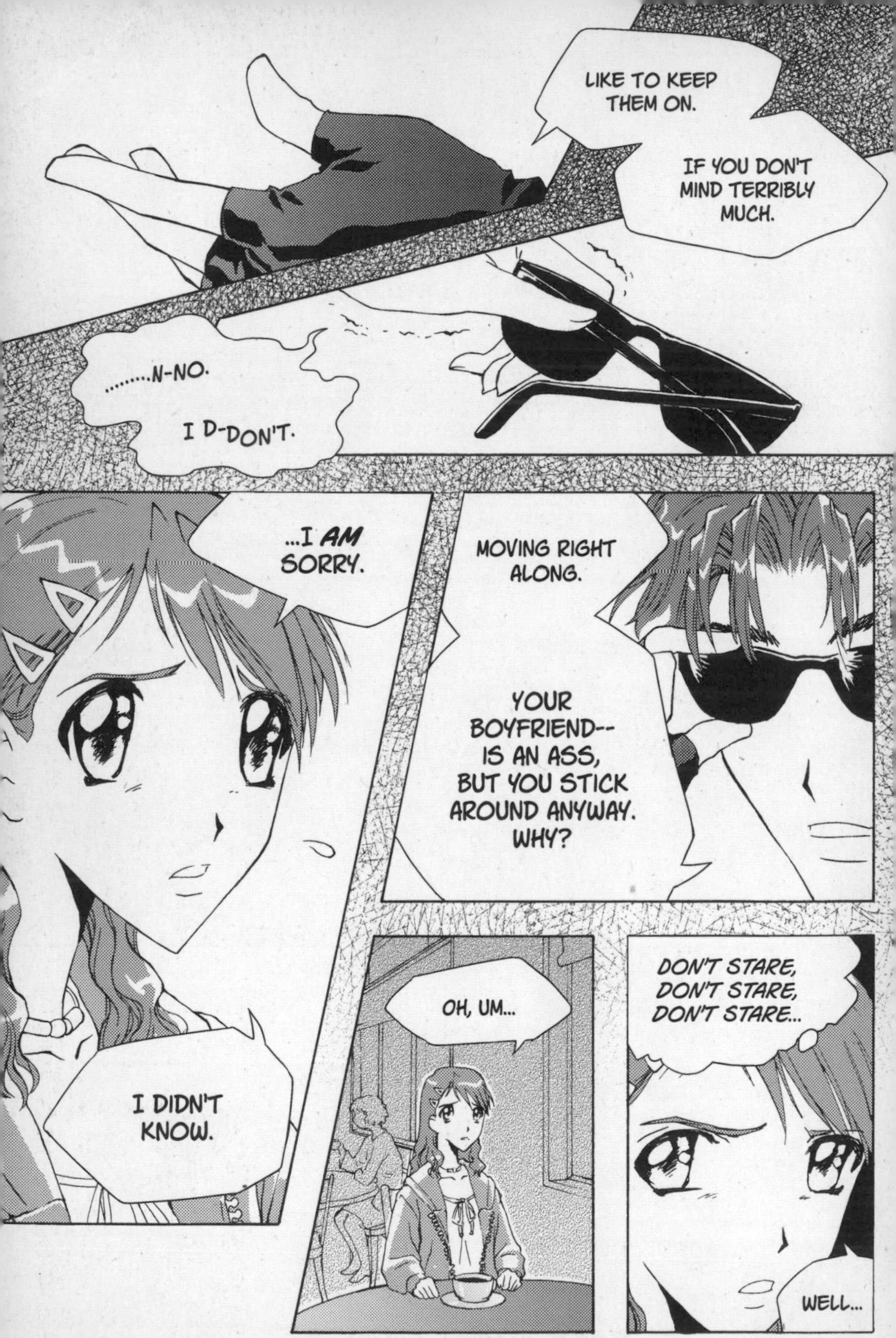
LIKE TO KEEP THEM ON.
IF YOU DON'T MIND TERRIBLY MUCH.
.........N-NO.
I D-DON'T.
...I *AM* SORRY.
I DIDN'T KNOW.
MOVING RIGHT ALONG.
YOUR BOYFRIEND-- IS AN ASS, BUT YOU STICK AROUND ANYWAY. WHY?
OH, UM...
DON'T STARE, DON'T STARE, DON'T STARE...
WELL...

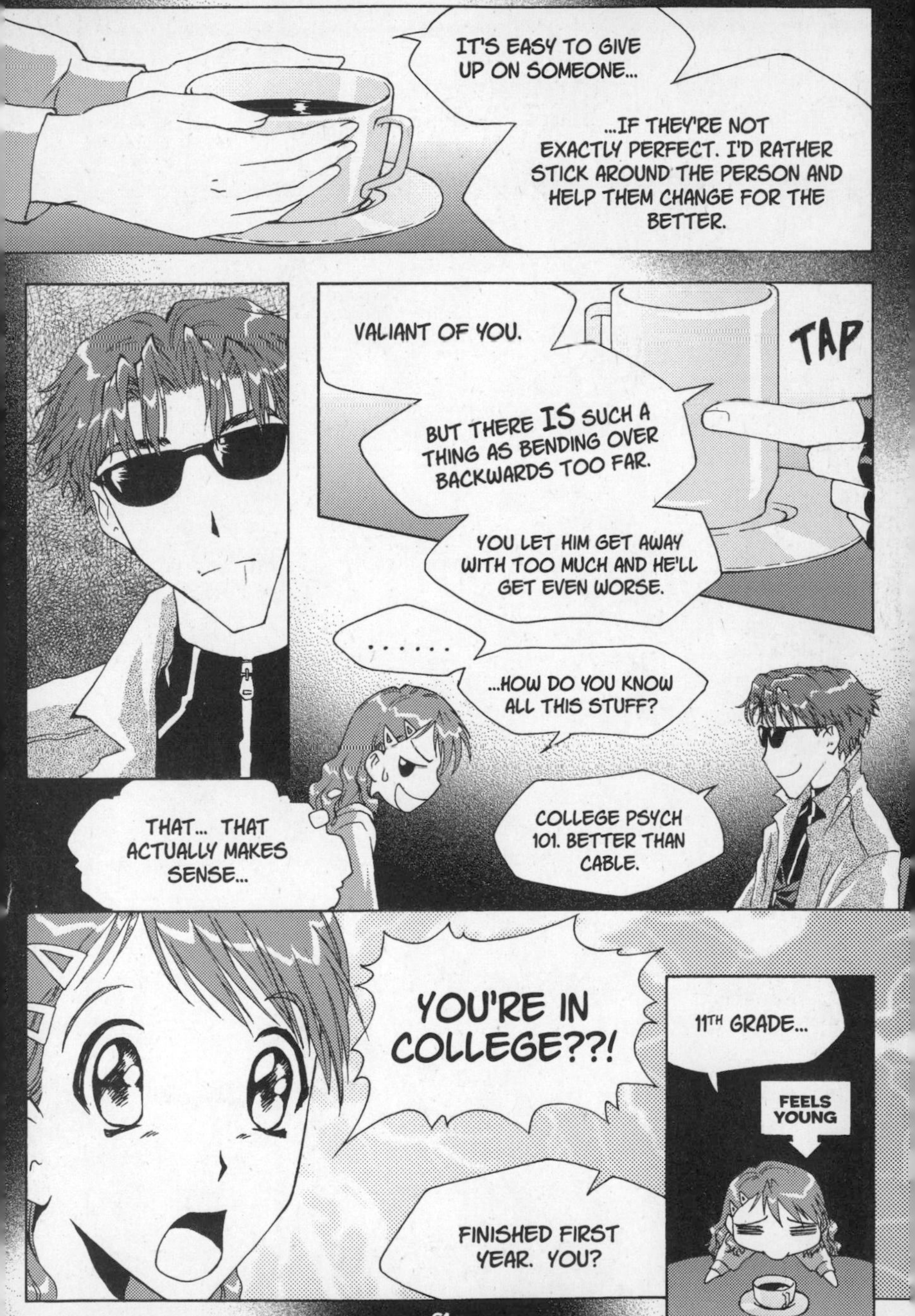
IT'S EASY TO GIVE UP ON SOMEONE...
...IF THEY'RE NOT EXACTLY PERFECT. I'D RATHER STICK AROUND THE PERSON AND HELP THEM CHANGE FOR THE BETTER.
VALIANT OF YOU.
TAP
BUT THERE IS SUCH A THING AS BENDING OVER BACKWARDS TOO FAR.
YOU LET HIM GET AWAY WITH TOO MUCH AND HE'LL GET EVEN WORSE.
......
...HOW DO YOU KNOW ALL THIS STUFF?
THAT... THAT ACTUALLY MAKES SENSE...
COLLEGE PSYCH 101. BETTER THAN CABLE.
YOU'RE IN COLLEGE??!
FINISHED FIRST YEAR. YOU?
11TH GRADE...
FEELS YOUNG

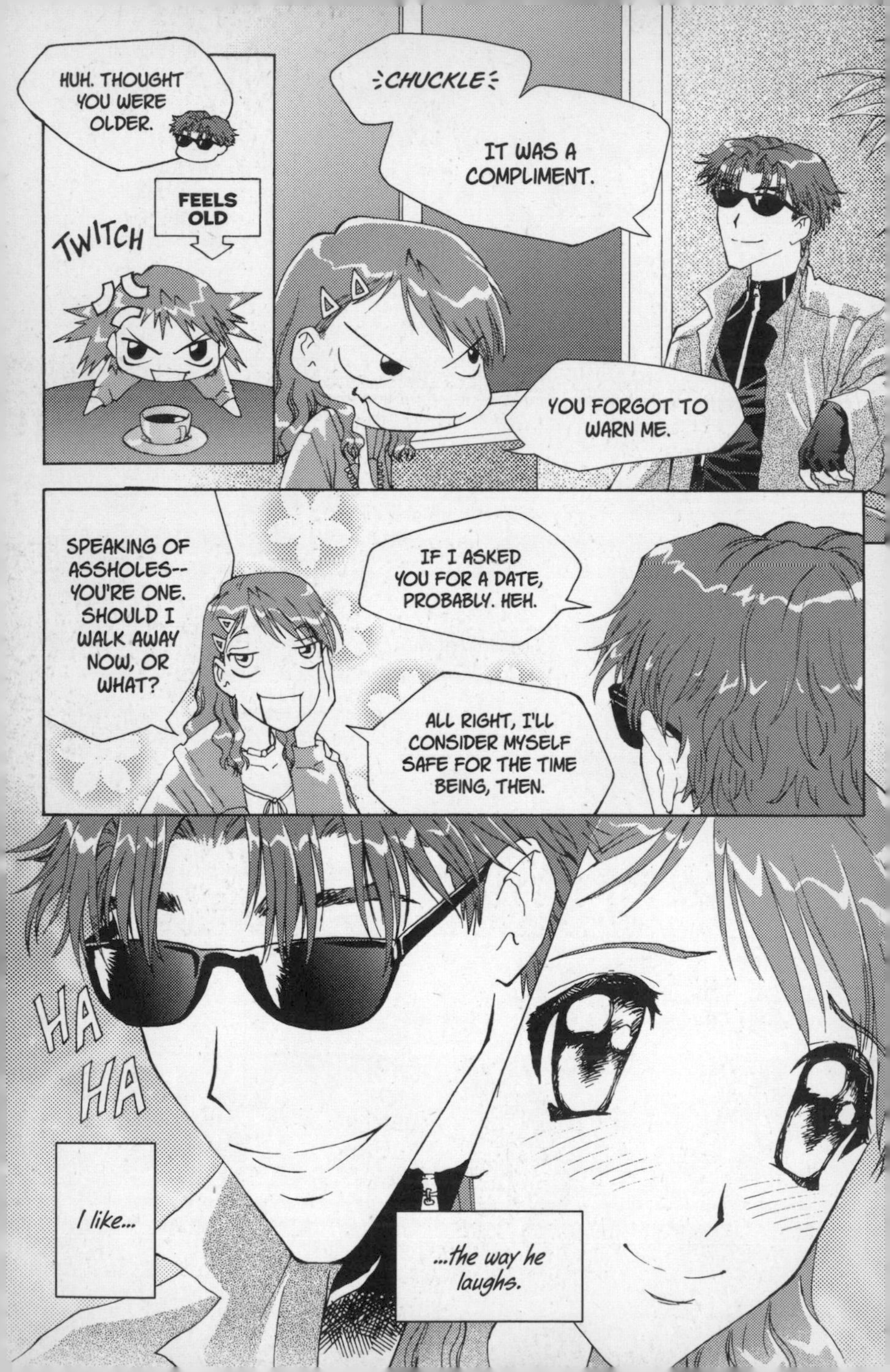
HUH. THOUGHT YOU WERE OLDER.
FEELS OLD
TWITCH
⁝CHUCKLE⁝
IT WAS A COMPLIMENT.
YOU FORGOT TO WARN ME.
SPEAKING OF ASSHOLES-- YOU'RE ONE. SHOULD I WALK AWAY NOW, OR WHAT?
IF I ASKED YOU FOR A DATE, PROBABLY. HEH.
ALL RIGHT, I'LL CONSIDER MYSELF SAFE FOR THE TIME BEING, THEN.
HA HA
I like...
...the way he laughs.

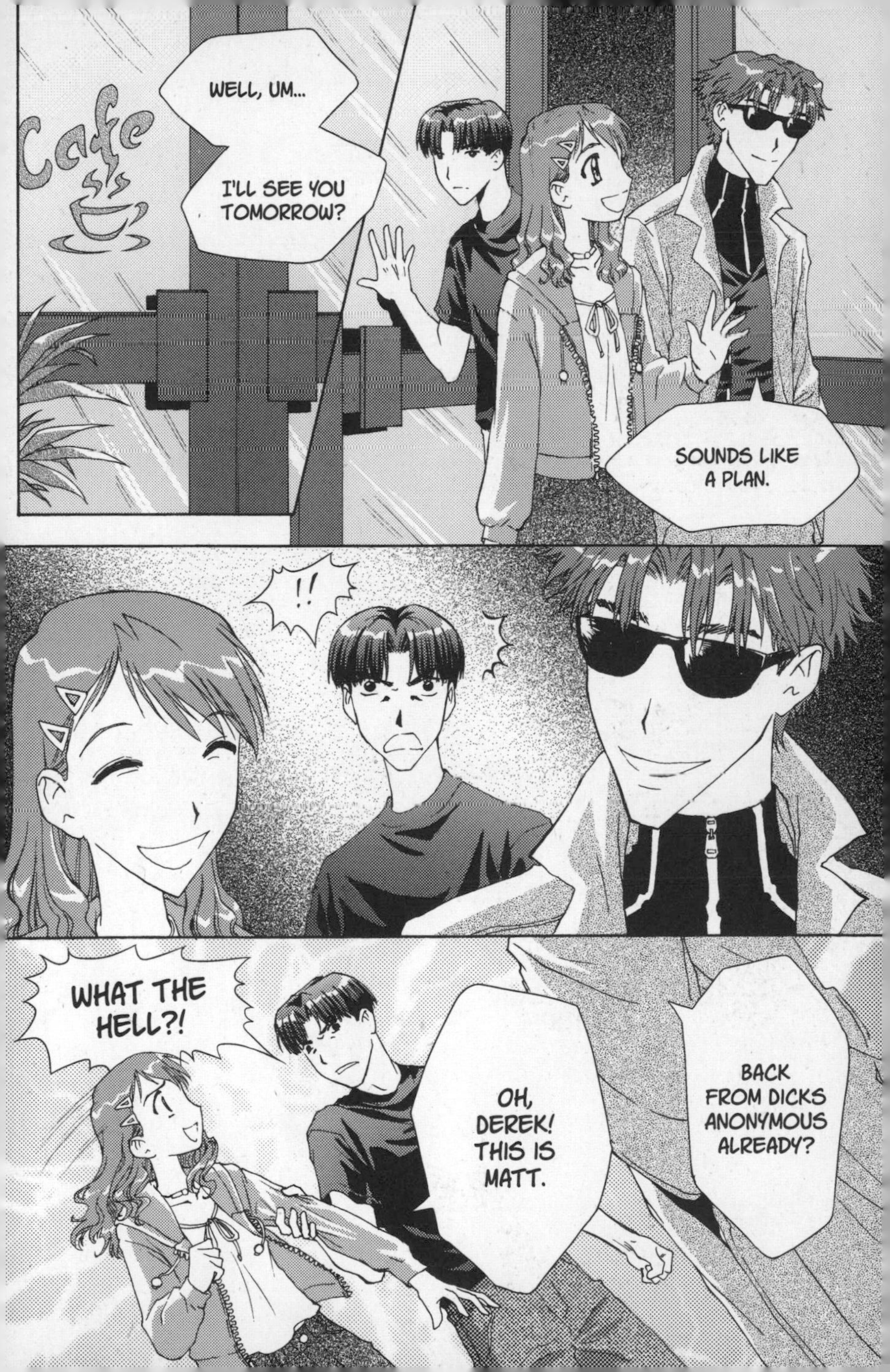
Cafe
WELL, UM...
I'LL SEE YOU TOMORROW?
SOUNDS LIKE A PLAN.
!!
WHAT THE HELL?!
OH, DEREK! THIS IS MATT.
BACK FROM DICKS ANONYMOUS ALREADY?

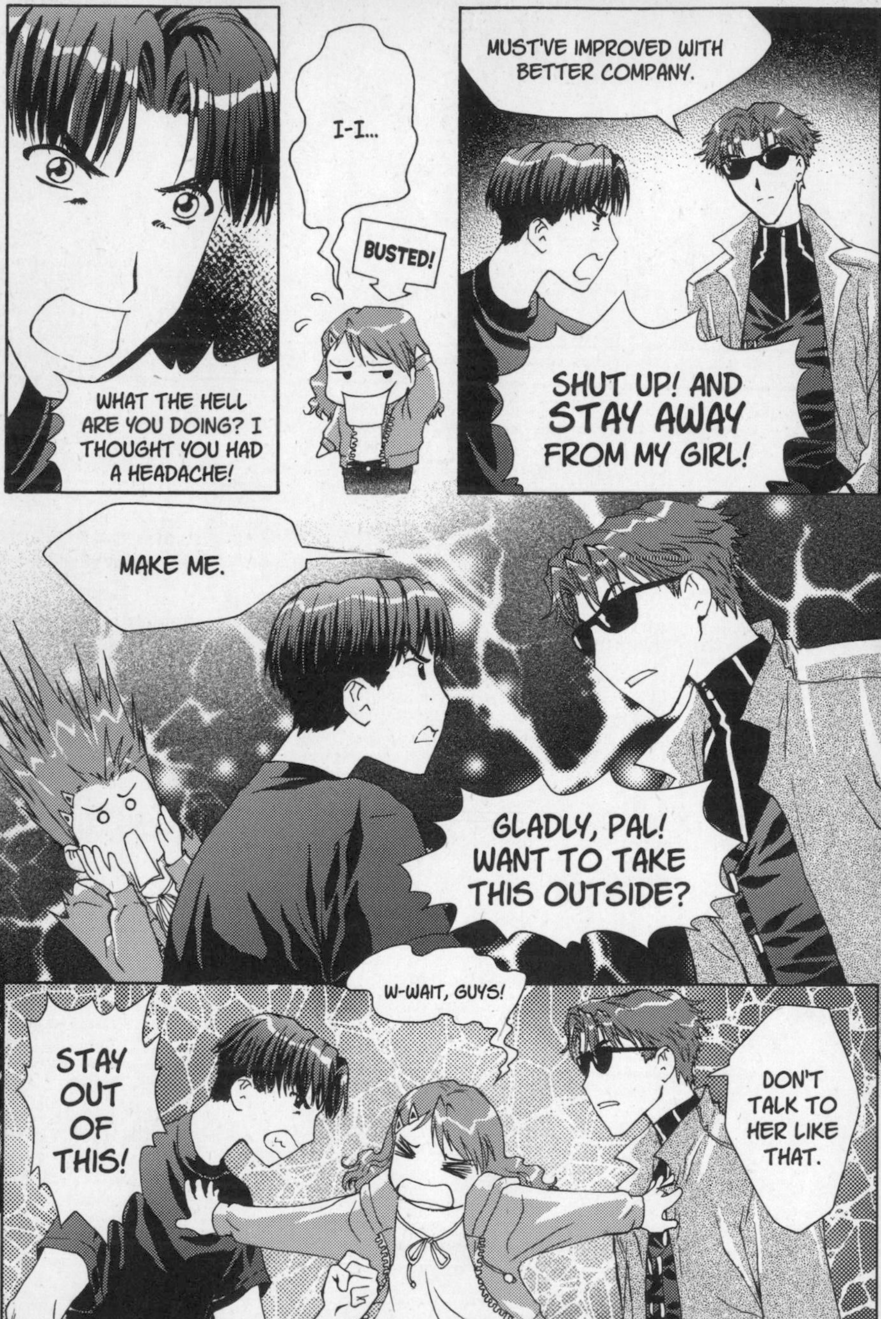
WHAT THE HELL ARE YOU DOING? I THOUGHT YOU HAD A HEADACHE!
I-I...
BUSTED!
MUST'VE IMPROVED WITH BETTER COMPANY.
SHUT UP! AND STAY AWAY FROM MY GIRL!
MAKE ME.
GLADLY, PAL! WANT TO TAKE THIS OUTSIDE?
STAY OUT OF THIS!
W-WAIT, GUYS!
DON'T TALK TO HER LIKE THAT.

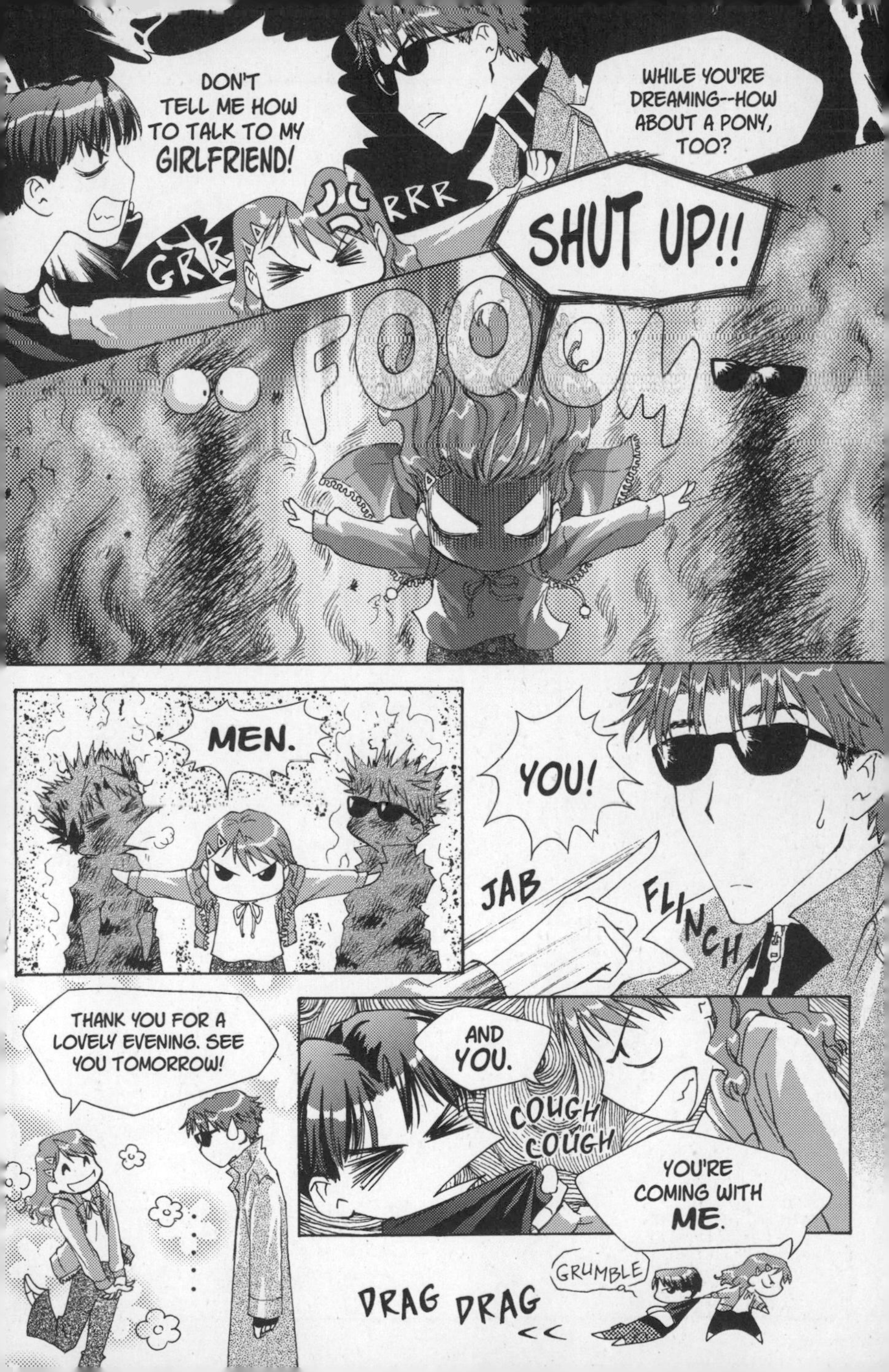
DON'T TELL ME HOW TO TALK TO MY GIRLFRIEND!
WHILE YOU'RE DREAMING--HOW ABOUT A PONY, TOO?
GRR
RRR
SHUT UP!!
FOOOM
MEN.
YOU!
JAB
FLINCH
THANK YOU FOR A LOVELY EVENING. SEE YOU TOMORROW!
AND YOU.
COUGH COUGH
YOU'RE COMING WITH ME.
GRUMBLE
DRAG DRAG

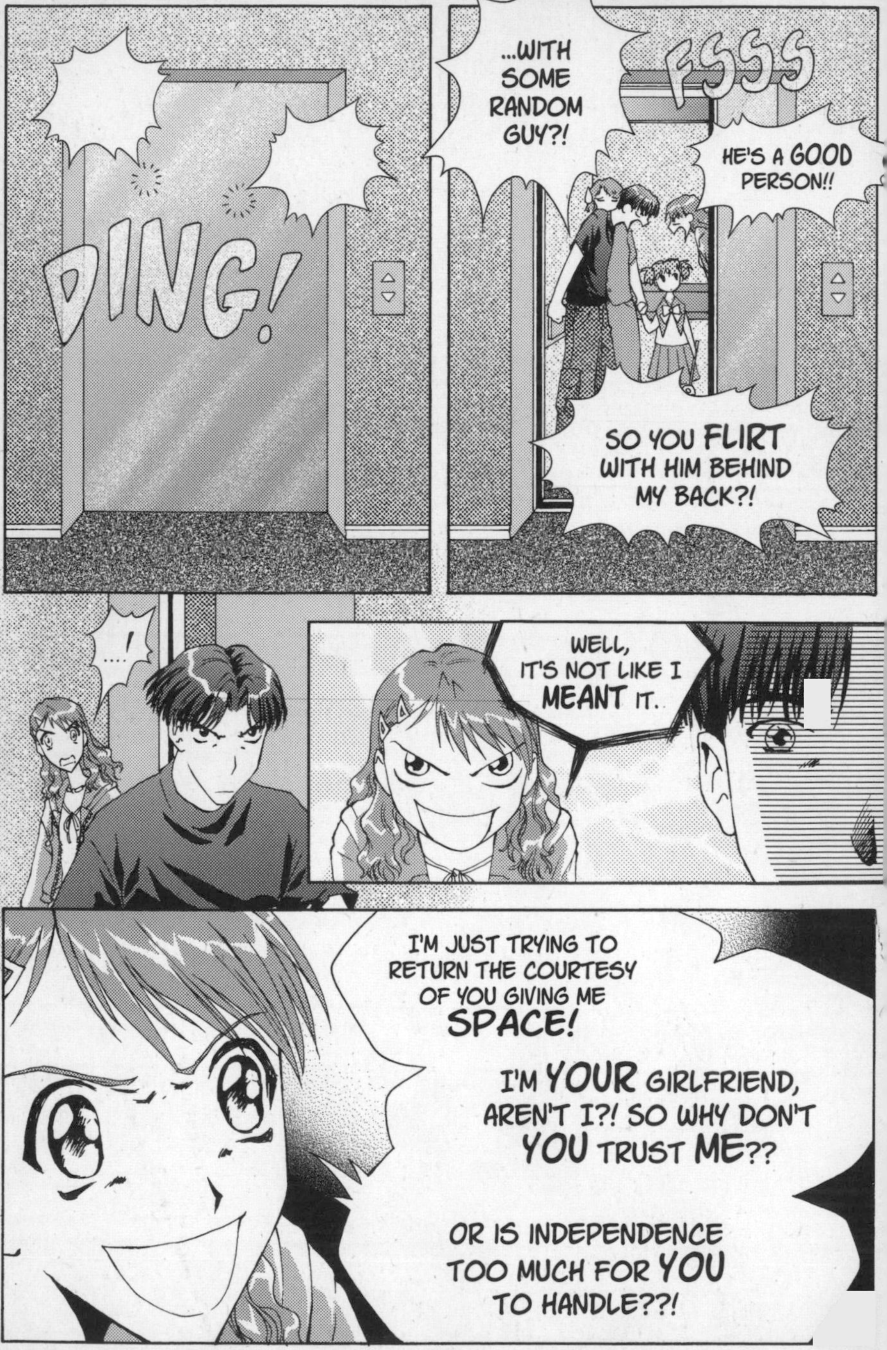
DING!
...WITH SOME RANDOM GUY?!
FSSS
HE'S A GOOD PERSON!!
SO YOU FLIRT WITH HIM BEHIND MY BACK?!
....!
WELL, IT'S NOT LIKE I MEANT IT.
I'M JUST TRYING TO RETURN THE COURTESY OF YOU GIVING ME SPACE!
I'M YOUR GIRLFRIEND, AREN'T I?! SO WHY DON'T YOU TRUST ME??
OR IS INDEPENDENCE TOO MUCH FOR YOU TO HANDLE??!

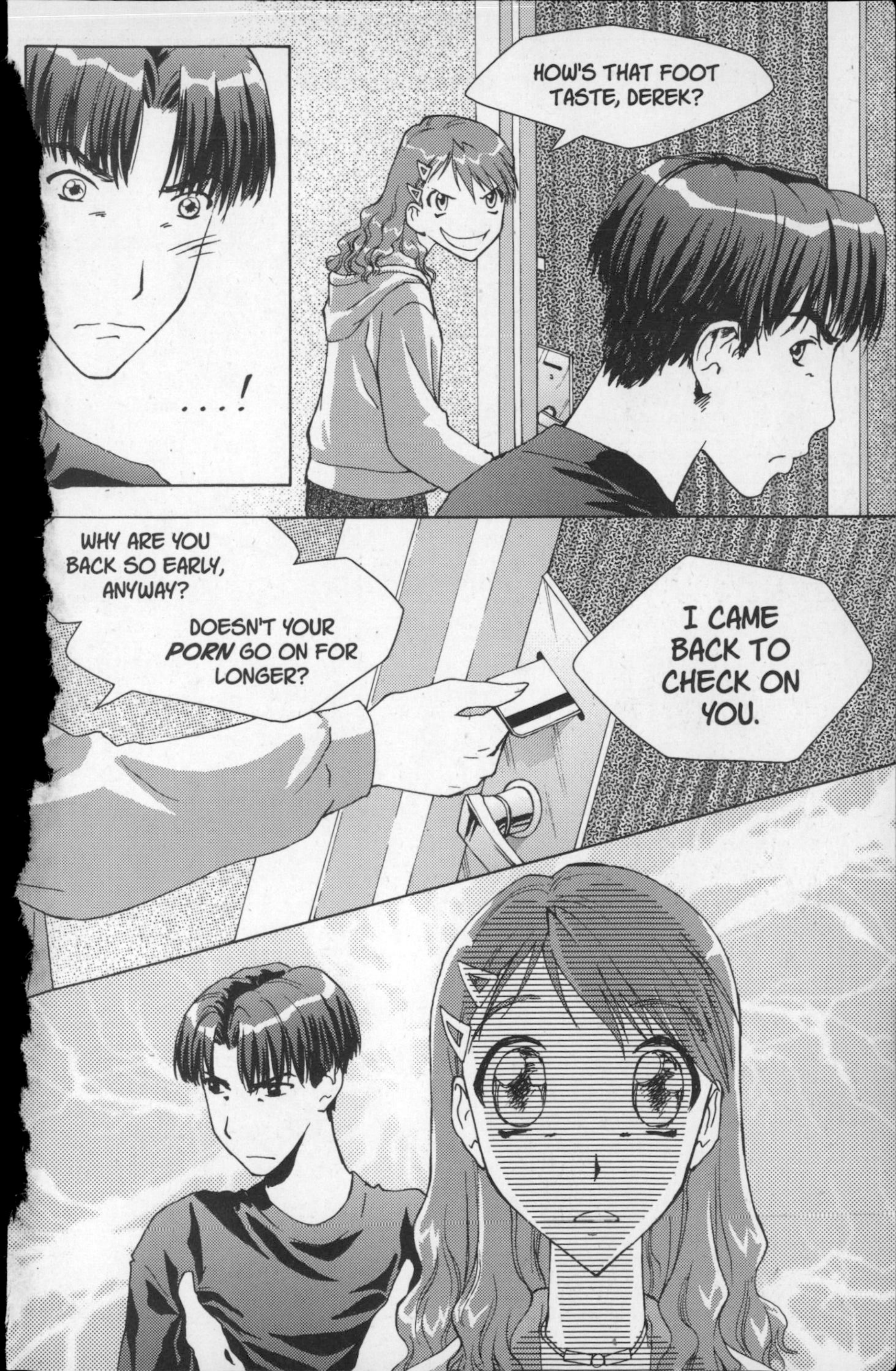
...!
HOW'S THAT FOOT TASTE, DEREK?
WHY ARE YOU BACK SO EARLY, ANYWAY?
DOESN'T YOUR *PORN* GO ON FOR LONGER?
I CAME BACK TO CHECK ON YOU.

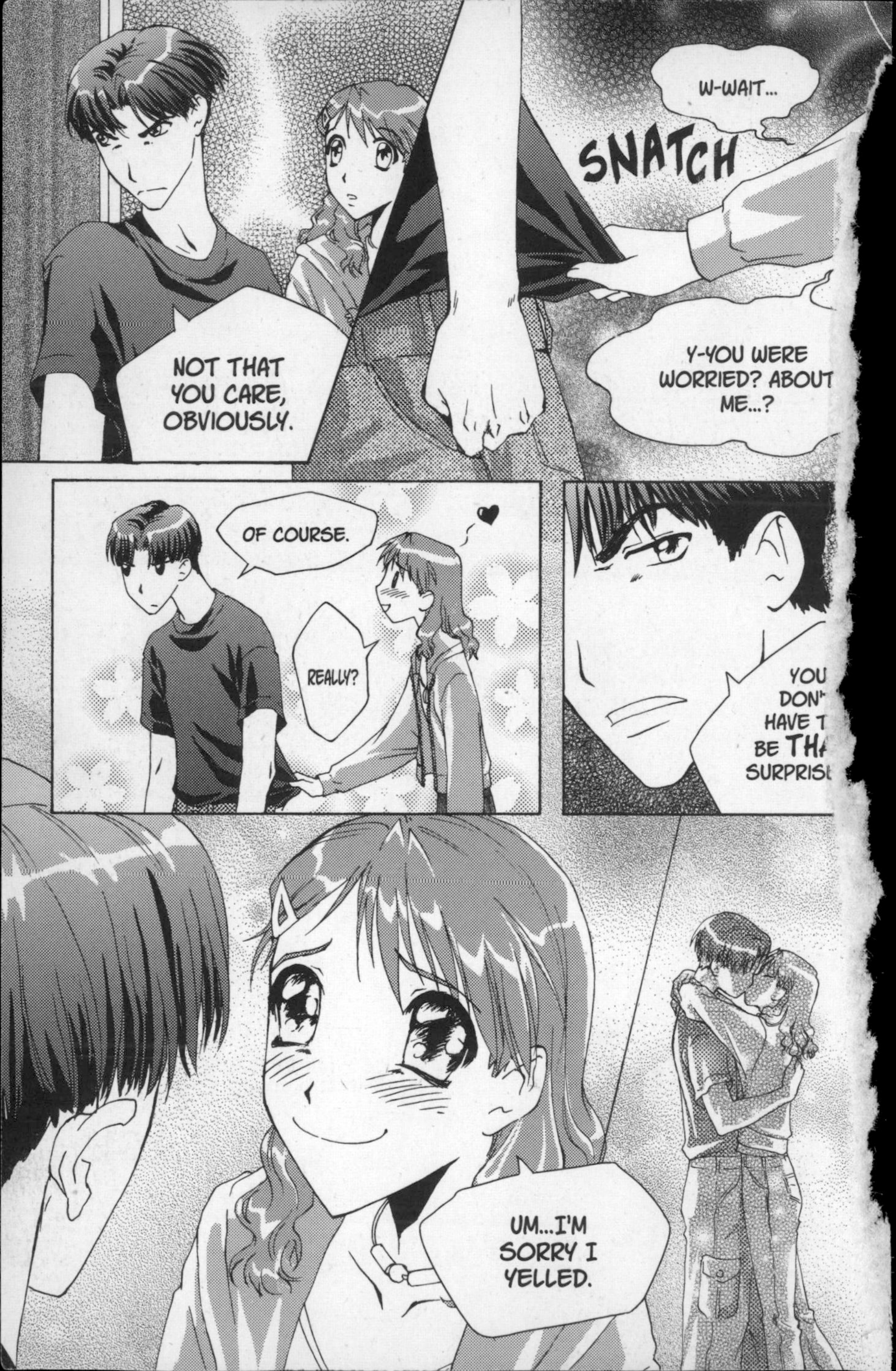
NOT THAT YOU CARE, OBVIOUSLY.
W-WAIT...
SNATCH
Y-YOU WERE WORRIED? ABOUT ME...?
OF COURSE.
REALLY?
YOU DON' HAVE T BE THA SURPRISE
UM...I'M SORRY I YELLED.

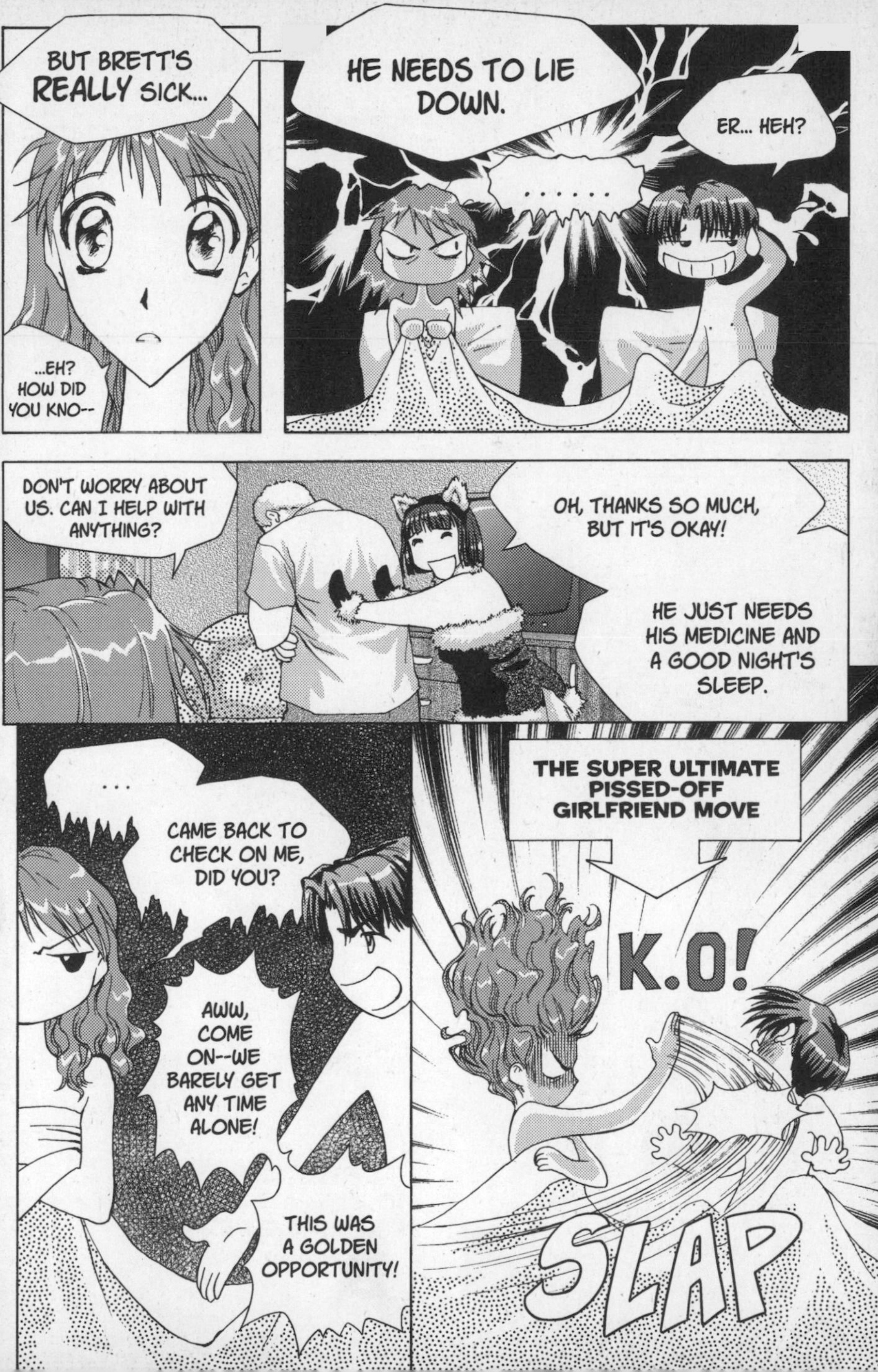

BUT BRETT'S REALLY SICK...
...EH? HOW DID YOU KNO--
HE NEEDS TO LIE DOWN.
....
ER... HEH?
DON'T WORRY ABOUT US. CAN I HELP WITH ANYTHING?
OH, THANKS SO MUCH, BUT IT'S OKAY!
HE JUST NEEDS HIS MEDICINE AND A GOOD NIGHT'S SLEEP.
...
CAME BACK TO CHECK ON ME, DID YOU?
AWW, COME ON--WE BARELY GET ANY TIME ALONE!
THIS WAS A GOLDEN OPPORTUNITY!
THE SUPER ULTIMATE PISSED-OFF GIRLFRIEND MOVE
K.O!
SLAP

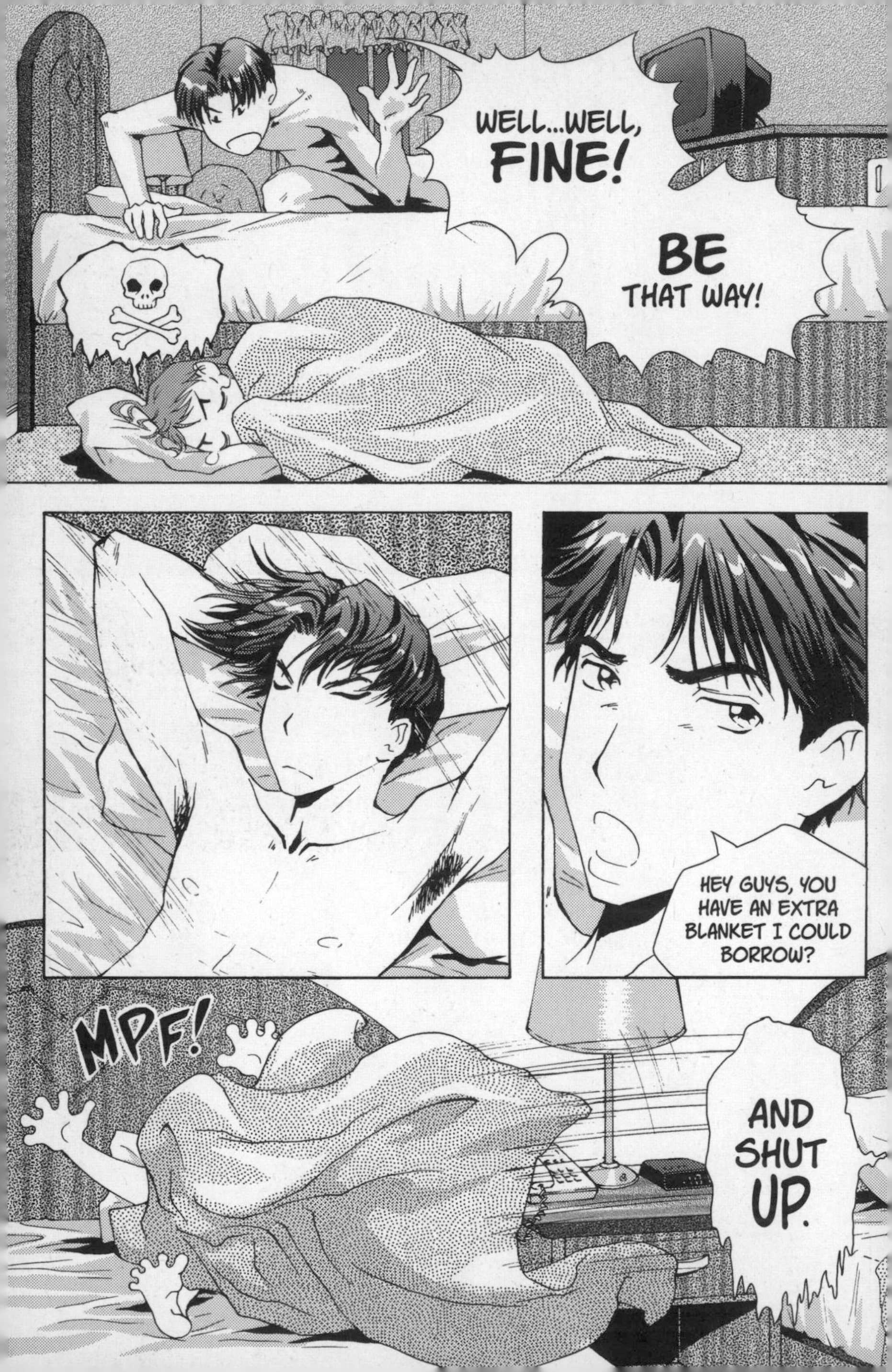
WELL...WELL, FINE!
BE THAT WAY!
HEY GUYS, YOU HAVE AN EXTRA BLANKET I COULD BORROW?
MPF!
AND SHUT UP.

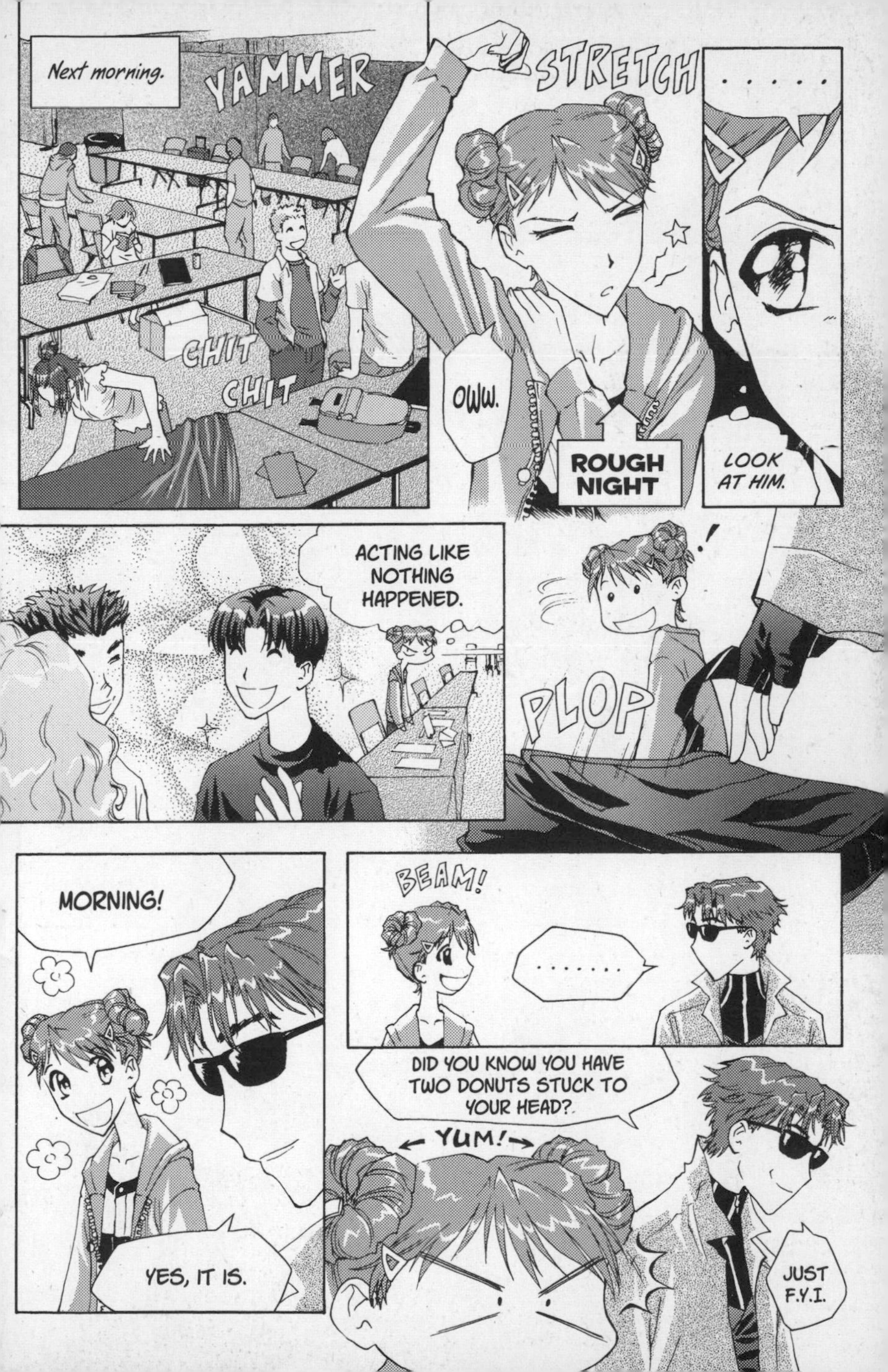
Next morning.
YAMMER
CHIT
CHIT
STRETCH
OWW.
ROUGH NIGHT
. . . . .
LOOK AT HIM.
ACTING LIKE NOTHING HAPPENED.
!
PLOP
MORNING!
YES, IT IS.
BEAM!
. . . .
DID YOU KNOW YOU HAVE TWO DONUTS STUCK TO YOUR HEAD?
YUM!
JUST F.Y.I.

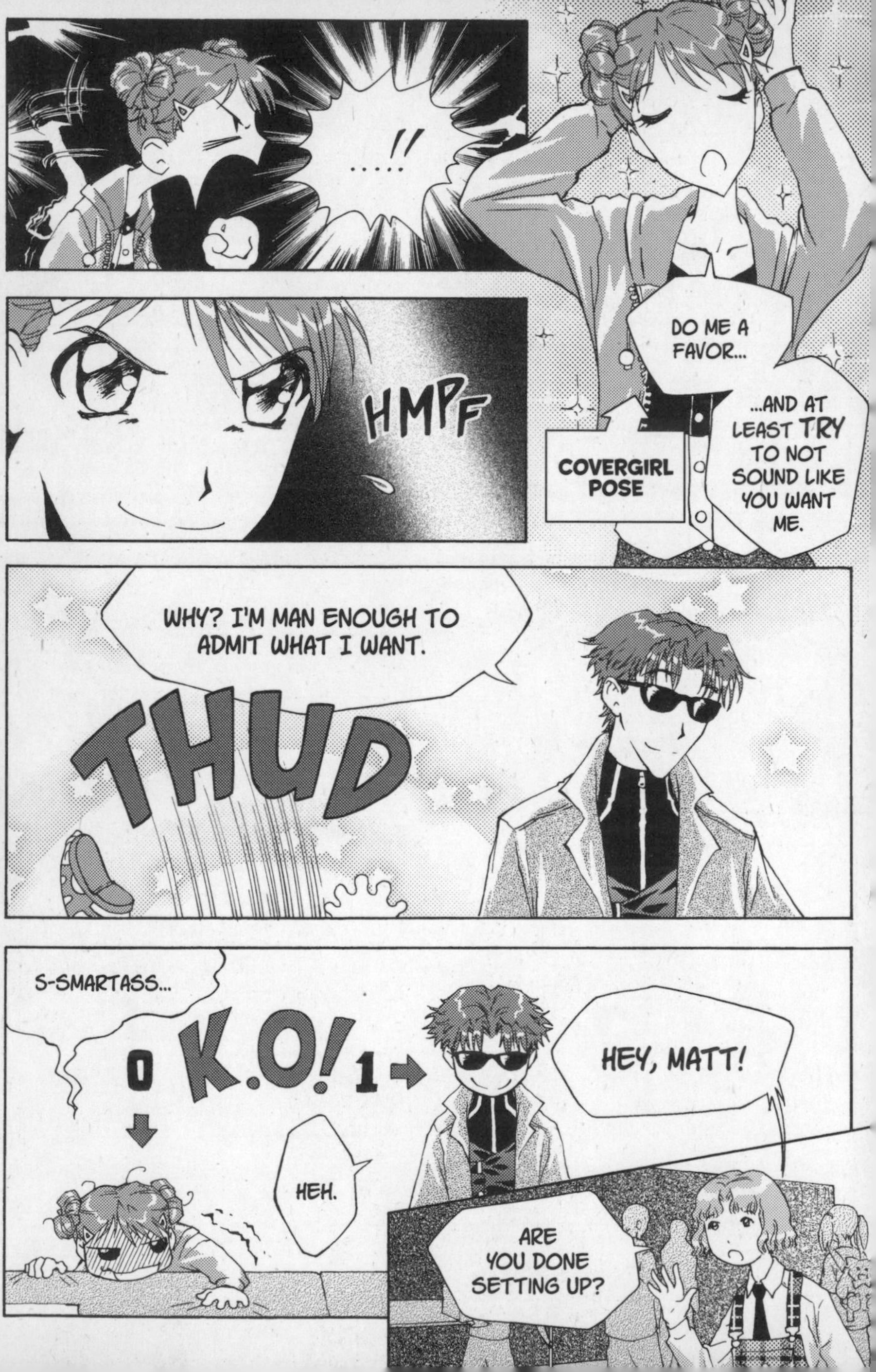
.....!!
HMPF
COVERGIRL POSE
DO ME A FAVOR...
...AND AT LEAST TRY TO NOT SOUND LIKE YOU WANT ME.
WHY? I'M MAN ENOUGH TO ADMIT WHAT I WANT.
THUD
S-SMARTASS...
0
K.O!
1
HEY, MATT!
HEH.
ARE YOU DONE SETTING UP?

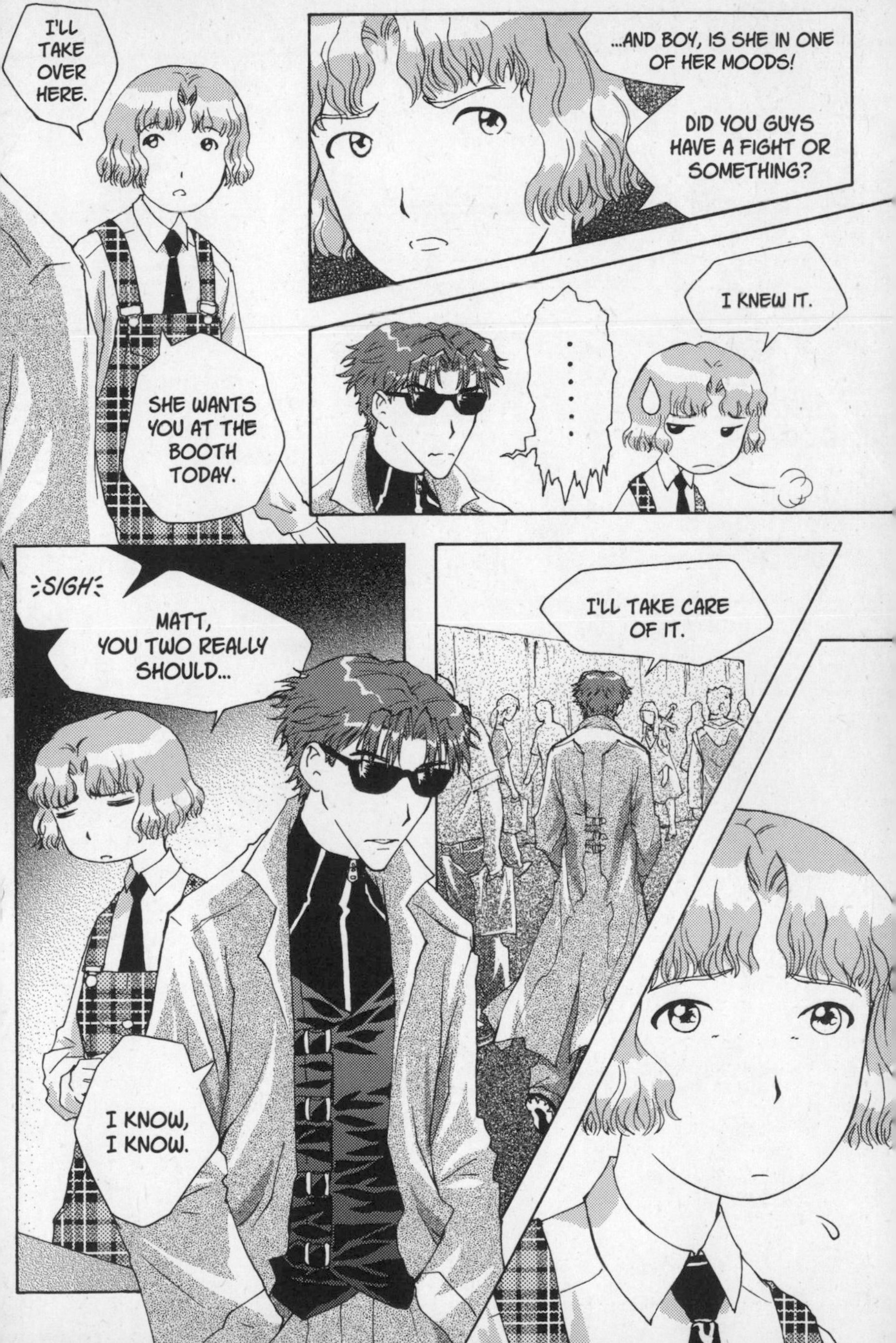

I'LL TAKE OVER HERE.
SHE WANTS YOU AT THE BOOTH TODAY.
...AND BOY, IS SHE IN ONE OF HER MOODS!
DID YOU GUYS HAVE A FIGHT OR SOMETHING?
......
I KNEW IT.
SIGH
MATT, YOU TWO REALLY SHOULD...
I KNOW, I KNOW.
I'LL TAKE CARE OF IT.

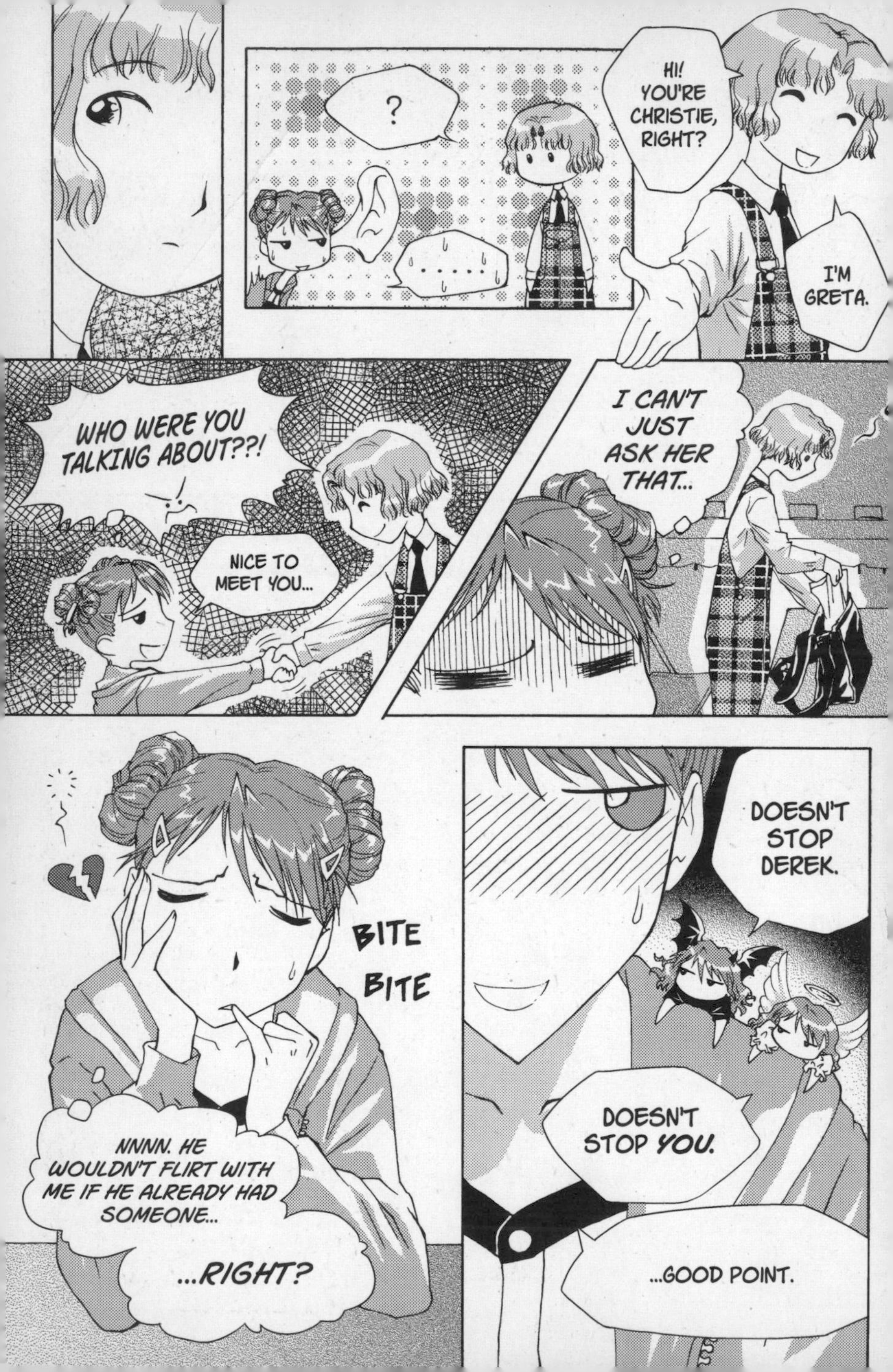
?
......
HI! YOU'RE CHRISTIE, RIGHT?
I'M GRETA.
WHO WERE YOU TALKING ABOUT??!
NICE TO MEET YOU...
I CAN'T JUST ASK HER THAT...
NNNN. HE WOULDN'T FLIRT WITH ME IF HE ALREADY HAD SOMEONE...
...RIGHT?
BITE
BITE
DOESN'T STOP DEREK.
DOESN'T STOP *YOU*.
...GOOD POINT.

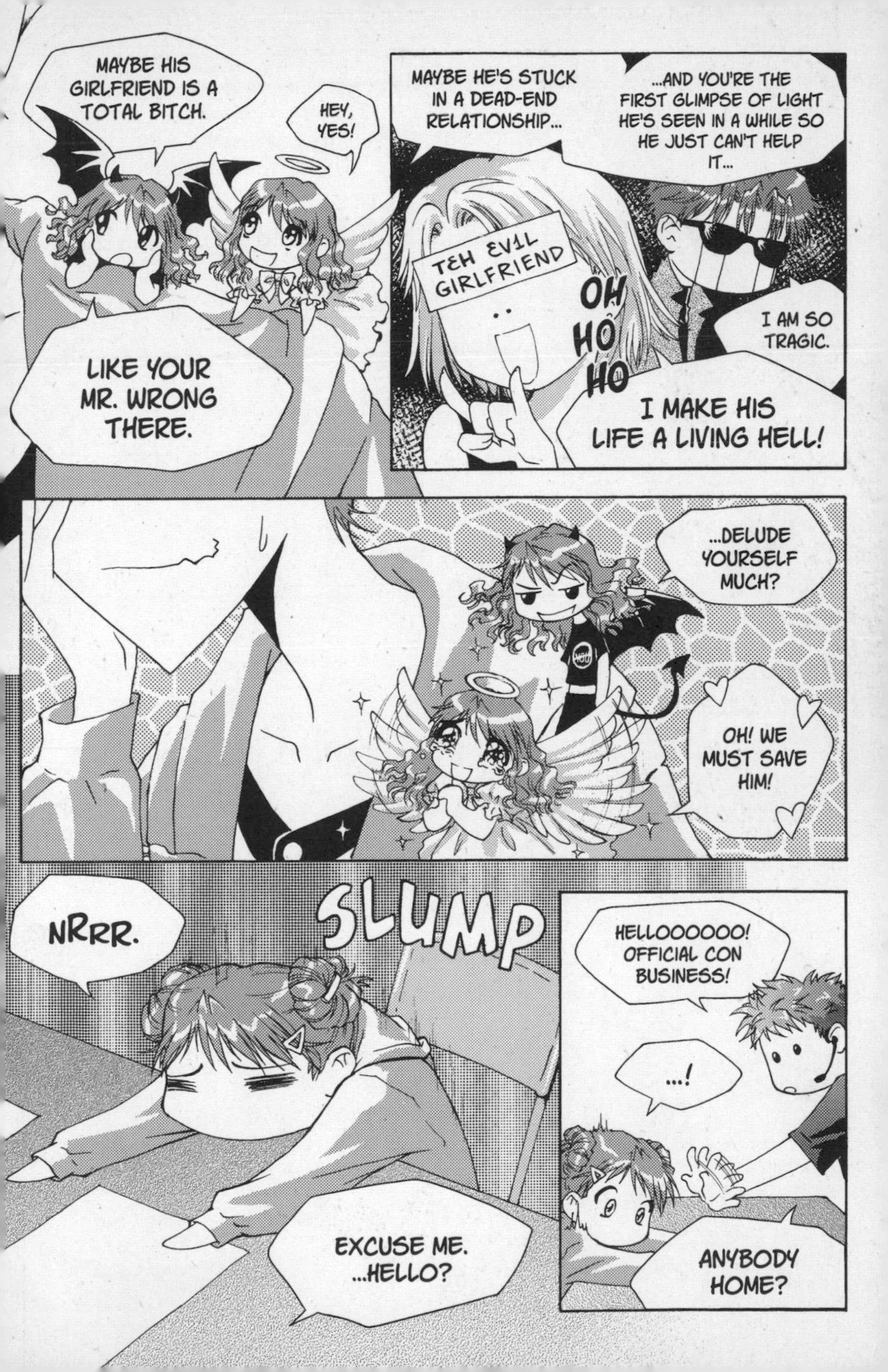
MAYBE HIS GIRLFRIEND IS A TOTAL BITCH.
HEY, YES!
LIKE YOUR MR. WRONG THERE.
MAYBE HE'S STUCK IN A DEAD-END RELATIONSHIP...
...AND YOU'RE THE FIRST GLIMPSE OF LIGHT HE'S SEEN IN A WHILE SO HE JUST CAN'T HELP IT...
TEH EV1L GIRLFRIEND
OH HO HO
I AM SO TRAGIC.
I MAKE HIS LIFE A LIVING HELL!
...DELUDE YOURSELF MUCH?
OH! WE MUST SAVE HIM!
NRRR.
SLUMP
EXCUSE ME. ...HELLO?
HELLOOOOOO! OFFICIAL CON BUSINESS!
...!
ANYBODY HOME?

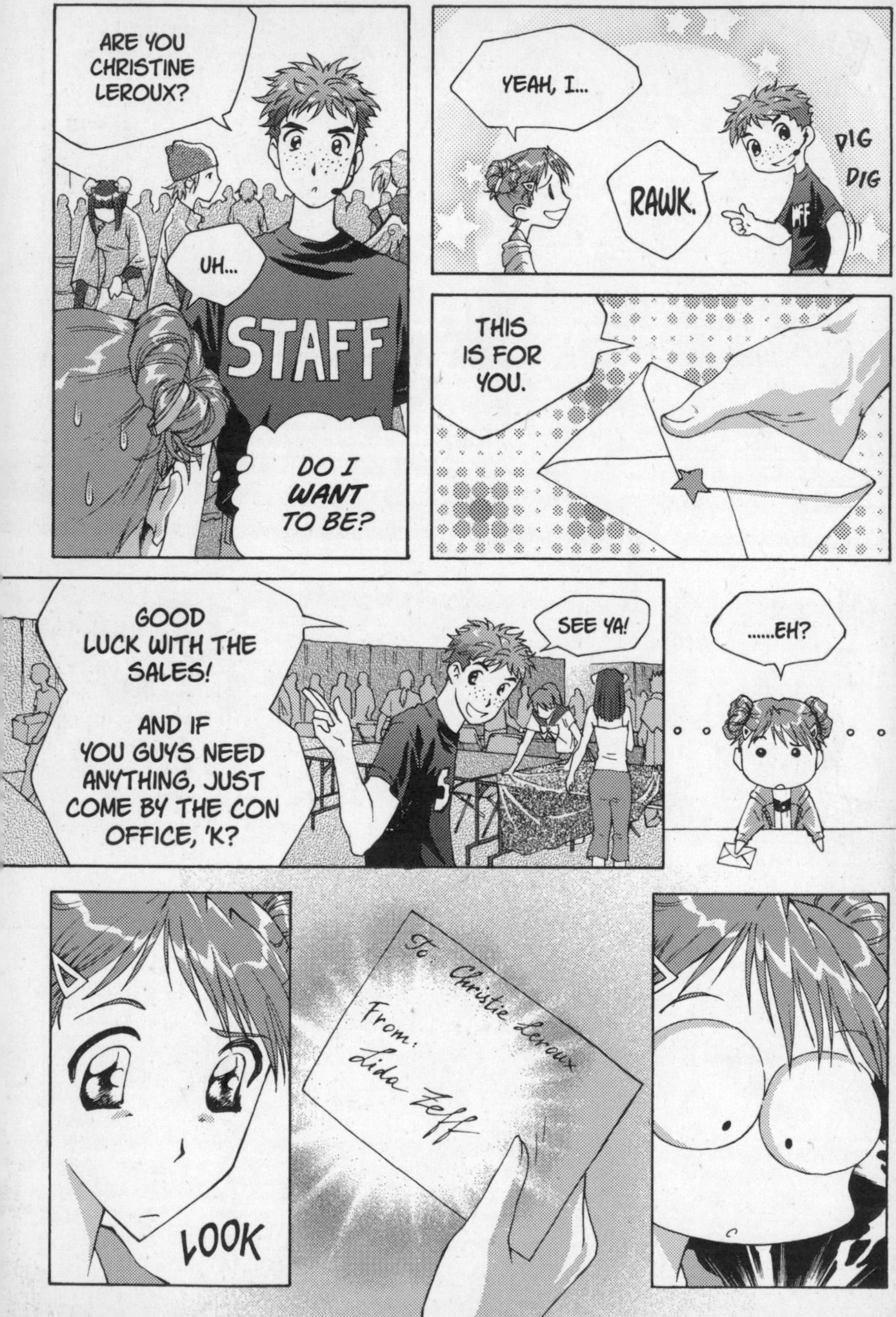
ARE YOU CHRISTINE LEROUX?
UH...
DO I WANT TO BE?
YEAH, I...
RAWK.
DIG DIG
THIS IS FOR YOU.
GOOD LUCK WITH THE SALES!
AND IF YOU GUYS NEED ANYTHING, JUST COME BY THE CON OFFICE, 'K?
SEE YA!
......EH?
LOOK
To Christie Leroux
From: Lida Zeff

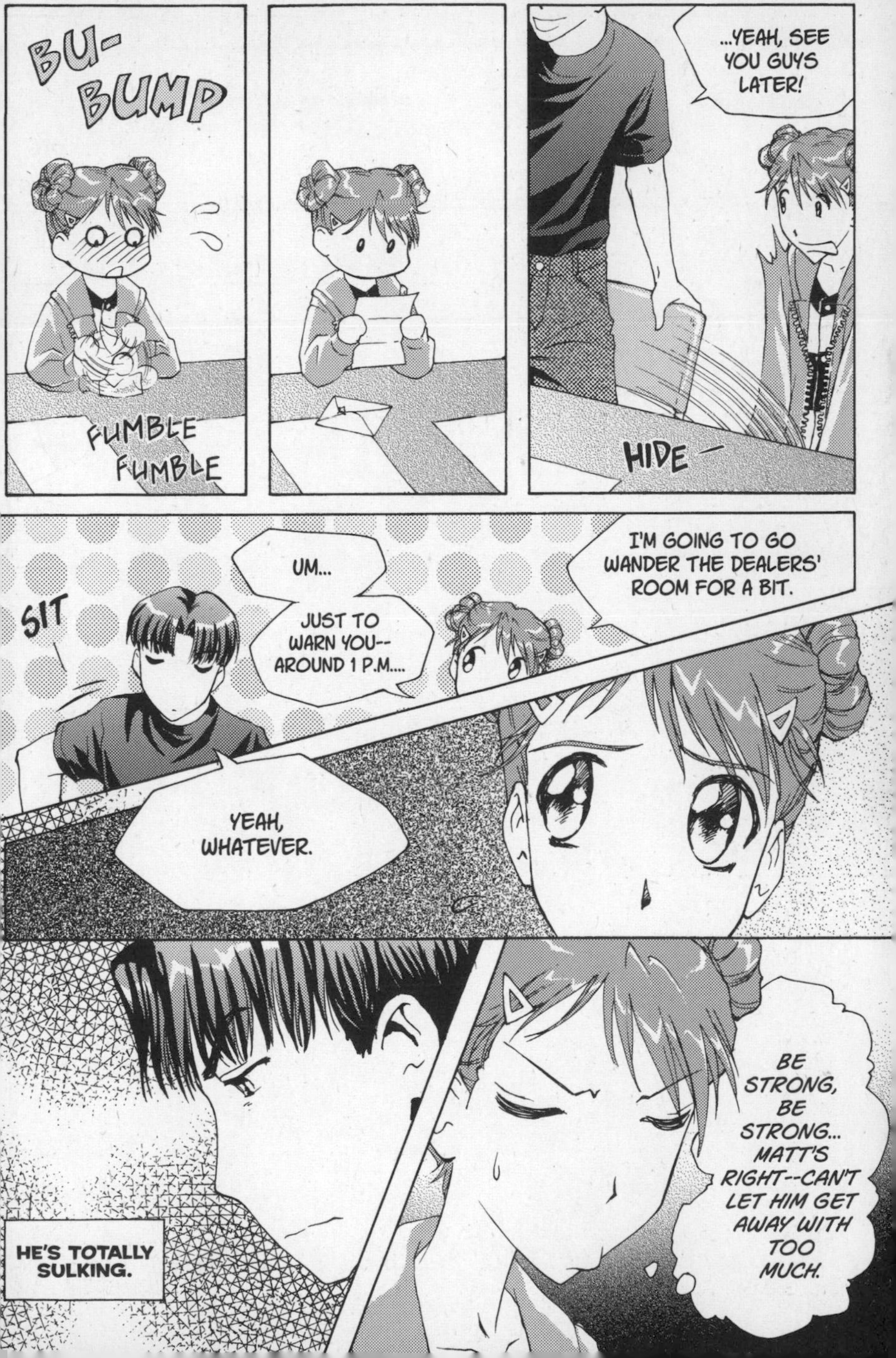
BU-BUMP
FUMBLE FUMBLE
...YEAH, SEE YOU GUYS LATER!
HIDE
SIT
UM...
JUST TO WARN YOU-- AROUND 1 P.M....
I'M GOING TO GO WANDER THE DEALERS' ROOM FOR A BIT.
YEAH, WHATEVER.
HE'S TOTALLY SULKING.
BE STRONG, BE STRONG... MATT'S RIGHT--CAN'T LET HIM GET AWAY WITH TOO MUCH.

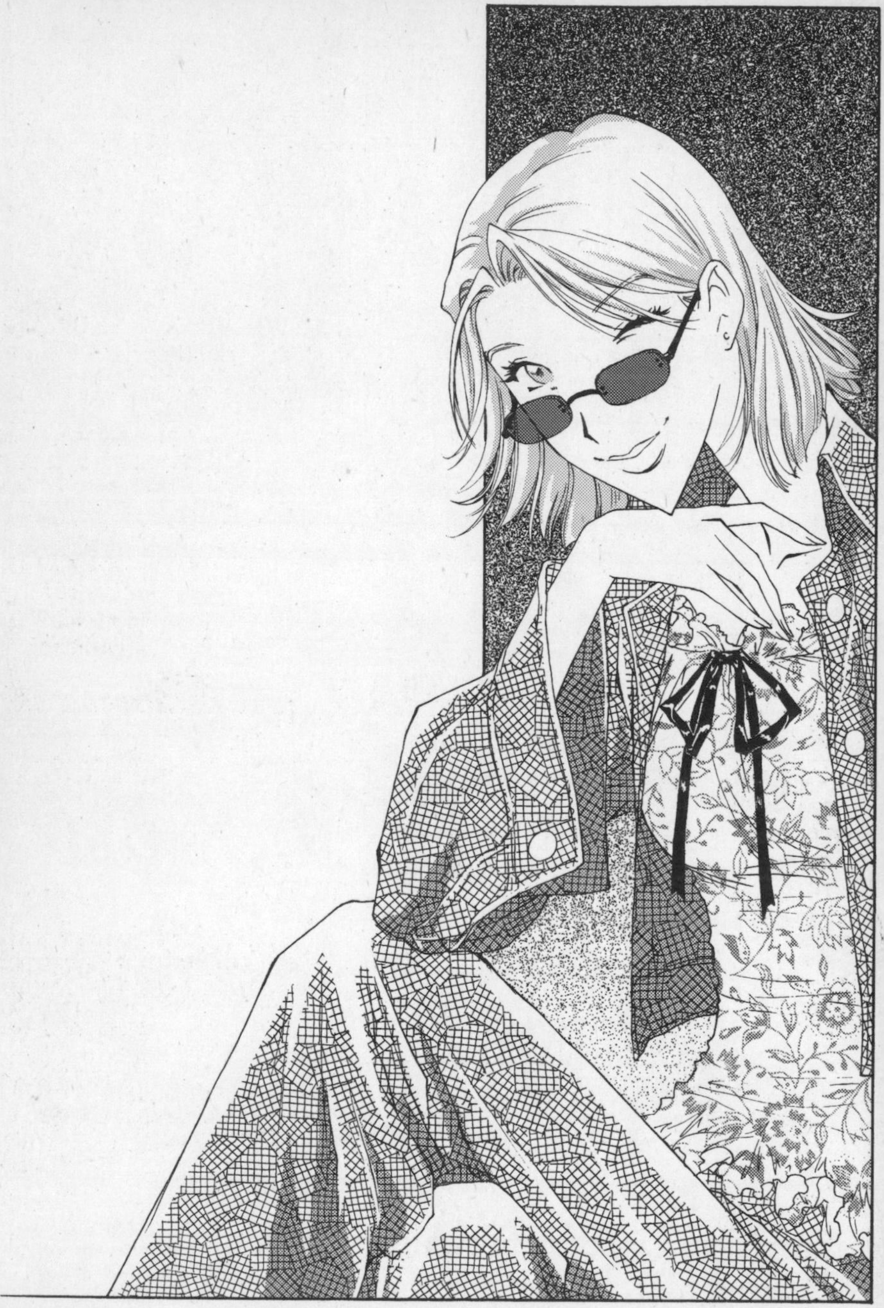

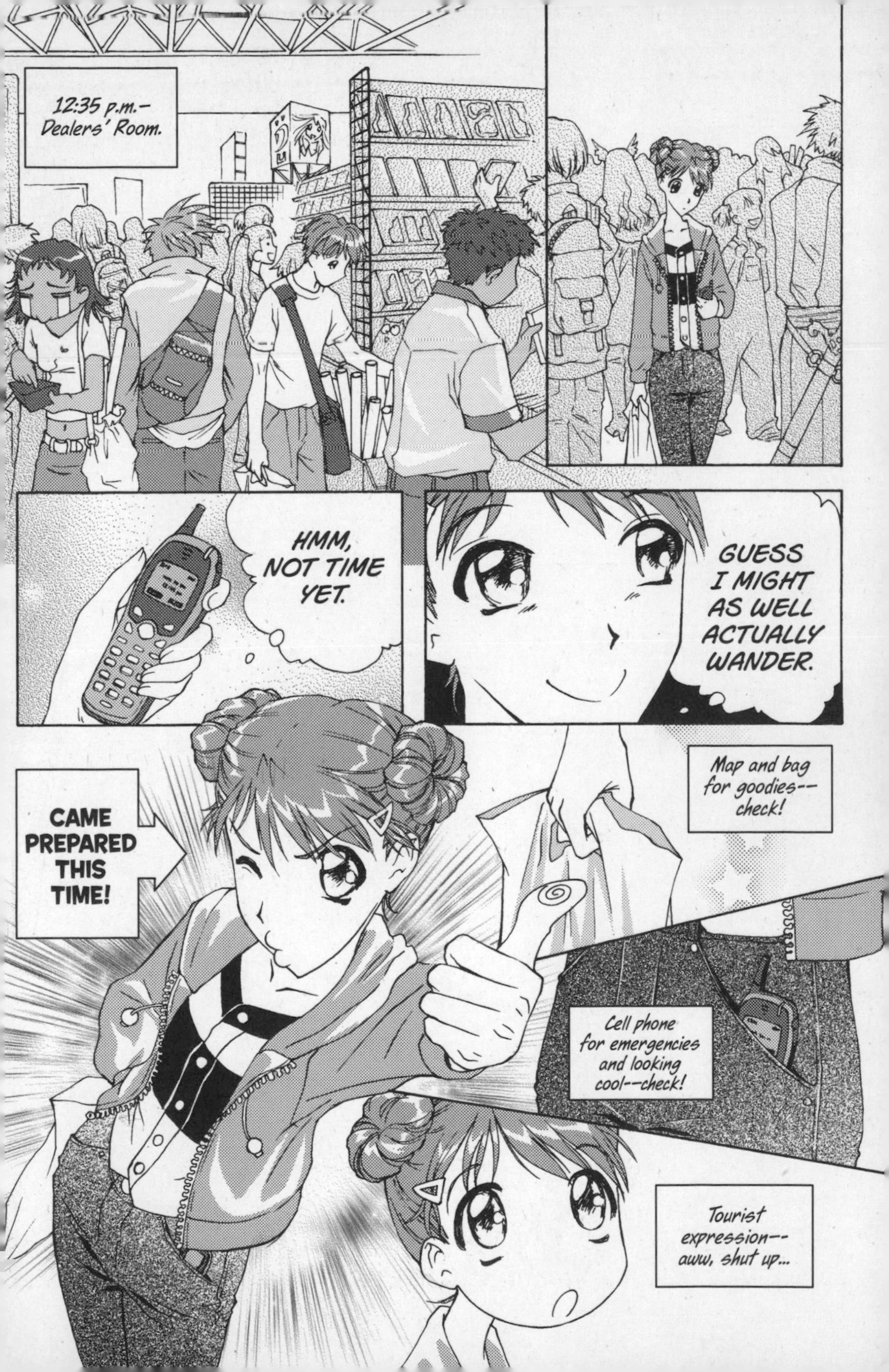
12:35 p.m.–
Dealers' Room.
HMM, NOT TIME YET.
GUESS I MIGHT AS WELL ACTUALLY WANDER.
CAME PREPARED THIS TIME!
Map and bag for goodies--check!
Cell phone for emergencies and looking cool--check!
Tourist expression--aww, shut up...

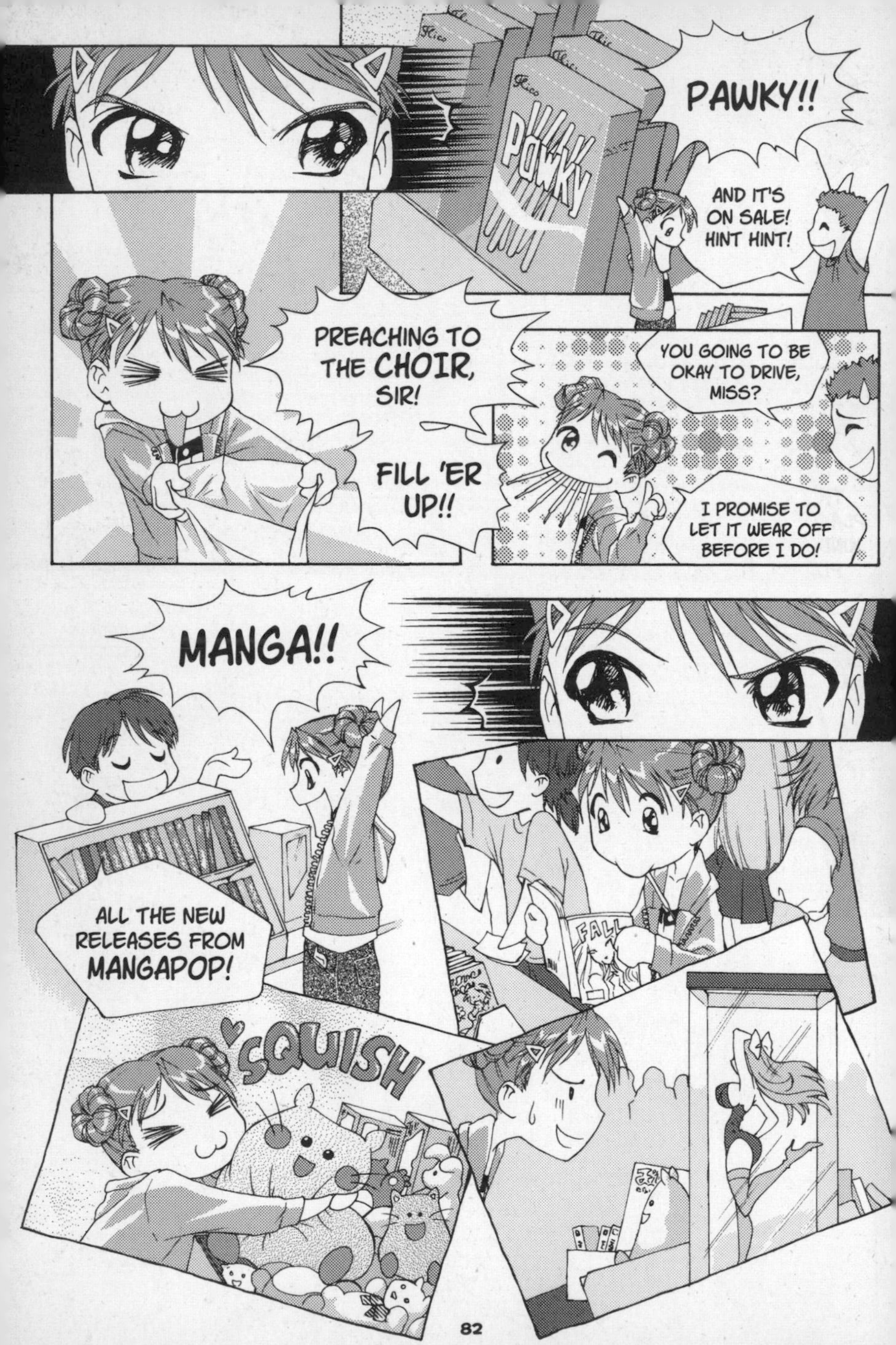
PAWKY!!
AND IT'S ON SALE! HINT HINT!
PREACHING TO THE CHOIR, SIR!
FILL 'ER UP!!
YOU GOING TO BE OKAY TO DRIVE, MISS?
I PROMISE TO LET IT WEAR OFF BEFORE I DO!
MANGA!!
ALL THE NEW RELEASES FROM MANGAPOP!
SQUISH

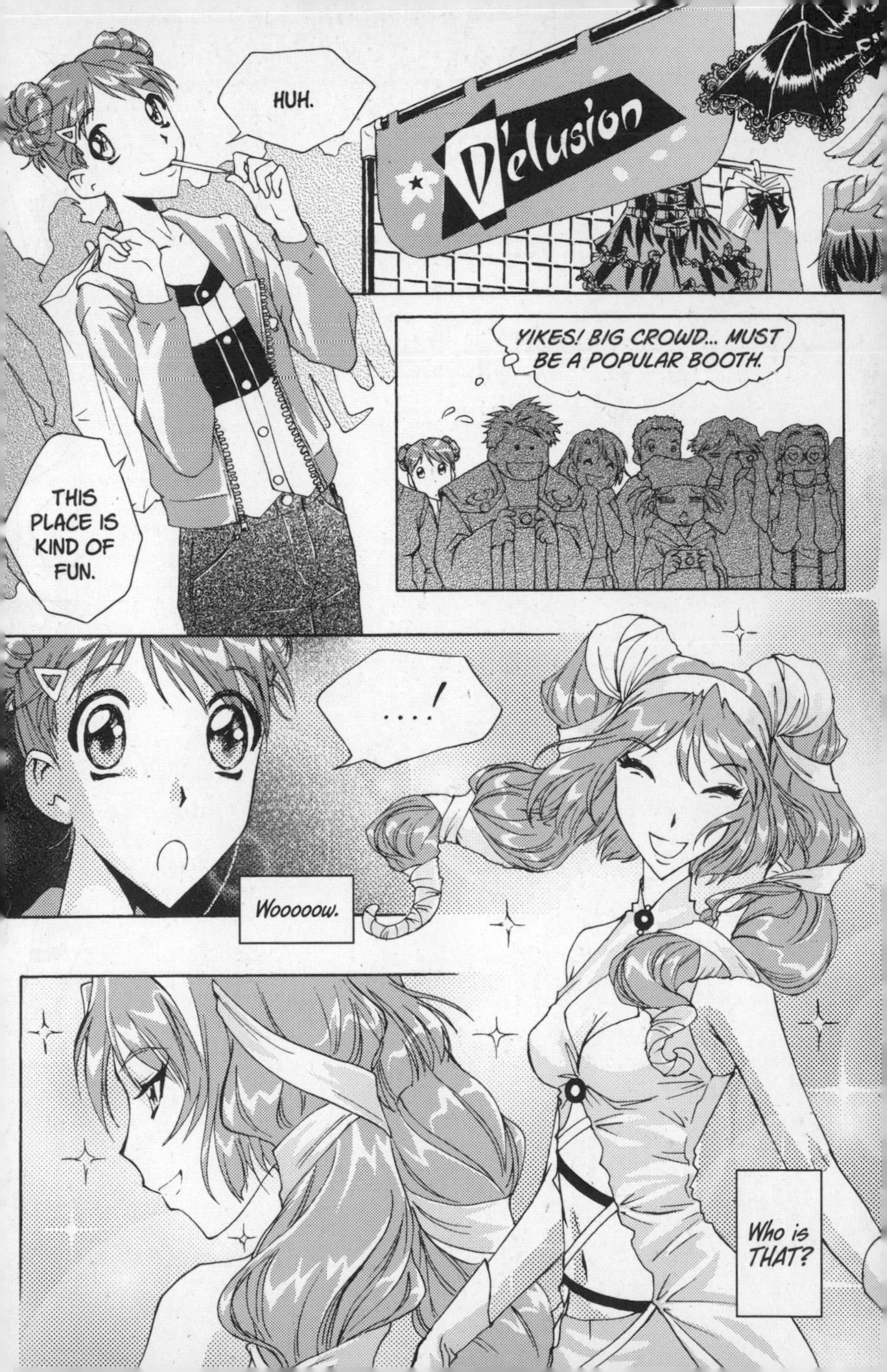
HUH.
THIS PLACE IS KIND OF FUN.
D'elusion
YIKES! BIG CROWD... MUST BE A POPULAR BOOTH.
....!
Wooooow.
Who is THAT?

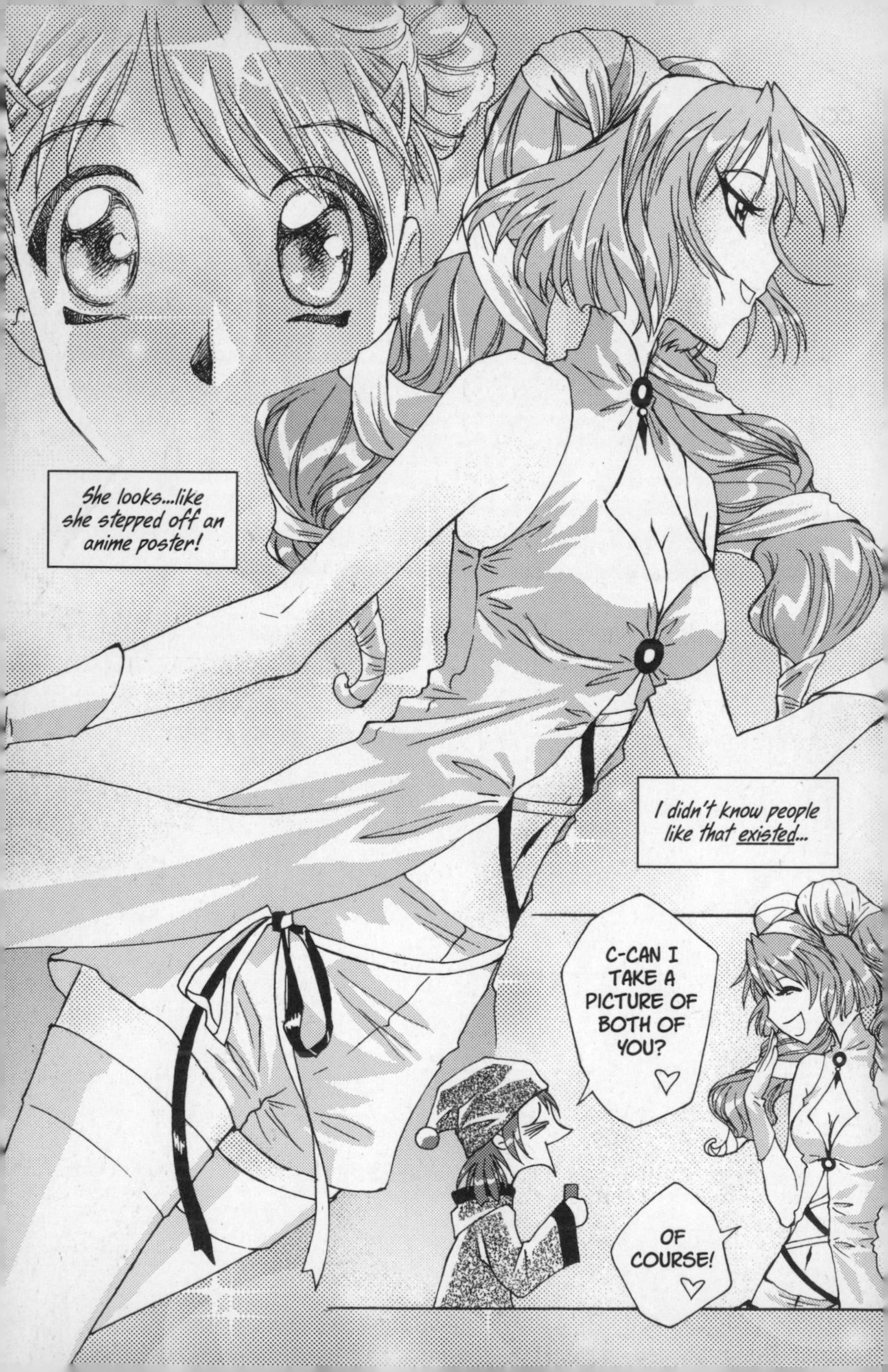
She looks...like she stepped off an anime poster!
I didn't know people like that existed...
C-CAN I TAKE A PICTURE OF BOTH OF YOU? ♡
OF COURSE! ♡

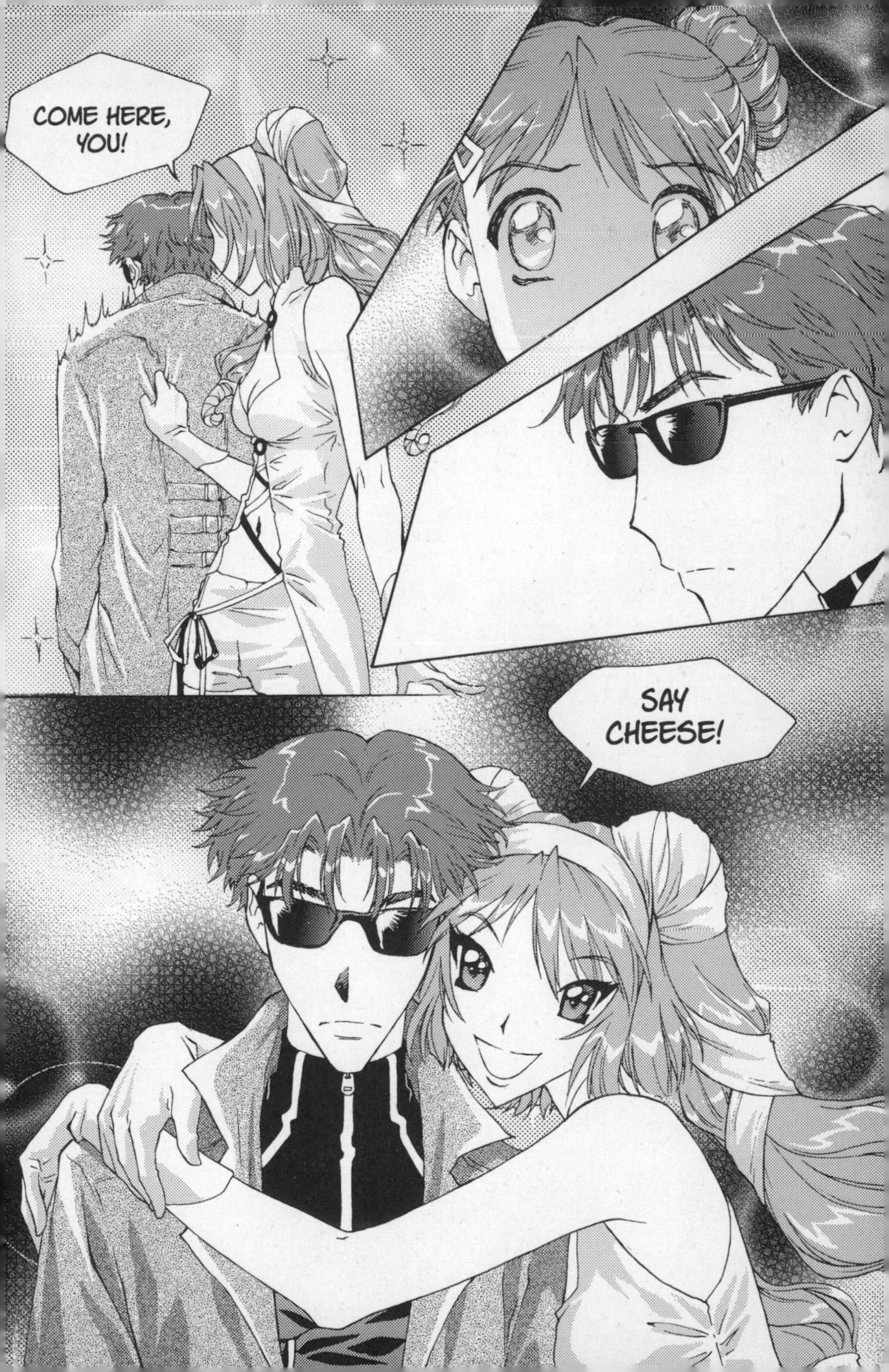
COME HERE, YOU!
SAY CHEESE!

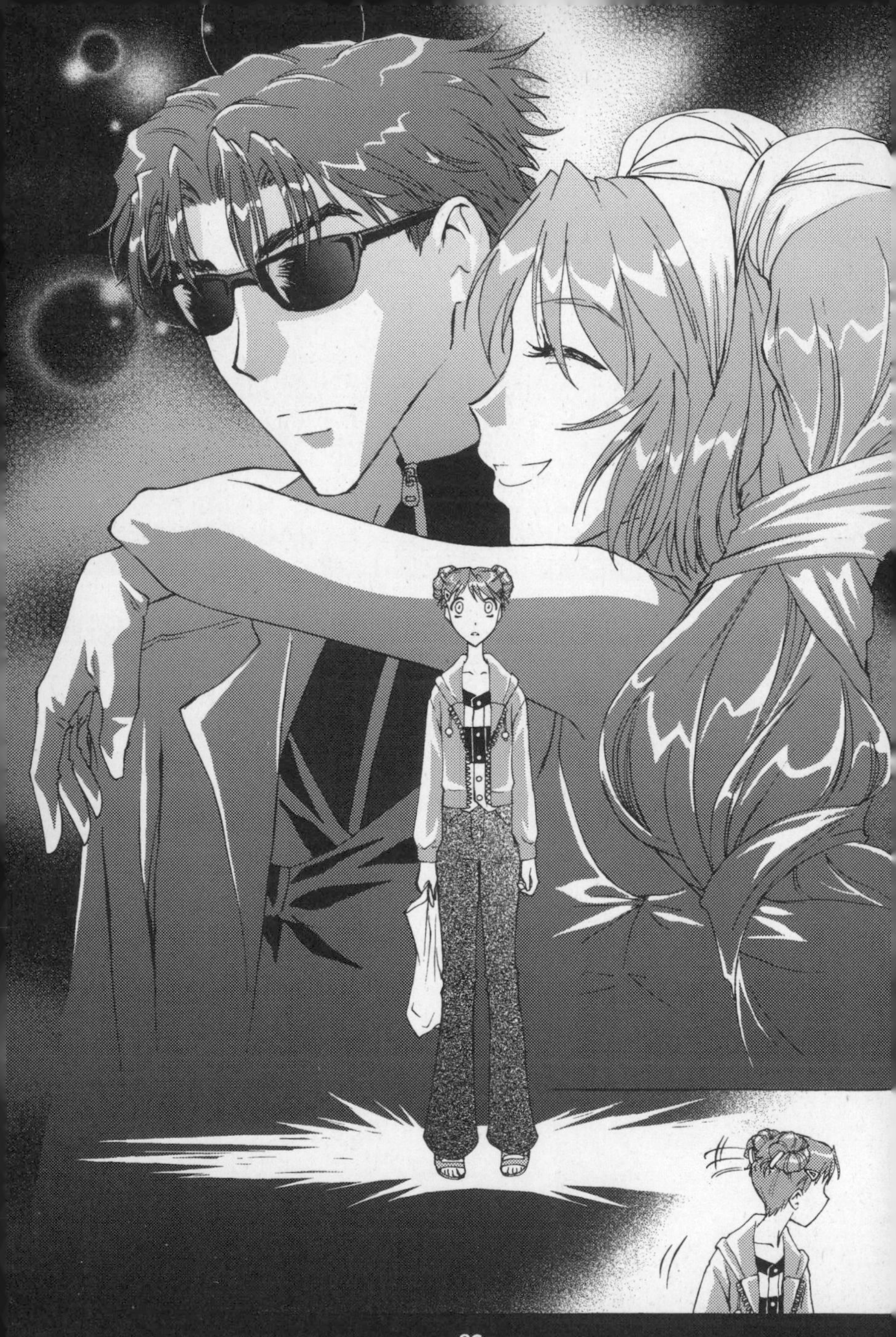

That wasn't the sound of my heart breaking.

I did NOT fall for a guy I knew for only half a day.

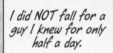

·············

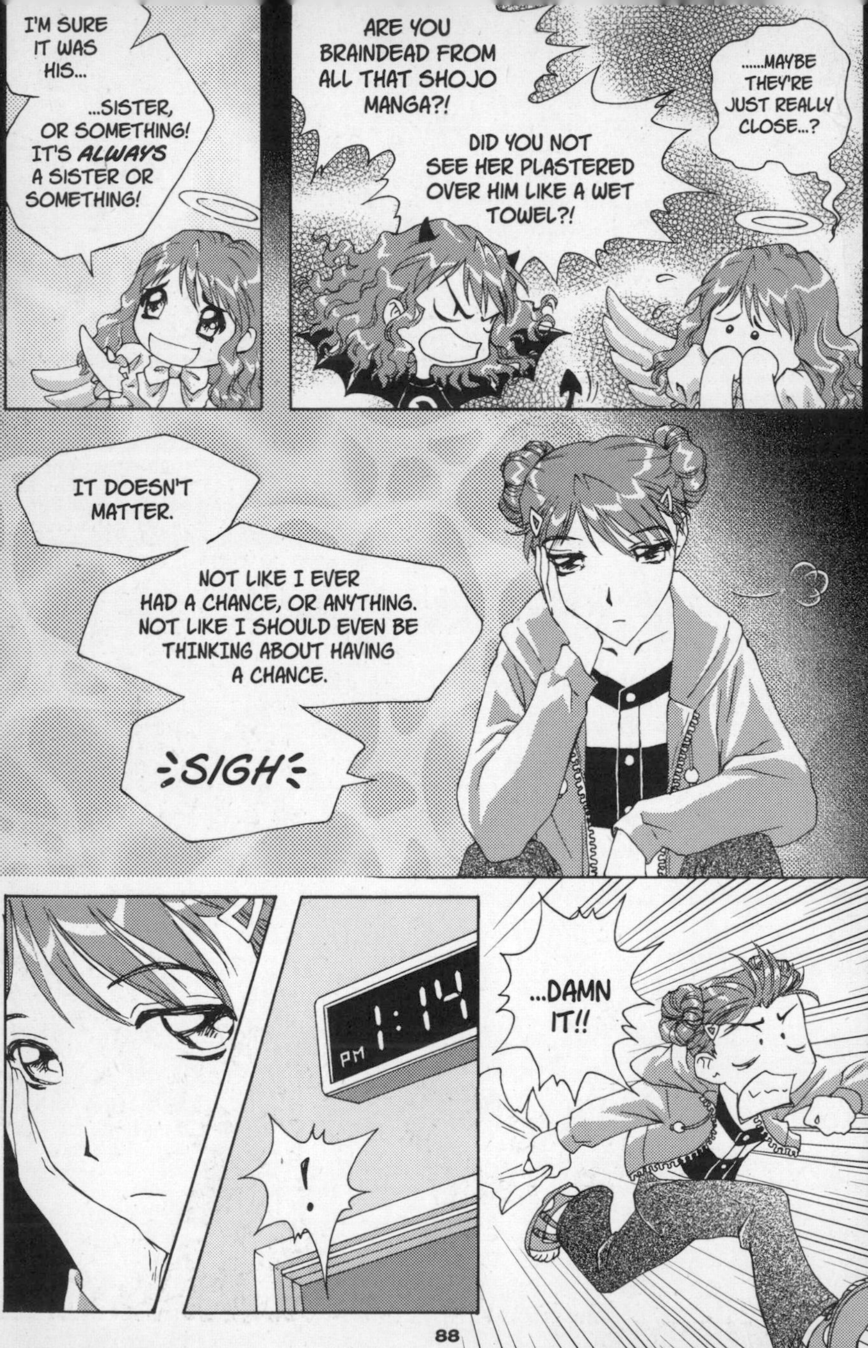
I'M SURE IT WAS HIS...
...SISTER, OR SOMETHING! IT'S ALWAYS A SISTER OR SOMETHING!
ARE YOU BRAINDEAD FROM ALL THAT SHOJO MANGA?!
DID YOU NOT SEE HER PLASTERED OVER HIM LIKE A WET TOWEL?!
......MAYBE THEY'RE JUST REALLY CLOSE...?
IT DOESN'T MATTER.
NOT LIKE I EVER HAD A CHANCE, OR ANYTHING. NOT LIKE I SHOULD EVEN BE THINKING ABOUT HAVING A CHANCE.
SIGH
PM 1:14
!
...DAMN IT!!

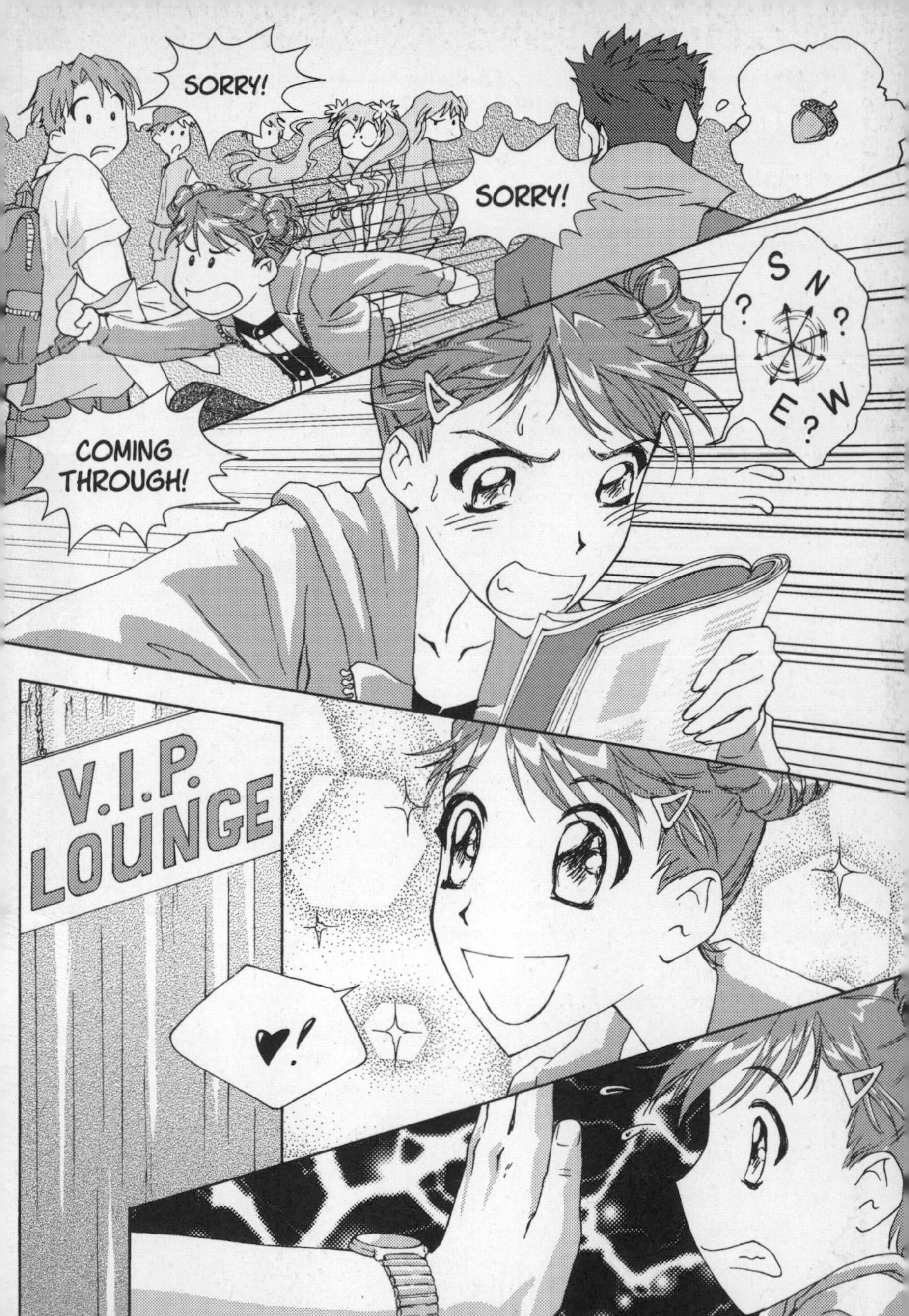
SORRY!
SORRY!
COMING THROUGH!
S N ? ? E ? W
V.I.P. LOUNGE
♥!

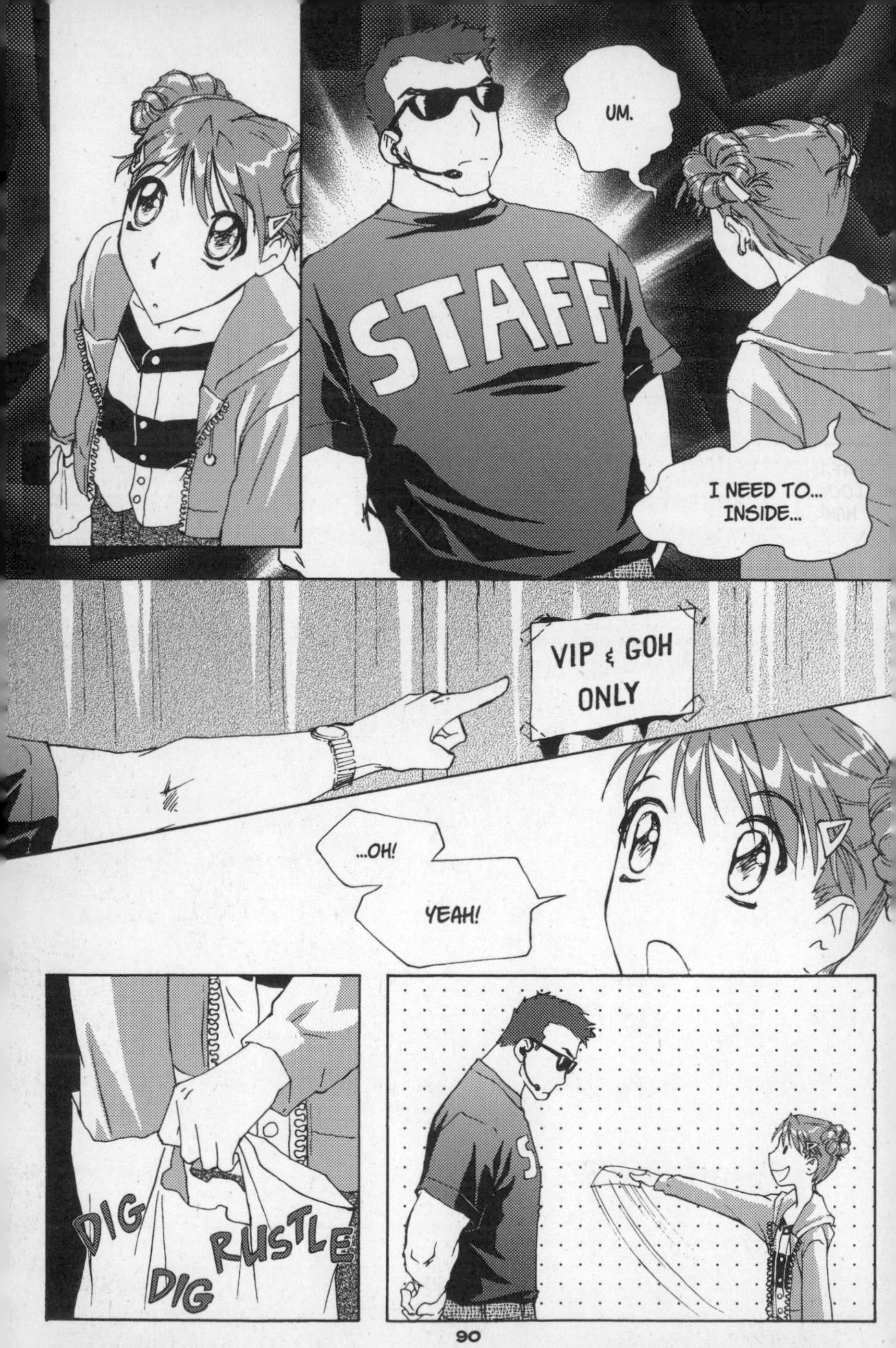
UM.
I NEED TO... INSIDE...
STAFF
VIP & GOH ONLY
...OH!
YEAH!
DIG
DIG
RUSTLE

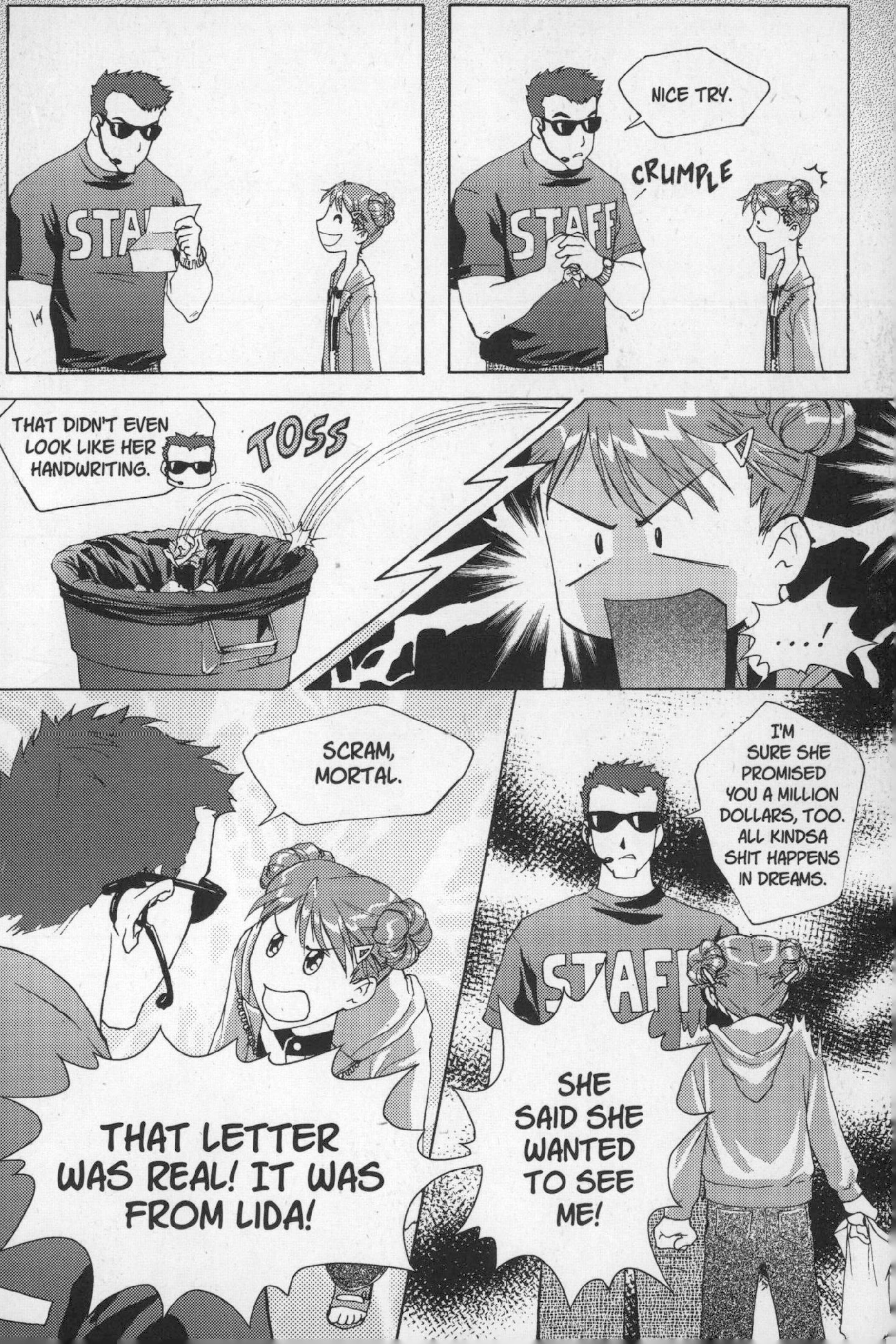
NICE TRY.
CRUMPLE
THAT DIDN'T EVEN LOOK LIKE HER HANDWRITING.
TOSS
...!
SCRAM, MORTAL.
THAT LETTER WAS REAL! IT WAS FROM LIDA!
I'M SURE SHE PROMISED YOU A MILLION DOLLARS, TOO. ALL KINDSA SHIT HAPPENS IN DREAMS.
SHE SAID SHE WANTED TO SEE ME!

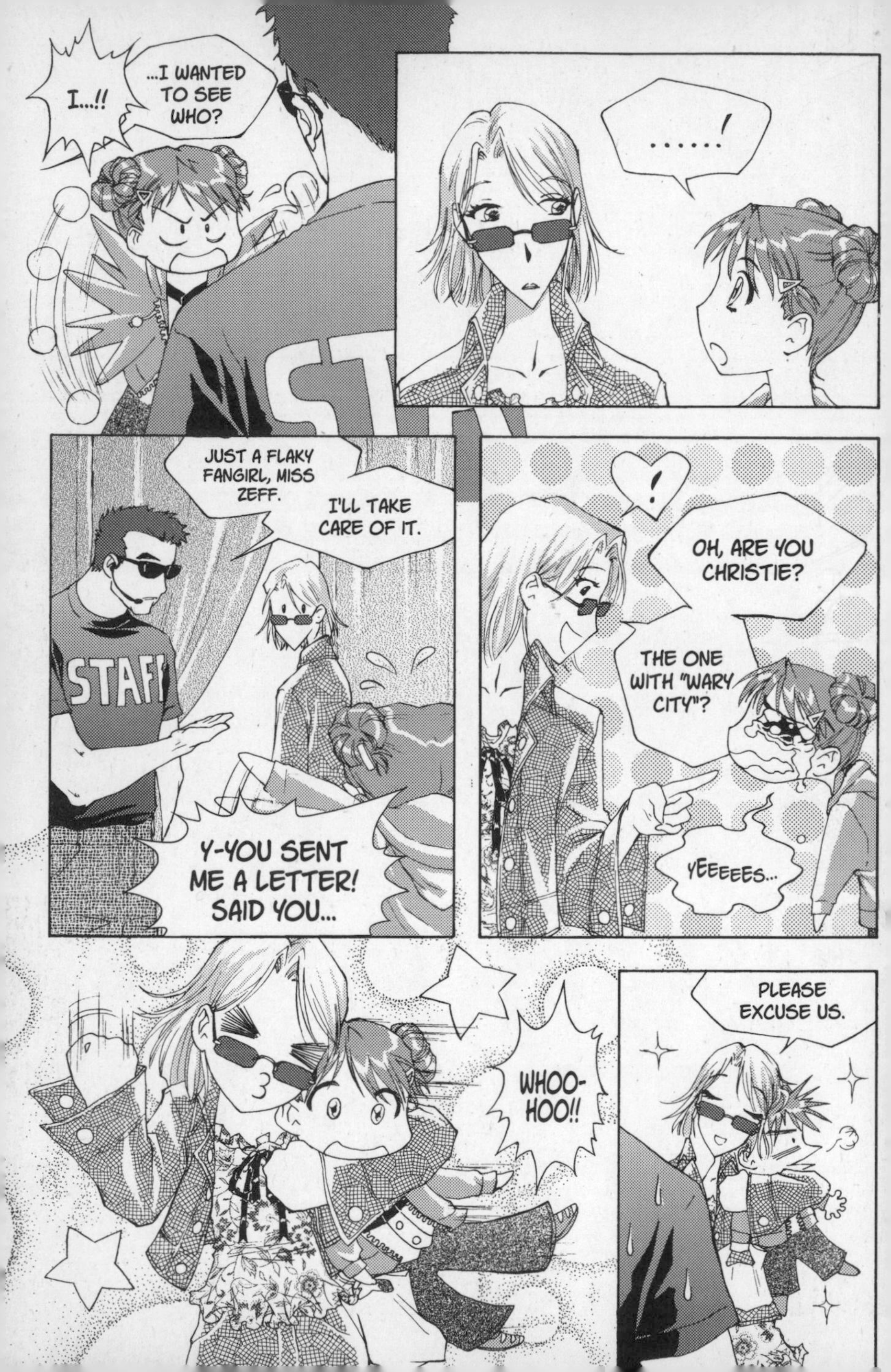
I...!!
...I WANTED TO SEE WHO?
......!
JUST A FLAKY FANGIRL, MISS ZEFF.
I'LL TAKE CARE OF IT.
Y-YOU SENT ME A LETTER! SAID YOU...
!
OH, ARE YOU CHRISTIE?
THE ONE WITH "WARY CITY"?
YEEEEEES...
WHOO-HOO!!
PLEASE EXCUSE US.

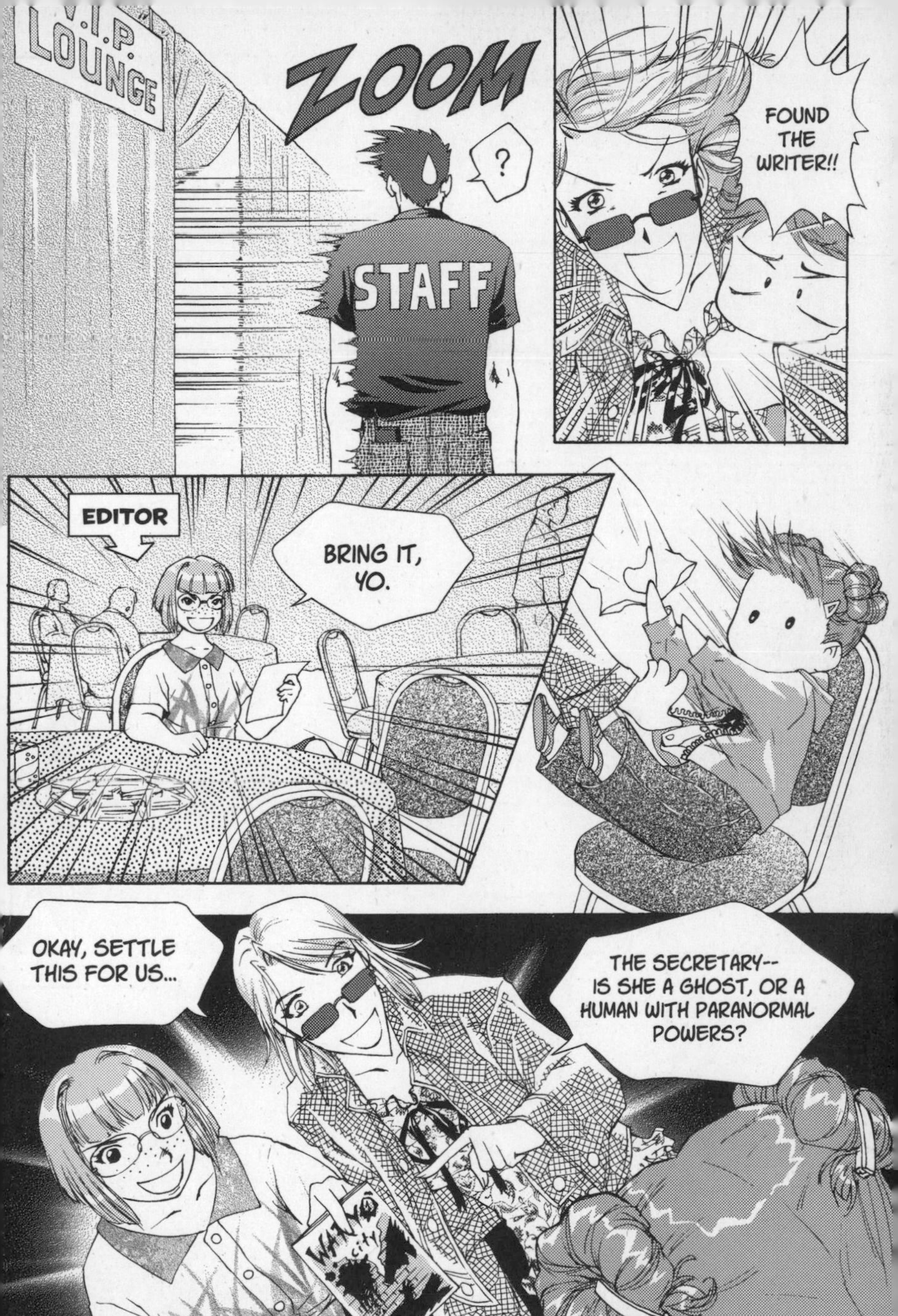
V.I.P. LOUNGE
ZOOM
?
STAFF
FOUND THE WRITER!!
EDITOR
BRING IT, YO.
OKAY, SETTLE THIS FOR US...
THE SECRETARY-- IS SHE A GHOST, OR A HUMAN WITH PARANORMAL POWERS?

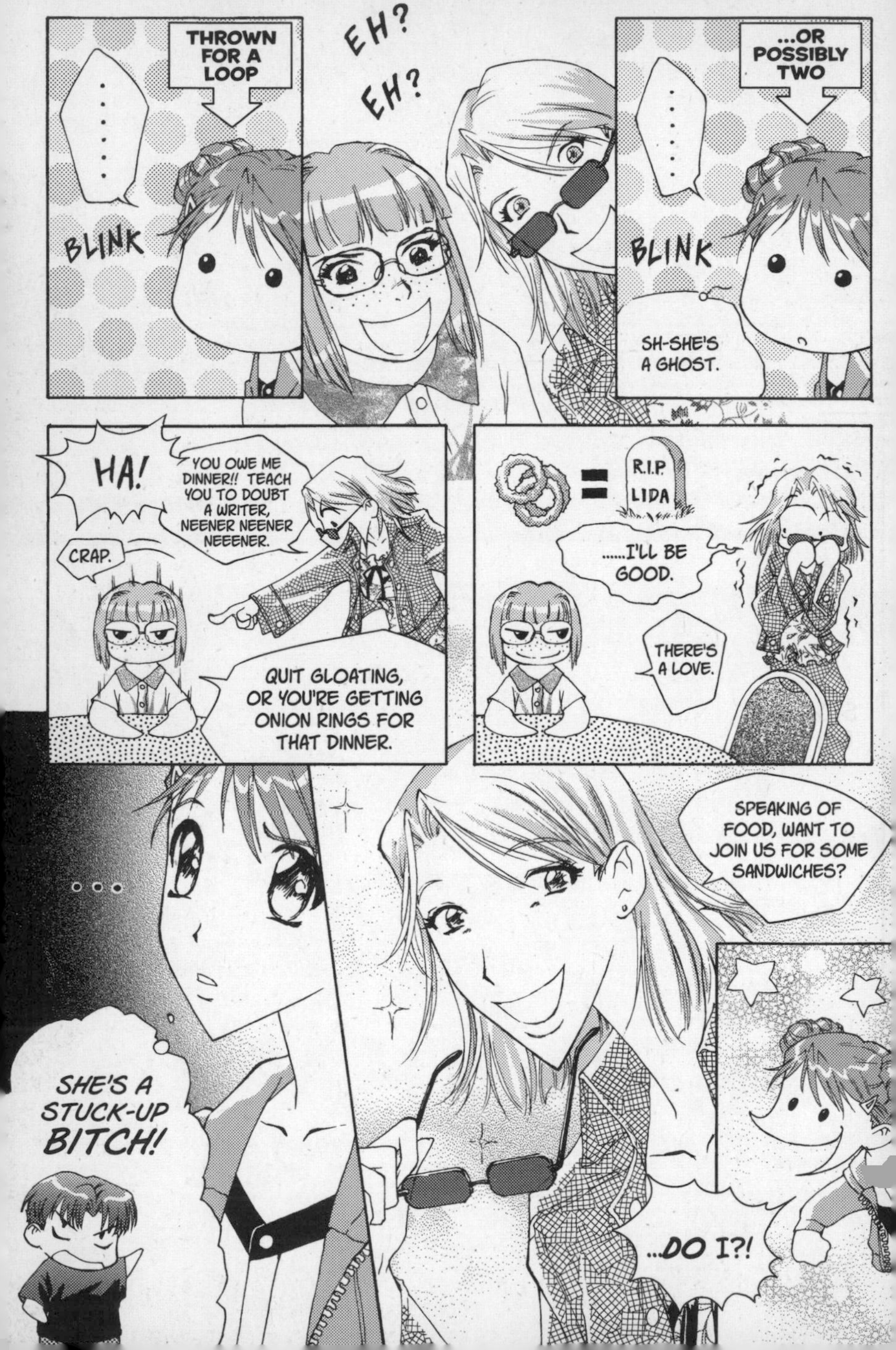
THROWN FOR A LOOP
......
BLINK
EH? EH?
...OR POSSIBLY TWO
......
BLINK
SH-SHE'S A GHOST.
HA!
YOU OWE ME DINNER!! TEACH YOU TO DOUBT A WRITER, NEENER NEENER NEEENER.
CRAP.
QUIT GLOATING, OR YOU'RE GETTING ONION RINGS FOR THAT DINNER.
R.I.P. LIDA
......I'LL BE GOOD.
THERE'S A LOVE.
...
SPEAKING OF FOOD, WANT TO JOIN US FOR SOME SANDWICHES?
SHE'S A STUCK-UP BITCH!
...DO I?!

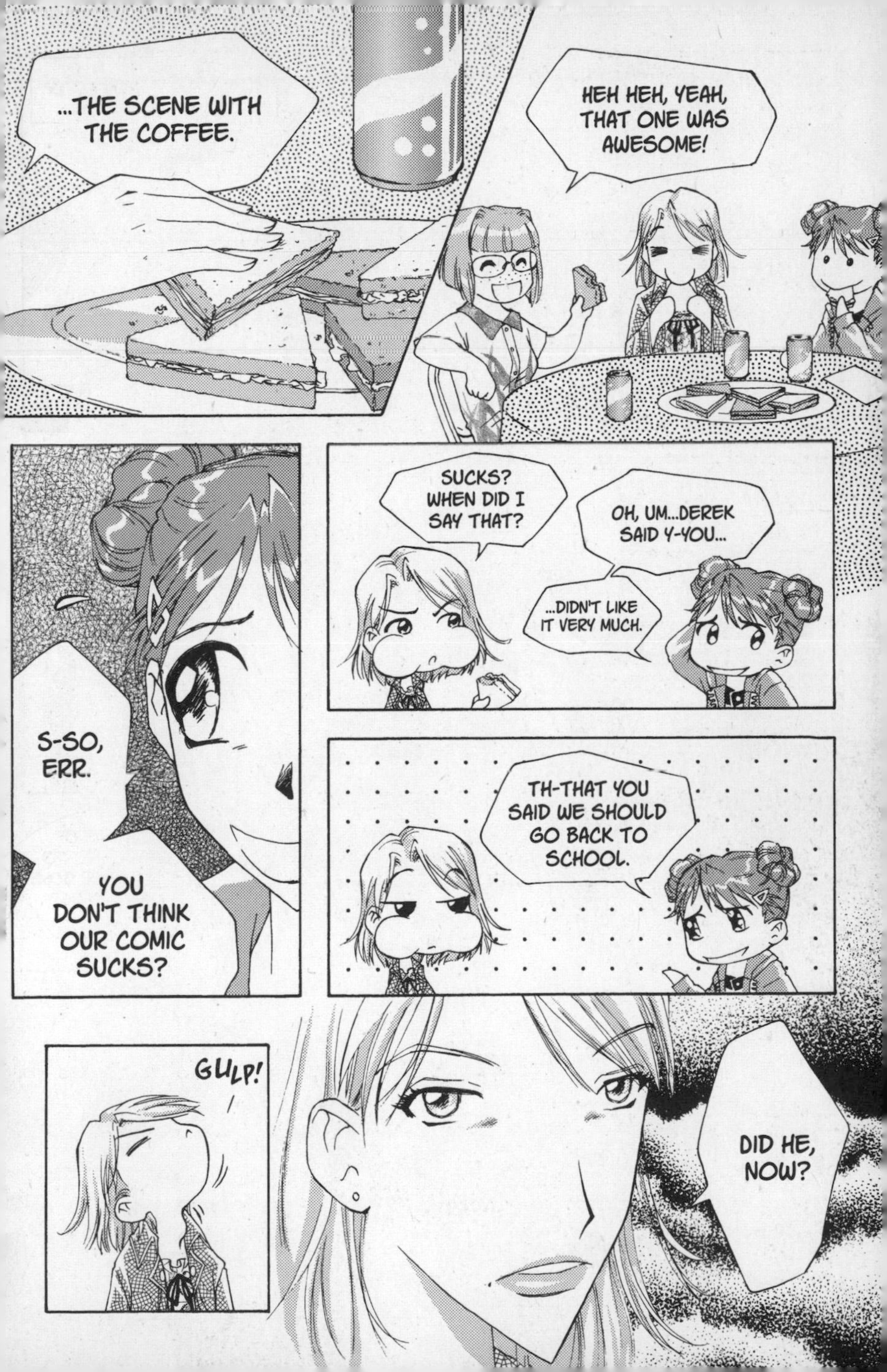
...THE SCENE WITH THE COFFEE.
HEH HEH, YEAH, THAT ONE WAS AWESOME!
S-SO, ERR.
YOU DON'T THINK OUR COMIC SUCKS?
SUCKS? WHEN DID I SAY THAT?
OH, UM...DEREK SAID Y-YOU...
...DIDN'T LIKE IT VERY MUCH.
TH-THAT YOU SAID WE SHOULD GO BACK TO SCHOOL.
GULP!
DID HE, NOW?

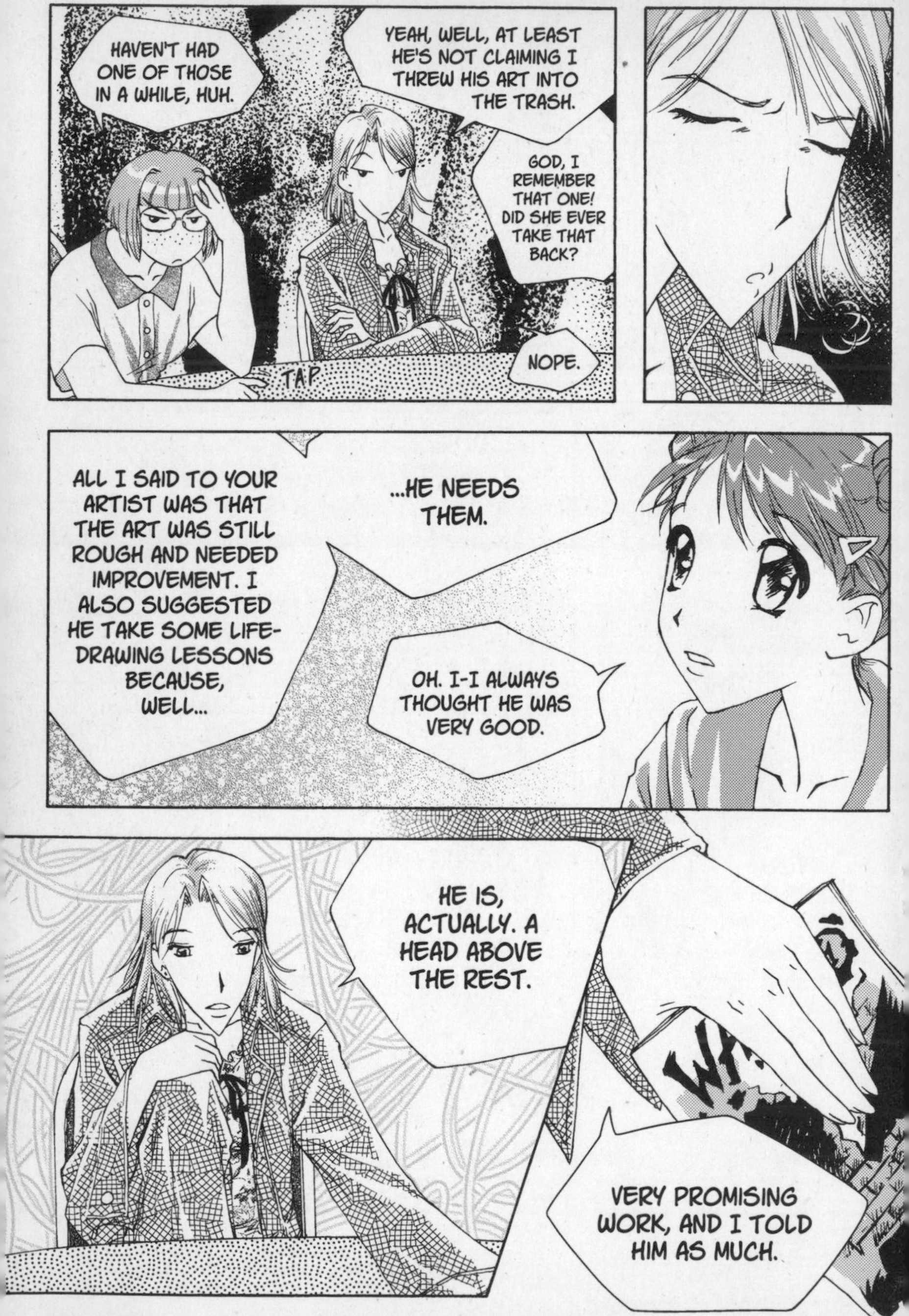
HAVEN'T HAD ONE OF THOSE IN A WHILE, HUH.
YEAH, WELL, AT LEAST HE'S NOT CLAIMING I THREW HIS ART INTO THE TRASH.
GOD, I REMEMBER THAT ONE! DID SHE EVER TAKE THAT BACK?
TAP
NOPE.
ALL I SAID TO YOUR ARTIST WAS THAT THE ART WAS STILL ROUGH AND NEEDED IMPROVEMENT. I ALSO SUGGESTED HE TAKE SOME LIFE-DRAWING LESSONS BECAUSE, WELL...
...HE NEEDS THEM.
OH. I-I ALWAYS THOUGHT HE WAS VERY GOOD.
HE IS, ACTUALLY. A HEAD ABOVE THE REST.
VERY PROMISING WORK, AND I TOLD HIM AS MUCH.

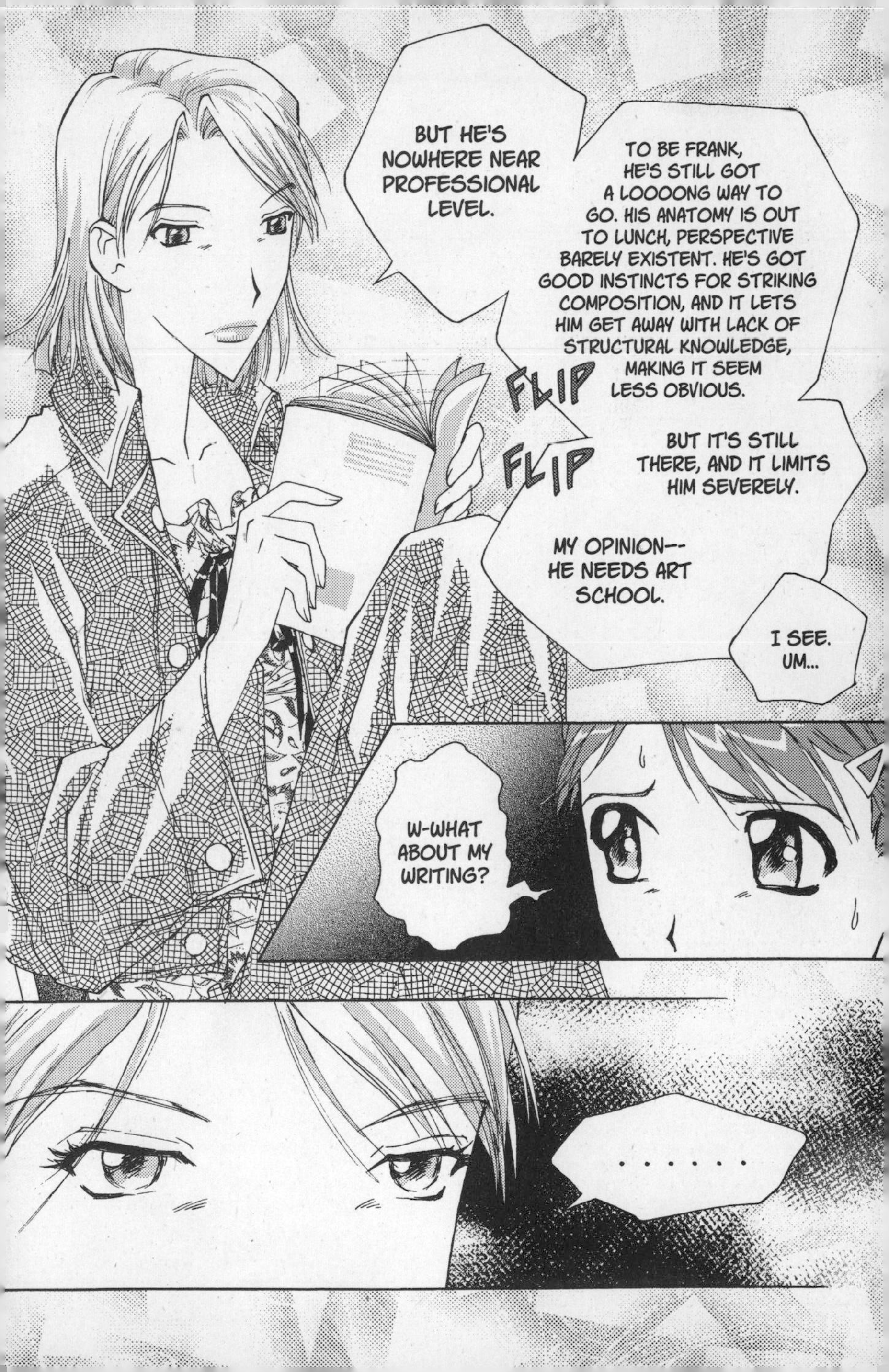
BUT HE'S NOWHERE NEAR PROFESSIONAL LEVEL.
TO BE FRANK, HE'S STILL GOT A LOOOONG WAY TO GO. HIS ANATOMY IS OUT TO LUNCH, PERSPECTIVE BARELY EXISTENT. HE'S GOT GOOD INSTINCTS FOR STRIKING COMPOSITION, AND IT LETS HIM GET AWAY WITH LACK OF STRUCTURAL KNOWLEDGE, MAKING IT SEEM LESS OBVIOUS.
FLIP
FLIP
BUT IT'S STILL THERE, AND IT LIMITS HIM SEVERELY.
MY OPINION-- HE NEEDS ART SCHOOL.
I SEE. UM...
W-WHAT ABOUT MY WRITING?
. . . . . .

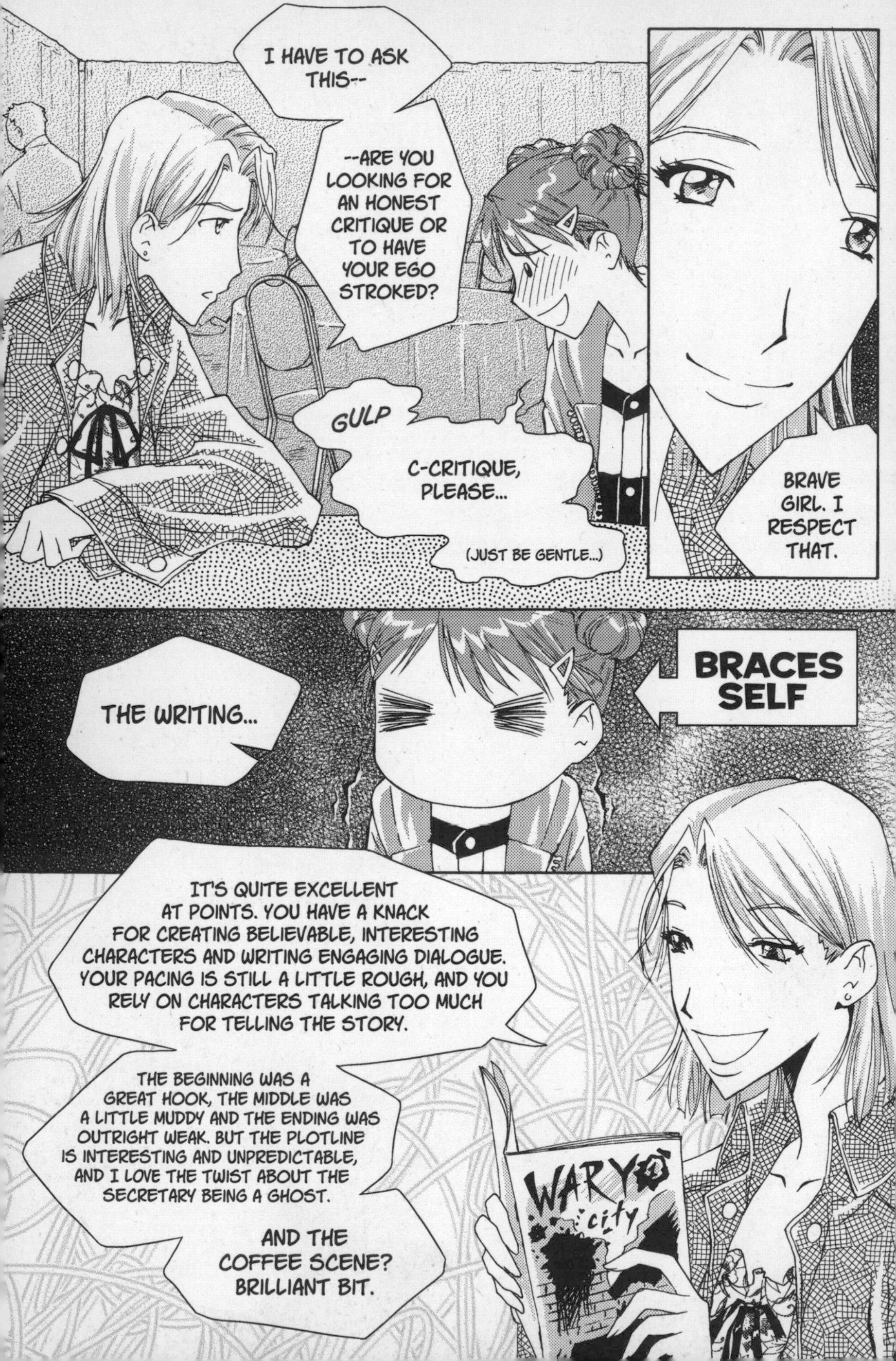

I HAVE TO ASK THIS--
--ARE YOU LOOKING FOR AN HONEST CRITIQUE OR TO HAVE YOUR EGO STROKED?
GULP
C-CRITIQUE, PLEASE...
(JUST BE GENTLE...)
BRAVE GIRL. I RESPECT THAT.
THE WRITING...
BRACES SELF
IT'S QUITE EXCELLENT AT POINTS. YOU HAVE A KNACK FOR CREATING BELIEVABLE, INTERESTING CHARACTERS AND WRITING ENGAGING DIALOGUE. YOUR PACING IS STILL A LITTLE ROUGH, AND YOU RELY ON CHARACTERS TALKING TOO MUCH FOR TELLING THE STORY.
THE BEGINNING WAS A GREAT HOOK, THE MIDDLE WAS A LITTLE MUDDY AND THE ENDING WAS OUTRIGHT WEAK. BUT THE PLOTLINE IS INTERESTING AND UNPREDICTABLE, AND I LOVE THE TWIST ABOUT THE SECRETARY BEING A GHOST.
AND THE COFFEE SCENE? BRILLIANT BIT.
WARYŌ city

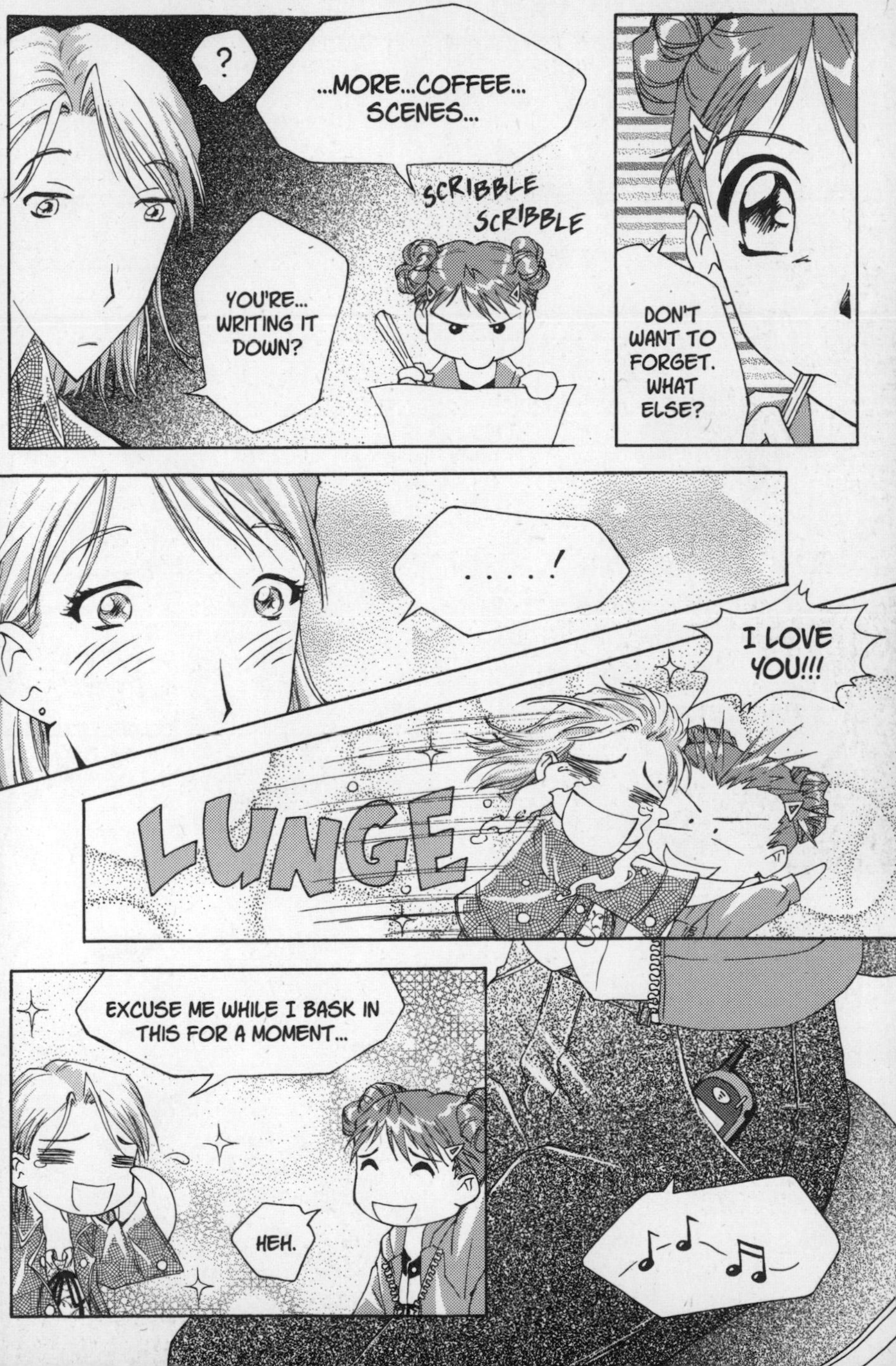
?
...MORE...COFFEE... SCENES...
SCRIBBLE SCRIBBLE
YOU'RE... WRITING IT DOWN?
DON'T WANT TO FORGET. WHAT ELSE?
.....!
I LOVE YOU!!!
LUNGE
EXCUSE ME WHILE I BASK IN THIS FOR A MOMENT...
HEH.

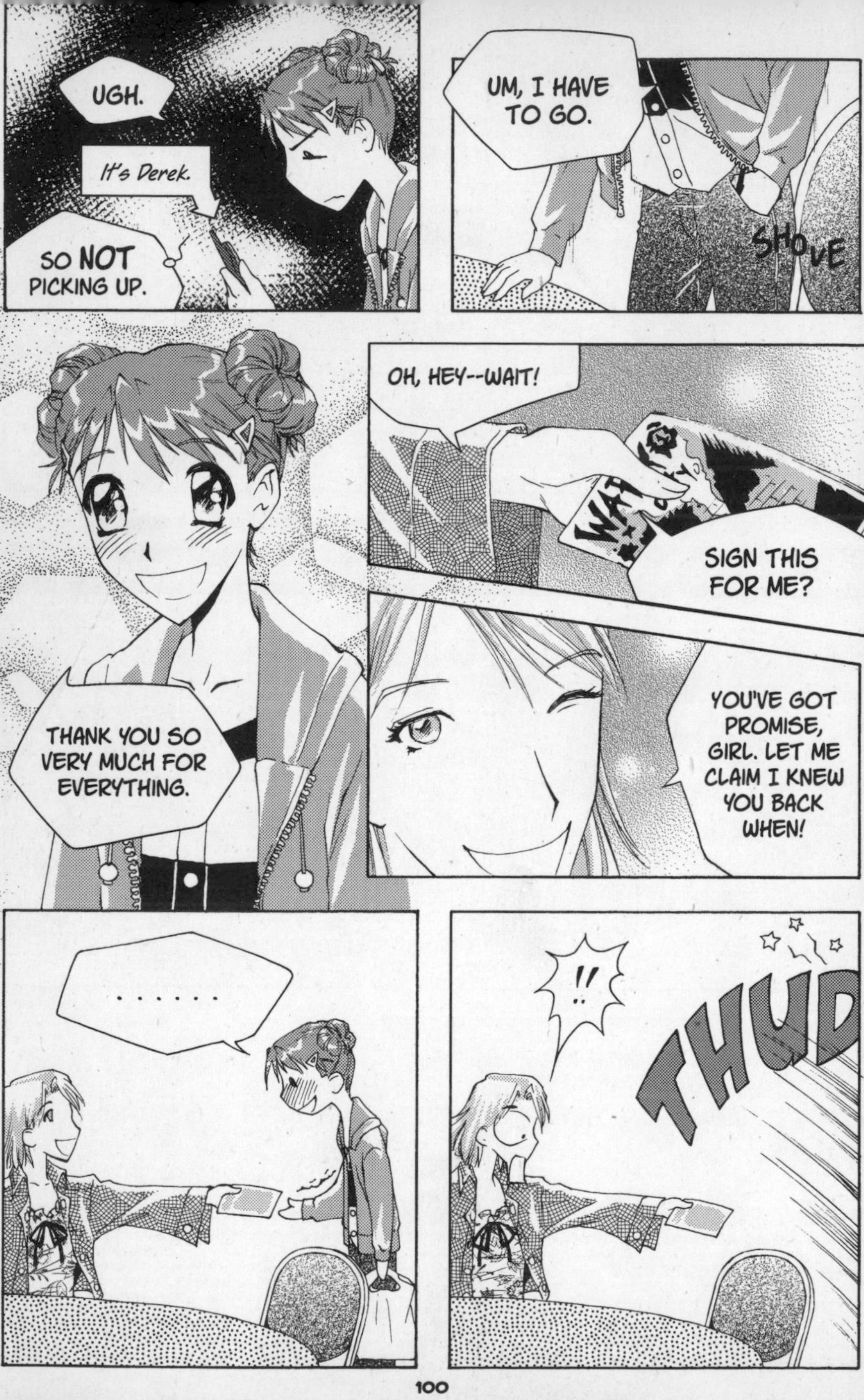
UGH.
It's Derek.
SO NOT PICKING UP.
UM, I HAVE TO GO.
SHOVE
THANK YOU SO VERY MUCH FOR EVERYTHING.
OH, HEY--WAIT!
SIGN THIS FOR ME?
YOU'VE GOT PROMISE, GIRL. LET ME CLAIM I KNEW YOU BACK WHEN!
......
!!
THUD

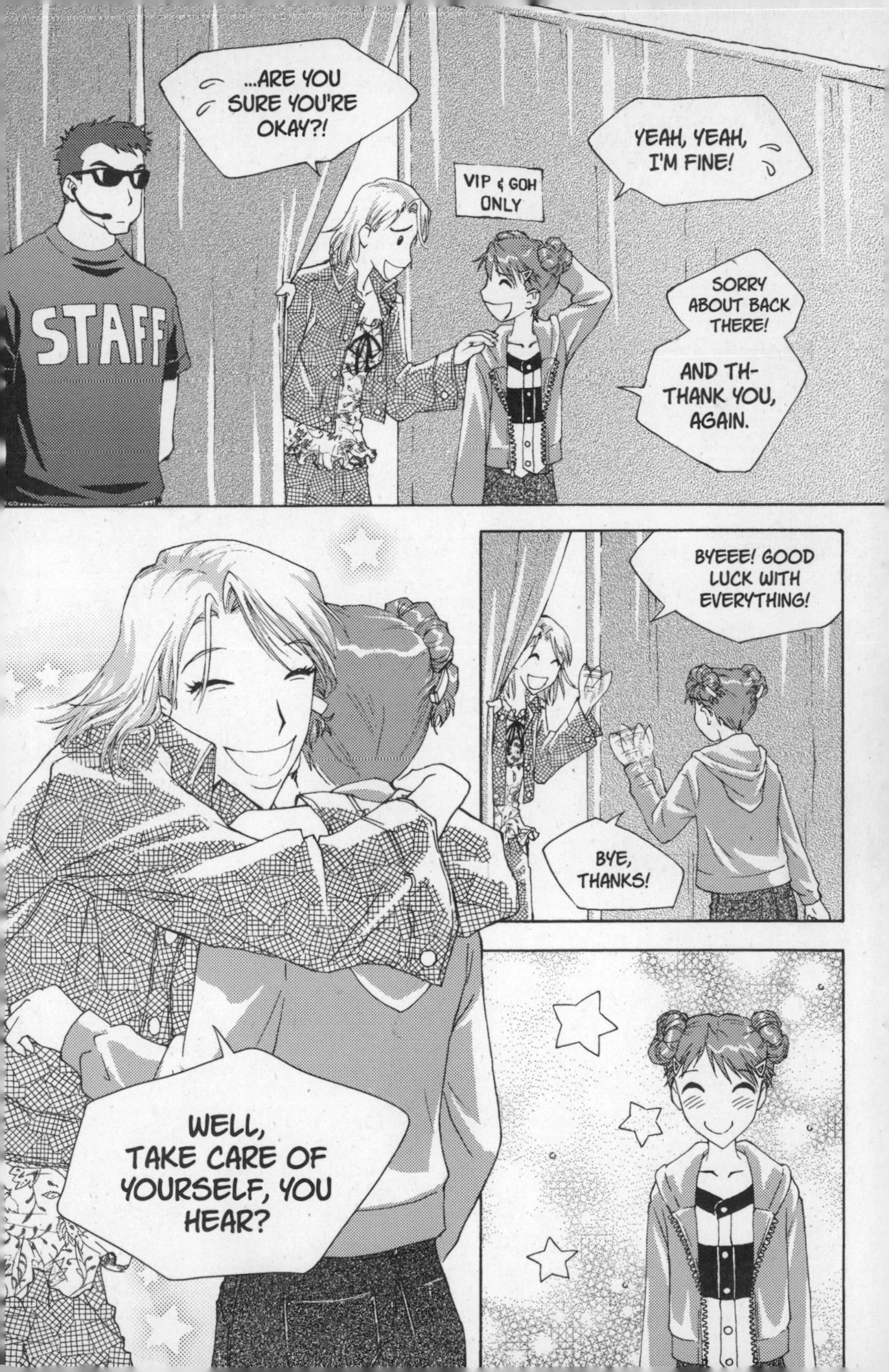
...ARE YOU SURE YOU'RE OKAY?!
STAFF
VIP & GOH ONLY
YEAH, YEAH, I'M FINE!
SORRY ABOUT BACK THERE!
AND TH- THANK YOU, AGAIN.
WELL, TAKE CARE OF YOURSELF, YOU HEAR?
BYEEE! GOOD LUCK WITH EVERYTHING!
BYE, THANKS!

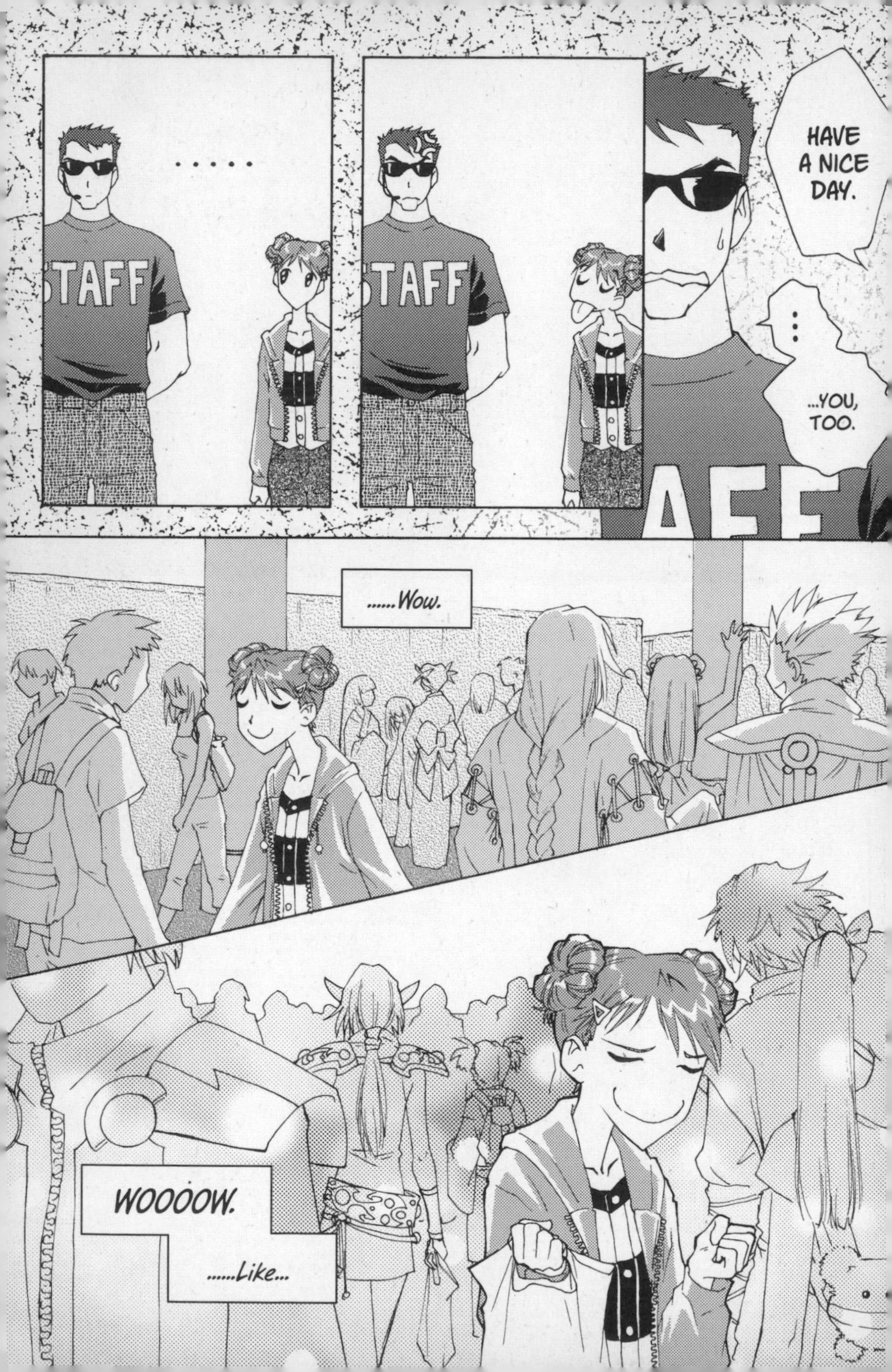
STAFF
.....
STAFF
HAVE A NICE DAY.
...
...YOU, TOO.
AFF
......Wow.
WOOOOW.
......Like...

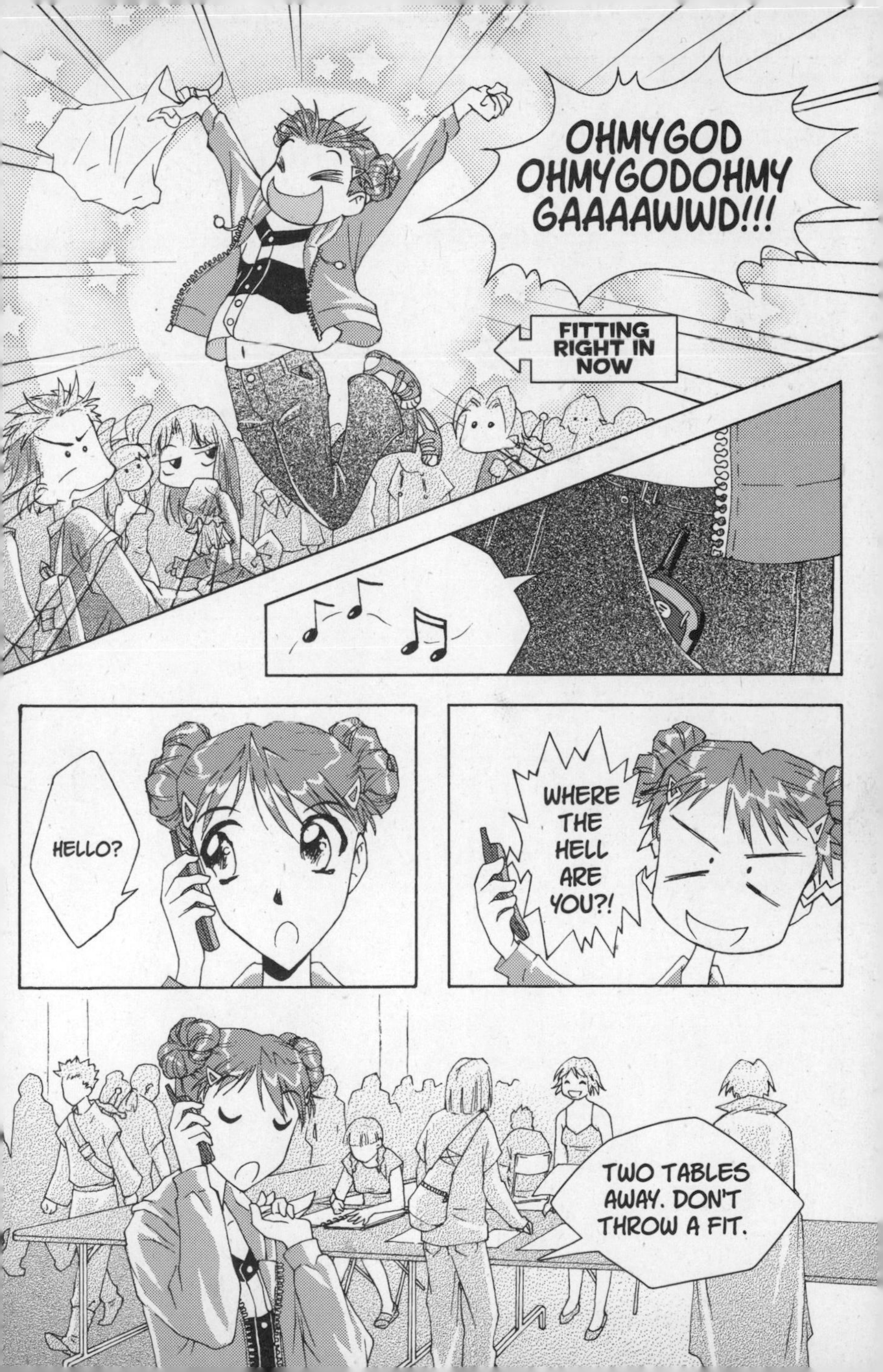
OHMYGOD OHMYGODOHMY GAAAAWWD!!!
FITTING RIGHT IN NOW
HELLO?
WHERE THE HELL ARE YOU?!
TWO TABLES AWAY. DON'T THROW A FIT.

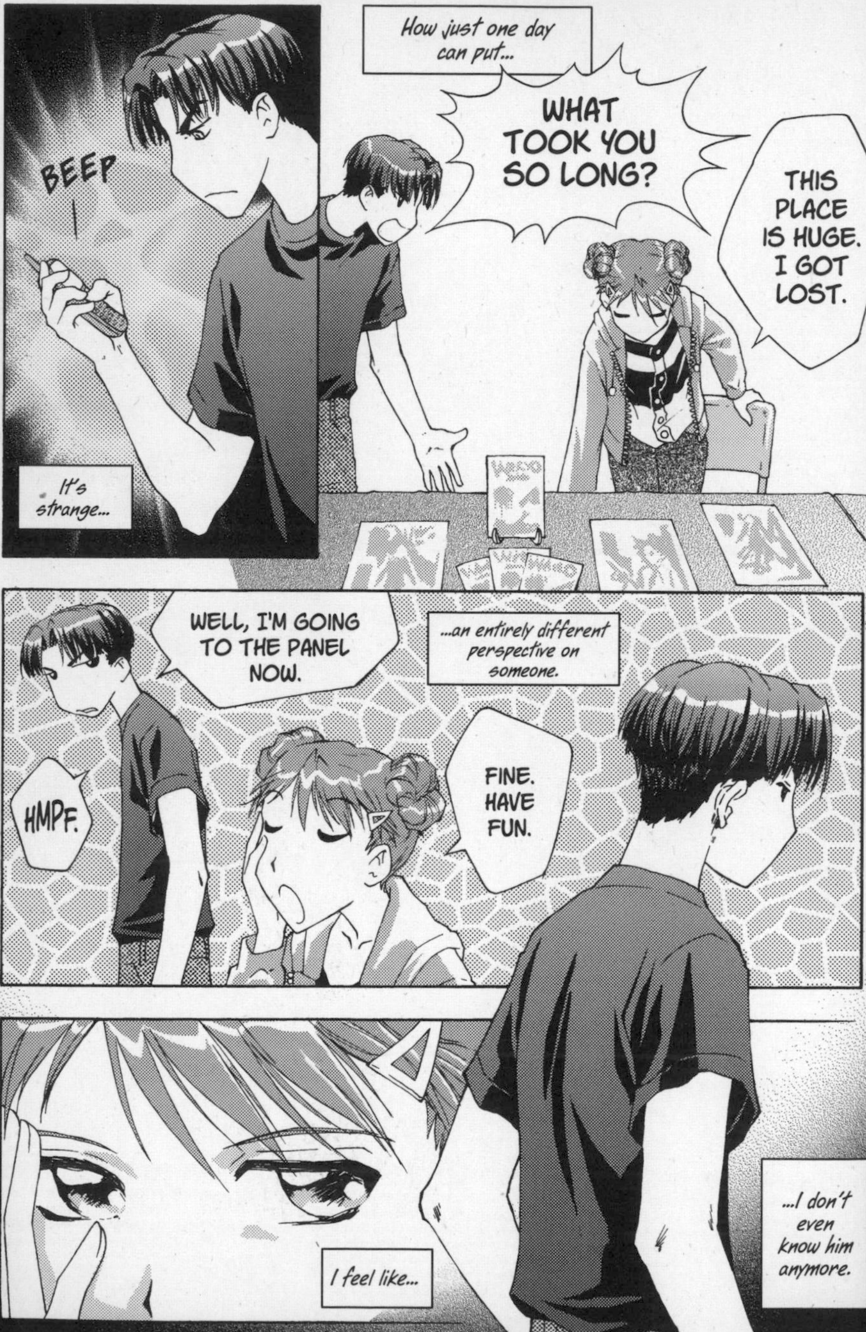
BEEP
It's strange...
How just one day can put...
WHAT TOOK YOU SO LONG?
THIS PLACE IS HUGE. I GOT LOST.
WELL, I'M GOING TO THE PANEL NOW.
...an entirely different perspective on someone.
HMPF.
FINE. HAVE FUN.
I feel like...
...I don't even know him anymore.

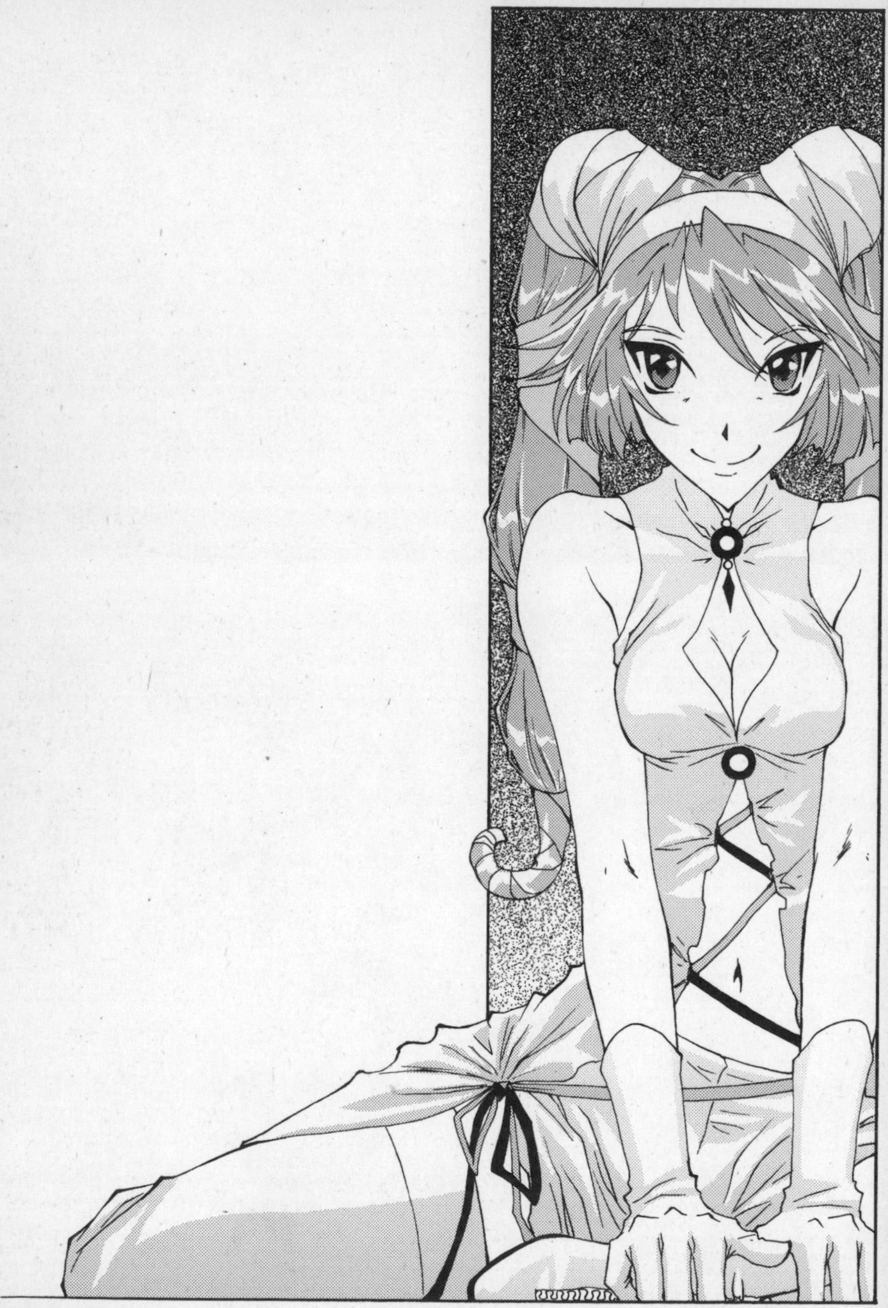

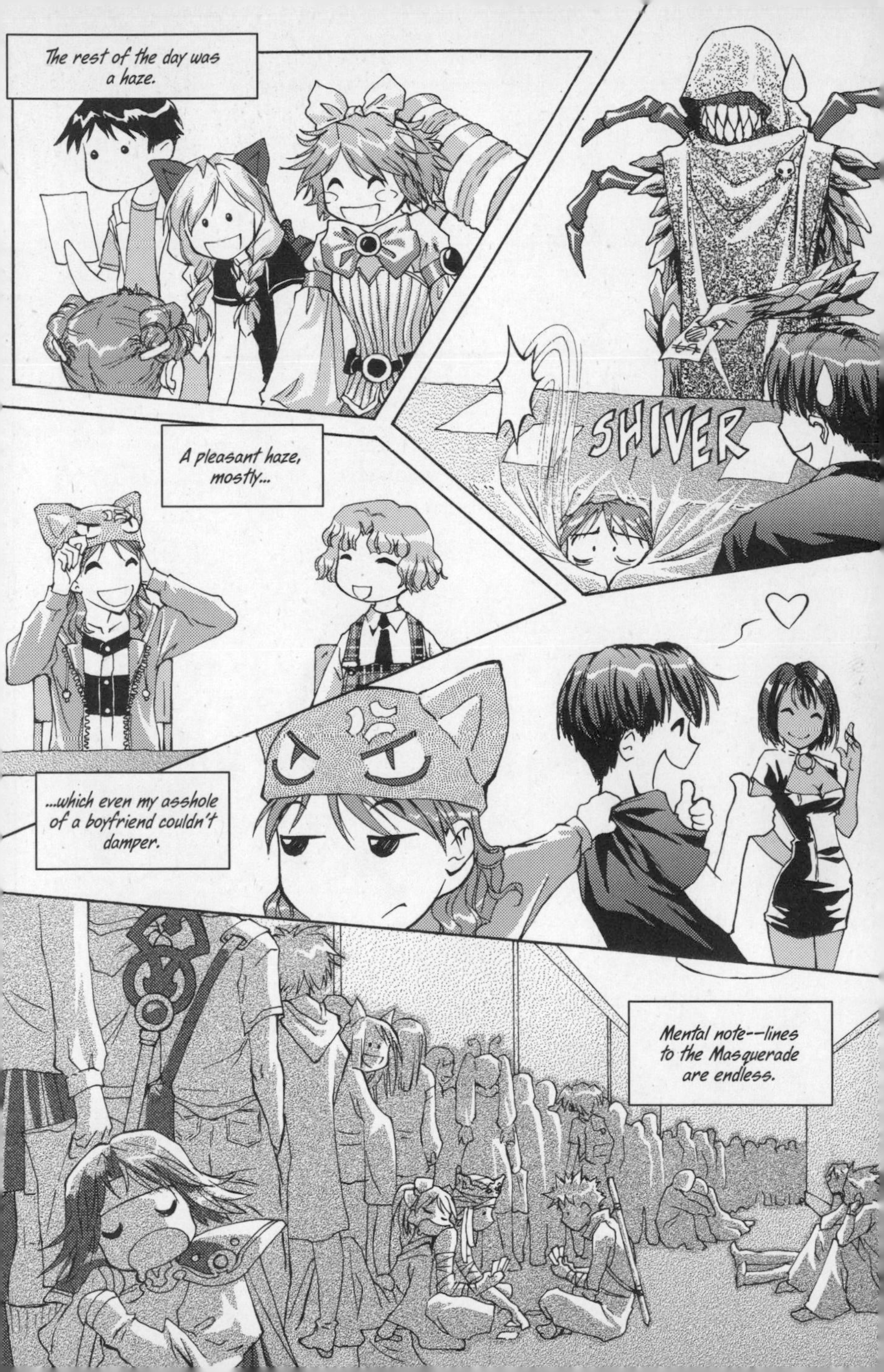
The rest of the day was a haze.
SHIVER
A pleasant haze, mostly...
...which even my asshole of a boyfriend couldn't damper.
Mental note--lines to the Masquerade are endless.

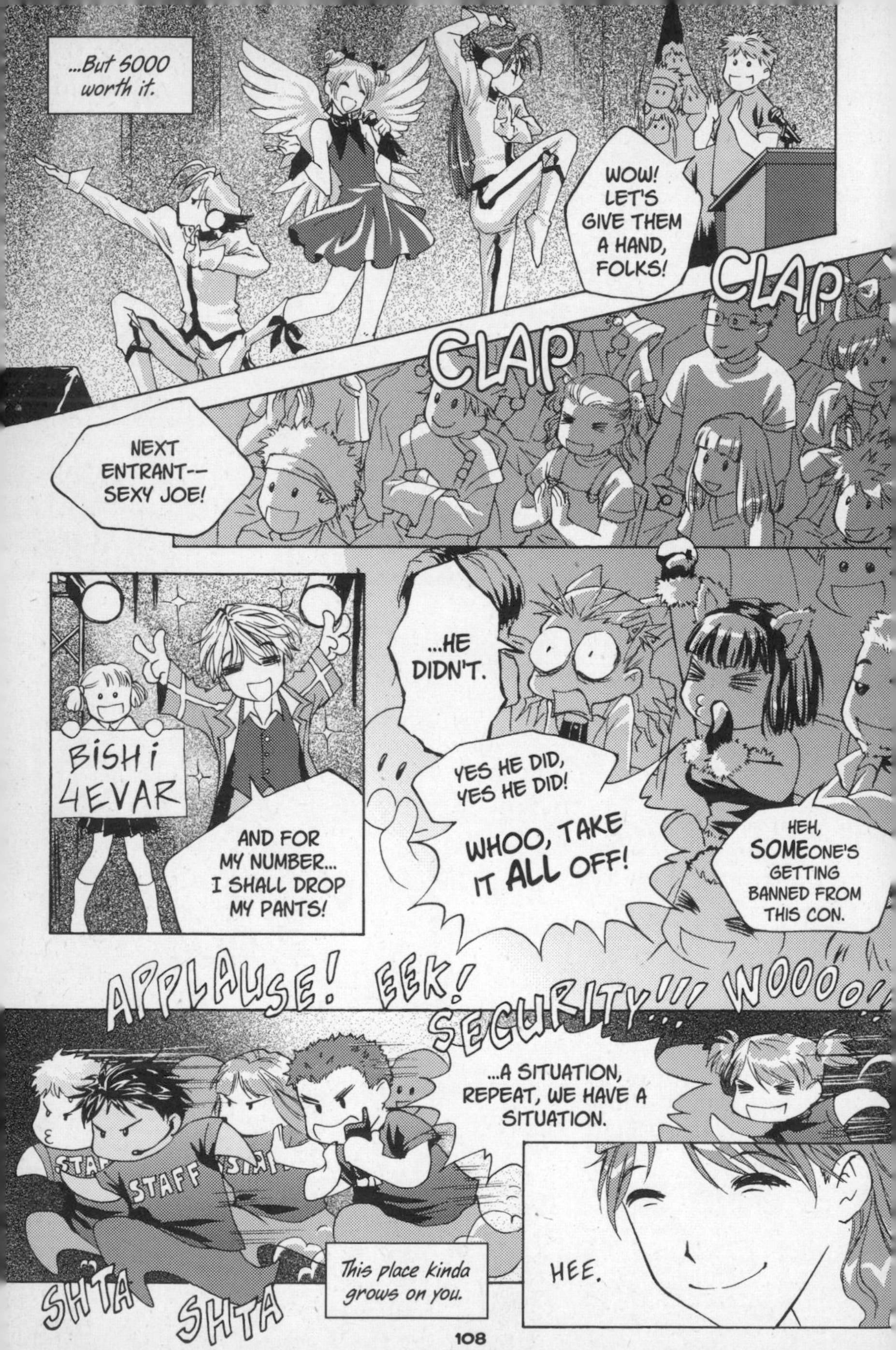
...But SOOO worth it.
WOW! LET'S GIVE THEM A HAND, FOLKS!
CLAP
CLAP
NEXT ENTRANT-- SEXY JOE!
BISHI 4EVAR
AND FOR MY NUMBER... I SHALL DROP MY PANTS!
...HE DIDN'T.
YES HE DID, YES HE DID!
WHOO, TAKE IT ALL OFF!
HEH, SOMEONE'S GETTING BANNED FROM THIS CON.
APPLAUSE! EEK! SECURITY!!! WOOOO!
...A SITUATION, REPEAT, WE HAVE A SITUATION.
STAFF
STAFF
SHTA
SHTA
This place kinda grows on you.
HEE.

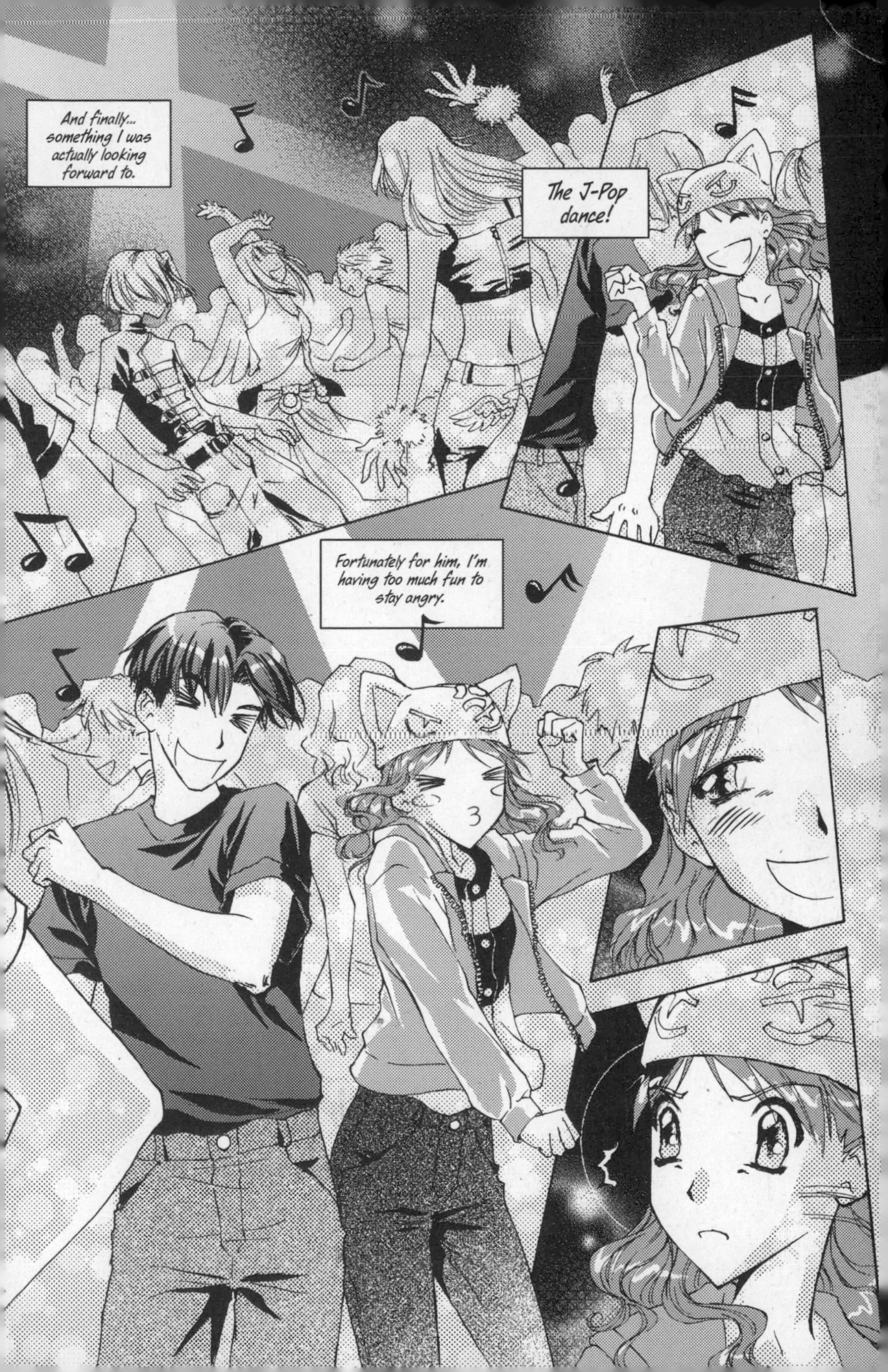
And finally... something I was actually looking forward to.
The J-Pop dance!
Fortunately for him, I'm having too much fun to stay angry.

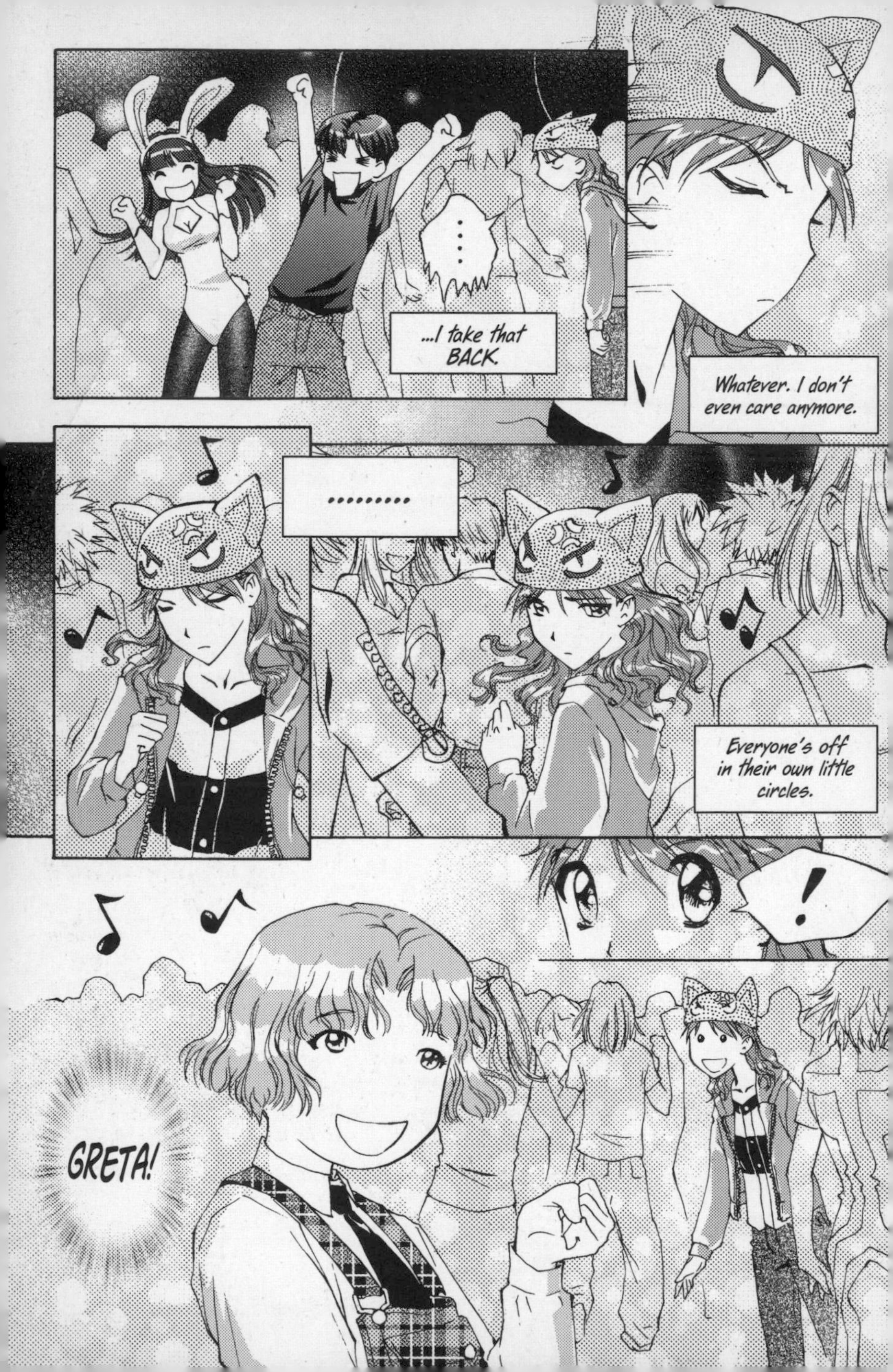
...I take that BACK.
Whatever. I don't even care anymore.
....
Everyone's off in their own little circles.
!
GRETA!

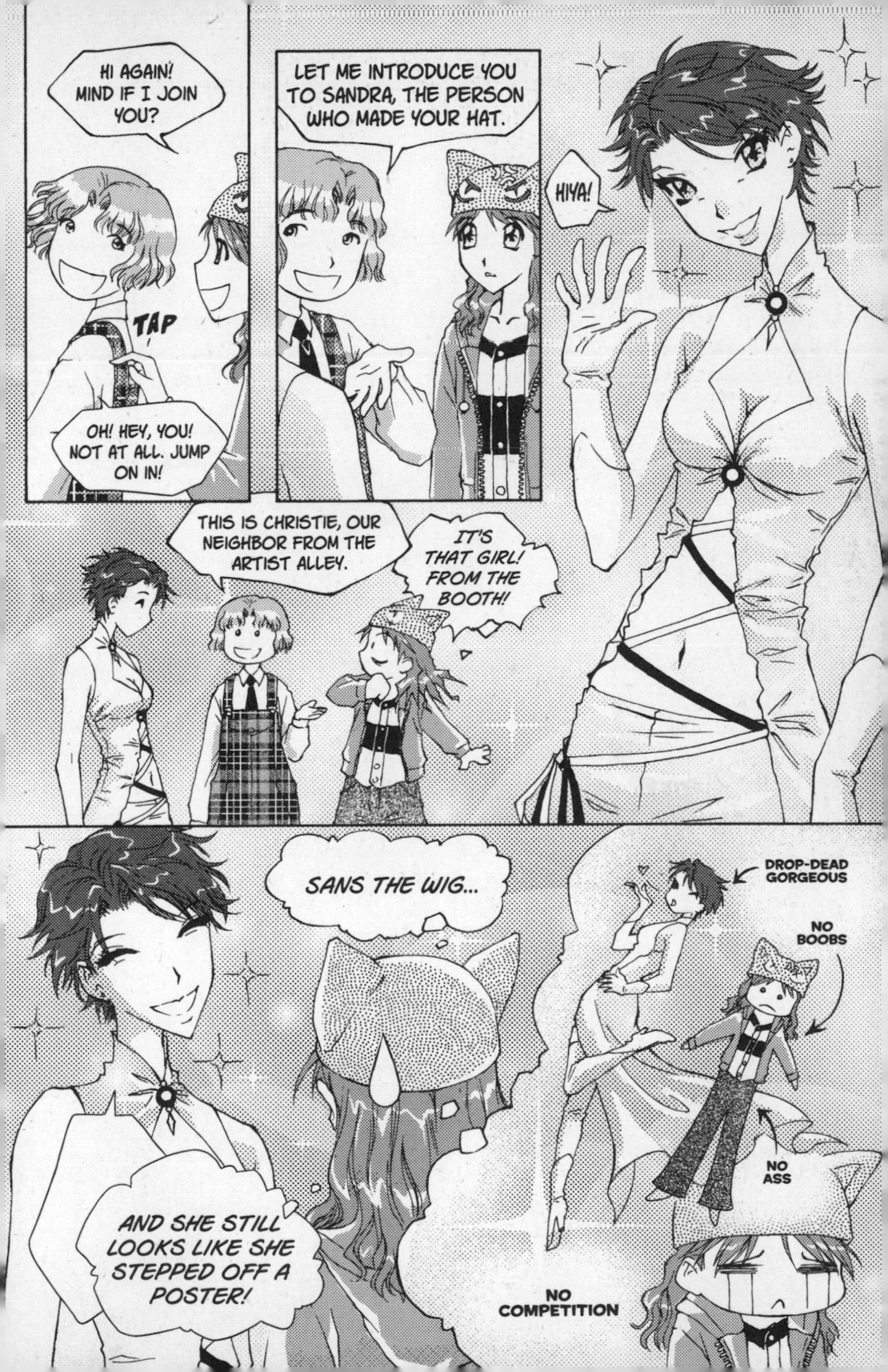
HI AGAIN! MIND IF I JOIN YOU?
TAP
OH! HEY, YOU! NOT AT ALL. JUMP ON IN!
LET ME INTRODUCE YOU TO SANDRA, THE PERSON WHO MADE YOUR HAT.
HIYA!
THIS IS CHRISTIE, OUR NEIGHBOR FROM THE ARTIST ALLEY.
IT'S THAT GIRL! FROM THE BOOTH!
SANS THE WIG...
AND SHE STILL LOOKS LIKE SHE STEPPED OFF A POSTER!
DROP-DEAD GORGEOUS
NO BOOBS
NO ASS
NO COMPETITION

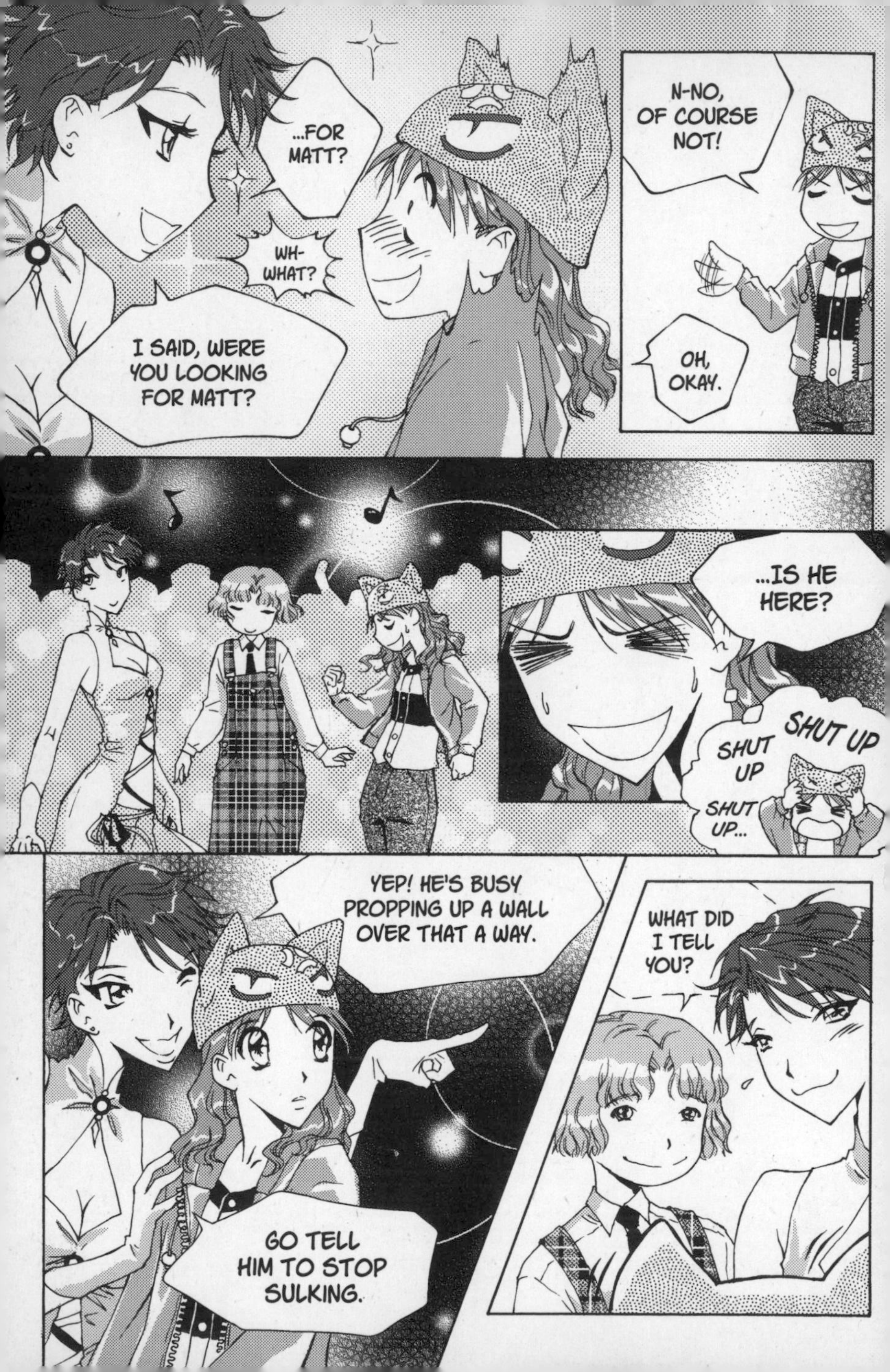
...FOR MATT?
WH- WHAT?
I SAID, WERE YOU LOOKING FOR MATT?
N-NO, OF COURSE NOT!
OH, OKAY.
...IS HE HERE?
SHUT UP
SHUT UP
SHUT UP...
YEP! HE'S BUSY PROPPING UP A WALL OVER THAT A WAY.
GO TELL HIM TO STOP SULKING.
WHAT DID I TELL YOU?

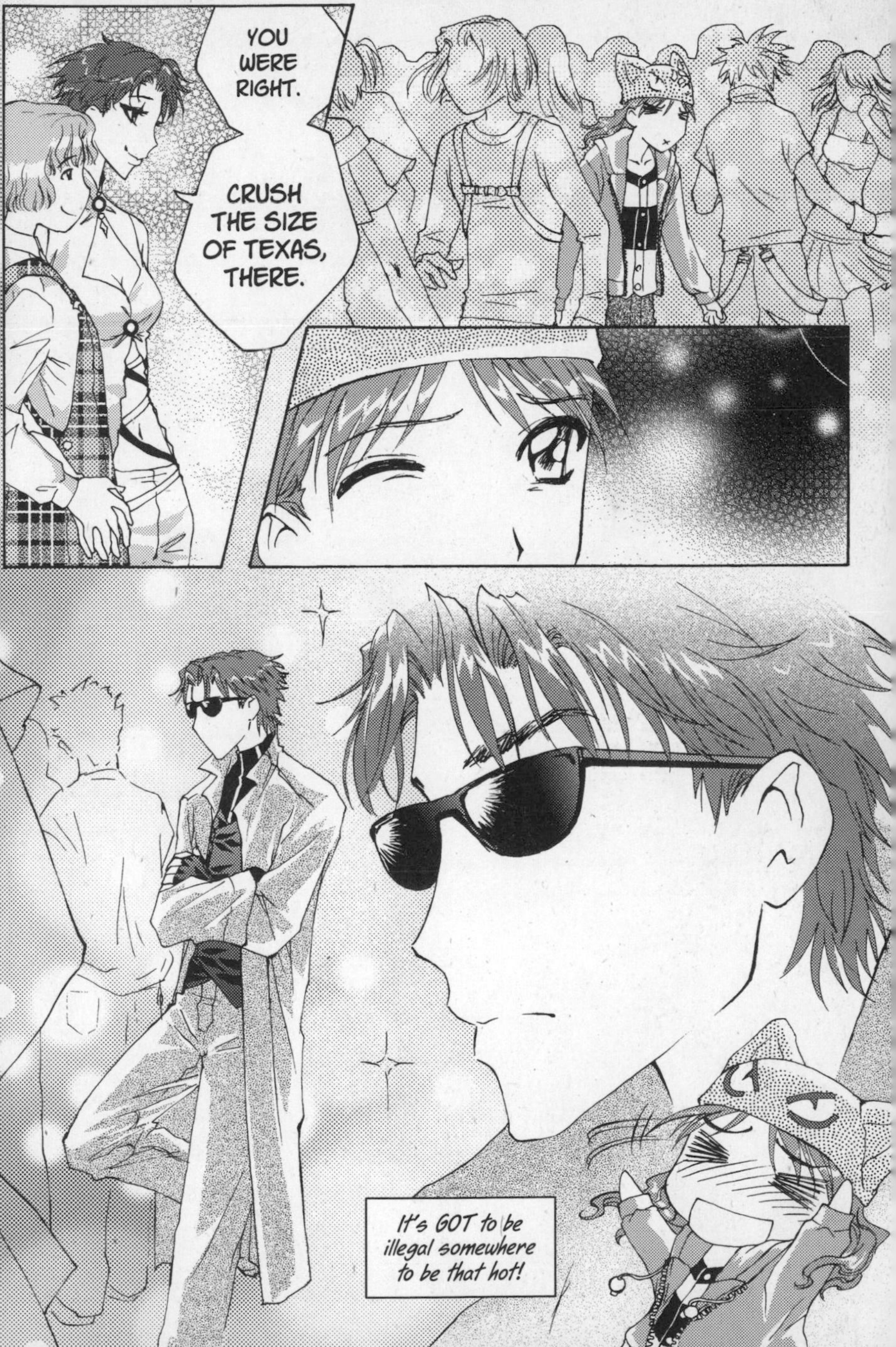
YOU WERE RIGHT.
CRUSH THE SIZE OF TEXAS, THERE.
It's GOT to be illegal somewhere to be that hot!

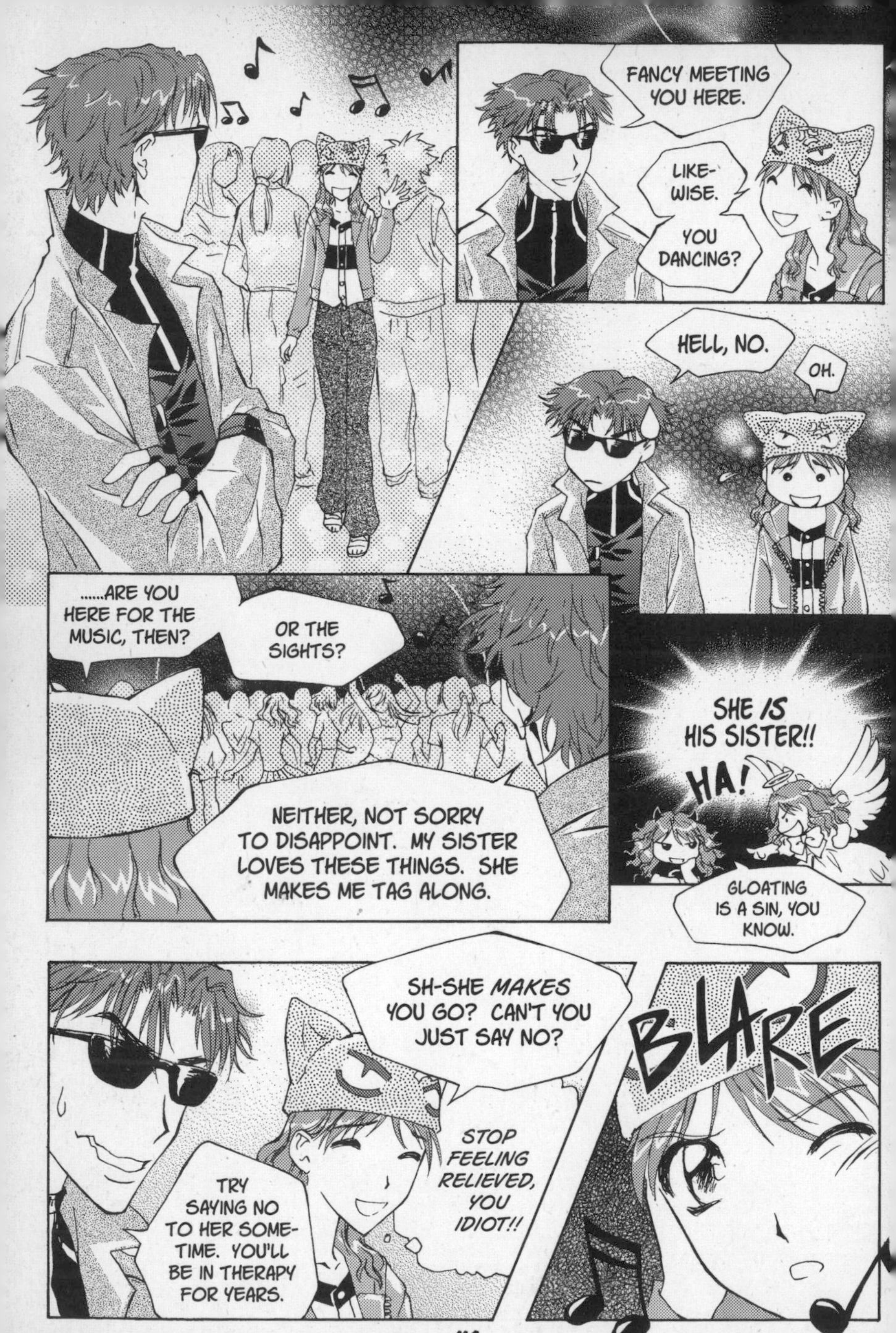

FANCY MEETING YOU HERE.
LIKE-WISE.
YOU DANCING?
HELL, NO.
OH.
......ARE YOU HERE FOR THE MUSIC, THEN?
OR THE SIGHTS?
NEITHER, NOT SORRY TO DISAPPOINT. MY SISTER LOVES THESE THINGS. SHE MAKES ME TAG ALONG.
SHE *IS* HIS SISTER!!
HA!
GLOATING IS A SIN, YOU KNOW.
SH-SHE *MAKES* YOU GO? CAN'T YOU JUST SAY NO?
TRY SAYING NO TO HER SOME-TIME. YOU'LL BE IN THERAPY FOR YEARS.
STOP FEELING RELIEVED, YOU IDIOT!!
BLARE

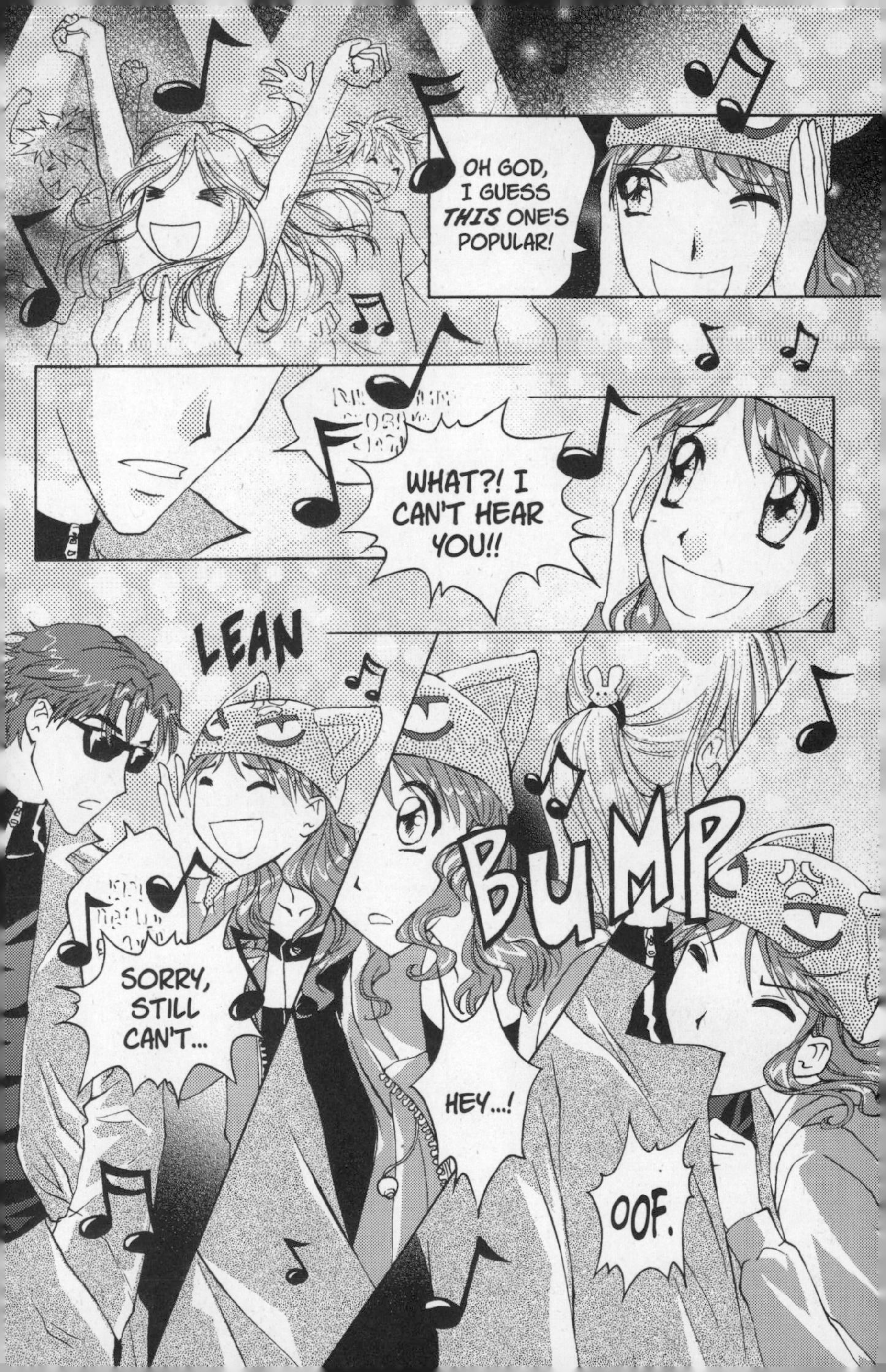
OH GOD, I GUESS *THIS* ONE'S POPULAR!
WHAT?! I CAN'T HEAR YOU!!
LEAN
SORRY, STILL CAN'T...
BUMP
HEY...!
OOF.

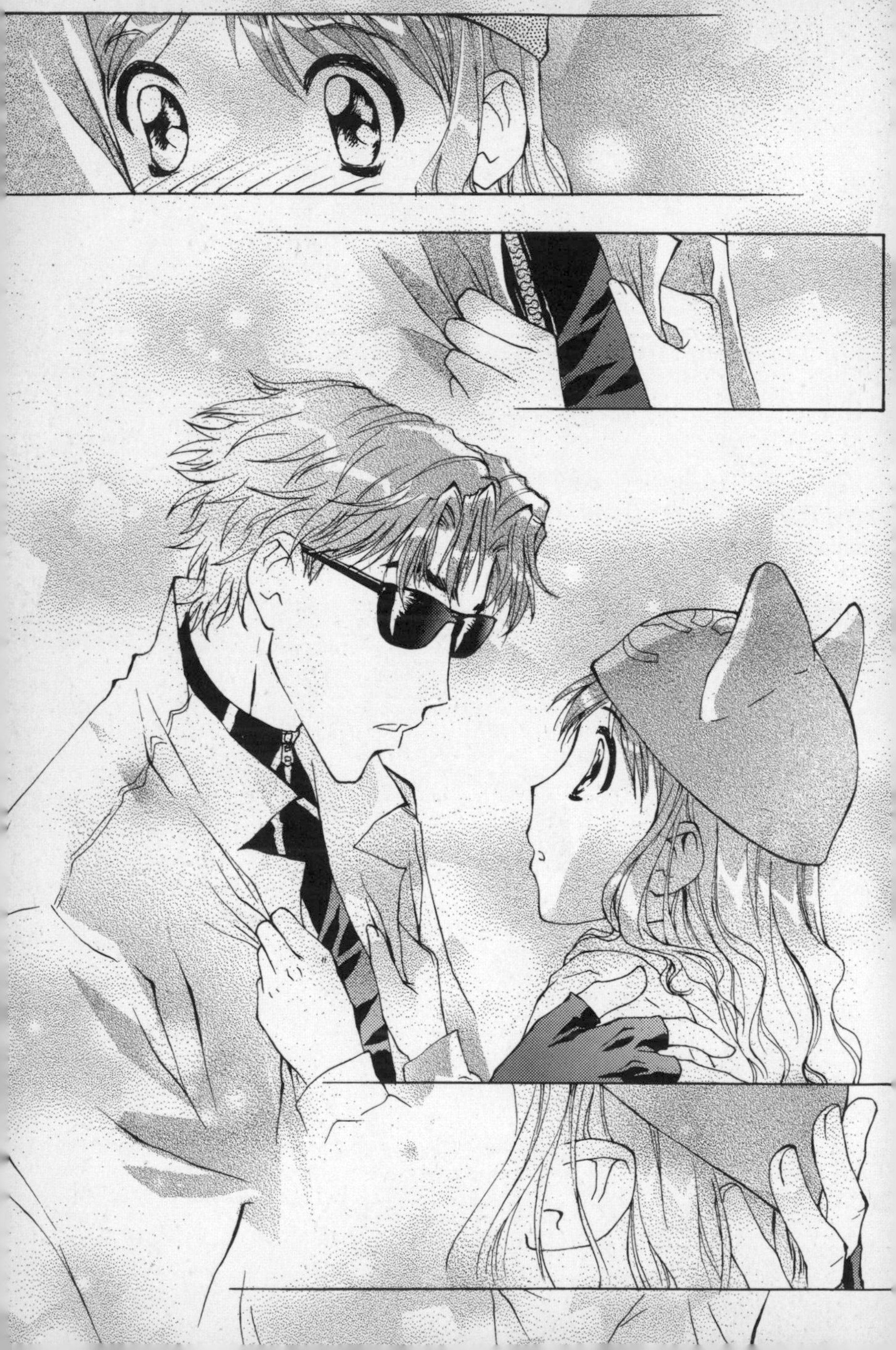

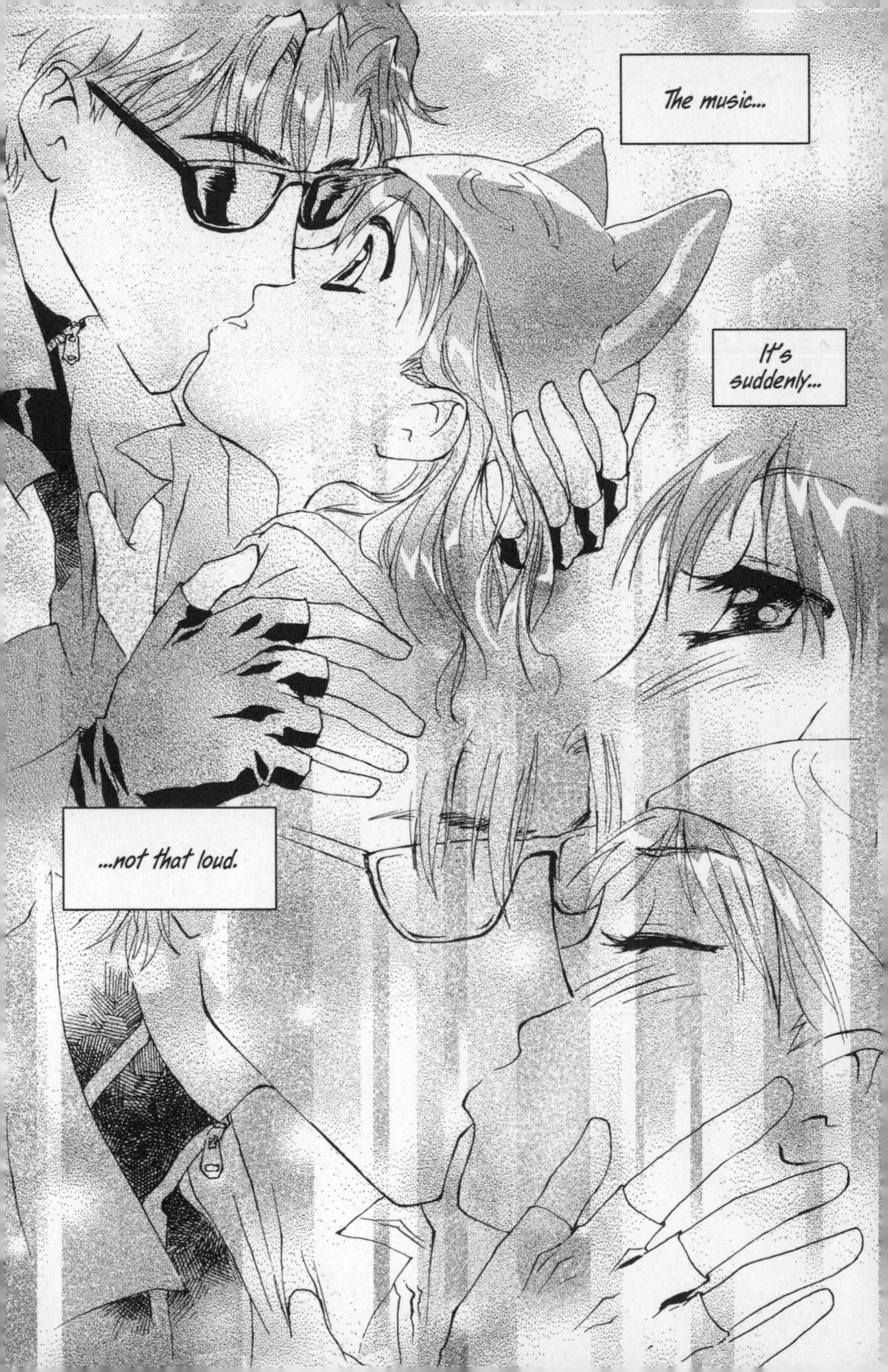
The music...
It's suddenly...
...not that loud.

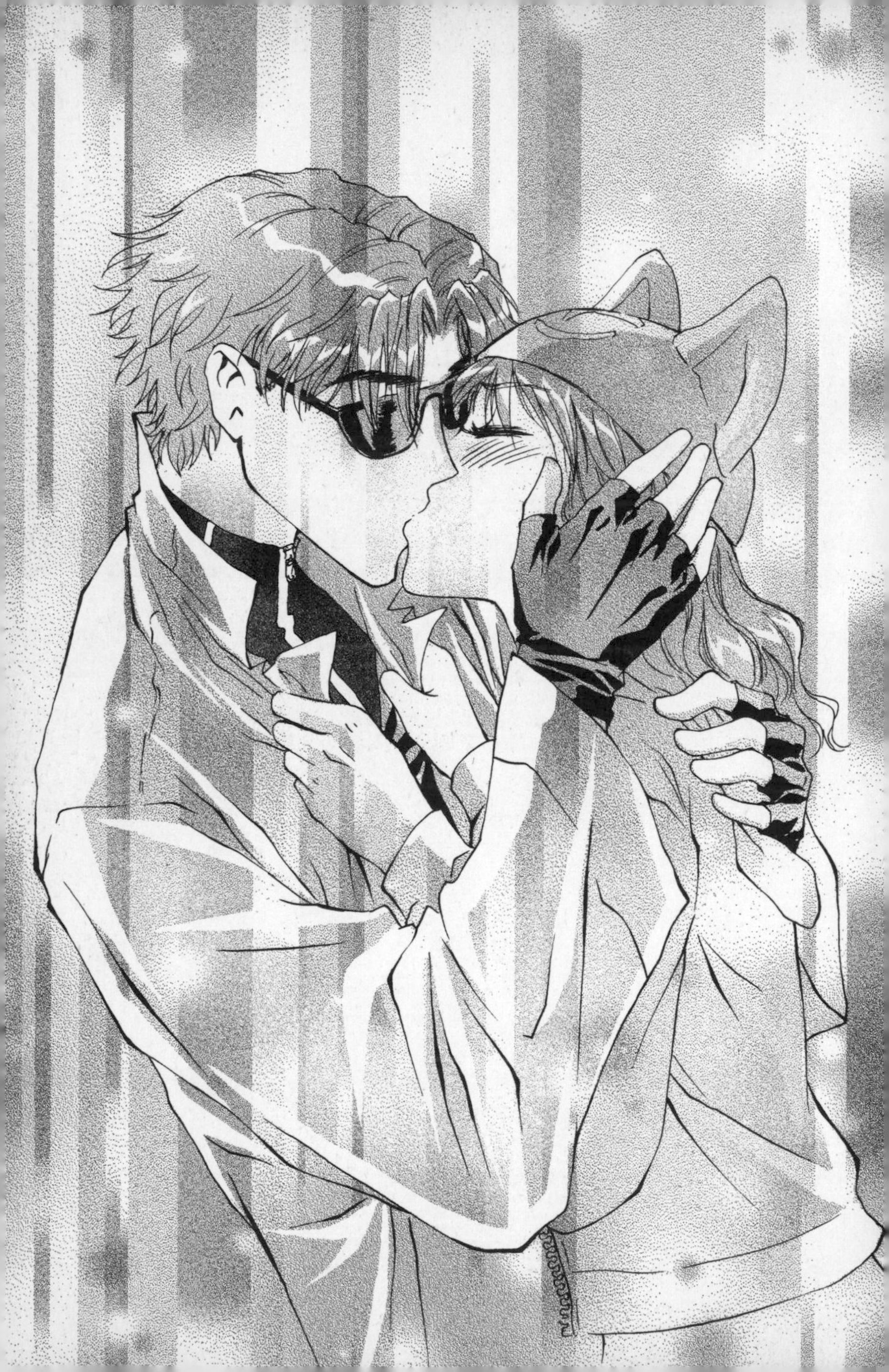

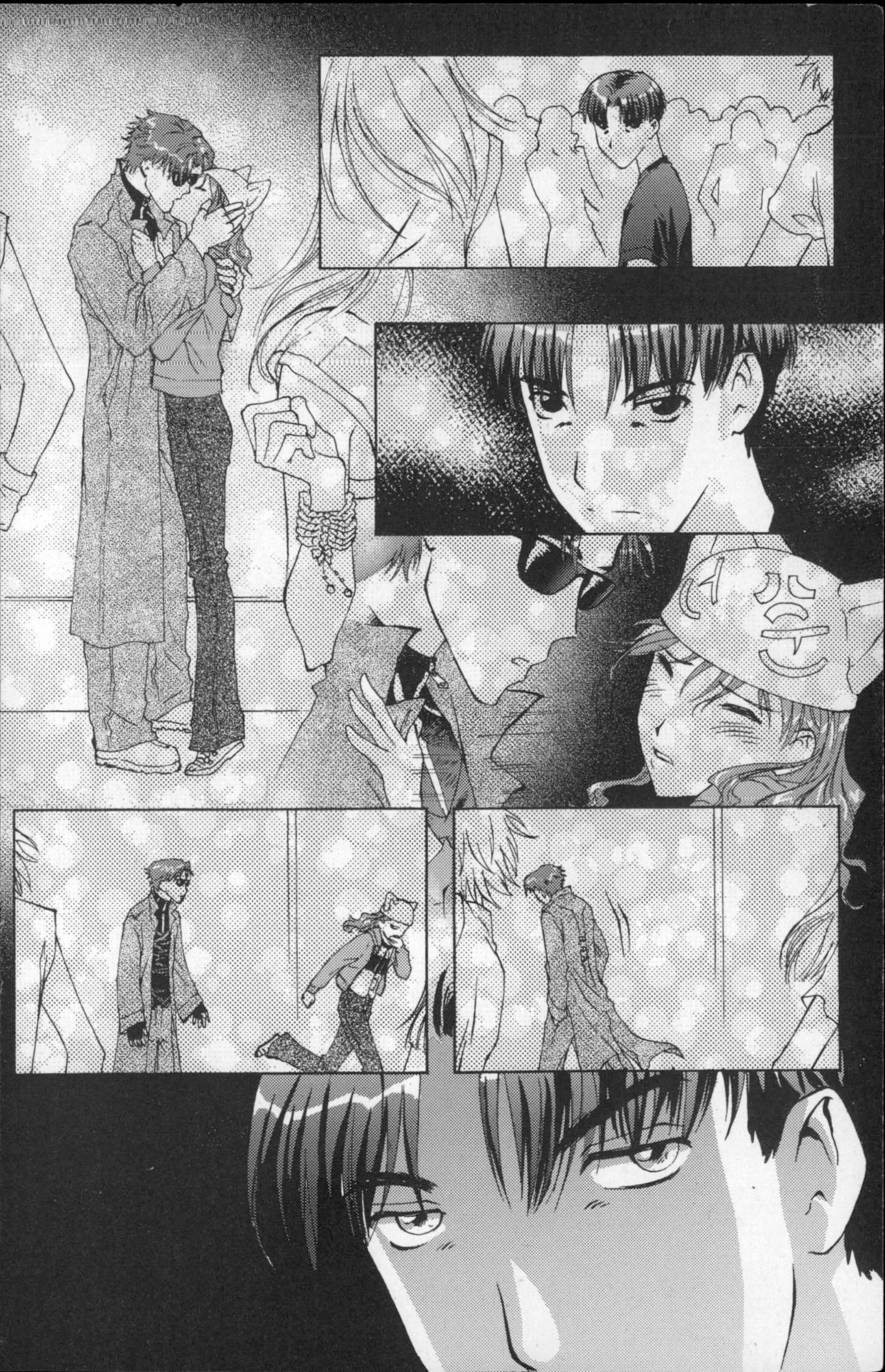

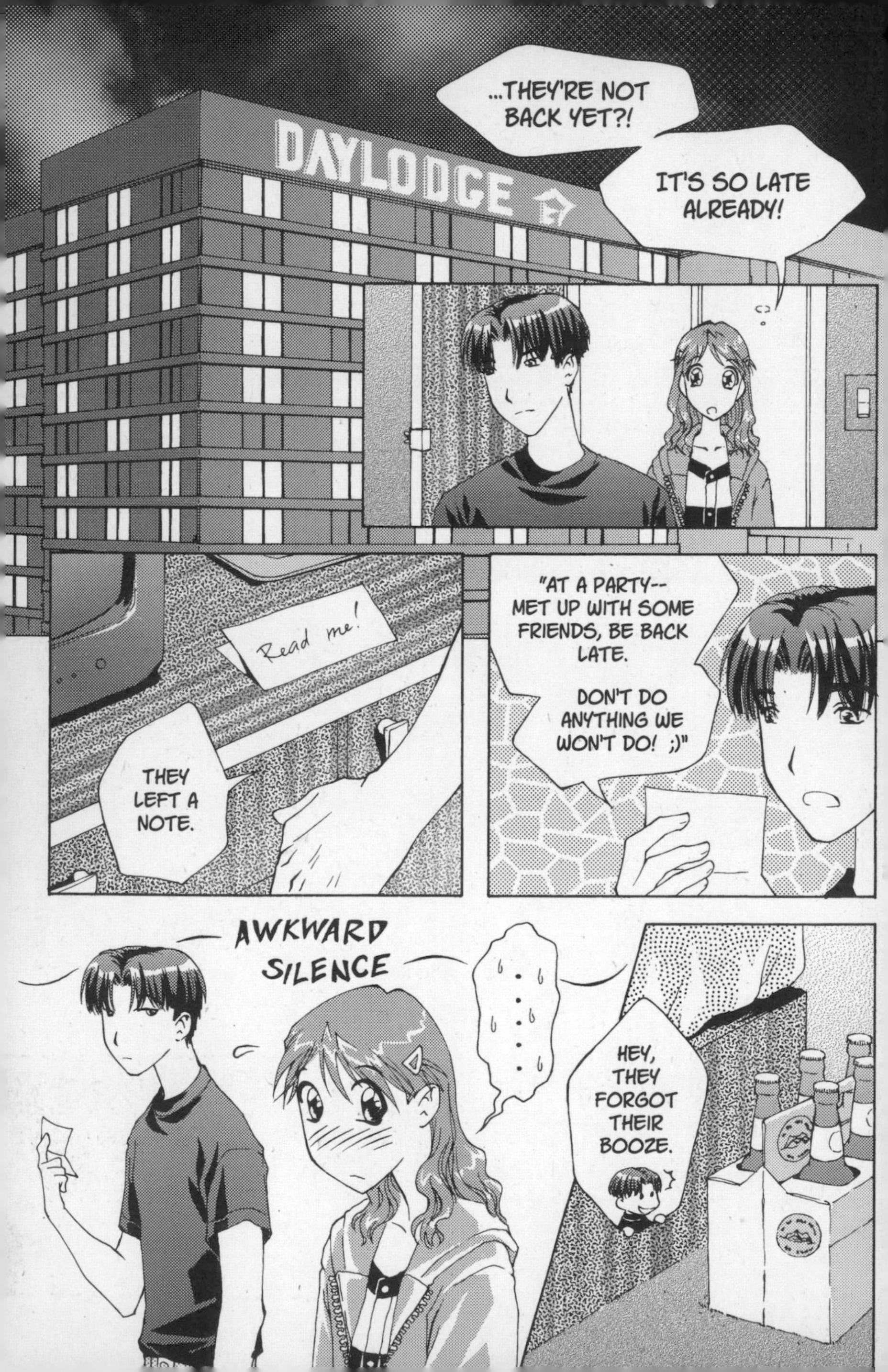
DAYLODGE
...THEY'RE NOT BACK YET?!
IT'S SO LATE ALREADY!
Read me!
THEY LEFT A NOTE.
"AT A PARTY-- MET UP WITH SOME FRIENDS, BE BACK LATE.
DON'T DO ANYTHING WE WON'T DO! ;)"
AWKWARD SILENCE
HEY, THEY FORGOT THEIR BOOZE.

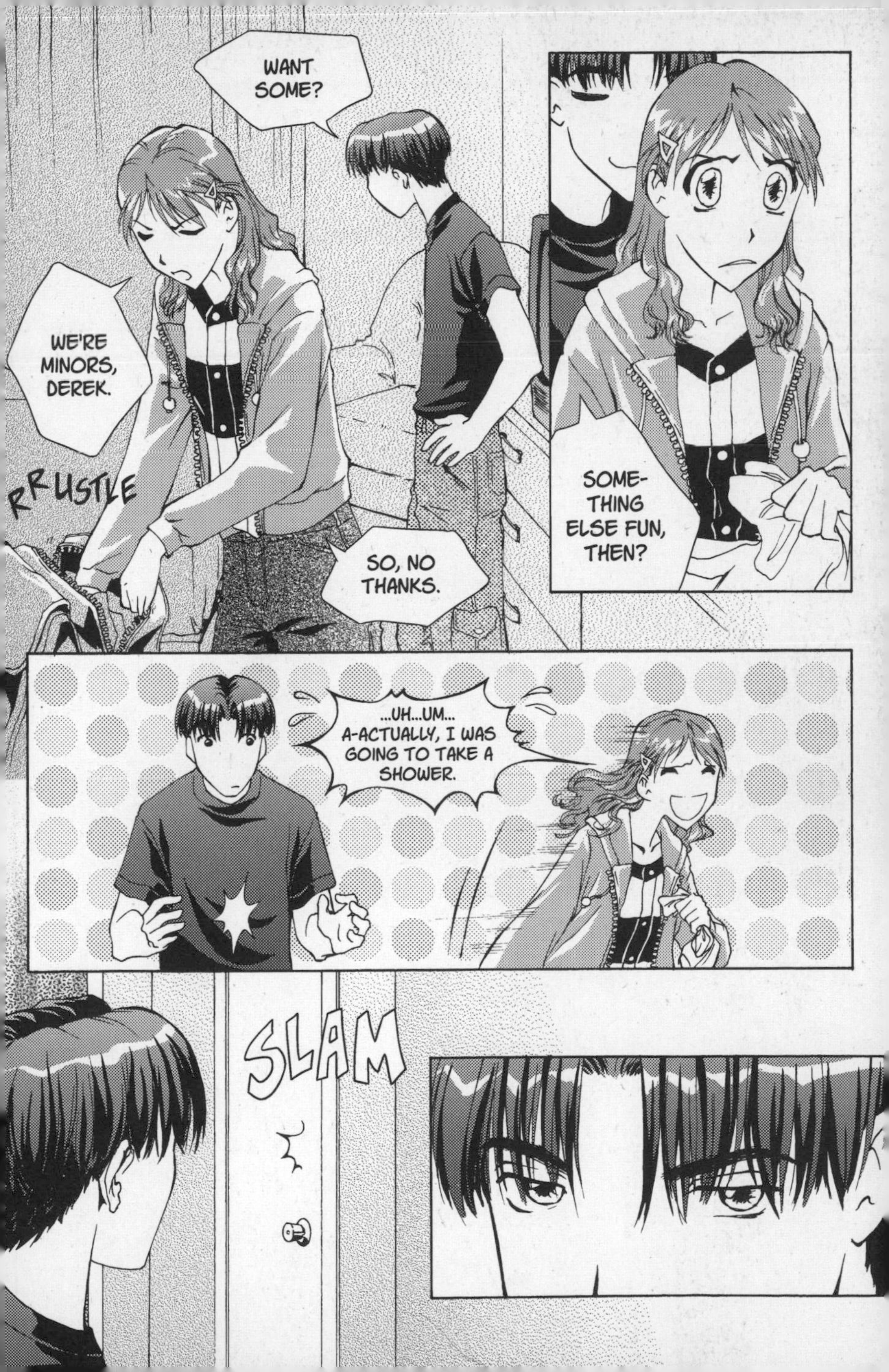
WANT SOME?
WE'RE MINORS, DEREK.
RRUSTLE
SO, NO THANKS.
SOME-THING ELSE FUN, THEN?
...UH...UM... A-ACTUALLY, I WAS GOING TO TAKE A SHOWER.
SLAM

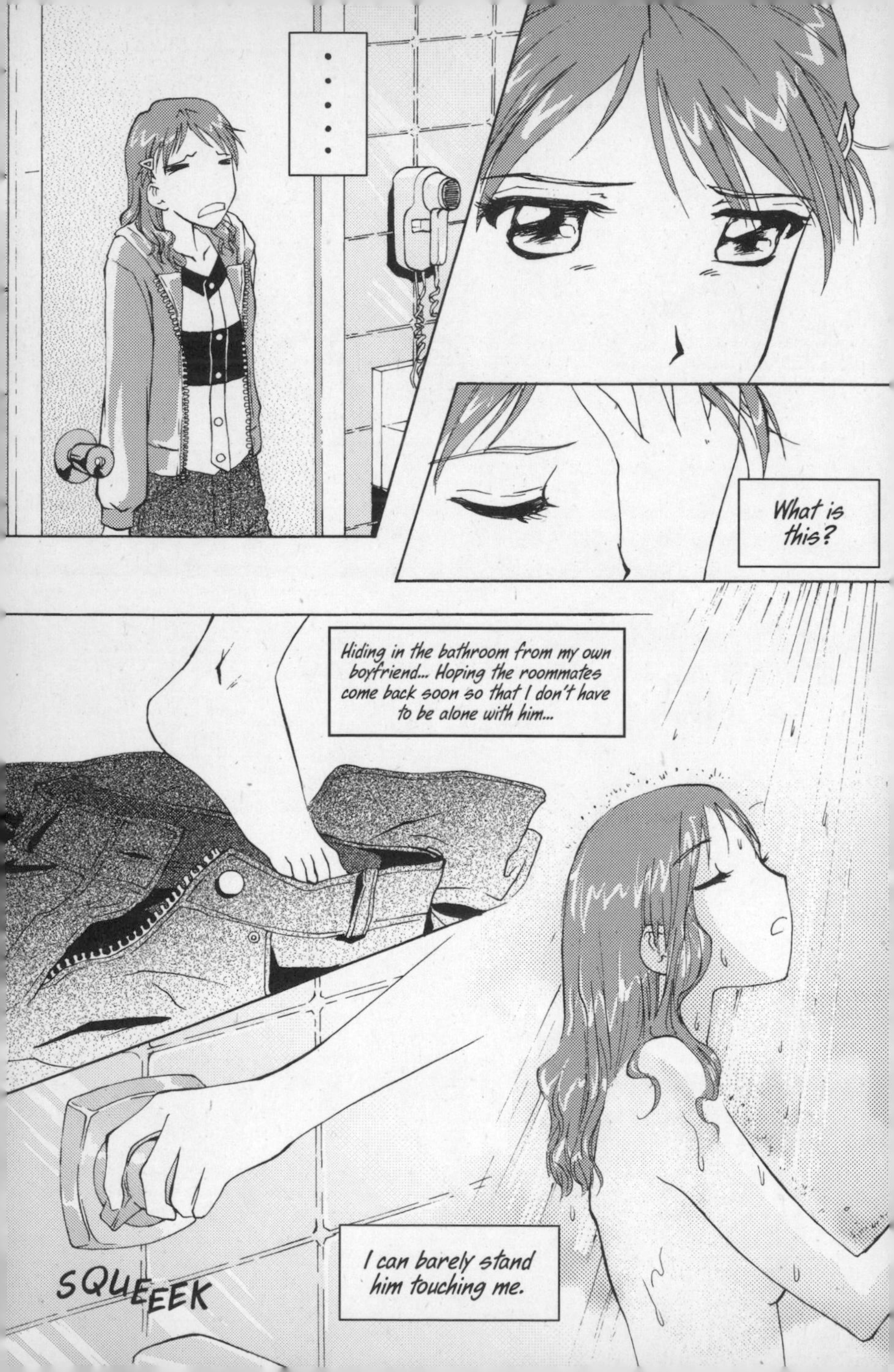
.....
What is this?
Hiding in the bathroom from my own boyfriend... Hoping the roommates come back soon so that I don't have to be alone with him...
I can barely stand him touching me.
SQUEEEK

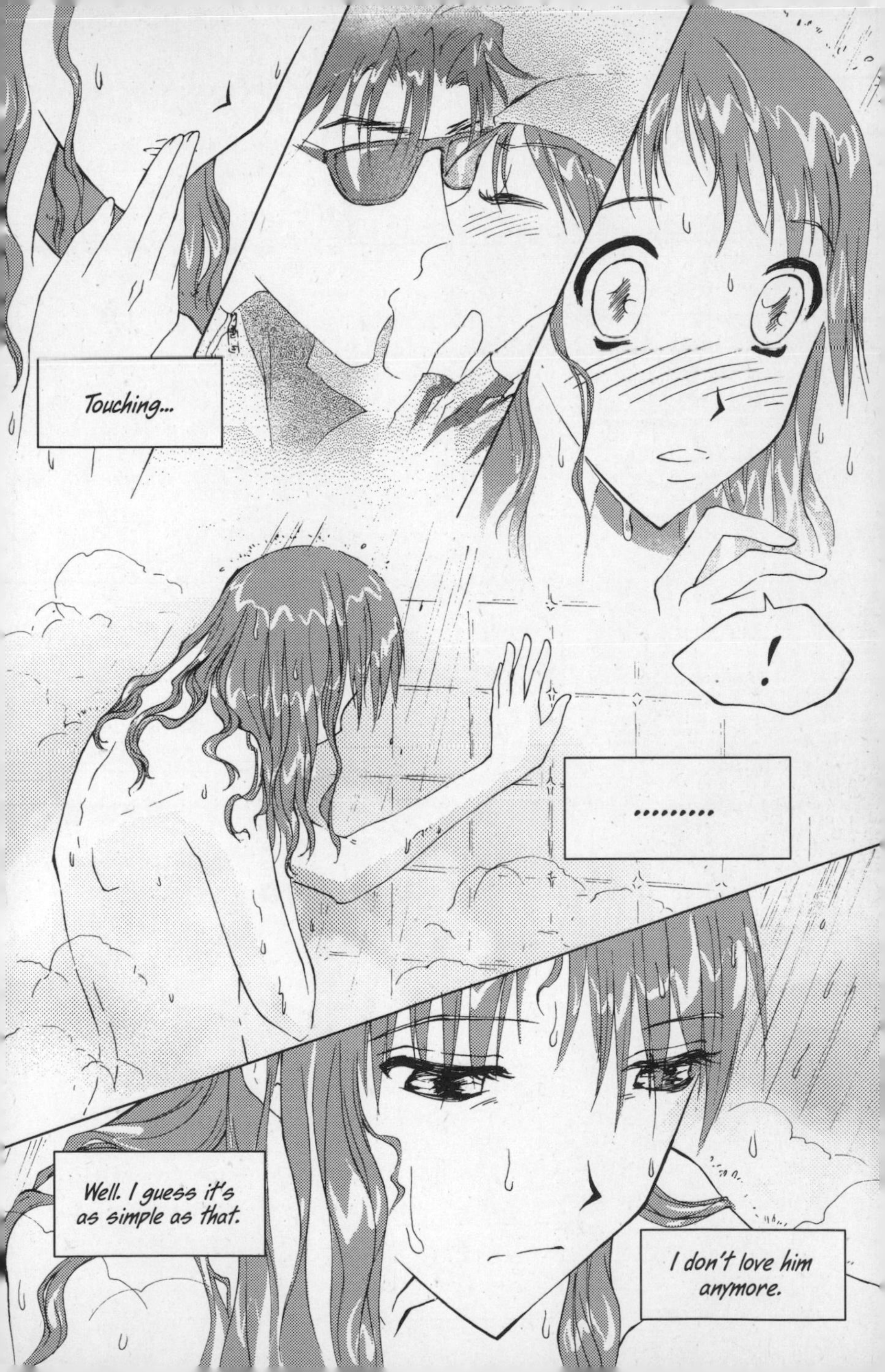
Touching...
!
....
Well. I guess it's as simple as that.
I don't love him anymore.

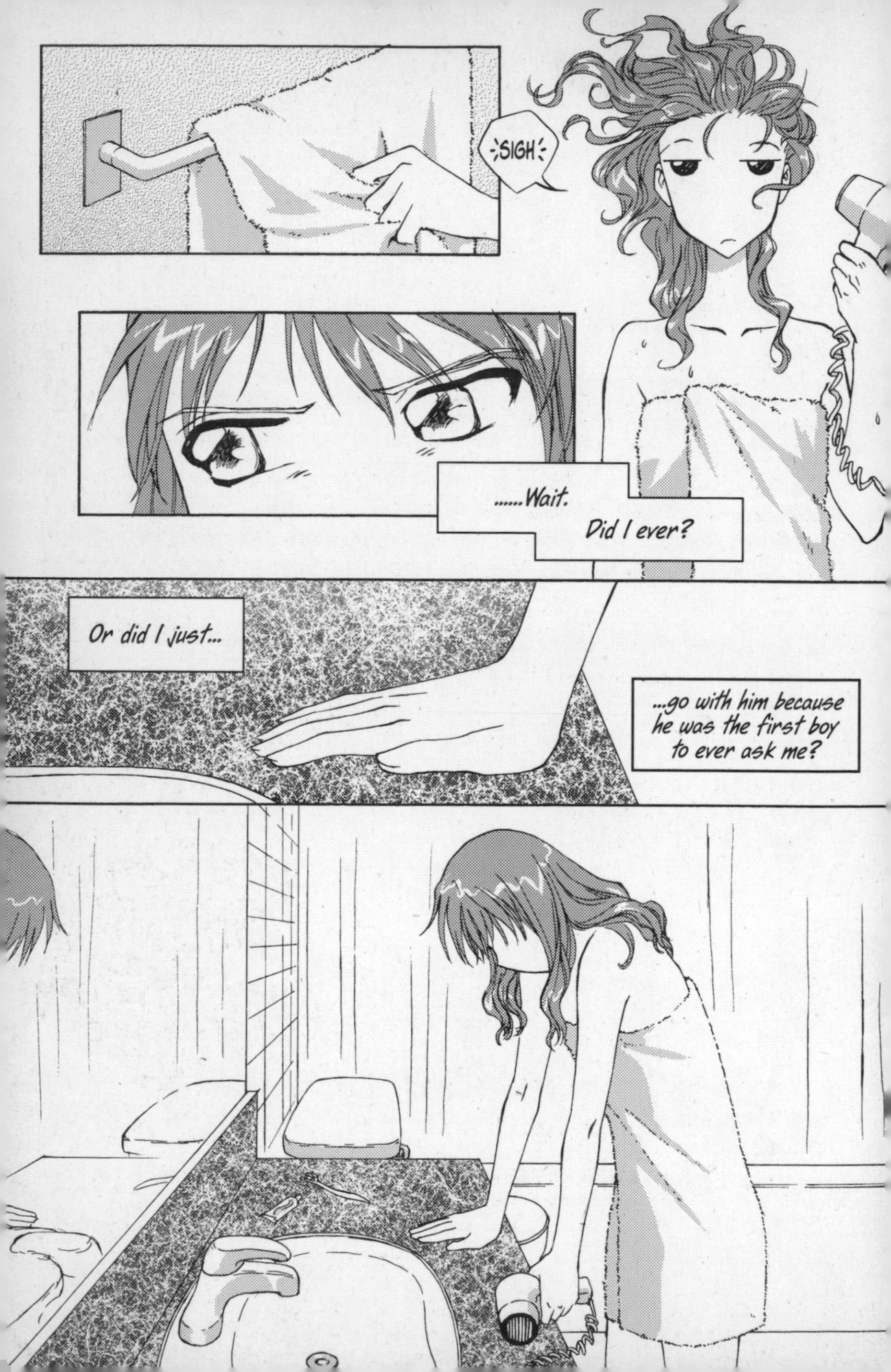
SIGH
......Wait.
Did I ever?
Or did I just...
...go with him because he was the first boy to ever ask me?

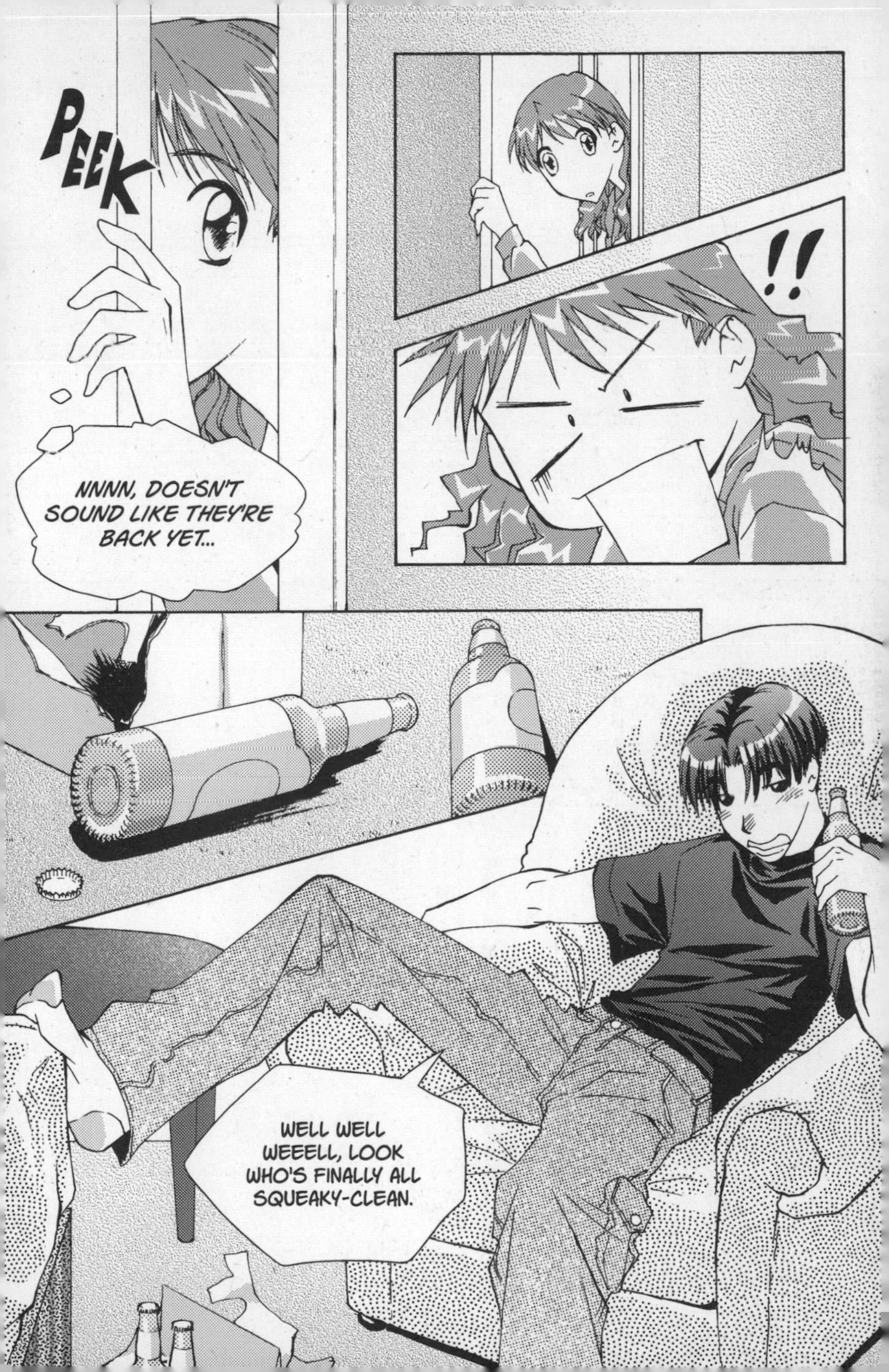
PEEK
NNNN, DOESN'T SOUND LIKE THEY'RE BACK YET...
!!
WELL WELL WEEELL, LOOK WHO'S FINALLY ALL SQUEAKY-CLEAN.

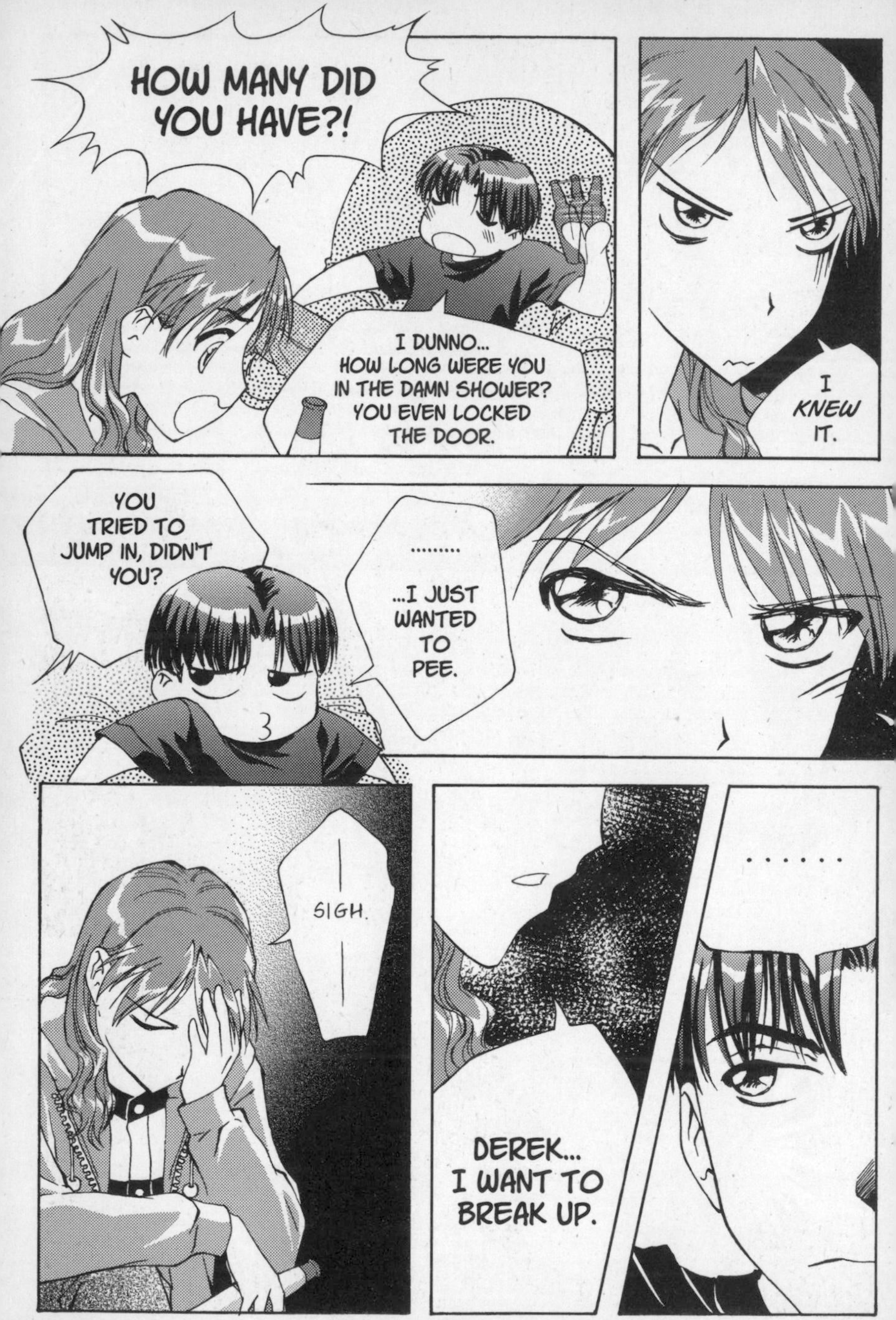
HOW MANY DID YOU HAVE?!
I DUNNO... HOW LONG WERE YOU IN THE DAMN SHOWER? YOU EVEN LOCKED THE DOOR.
I KNEW IT.
YOU TRIED TO JUMP IN, DIDN'T YOU?
....
...I JUST WANTED TO PEE.
SIGH.
......
DEREK... I WANT TO BREAK UP.

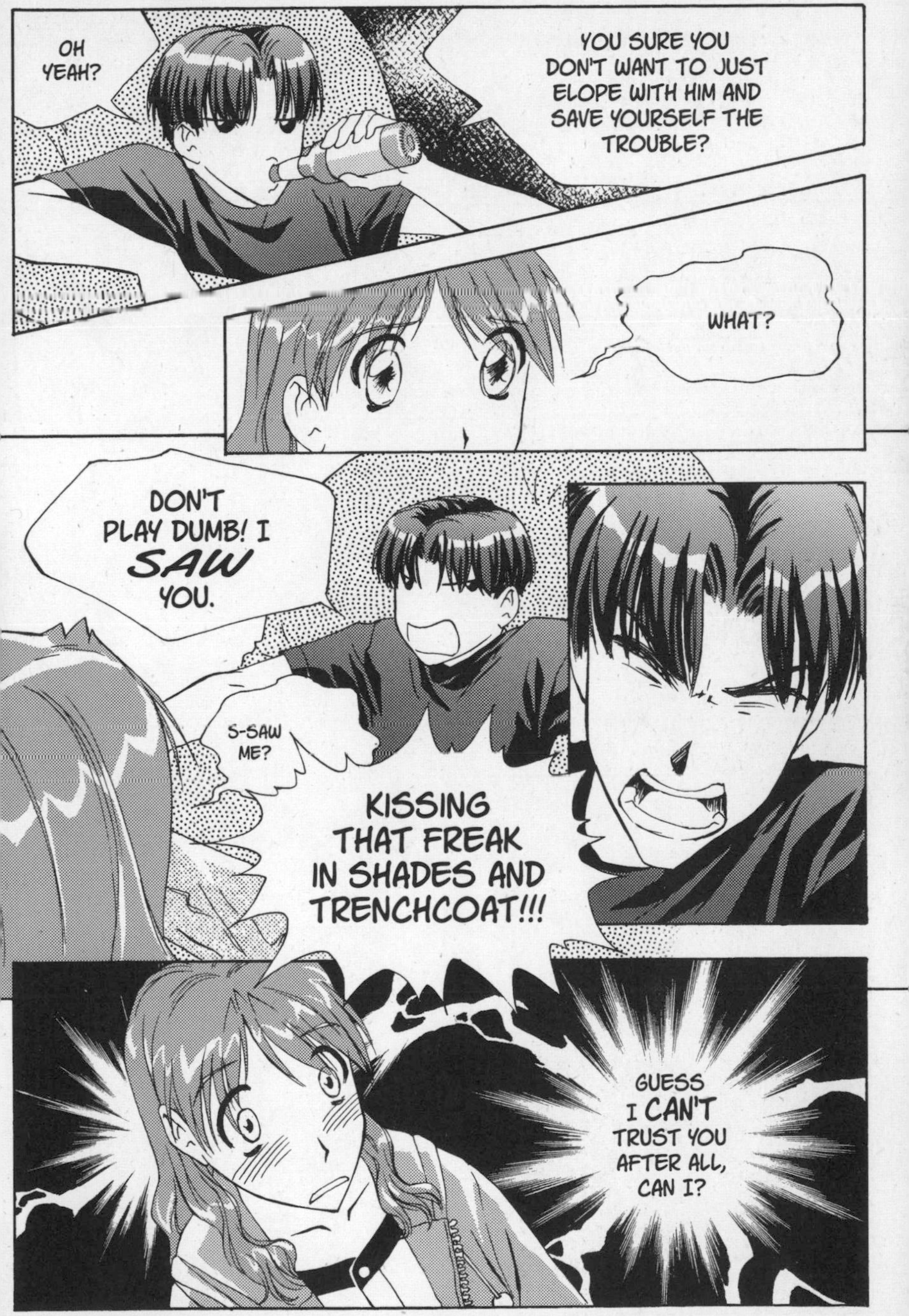
OH YEAH?
YOU SURE YOU DON'T WANT TO JUST ELOPE WITH HIM AND SAVE YOURSELF THE TROUBLE?
WHAT?
DON'T PLAY DUMB! I *SAW* YOU.
S-SAW ME?
KISSING THAT FREAK IN SHADES AND TRENCHCOAT!!!
GUESS I **CAN'T** TRUST YOU AFTER ALL, CAN I?

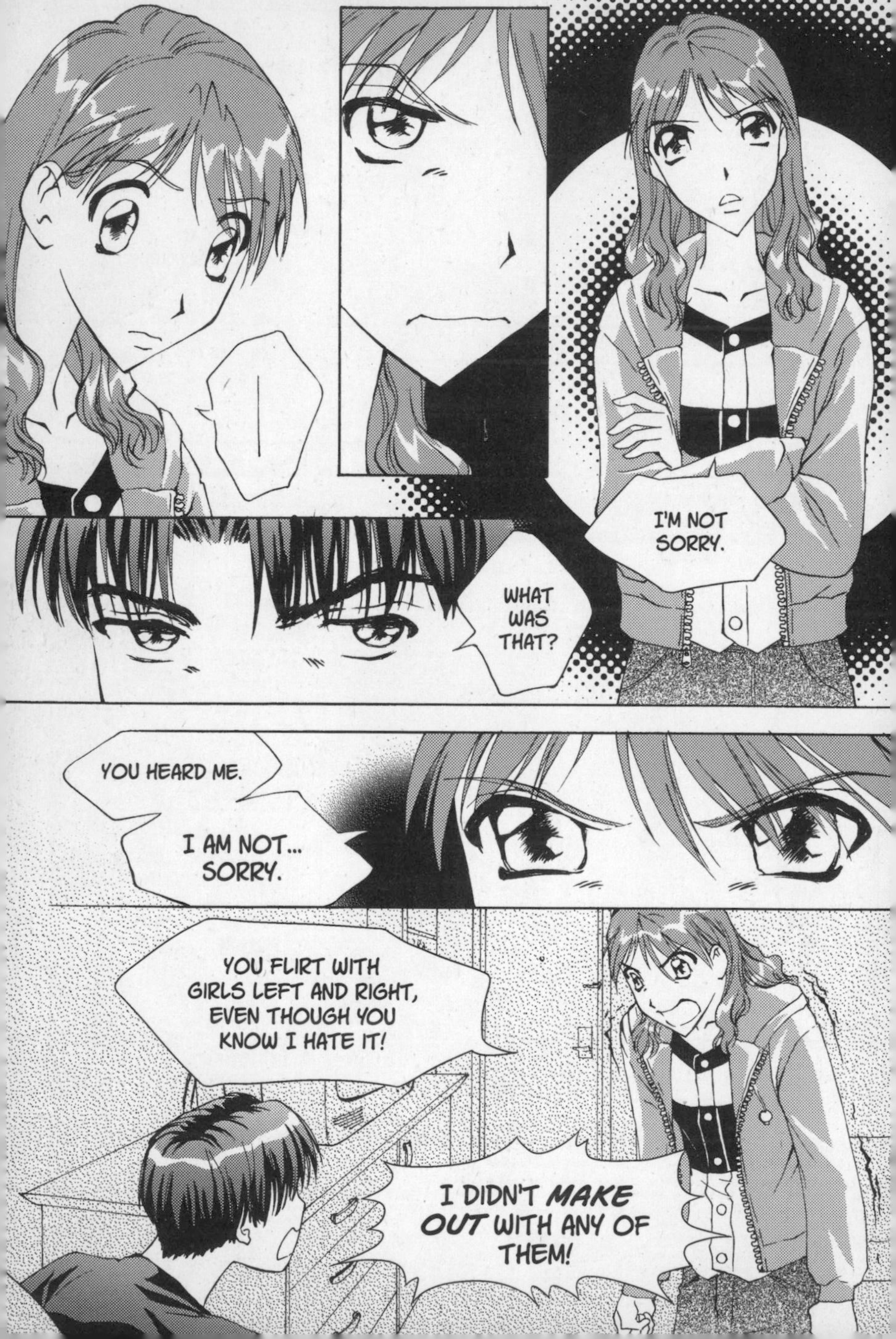
I'M NOT SORRY.
WHAT WAS THAT?
YOU HEARD ME.
I AM NOT... SORRY.
YOU FLIRT WITH GIRLS LEFT AND RIGHT, EVEN THOUGH YOU KNOW I HATE IT!
I DIDN'T *MAKE OUT* WITH ANY OF THEM!

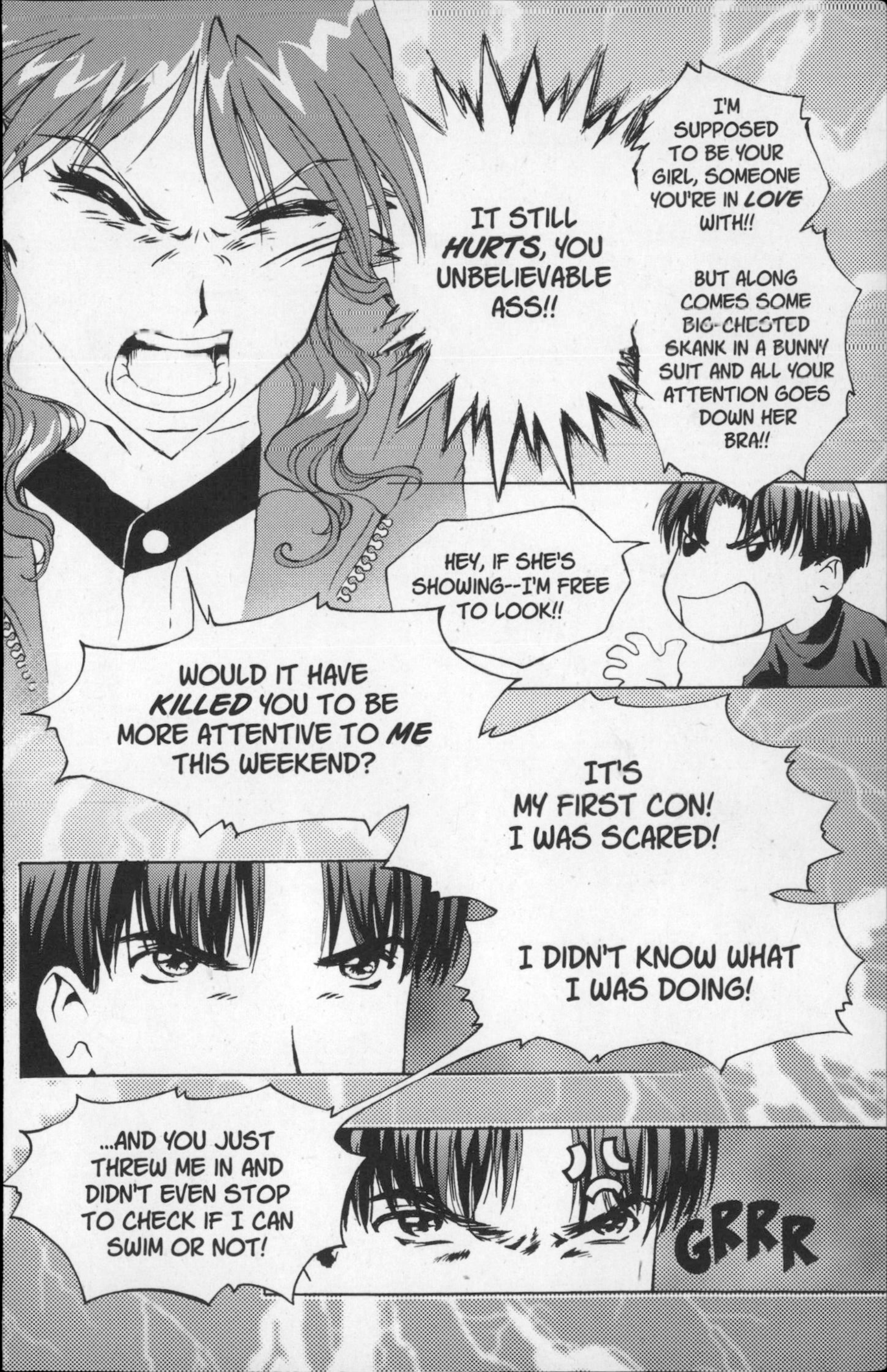
IT STILL *HURTS*, YOU UNBELIEVABLE ASS!!
I'M SUPPOSED TO BE YOUR GIRL, SOMEONE YOU'RE IN *LOVE* WITH!!
BUT ALONG COMES SOME BIG-CHESTED SKANK IN A BUNNY SUIT AND ALL YOUR ATTENTION GOES DOWN HER BRA!!
HEY, IF SHE'S SHOWING--I'M FREE TO LOOK!!
WOULD IT HAVE *KILLED* YOU TO BE MORE ATTENTIVE TO *ME* THIS WEEKEND?
IT'S MY FIRST CON! I WAS SCARED!
I DIDN'T KNOW WHAT I WAS DOING!
...AND YOU JUST THREW ME IN AND DIDN'T EVEN STOP TO CHECK IF I CAN SWIM OR NOT!
GRRR

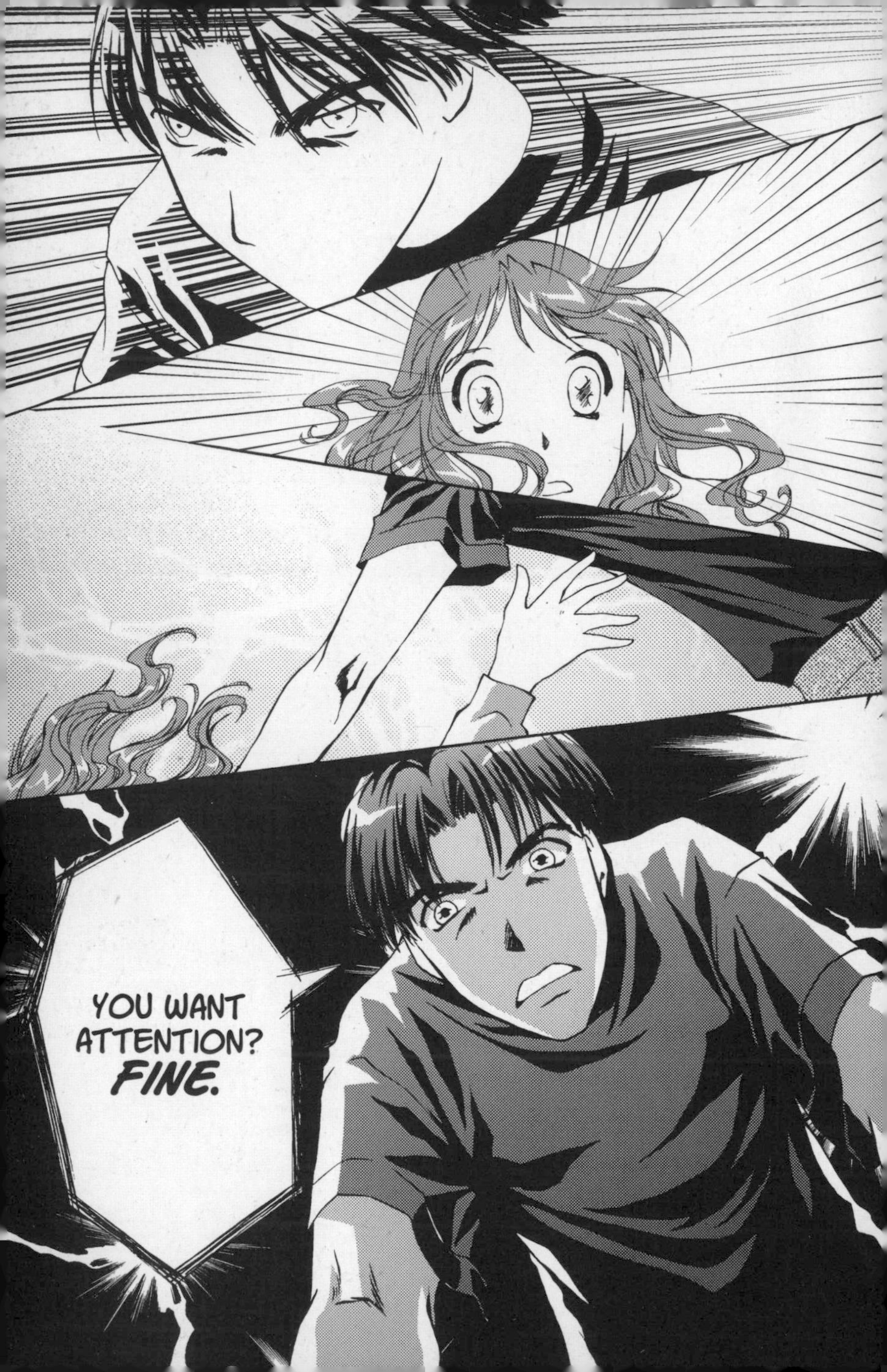
YOU WANT ATTENTION? FINE.

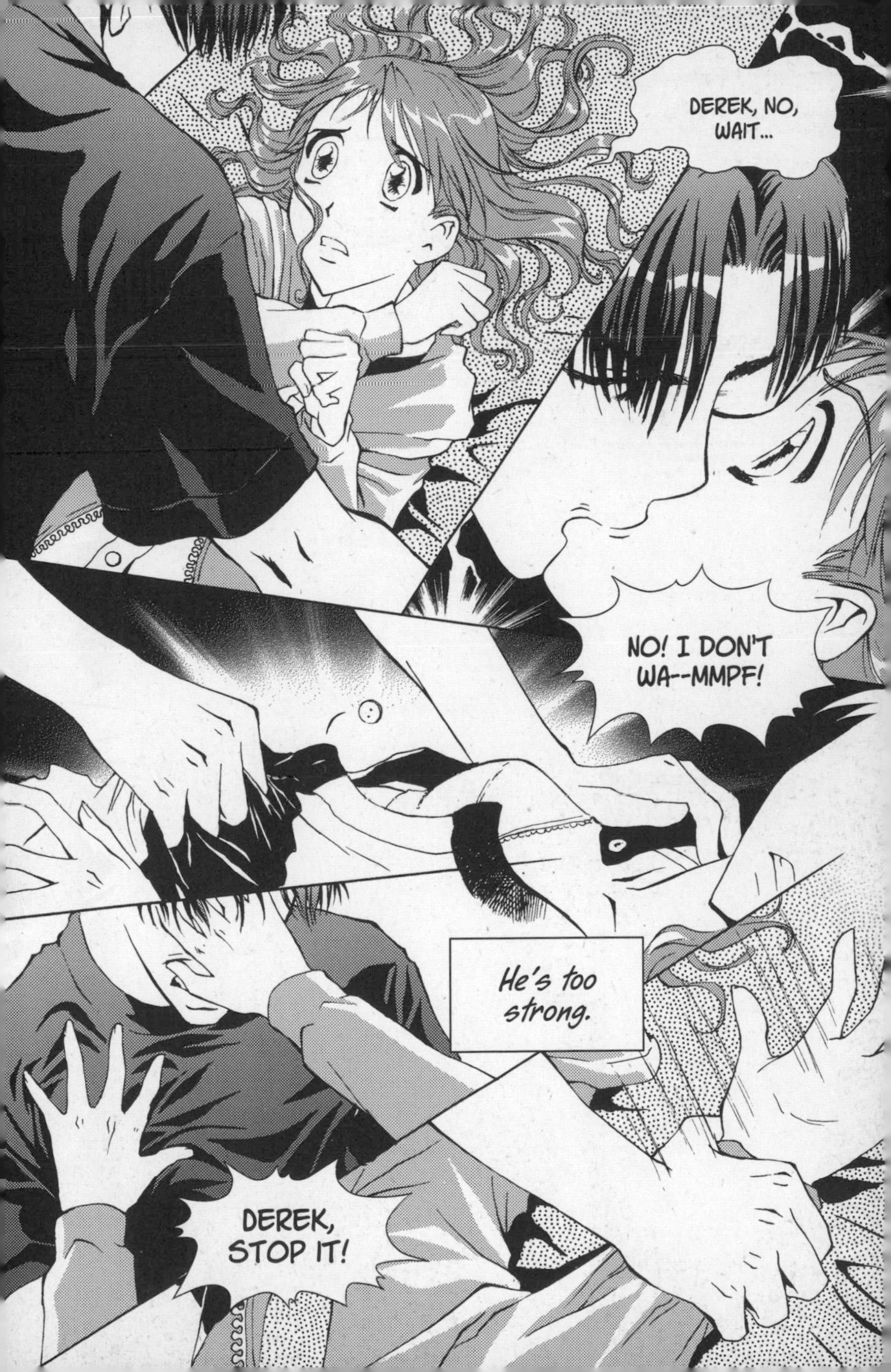
DEREK, NO, WAIT...
NO! I DON'T WA--MMPF!
He's too strong.
DEREK, STOP IT!

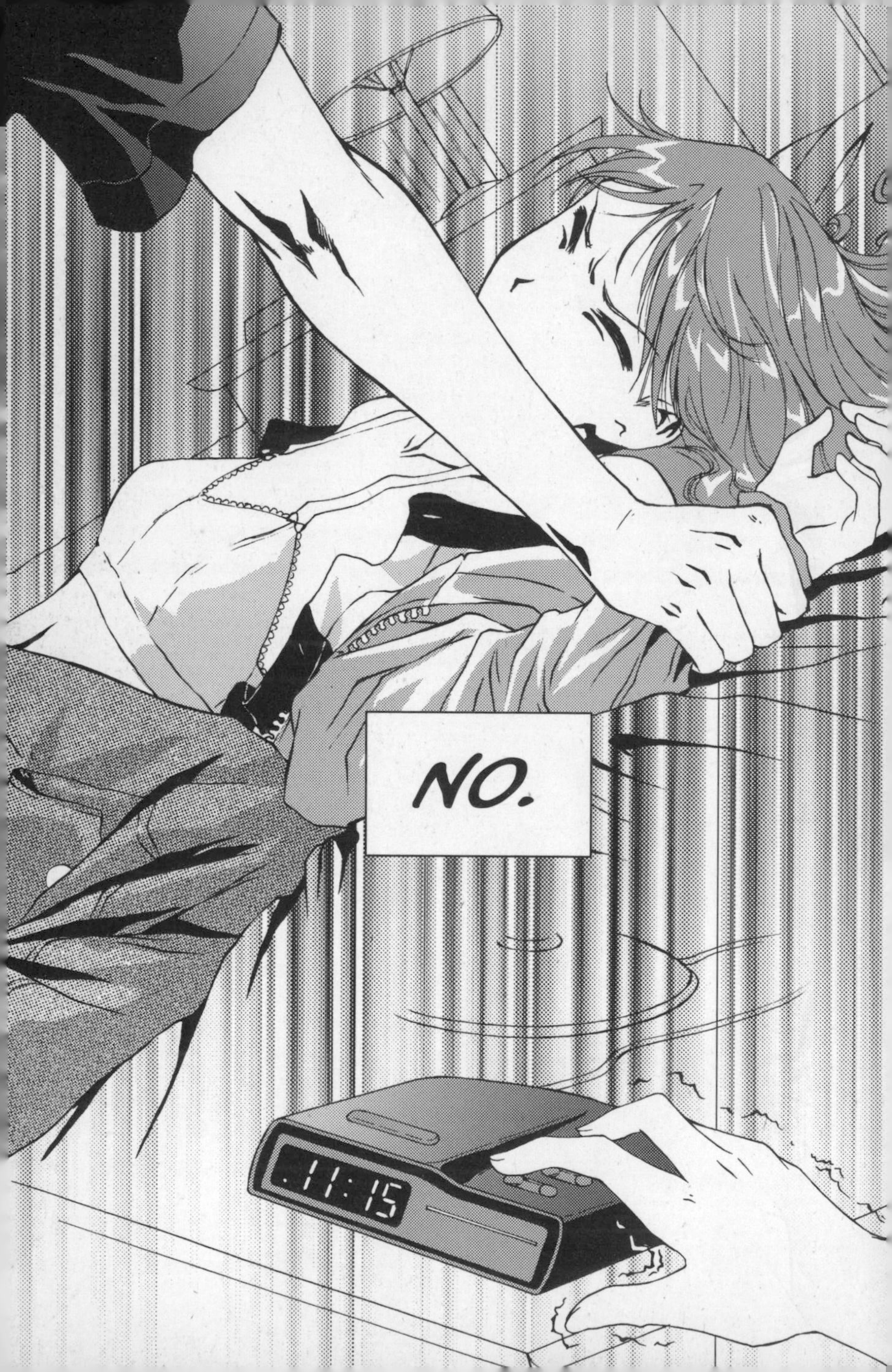
NO.
11:15

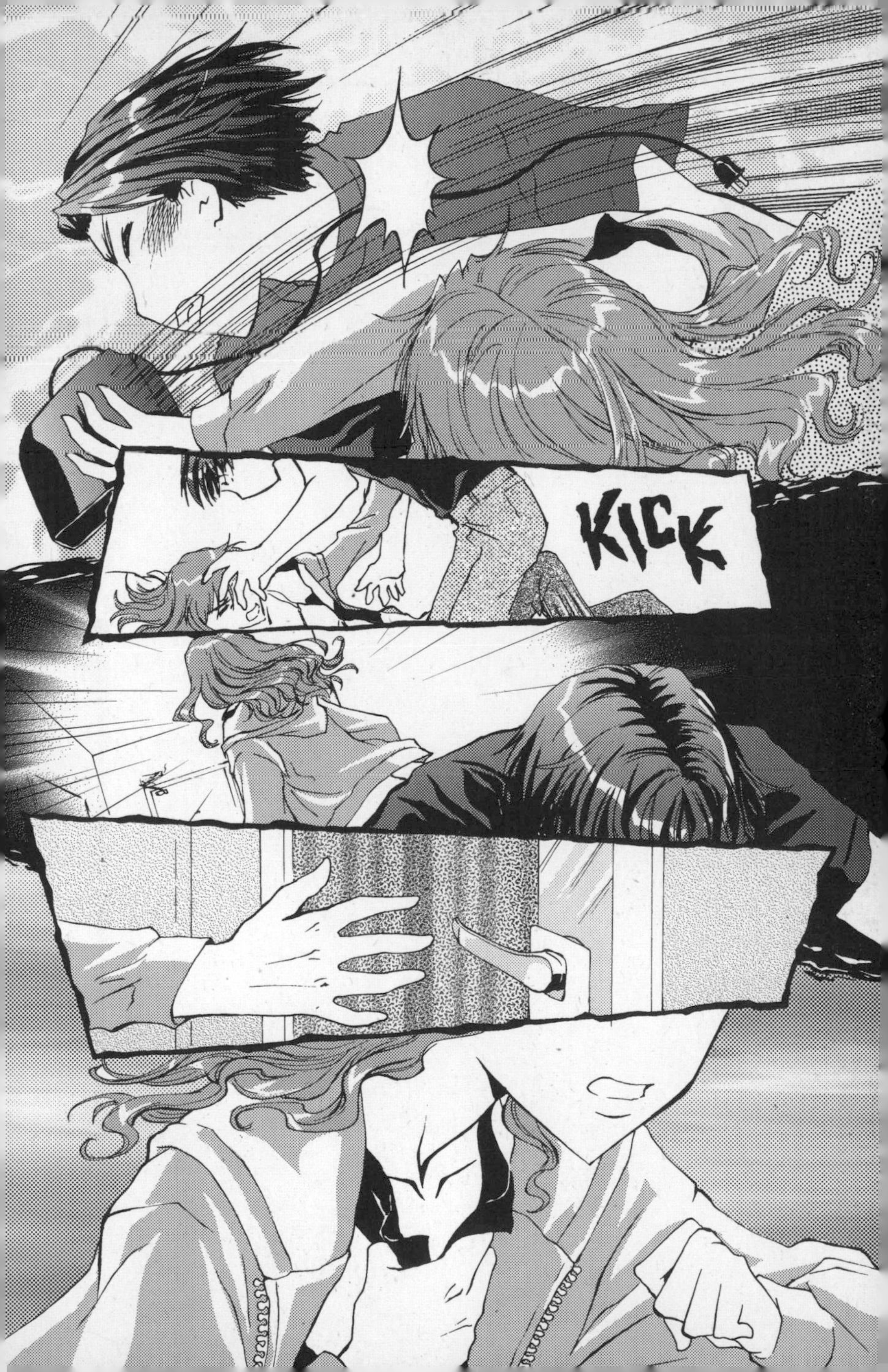
KICK

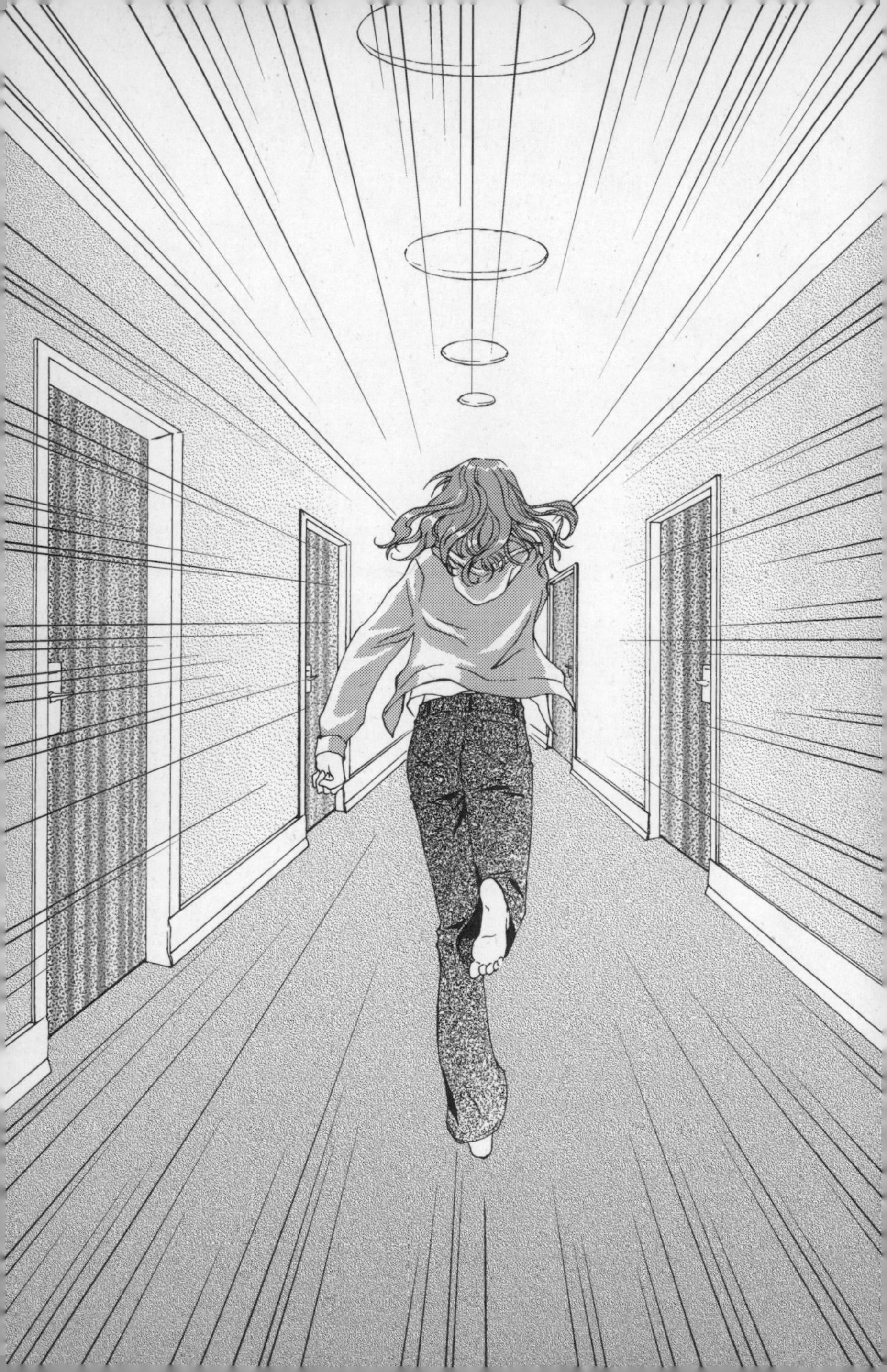

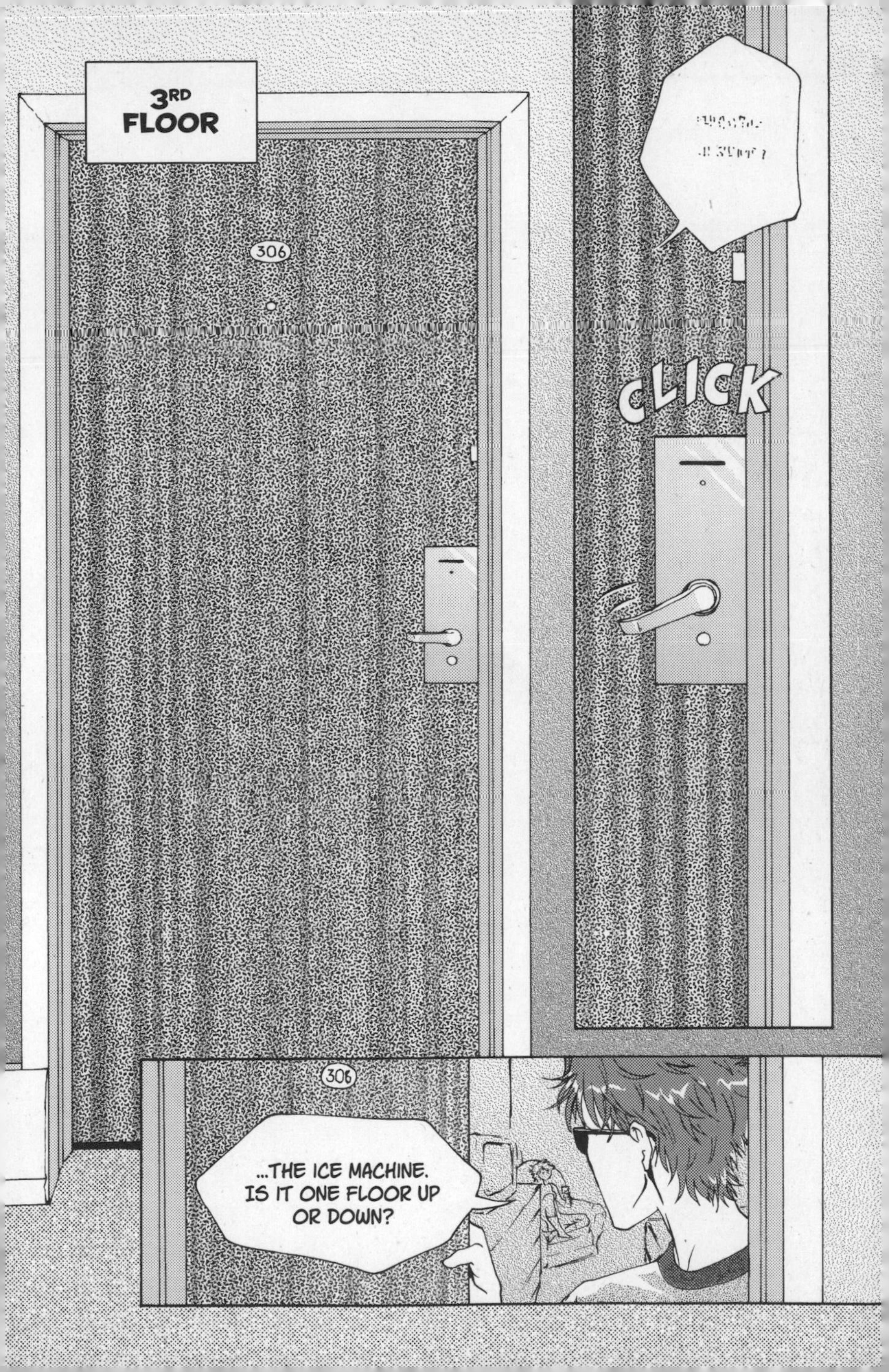
3RD FLOOR
306
CLICK
306
...THE ICE MACHINE. IS IT ONE FLOOR UP OR DOWN?

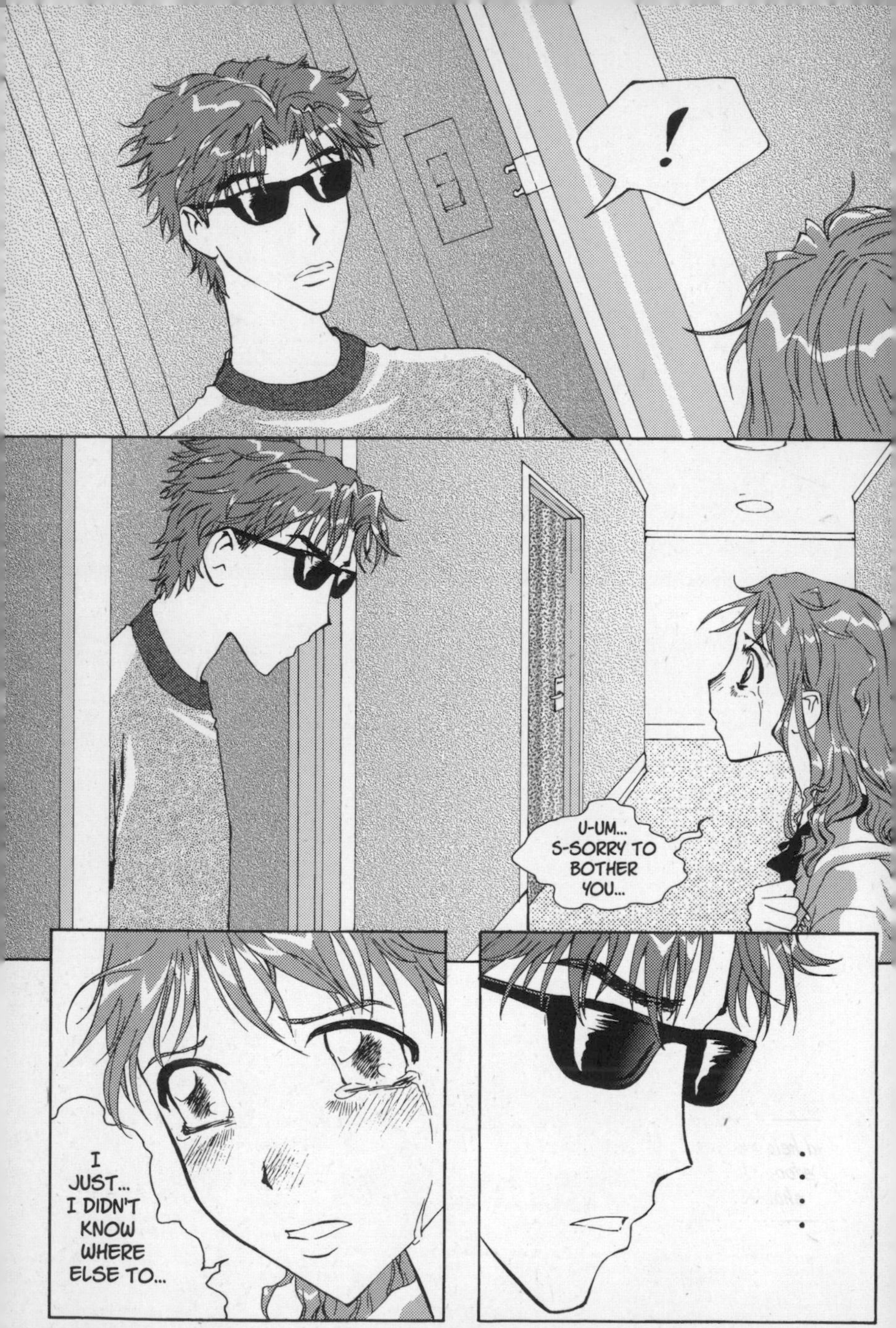
!
U-UM... S-SORRY TO BOTHER YOU...
I JUST... I DIDN'T KNOW WHERE ELSE TO...
....

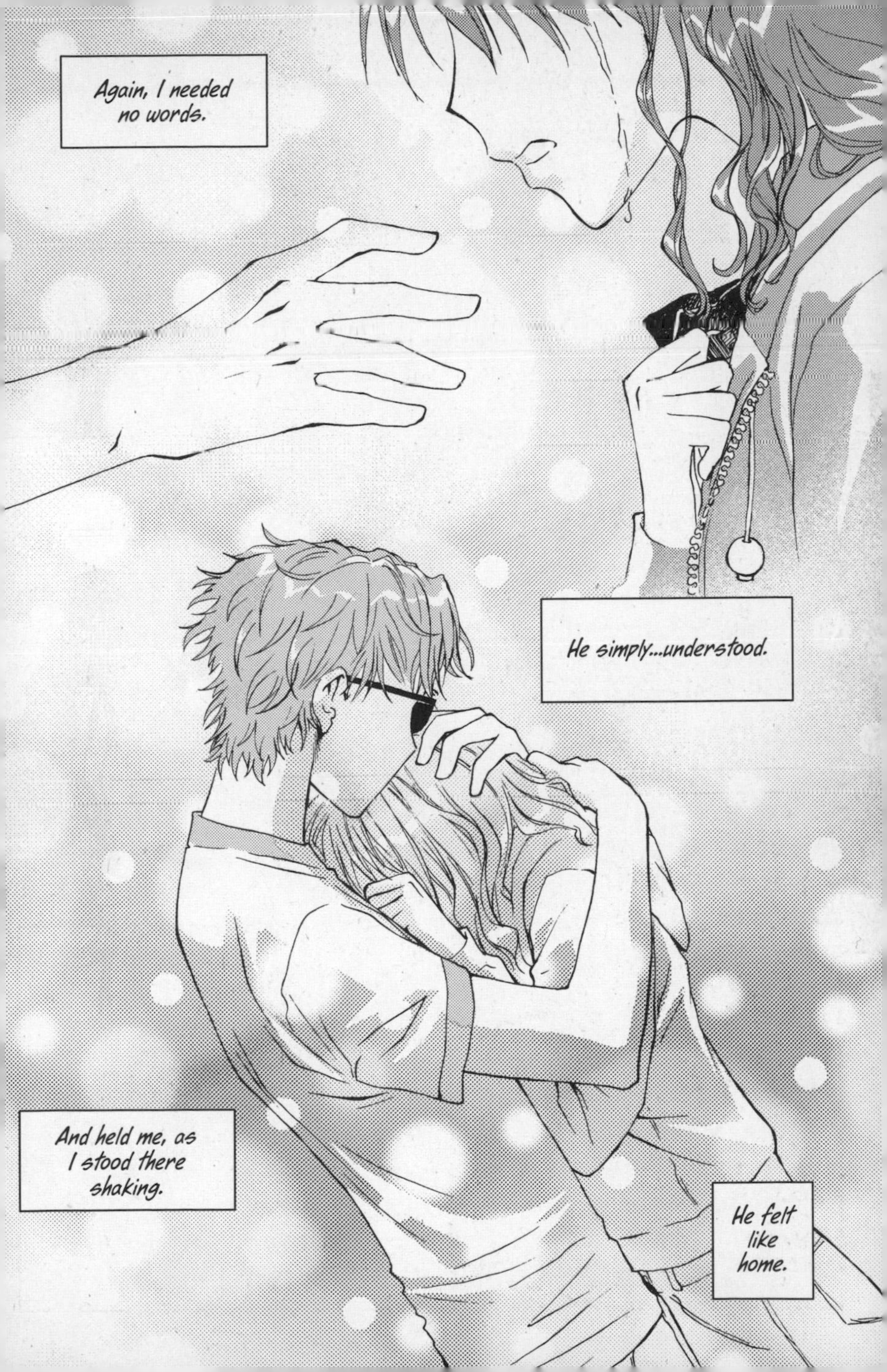
Again, I needed no words.
He simply...understood.
And held me, as I stood there shaking.
He felt like home.

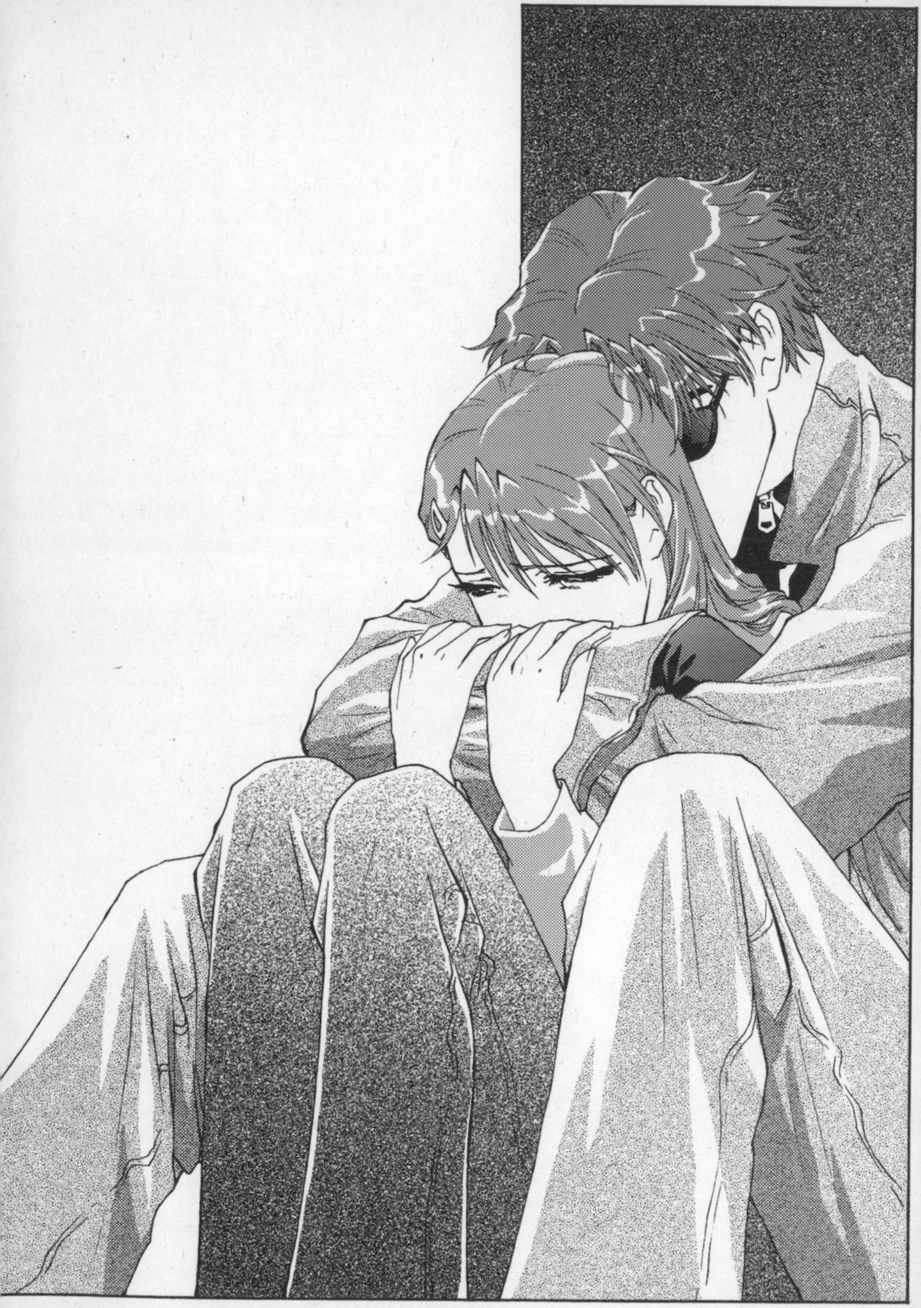

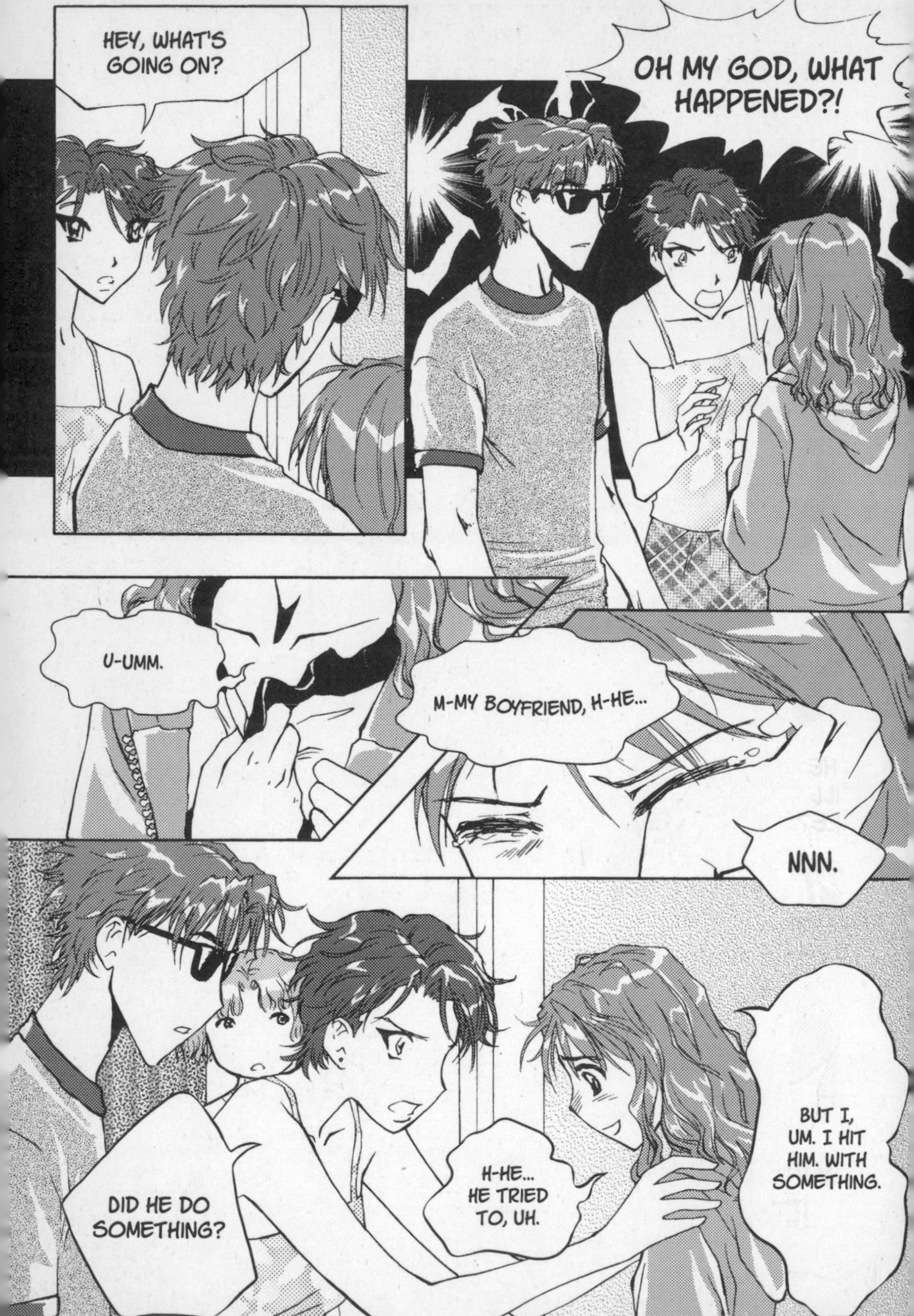
HEY, WHAT'S GOING ON?
OH MY GOD, WHAT HAPPENED?!
U-UMM.
M-MY BOYFRIEND, H-HE...
NNN.
DID HE DO SOMETHING?
H-HE... HE TRIED TO, UH.
BUT I, UM. I HIT HIM. WITH SOMETHING.

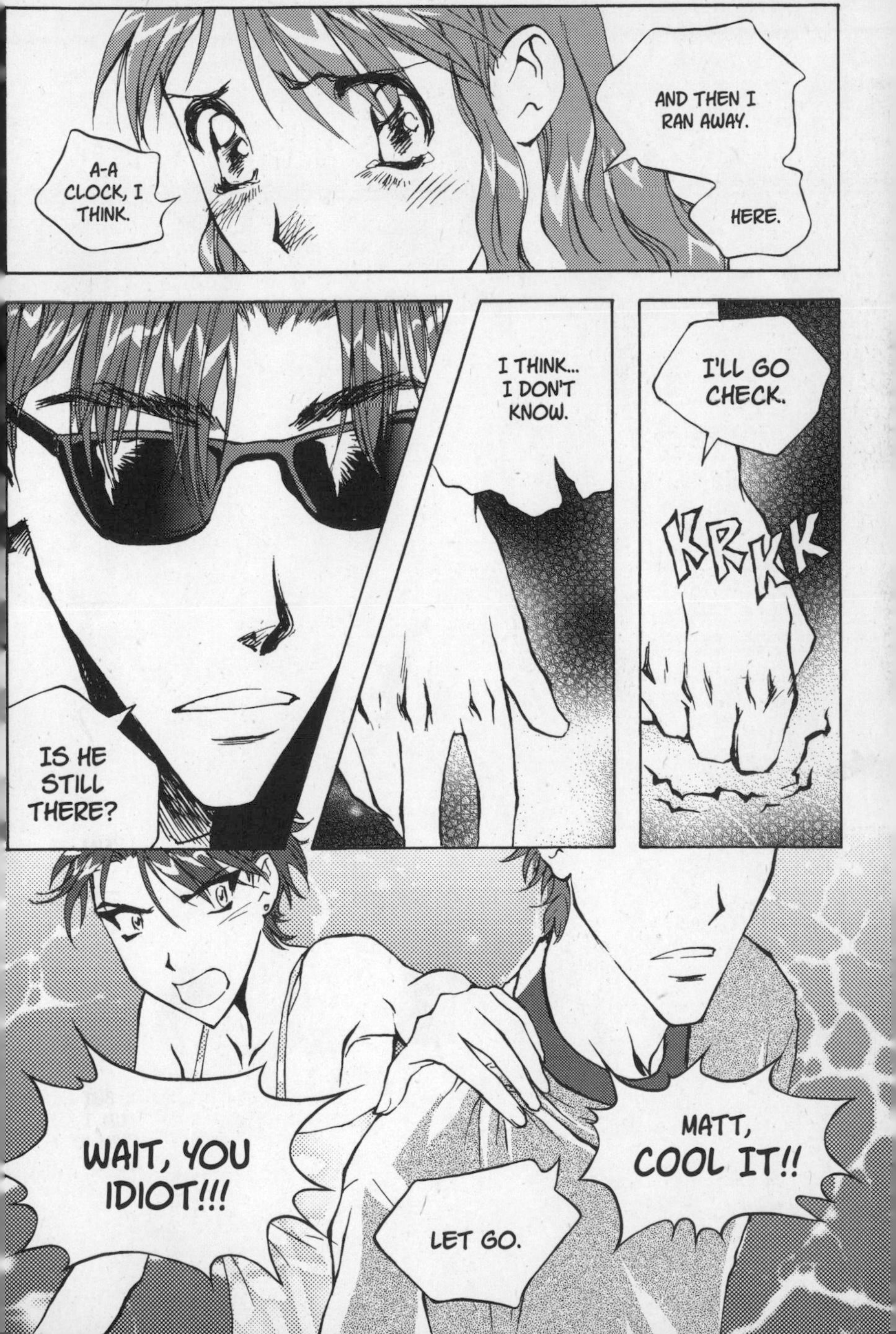
A-A CLOCK, I THINK.
AND THEN I RAN AWAY.
HERE.
IS HE STILL THERE?
I THINK... I DON'T KNOW.
I'LL GO CHECK.
KRKK
WAIT, YOU IDIOT!!!
LET GO.
MATT, COOL IT!!

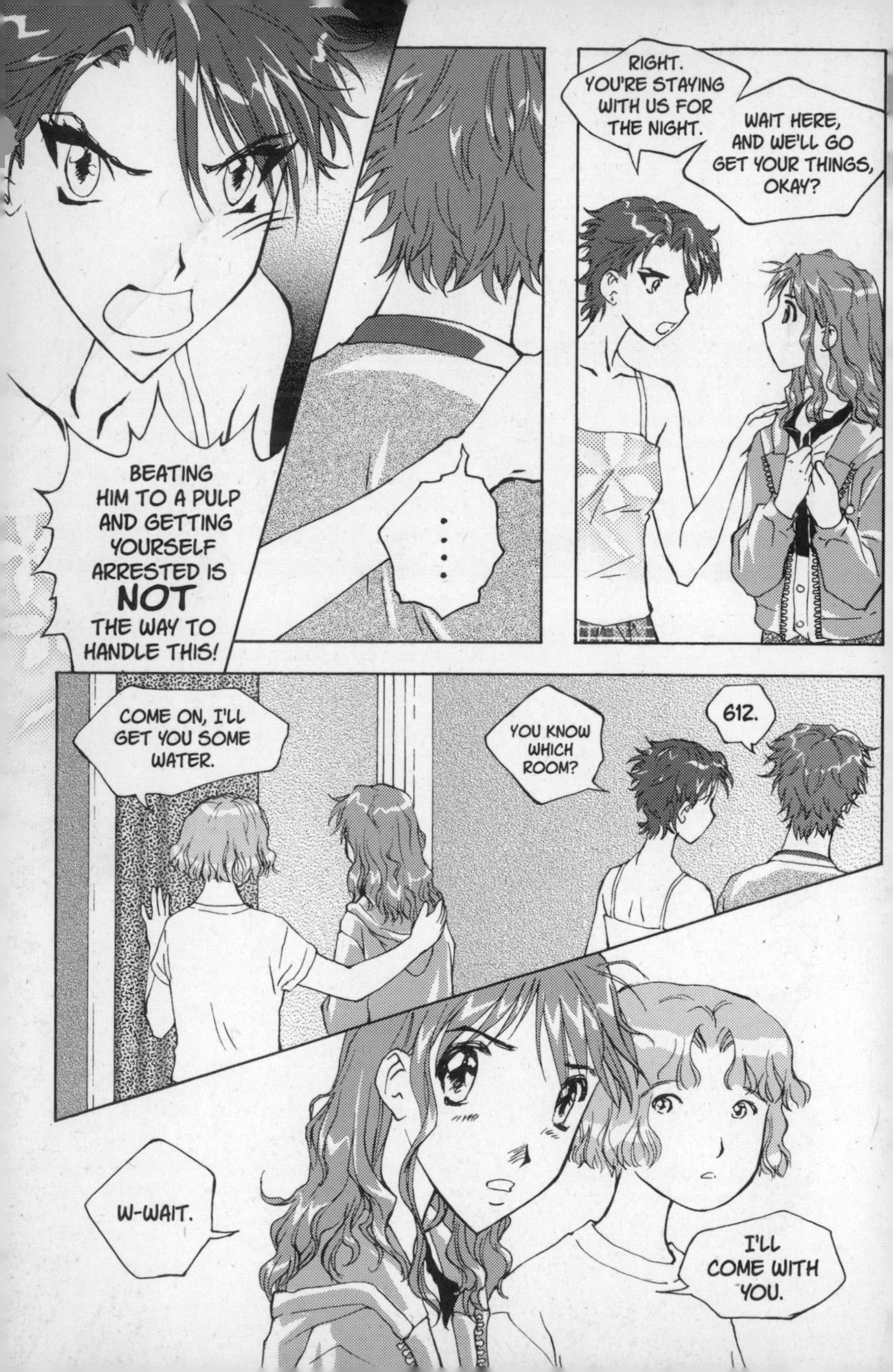
BEATING HIM TO A PULP AND GETTING YOURSELF ARRESTED IS NOT THE WAY TO HANDLE THIS!
....
RIGHT. YOU'RE STAYING WITH US FOR THE NIGHT.
WAIT HERE, AND WE'LL GO GET YOUR THINGS, OKAY?
COME ON, I'LL GET YOU SOME WATER.
YOU KNOW WHICH ROOM?
612.
W-WAIT.
I'LL COME WITH YOU.

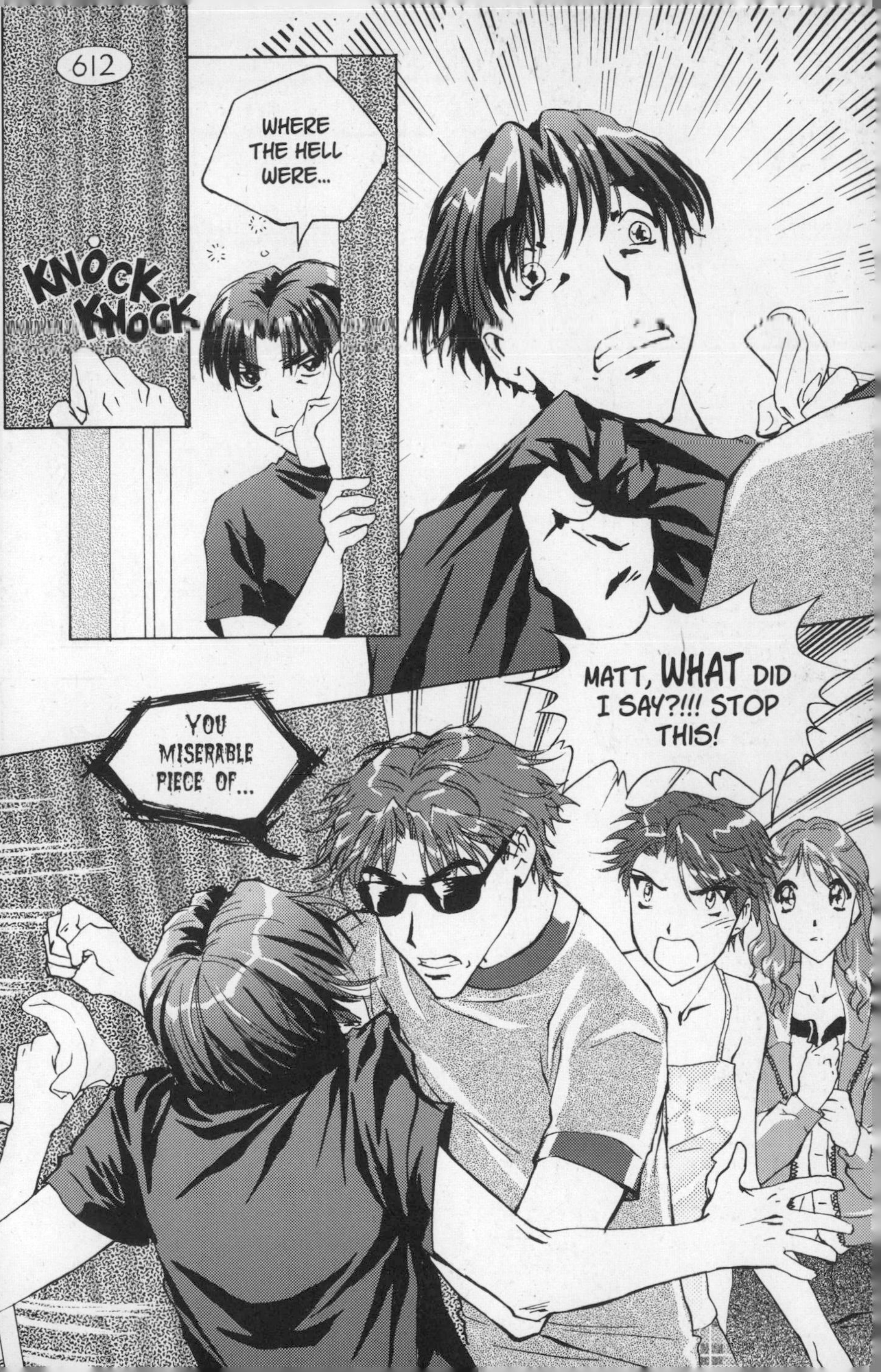
KNOCK KNOCK
WHERE THE HELL WERE...
YOU MISERABLE PIECE OF...
MATT, WHAT DID I SAY?!!! STOP THIS!

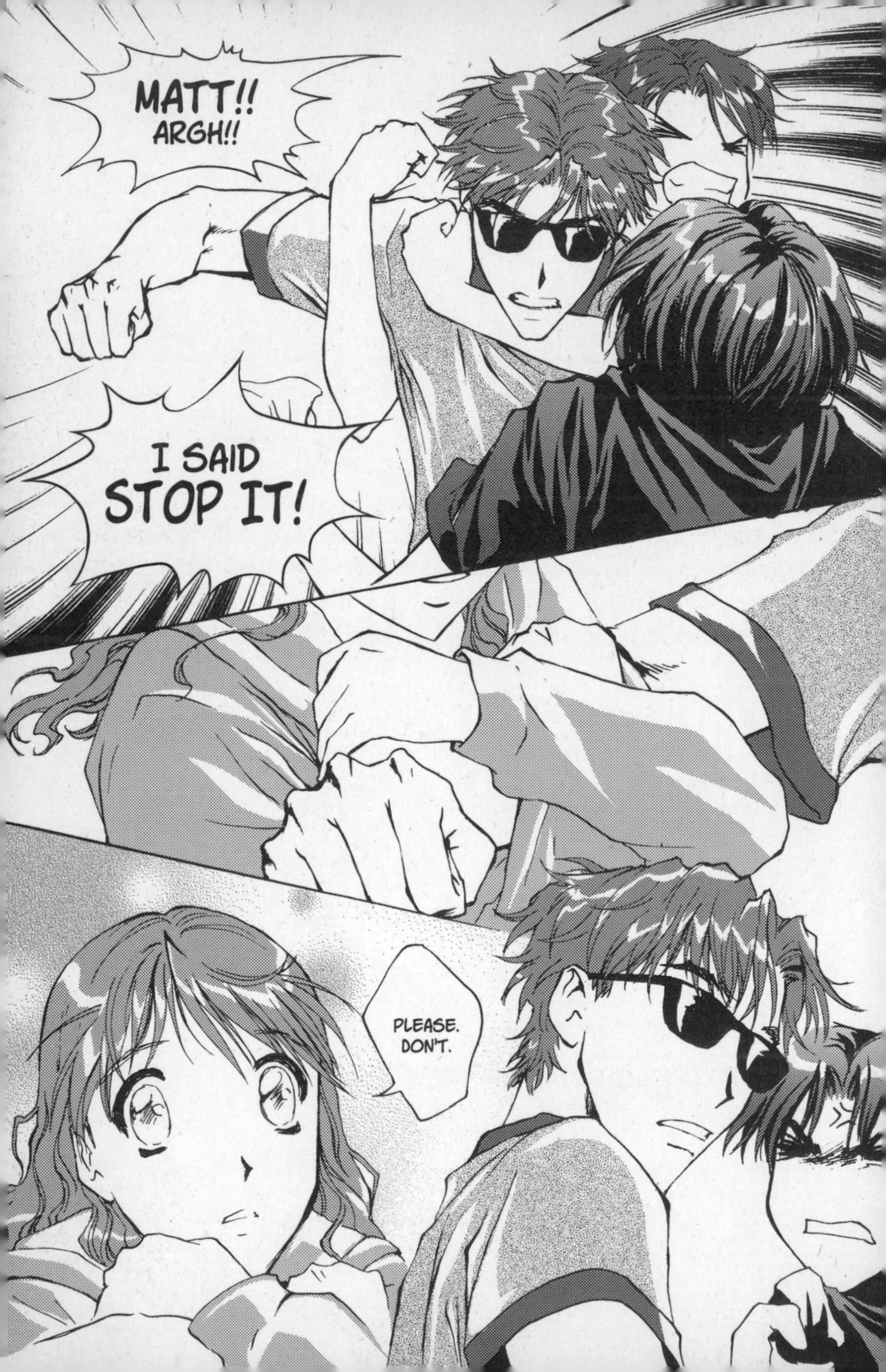
MATT!! ARGH!!
I SAID STOP IT!
PLEASE. DON'T.

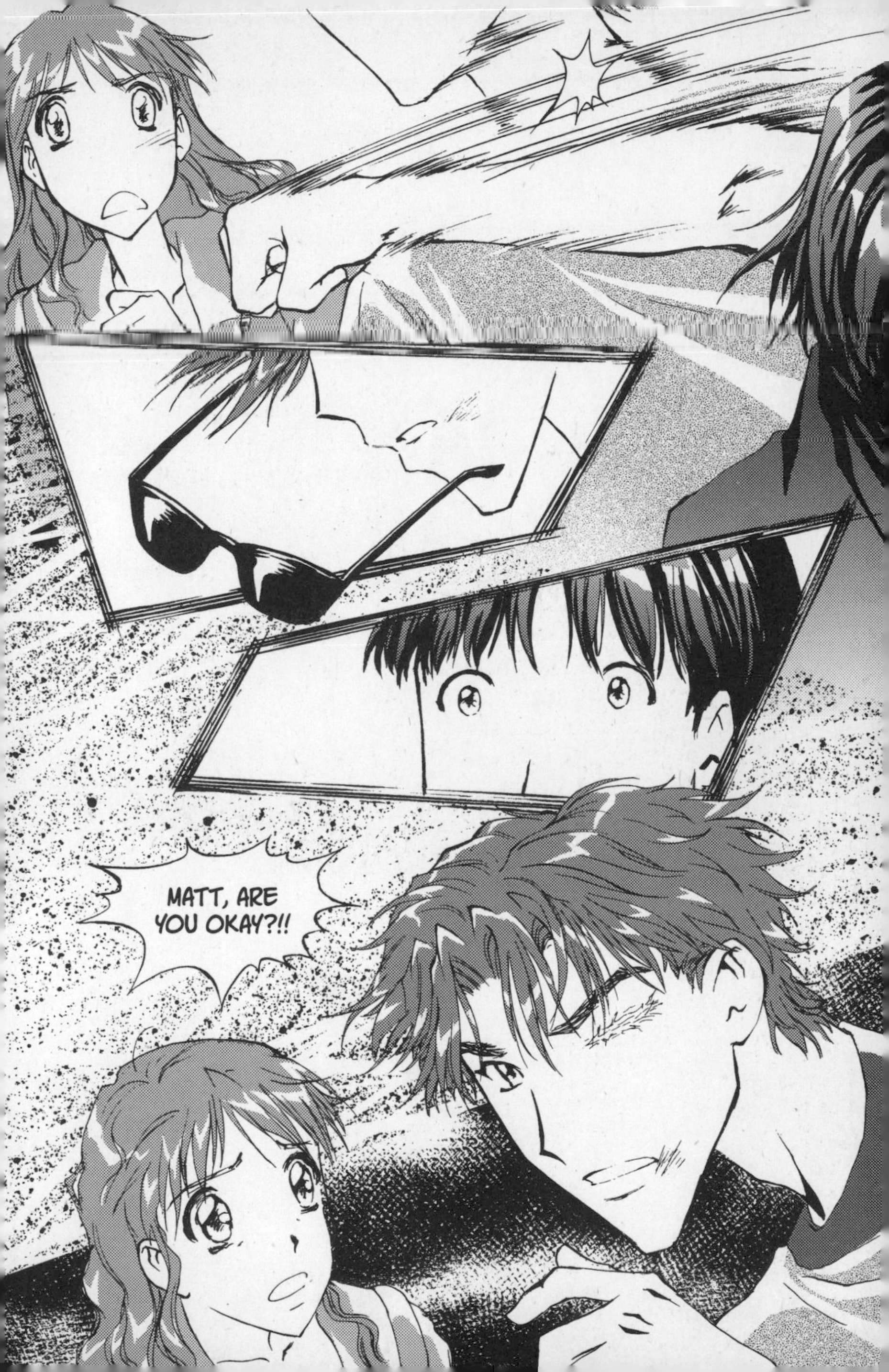
MATT, ARE
YOU OKAY?!!

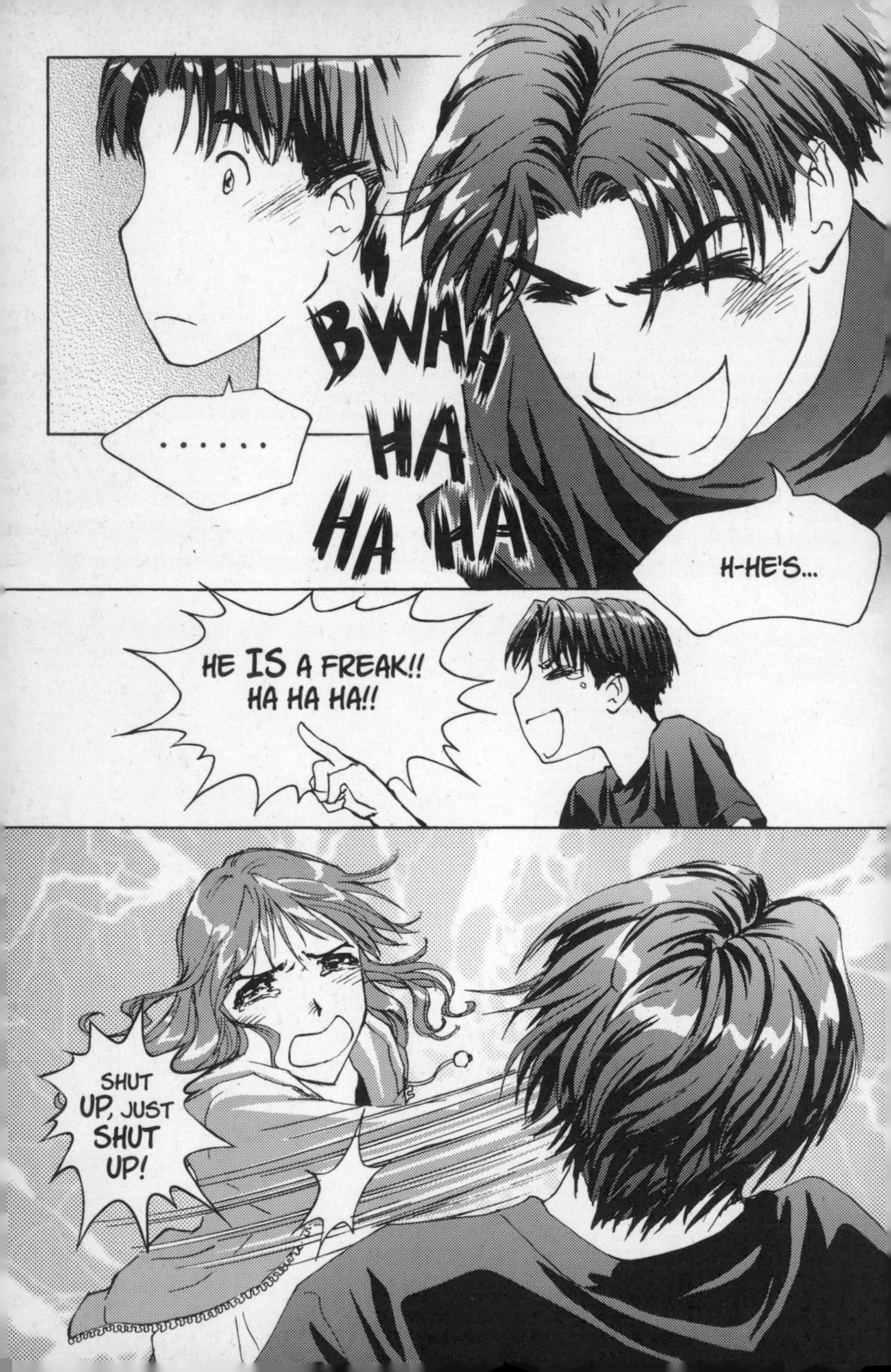

......
BWAH HA HA HA HA
H-HE'S...
HE IS A FREAK!! HA HA HA!!
SHUT UP, JUST SHUT UP!

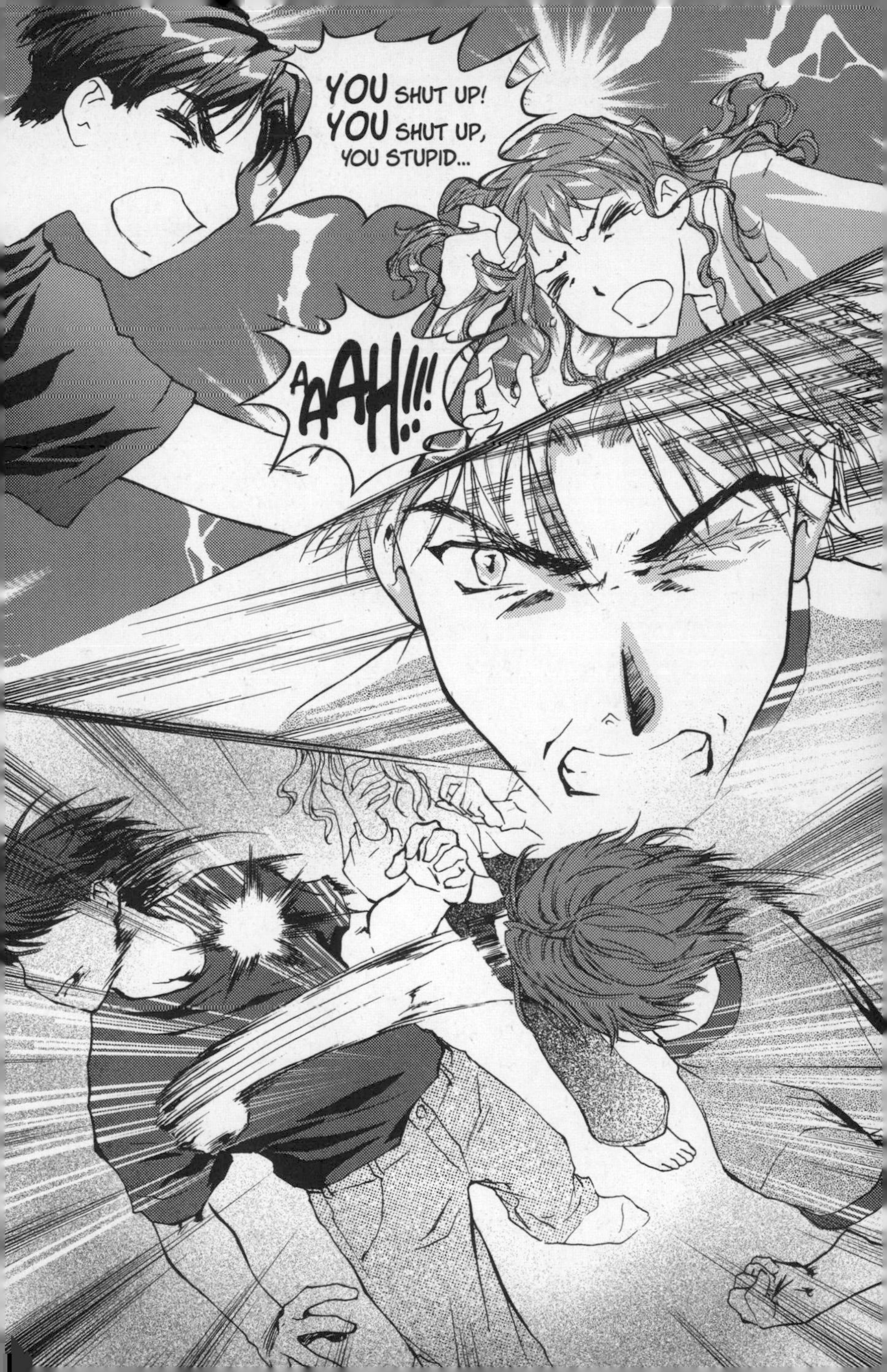
YOU SHUT UP!
YOU SHUT UP,
YOU STUPID...
AAAH!!!

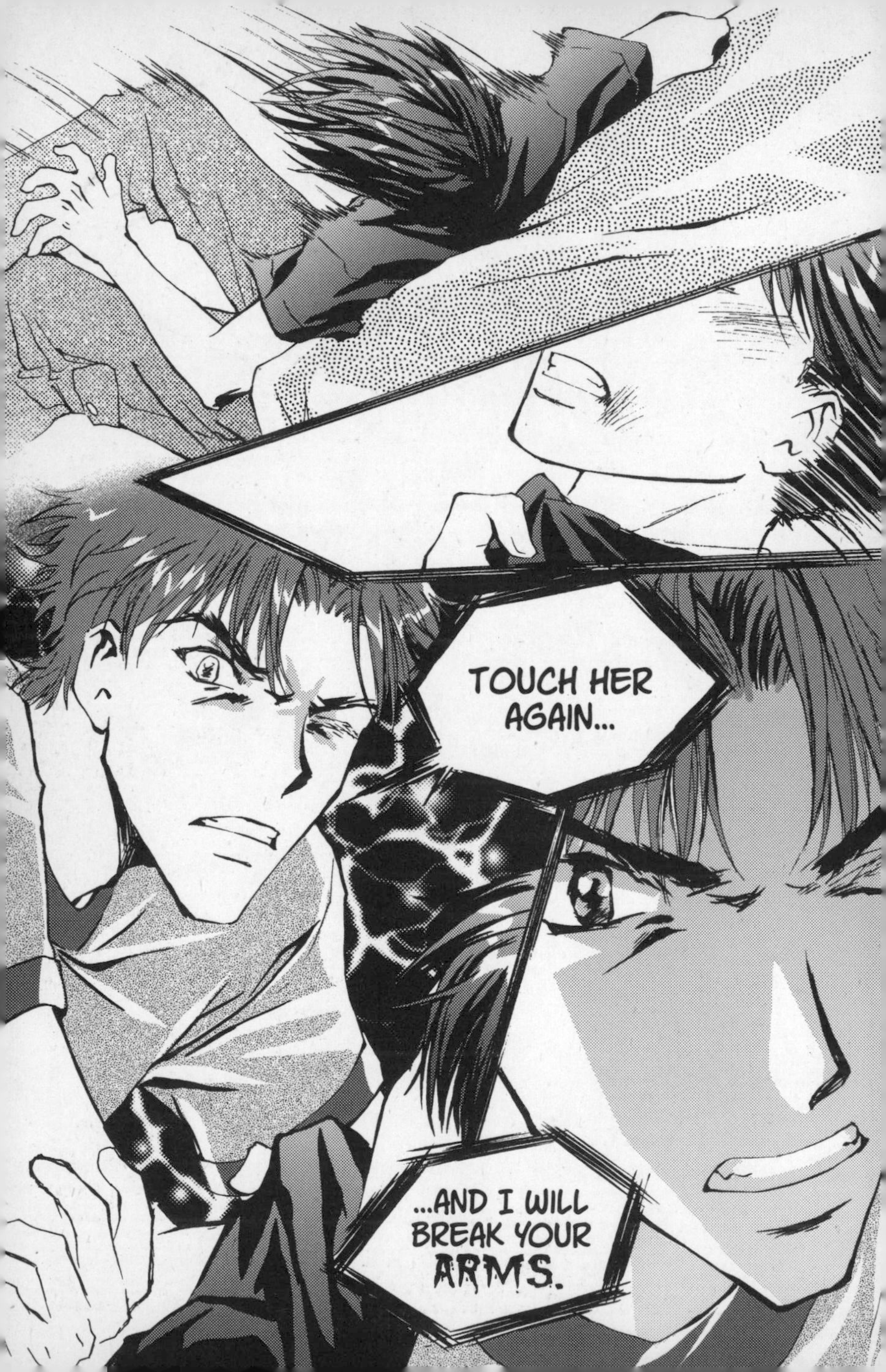
TOUCH HER AGAIN...
...AND I WILL BREAK YOUR ARMS.

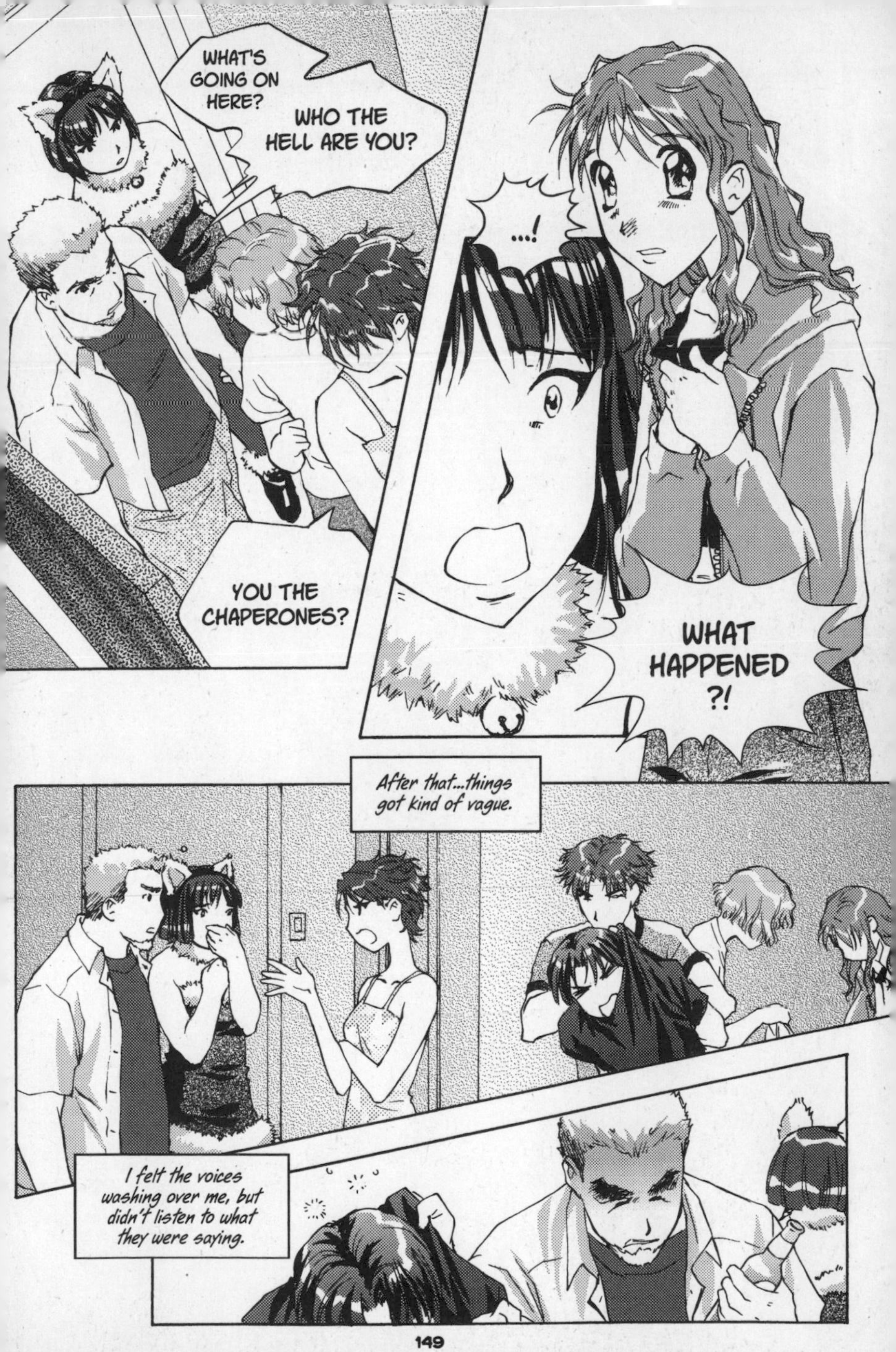

WHAT'S GOING ON HERE?
WHO THE HELL ARE YOU?
YOU THE CHAPERONES?
...!
WHAT HAPPENED ?!
After that...things got kind of vague.
I felt the voices washing over me, but didn't listen to what they were saying.

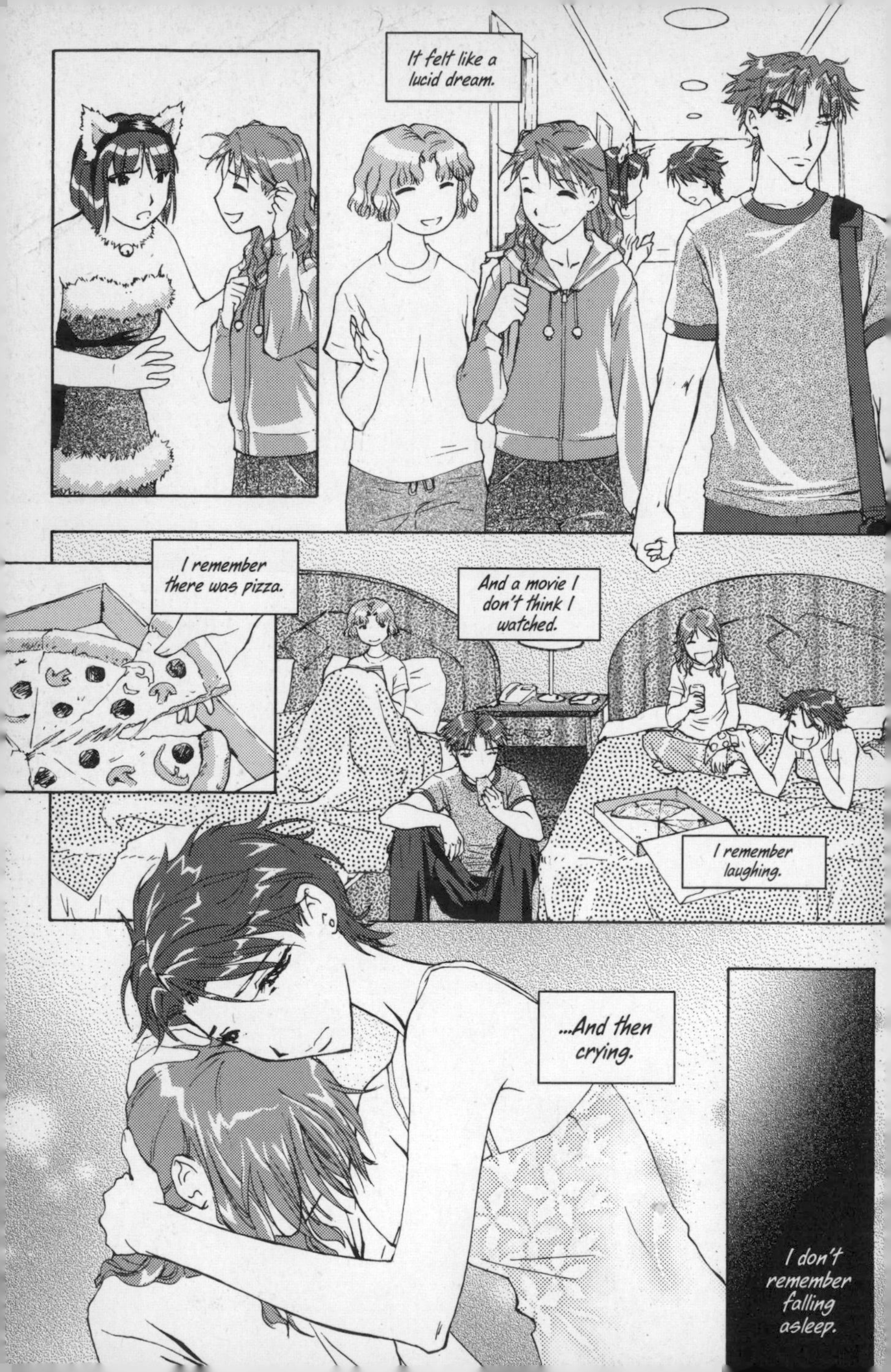
It felt like a lucid dream.
I remember there was pizza.
And a movie I don't think I watched.
I remember laughing.
...And then crying.
I don't remember falling asleep.

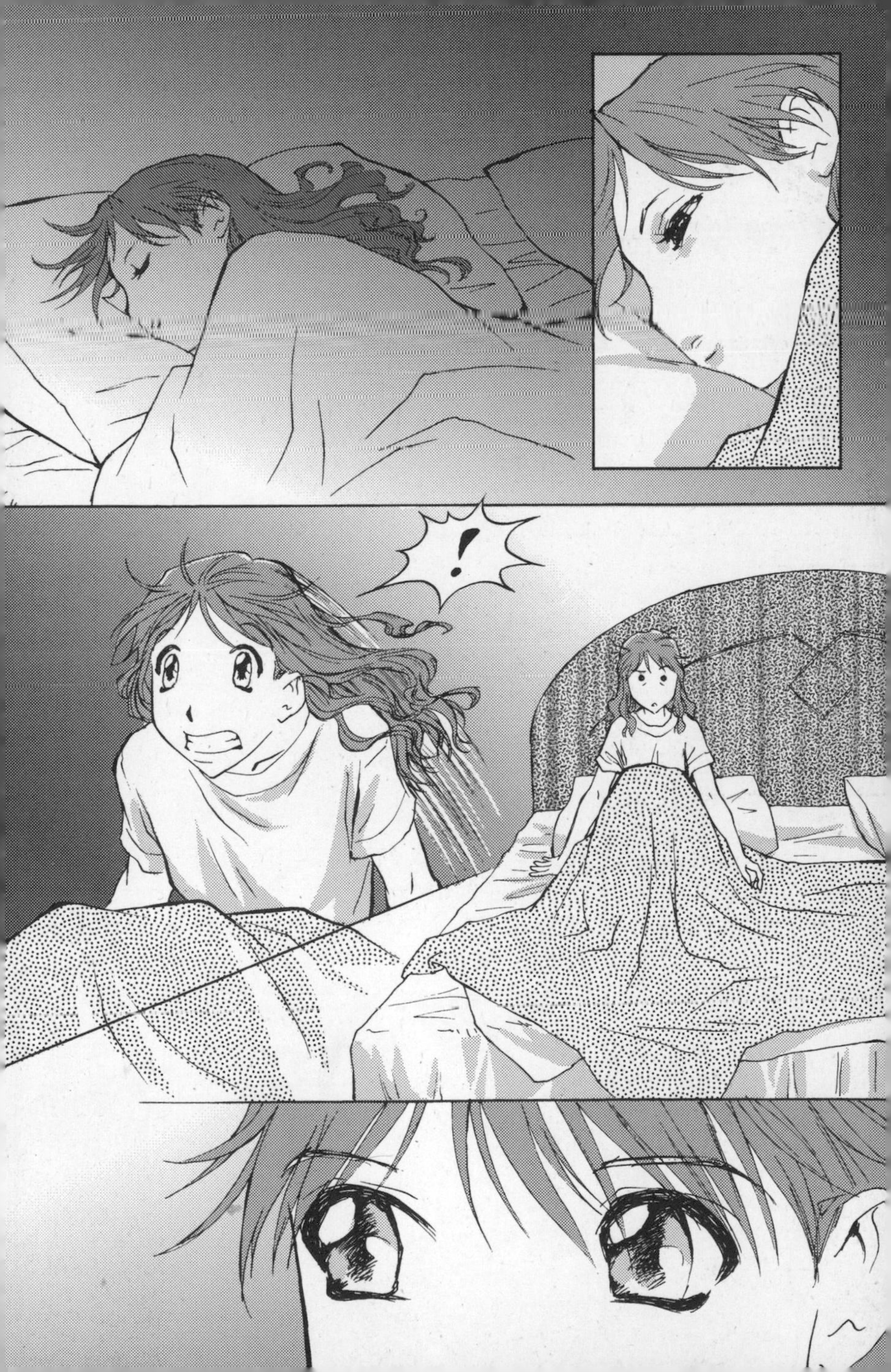
!

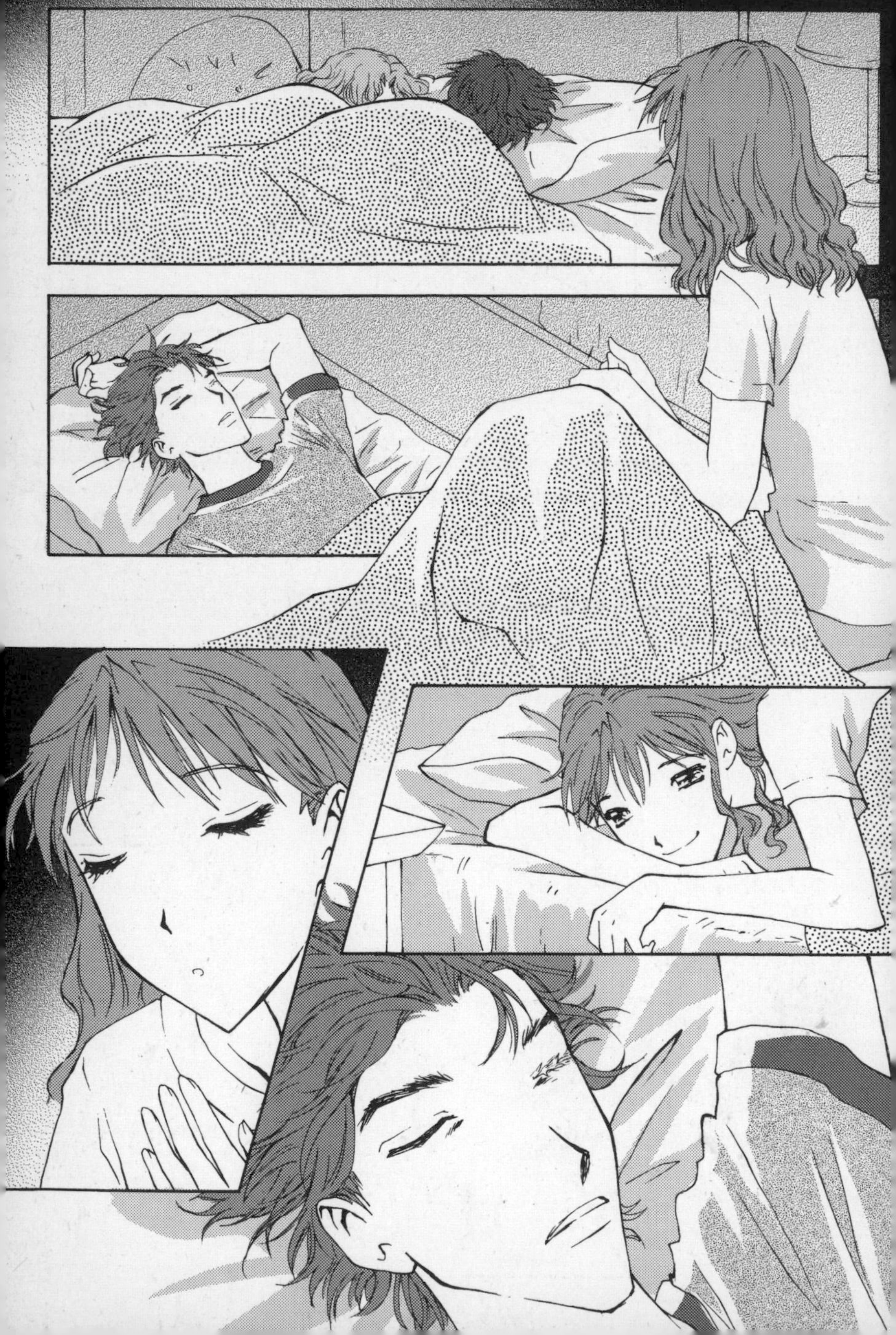

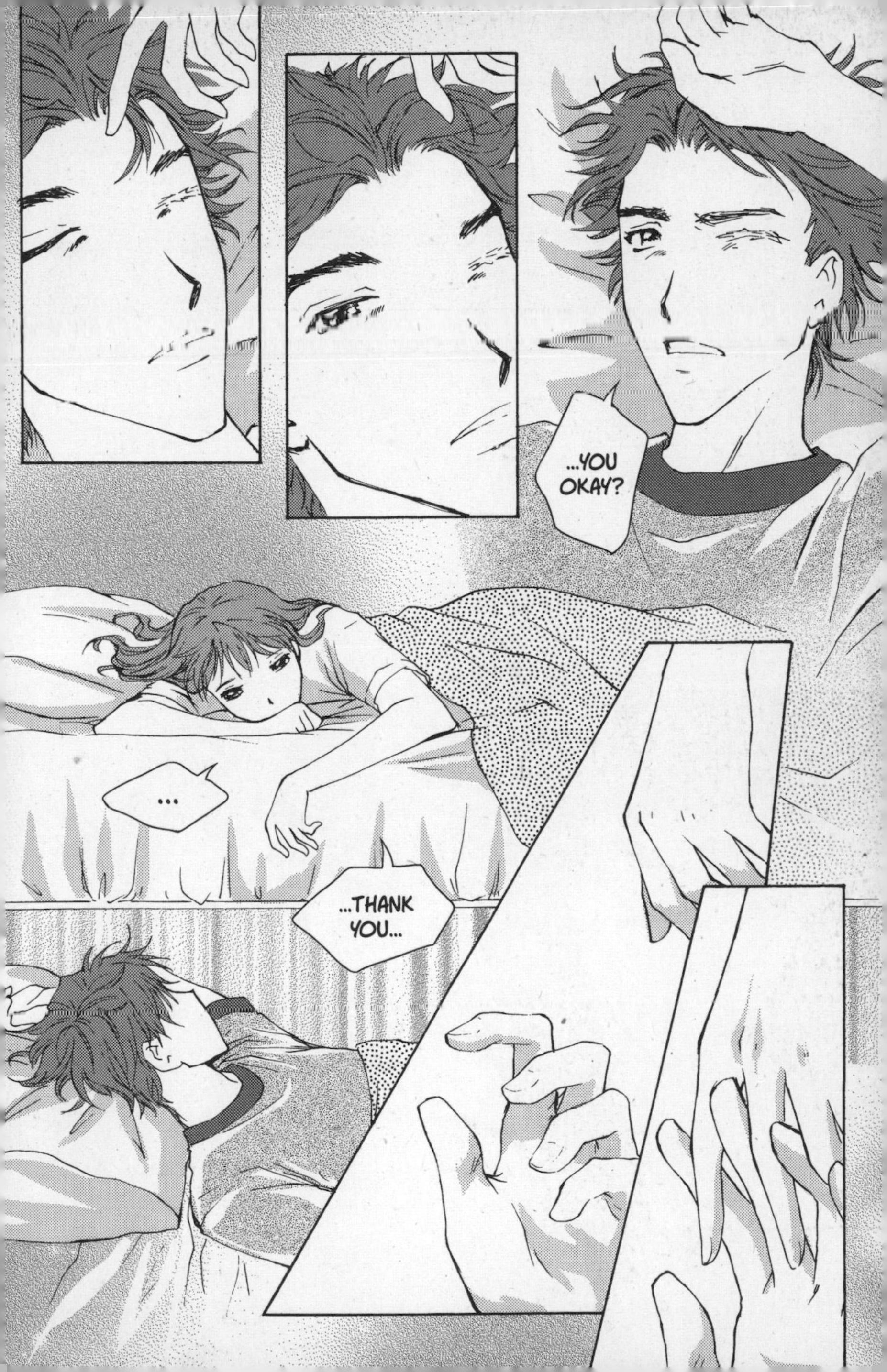
...YOU OKAY?
...
...THANK YOU...

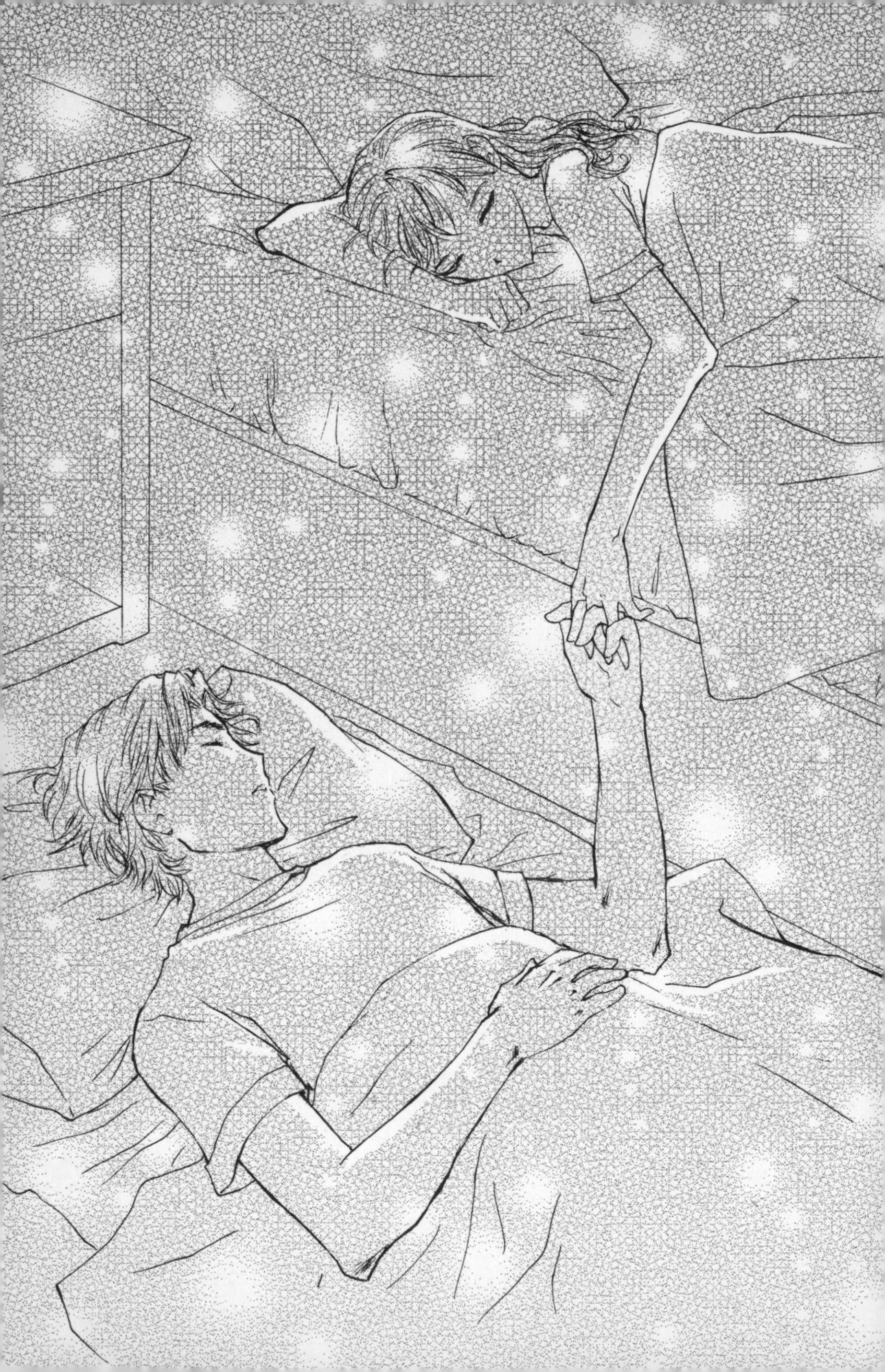

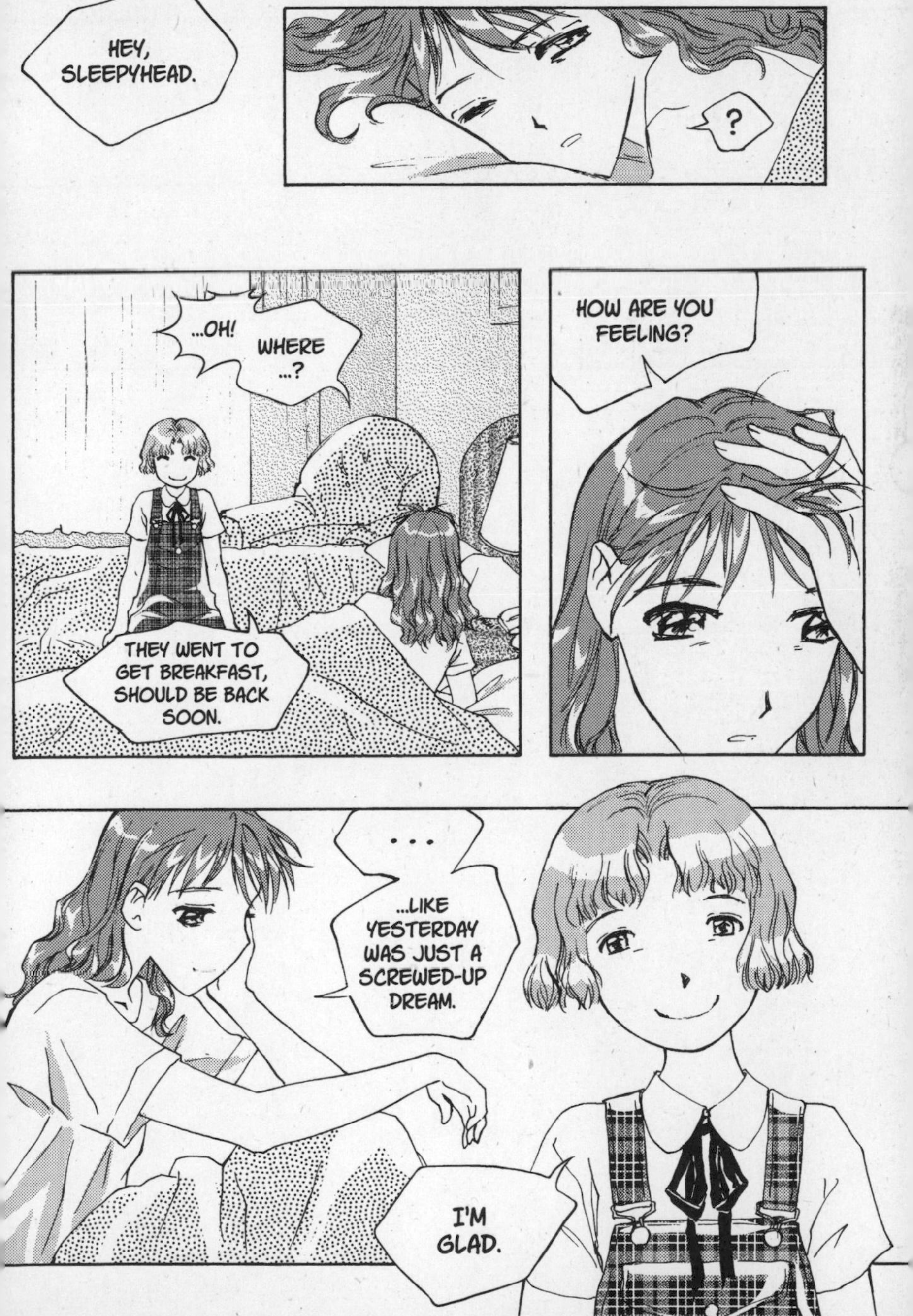
HEY, SLEEPYHEAD.
?
...OH!
WHERE ...?
THEY WENT TO GET BREAKFAST, SHOULD BE BACK SOON.
HOW ARE YOU FEELING?
. . .
...LIKE YESTERDAY WAS JUST A SCREWED-UP DREAM.
I'M GLAD.

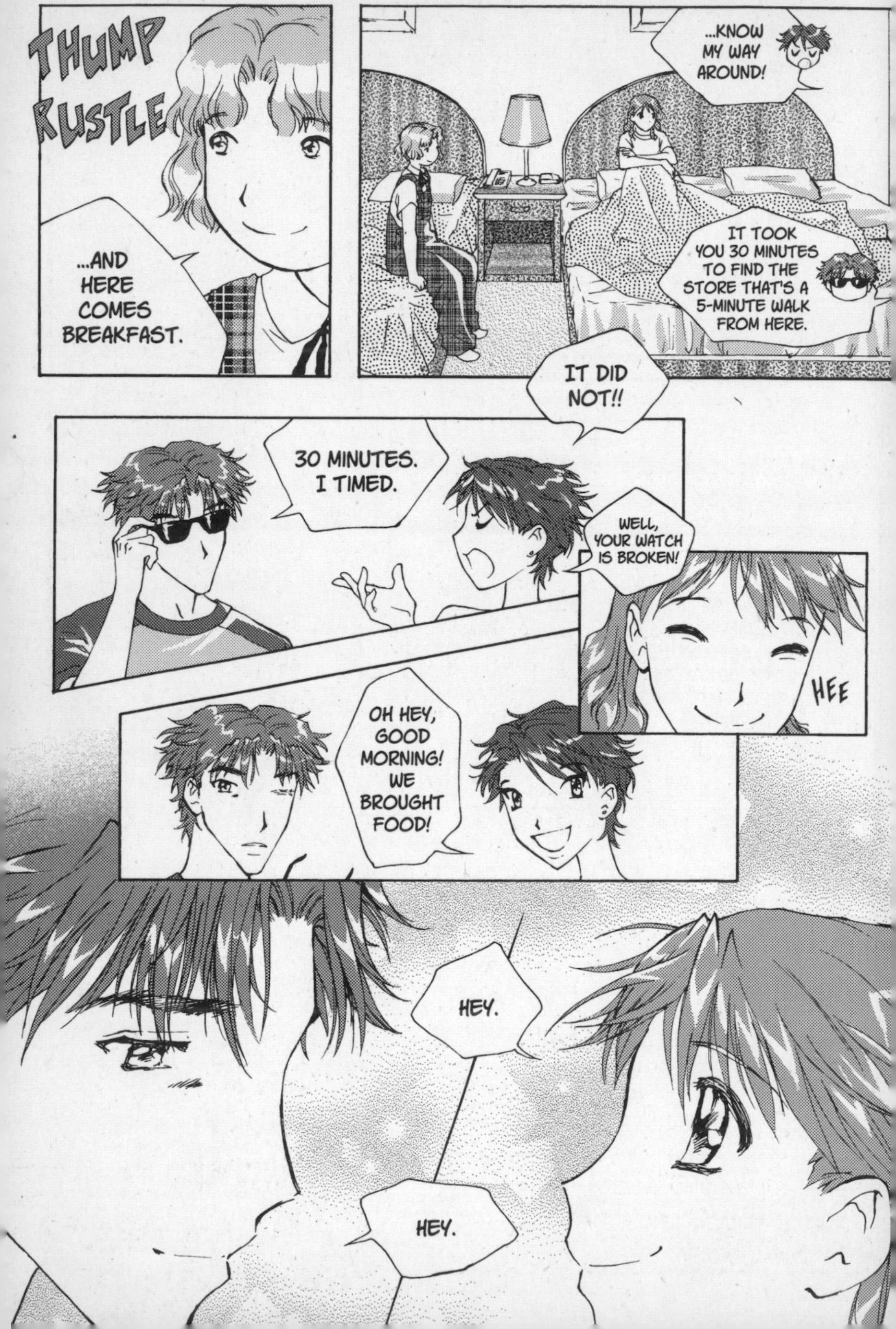
THUMP
RUSTLE
...AND HERE COMES BREAKFAST.
...KNOW MY WAY AROUND!
IT TOOK YOU 30 MINUTES TO FIND THE STORE THAT'S A 5-MINUTE WALK FROM HERE.
IT DID NOT!!
30 MINUTES. I TIMED.
WELL, YOUR WATCH IS BROKEN!
HEE
OH HEY, GOOD MORNING! WE BROUGHT FOOD!
HEY.
HEY.

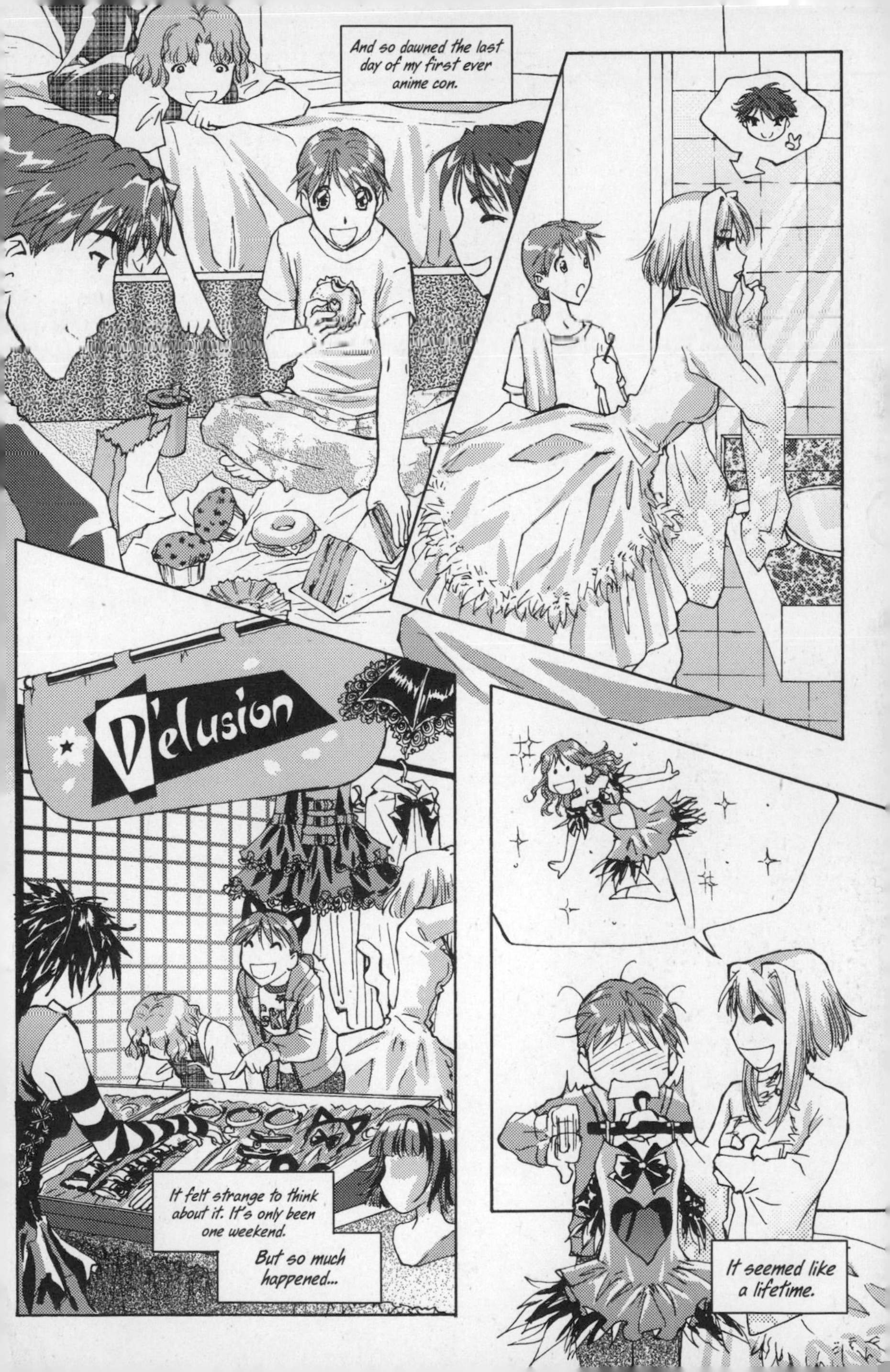
And so dawned the last day of my first ever anime con.
D'elusion
It felt strange to think about it. It's only been one weekend.
But so much happened...
It seemed like a lifetime.

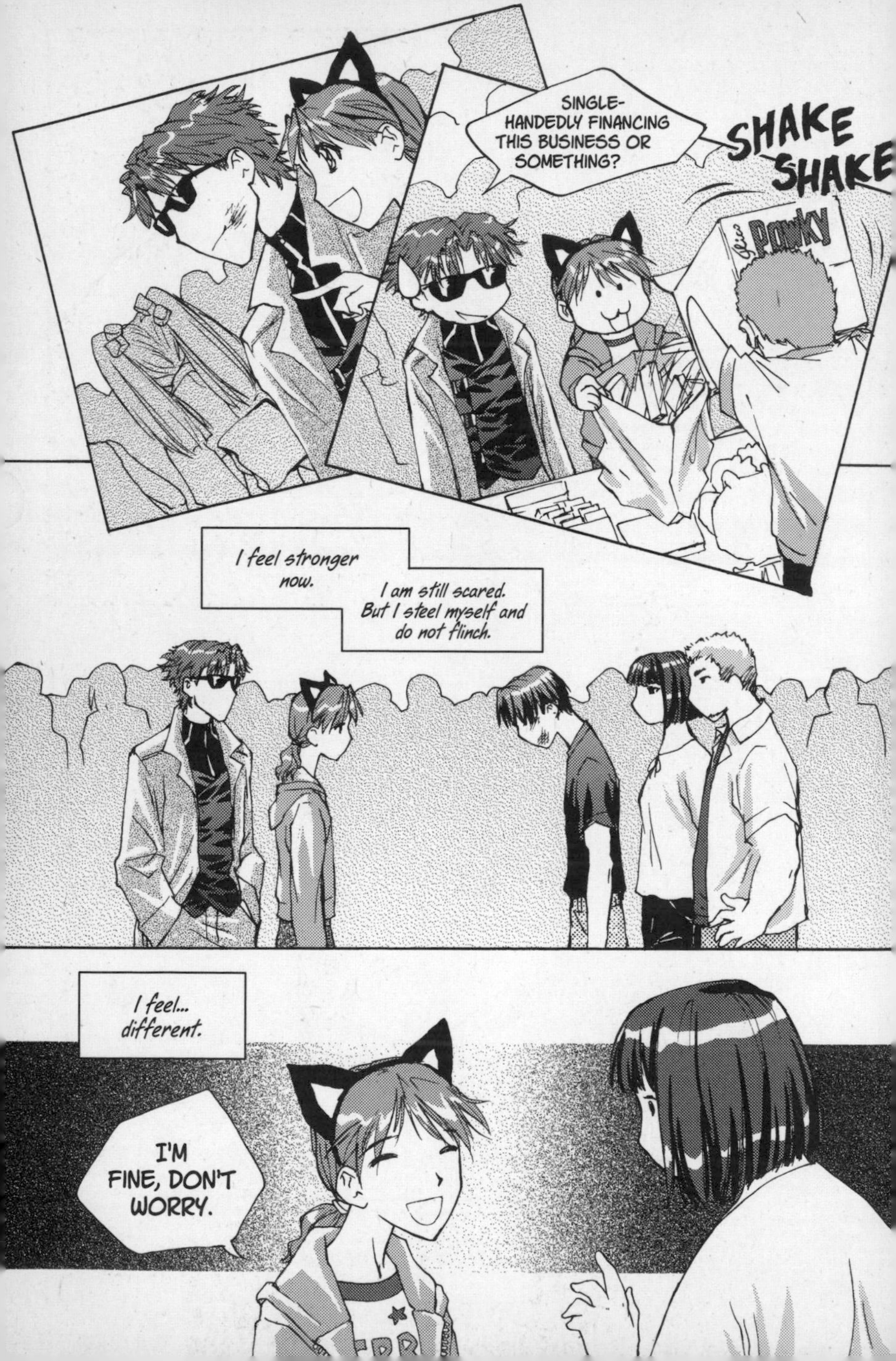
SINGLE-HANDEDLY FINANCING THIS BUSINESS OR SOMETHING?
SHAKE SHAKE
Pawky
I feel stronger now.
I am still scared. But I steel myself and do not flinch.
I feel... different.
I'M FINE, DON'T WORRY.

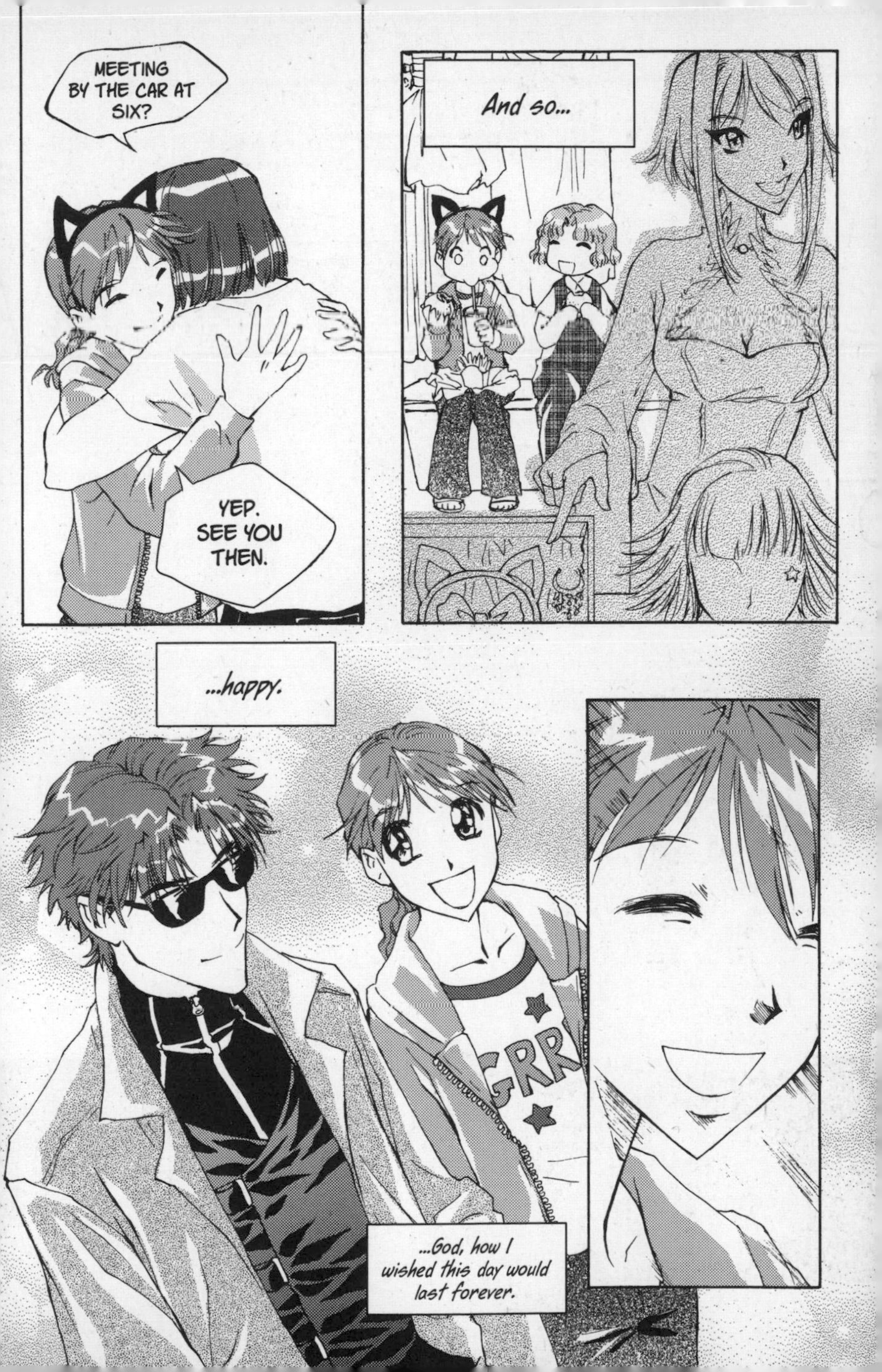
MEETING BY THE CAR AT SIX?
YEP. SEE YOU THEN.
And so...
...happy.
...God, how I wished this day would last forever.
GRR

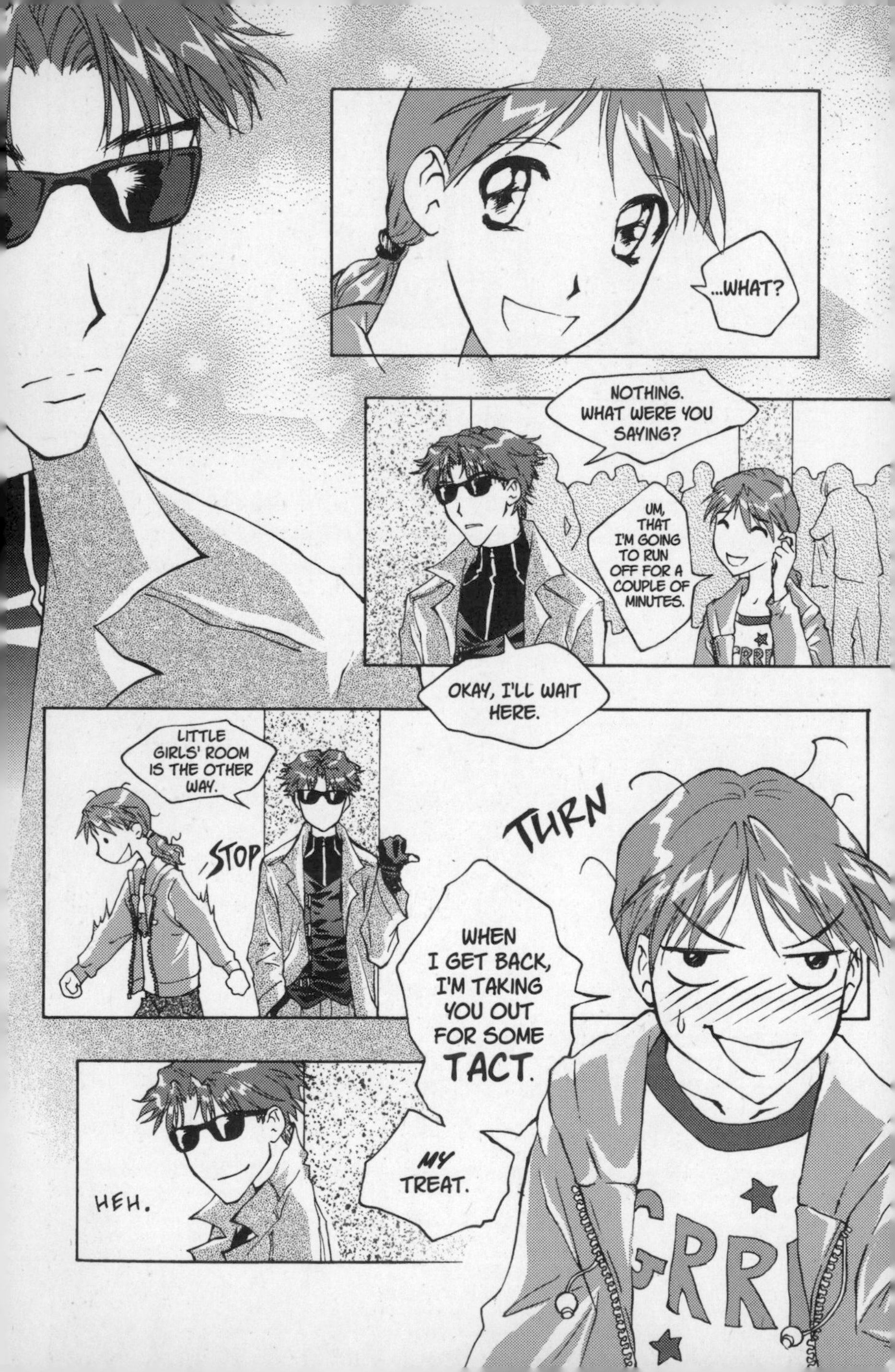

...WHAT?
NOTHING. WHAT WERE YOU SAYING?
UM, THAT I'M GOING TO RUN OFF FOR A COUPLE OF MINUTES.
OKAY, I'LL WAIT HERE.
LITTLE GIRLS' ROOM IS THE OTHER WAY.
STOP
HEH.
MY TREAT.
TURN
WHEN I GET BACK, I'M TAKING YOU OUT FOR SOME TACT.

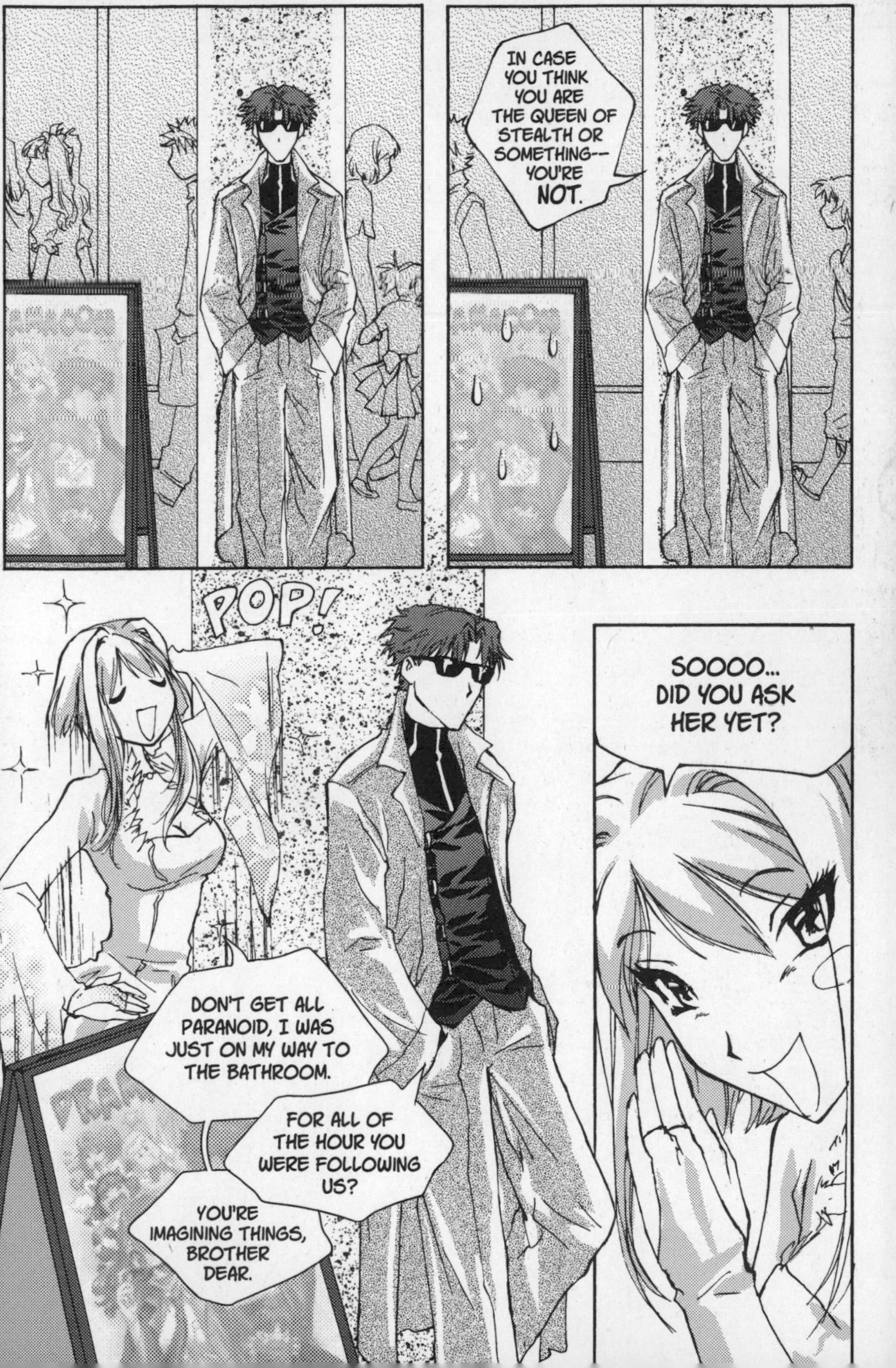
IN CASE YOU THINK YOU ARE THE QUEEN OF STEALTH OR SOMETHING-- YOU'RE NOT.
POP!
DON'T GET ALL PARANOID, I WAS JUST ON MY WAY TO THE BATHROOM.
FOR ALL OF THE HOUR YOU WERE FOLLOWING US?
YOU'RE IMAGINING THINGS, BROTHER DEAR.
SOOOO... DID YOU ASK HER YET?

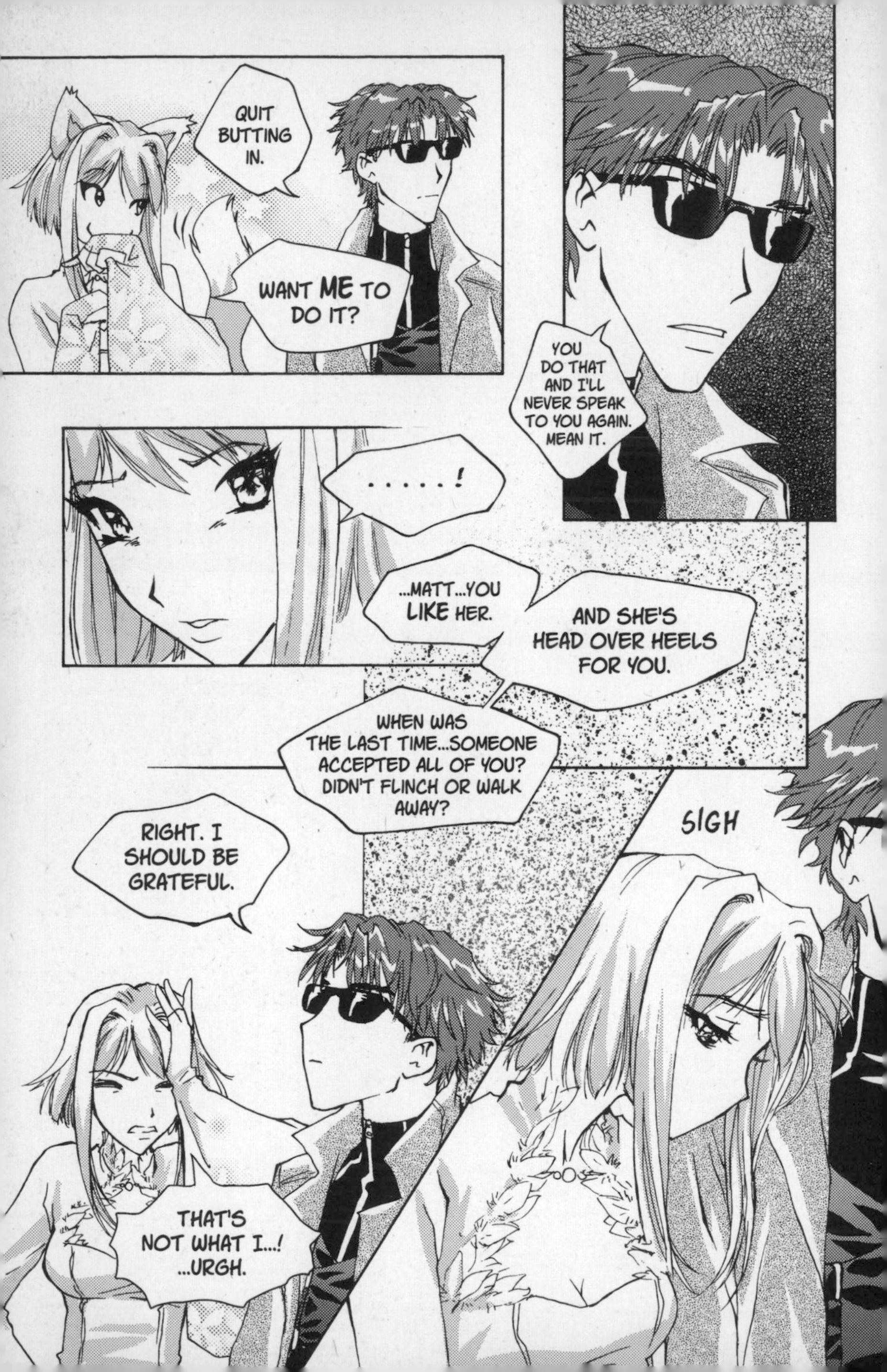
QUIT BUTTING IN.
WANT ME TO DO IT?
. . . . . !
YOU DO THAT AND I'LL NEVER SPEAK TO YOU AGAIN. MEAN IT.
...MATT...YOU LIKE HER.
AND SHE'S HEAD OVER HEELS FOR YOU.
WHEN WAS THE LAST TIME...SOMEONE ACCEPTED ALL OF YOU? DIDN'T FLINCH OR WALK AWAY?
RIGHT. I SHOULD BE GRATEFUL.
THAT'S NOT WHAT I...! ...URGH.
SIGH

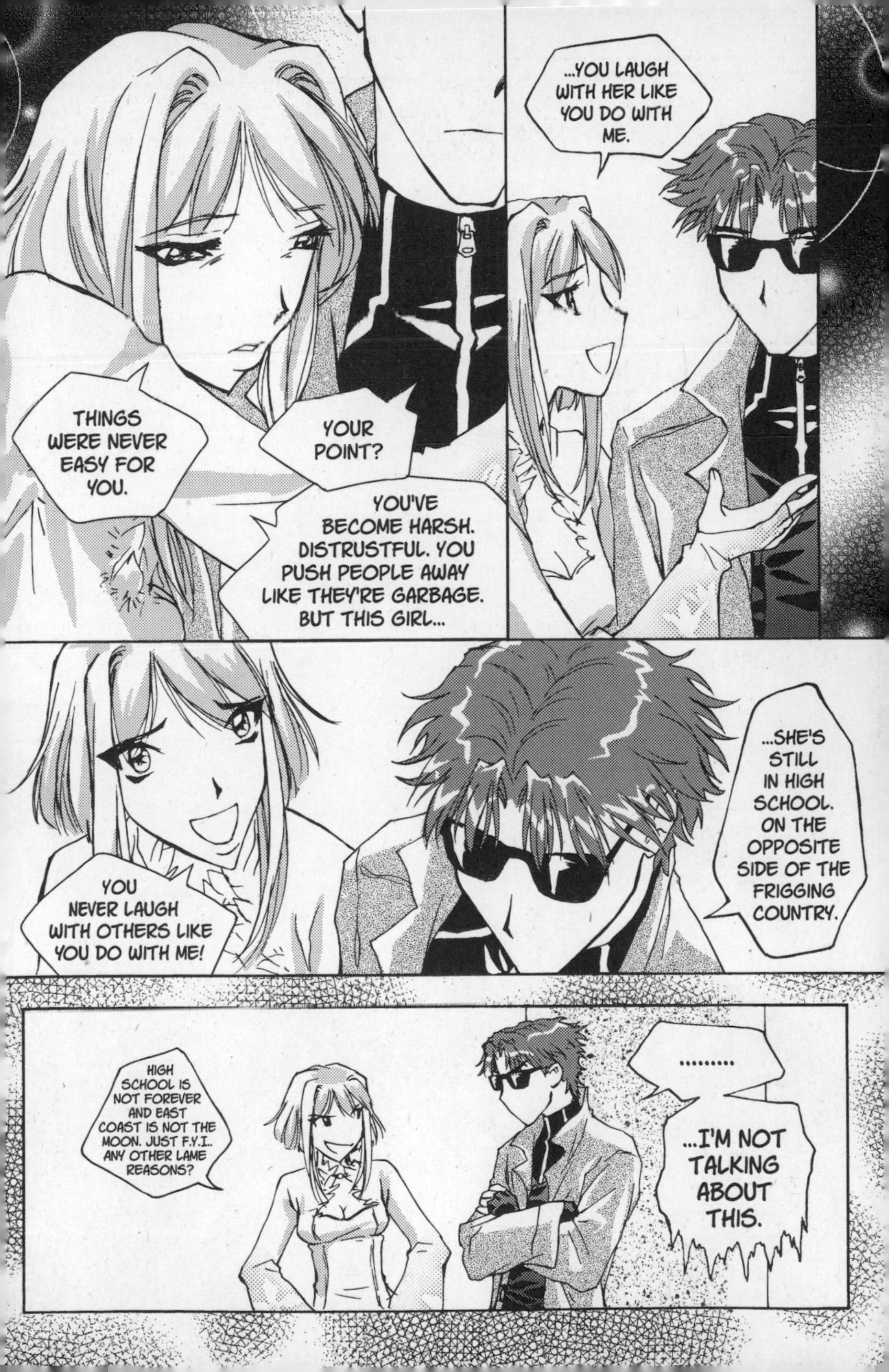
THINGS WERE NEVER EASY FOR YOU.
YOUR POINT?
YOU'VE BECOME HARSH. DISTRUSTFUL. YOU PUSH PEOPLE AWAY LIKE THEY'RE GARBAGE. BUT THIS GIRL...
...YOU LAUGH WITH HER LIKE YOU DO WITH ME.
YOU NEVER LAUGH WITH OTHERS LIKE YOU DO WITH ME!
...SHE'S STILL IN HIGH SCHOOL. ON THE OPPOSITE SIDE OF THE FRIGGING COUNTRY.
HIGH SCHOOL IS NOT FOREVER AND EAST COAST IS NOT THE MOON. JUST F.Y.I.. ANY OTHER LAME REASONS?
....
...I'M NOT TALKING ABOUT THIS.

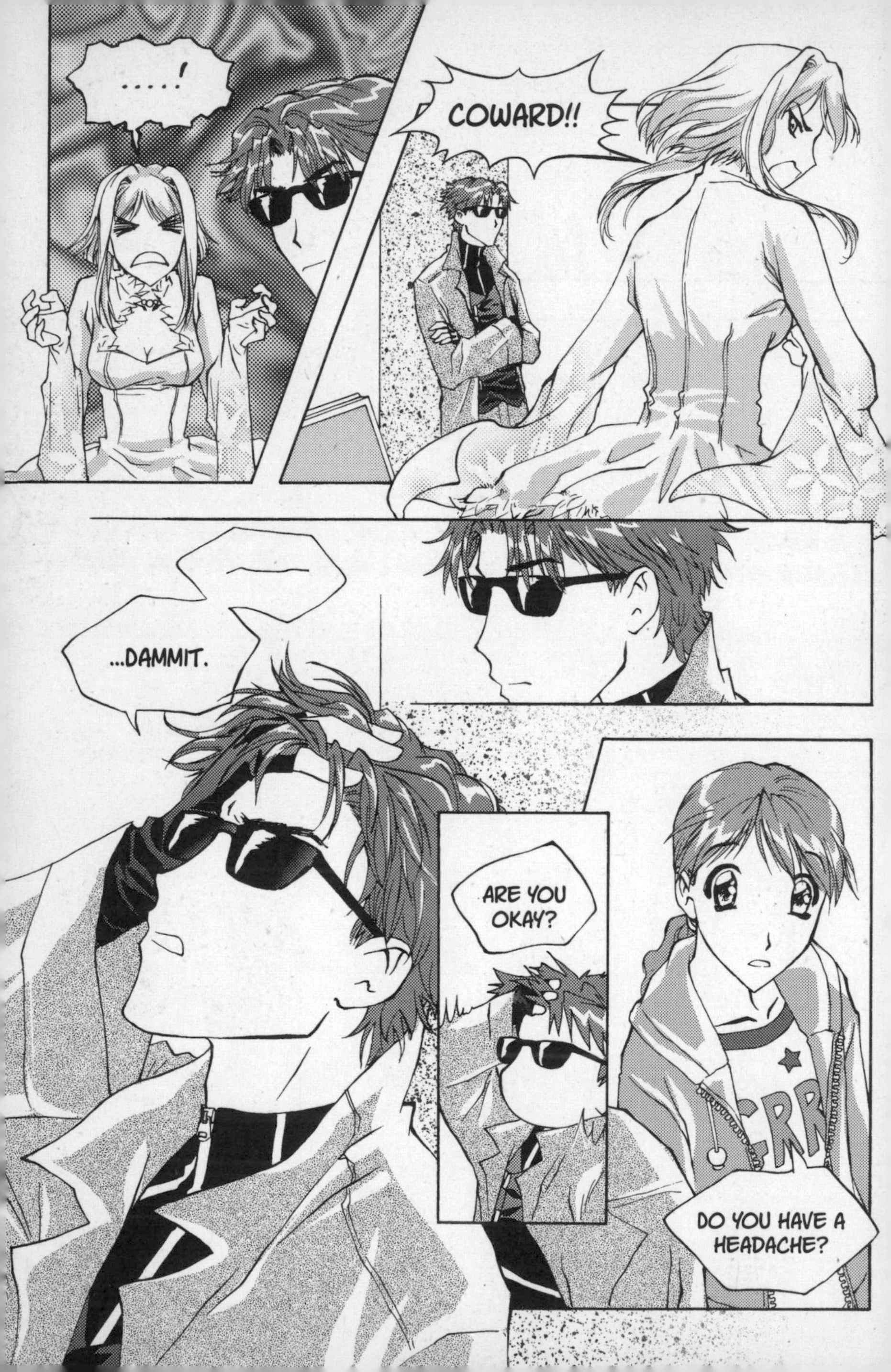

.....!
COWARD!!
...DAMMIT.
ARE YOU OKAY?
DO YOU HAVE A HEADACHE?

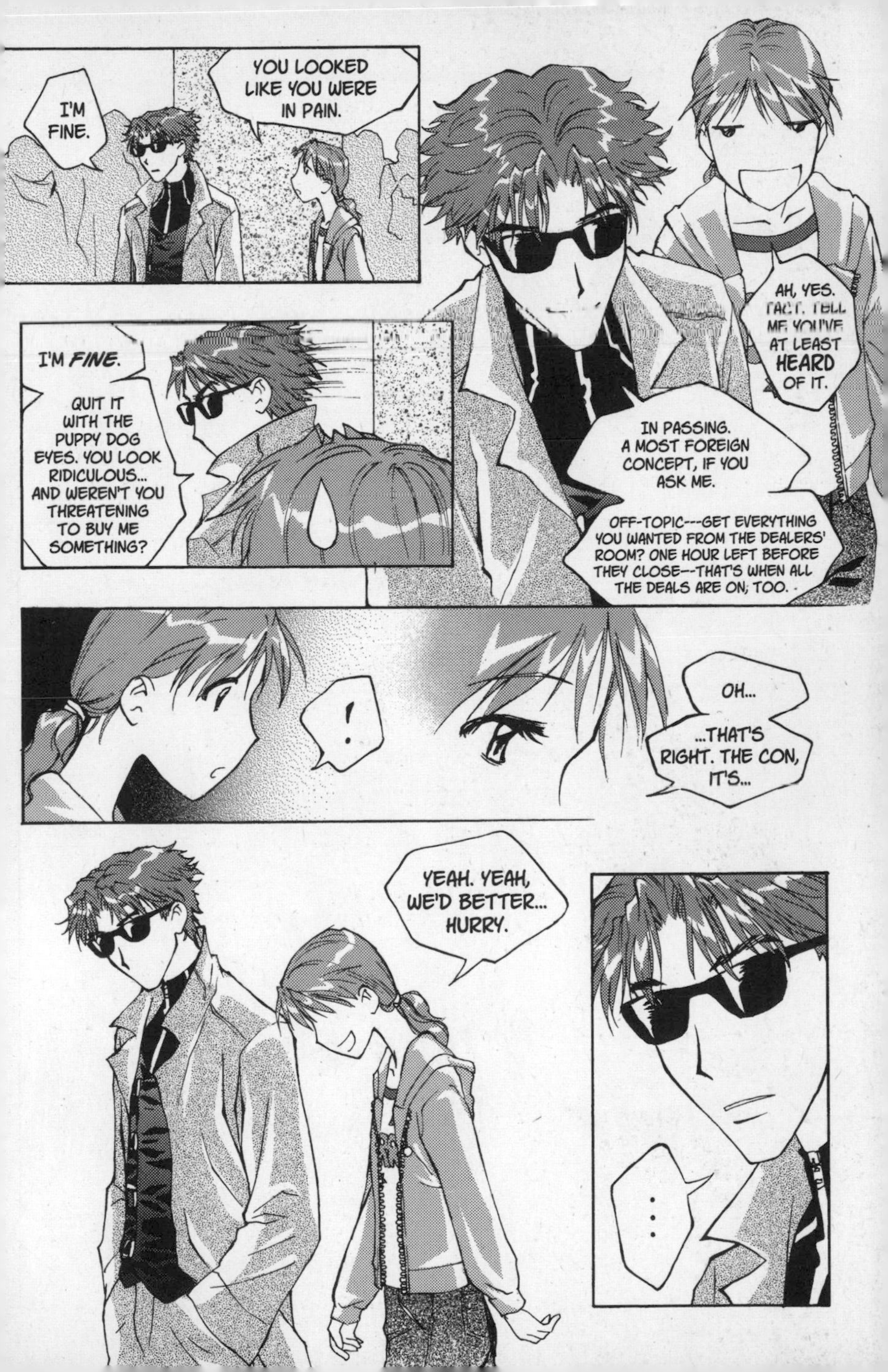
YOU LOOKED LIKE YOU WERE IN PAIN.
I'M FINE.
I'M *FINE*.
QUIT IT WITH THE PUPPY DOG EYES. YOU LOOK RIDICULOUS... AND WEREN'T YOU THREATENING TO BUY ME SOMETHING?
AH, YES. TACT. TELL ME YOU'VE AT LEAST **HEARD** OF IT.
IN PASSING. A MOST FOREIGN CONCEPT, IF YOU ASK ME.
OFF-TOPIC---GET EVERYTHING YOU WANTED FROM THE DEALERS' ROOM? ONE HOUR LEFT BEFORE THEY CLOSE--THAT'S WHEN ALL THE DEALS ARE ON, TOO.
!
OH...
...THAT'S RIGHT. THE CON, IT'S...
YEAH. YEAH, WE'D BETTER... HURRY.
...

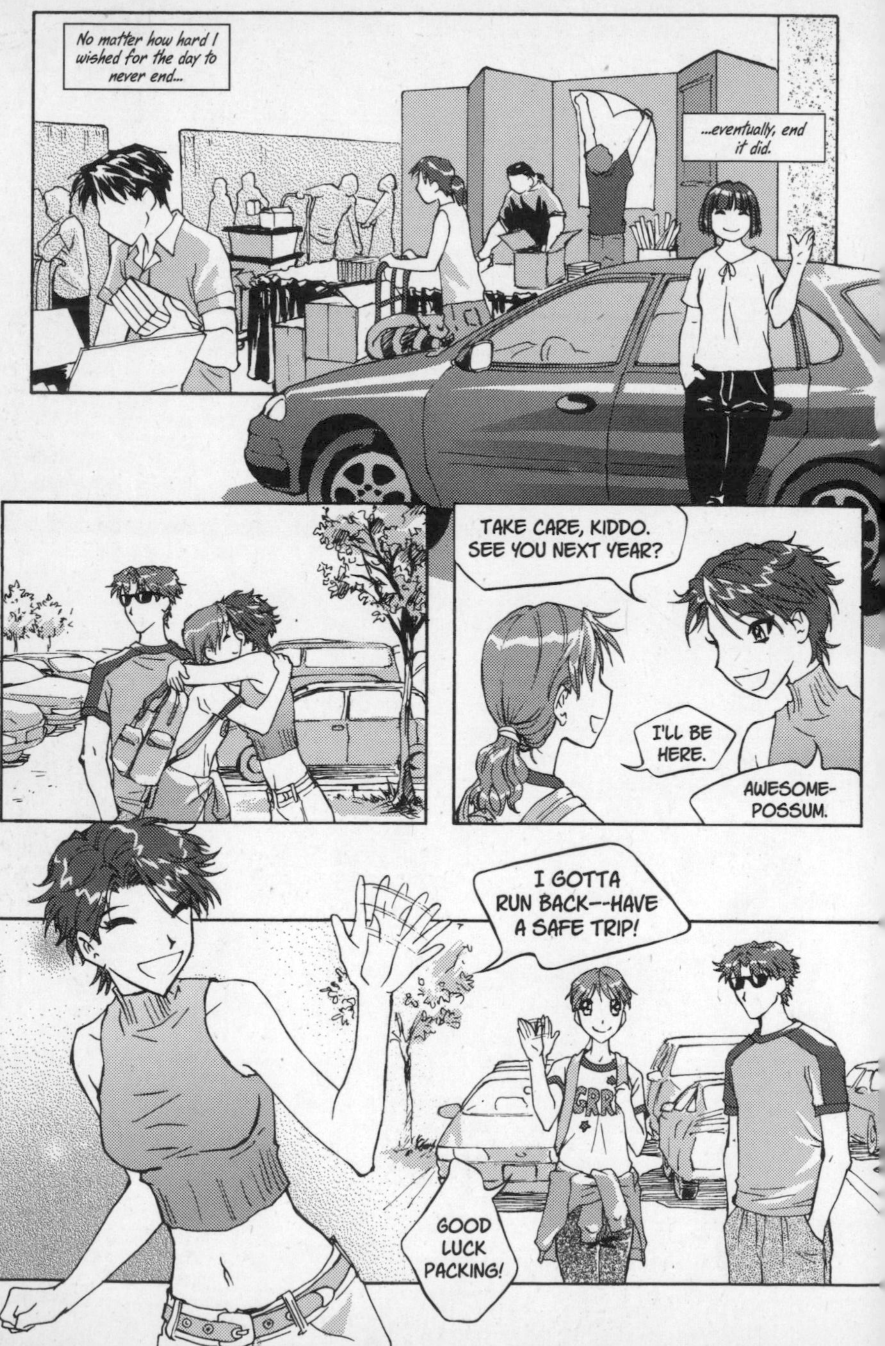
No matter how hard I wished for the day to never end...
...eventually, end it did.
TAKE CARE, KIDDO. SEE YOU NEXT YEAR?
I'LL BE HERE.
AWESOME-POSSUM.
I GOTTA RUN BACK--HAVE A SAFE TRIP!
GOOD LUCK PACKING!

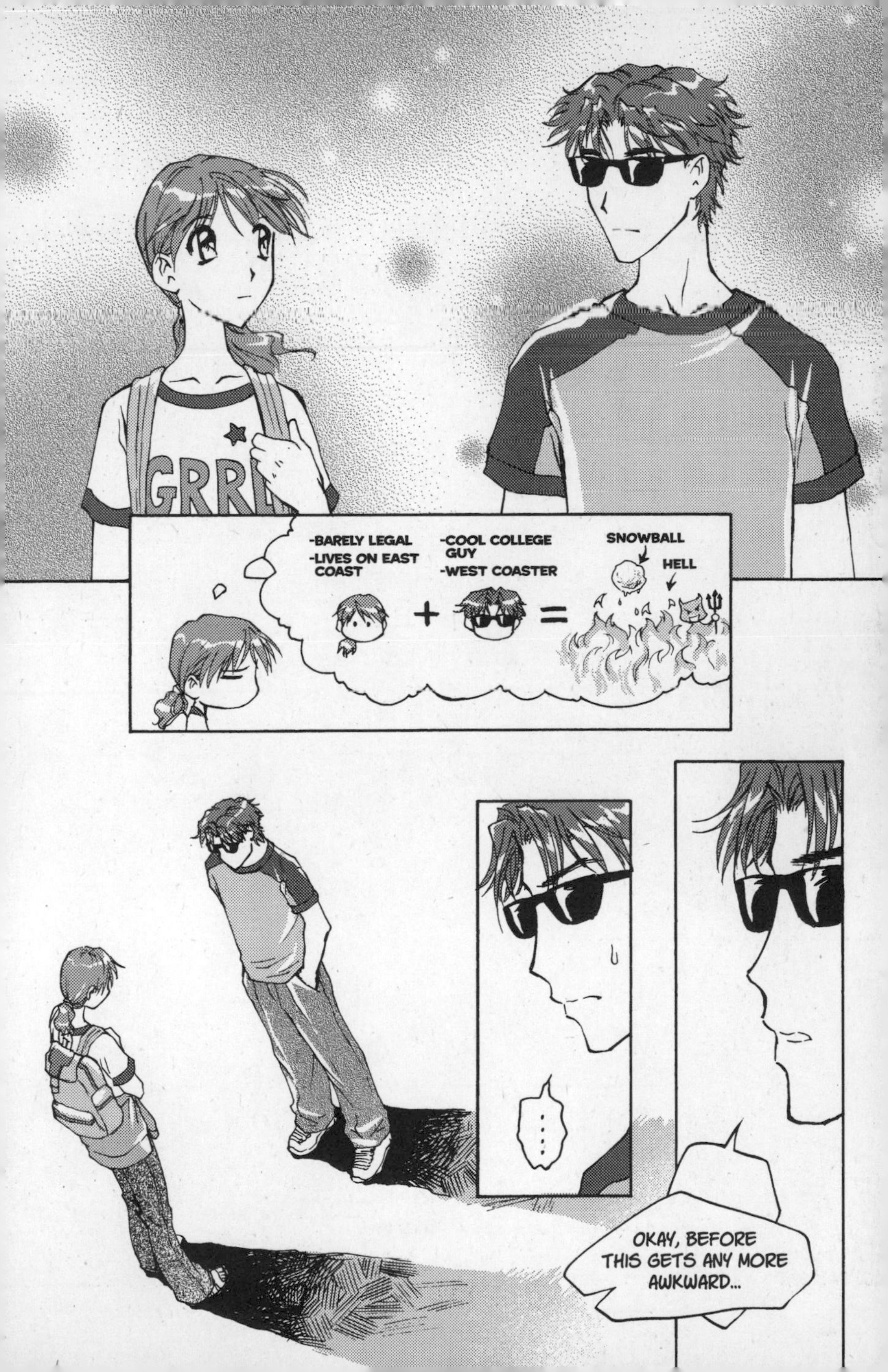
-BARELY LEGAL
-LIVES ON EAST COAST
-COOL COLLEGE GUY
-WEST COASTER
SNOWBALL
HELL
+
=
...
OKAY, BEFORE THIS GETS ANY MORE AWKWARD...

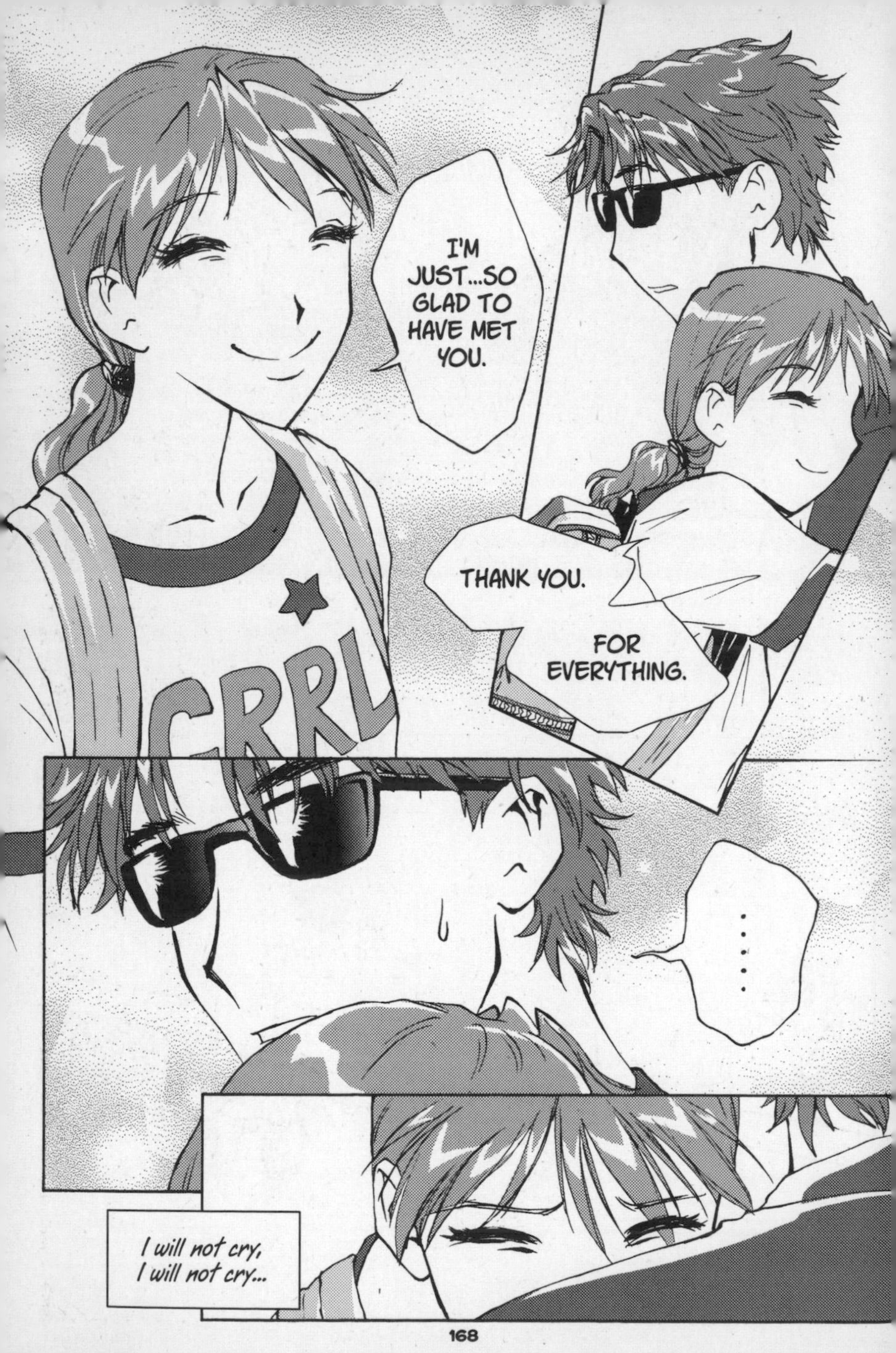
I'M JUST...SO GLAD TO HAVE MET YOU.
THANK YOU.
FOR EVERYTHING.
CRRL
......
I will not cry, I will not cry...

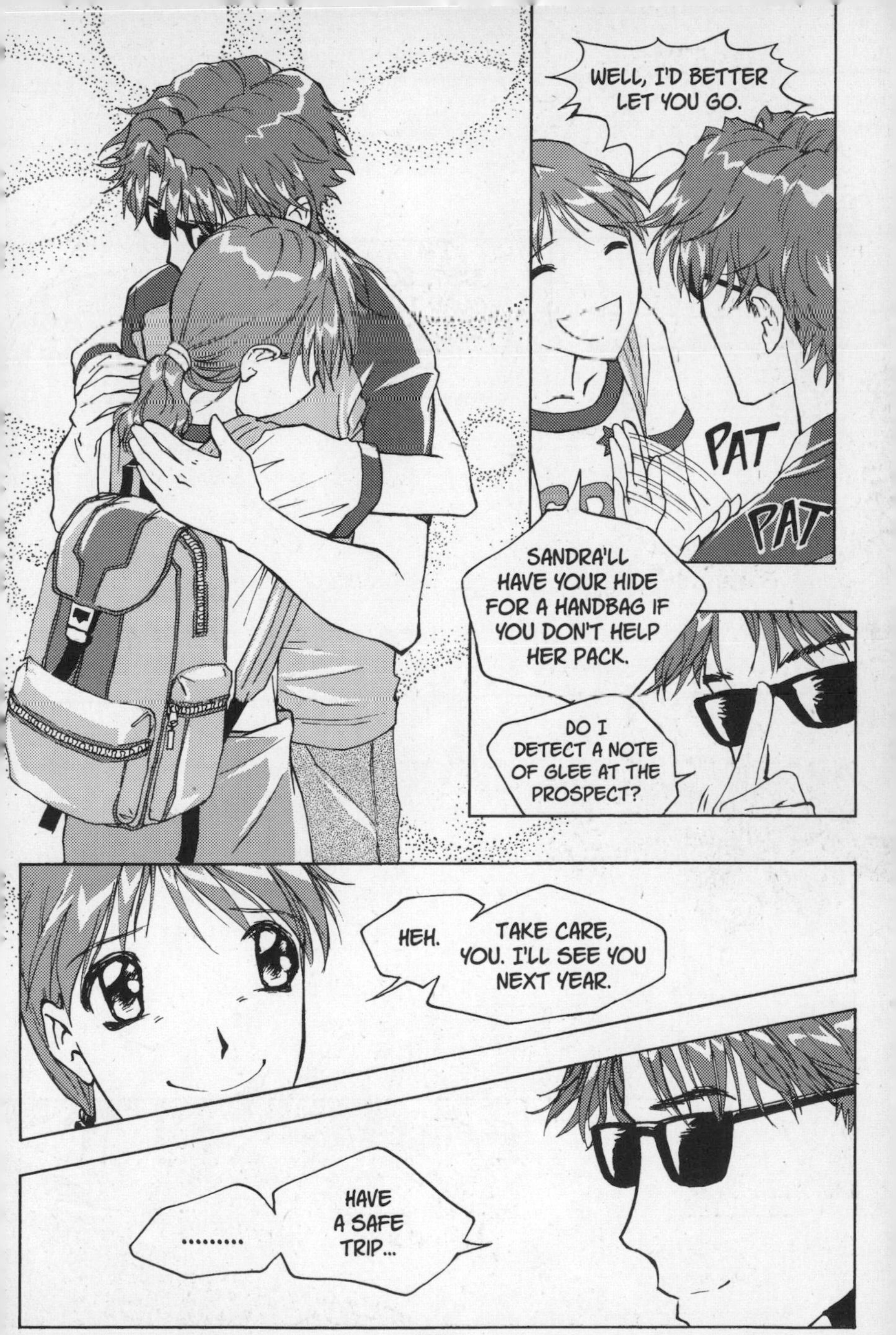
WELL, I'D BETTER LET YOU GO.
PAT
PAT
SANDRA'LL HAVE YOUR HIDE FOR A HANDBAG IF YOU DON'T HELP HER PACK.
DO I DETECT A NOTE OF GLEE AT THE PROSPECT?
HEH. TAKE CARE, YOU. I'LL SEE YOU NEXT YEAR.
....
HAVE A SAFE TRIP...

...And this is how you break your own heart into itty-bitty little pieces.

I should give lessons.

ALL READY TO GO HOME?

YEAH.

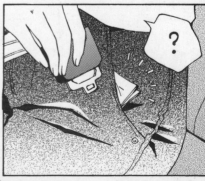

And I am.

?

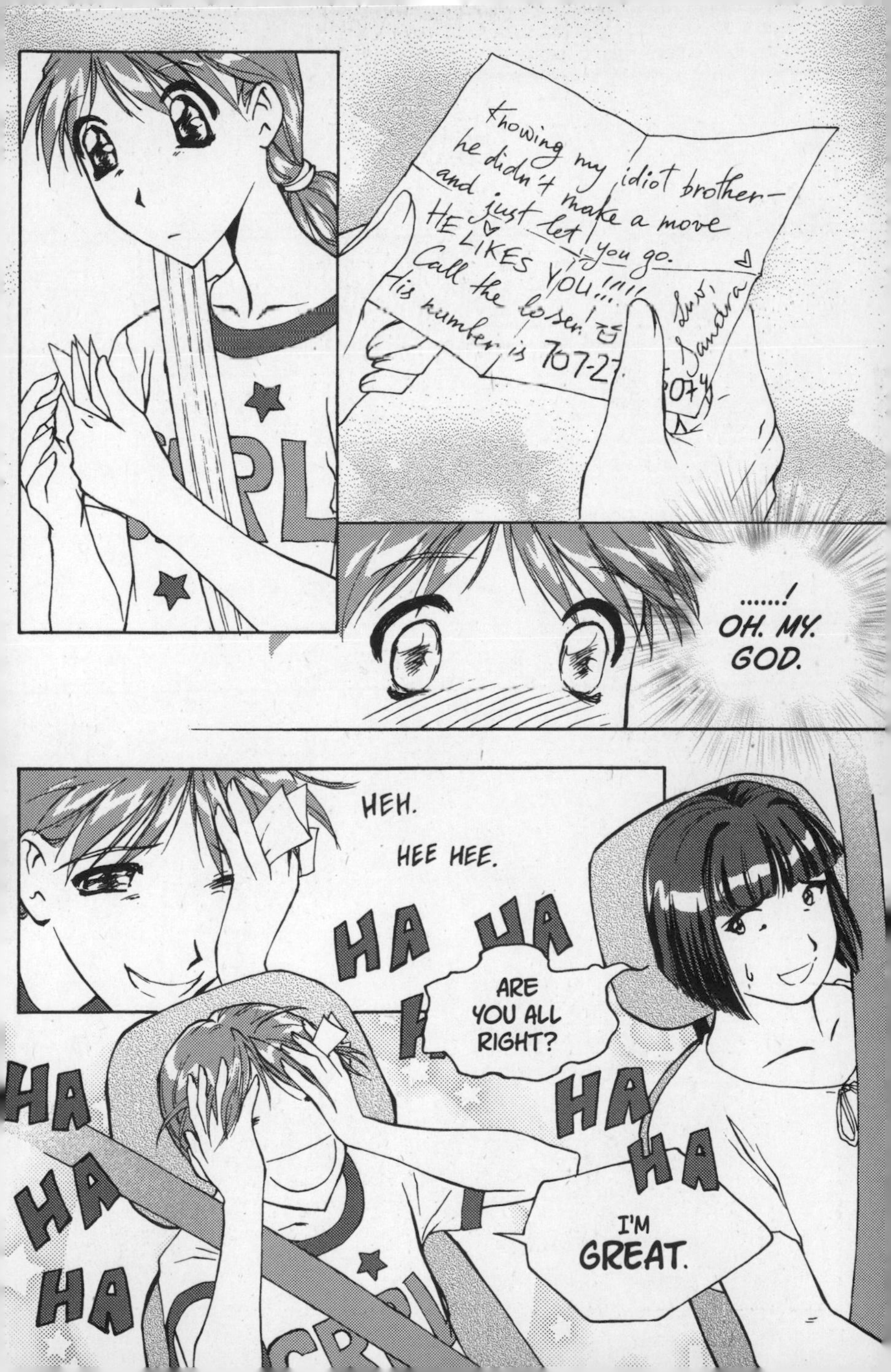
Knowing my idiot brother—
he didn't make a move
and just let you go.
HE LIKES YOU!!!!!
Call the loser!
His number is 707-27
Luv, Sandra
......!
OH. MY. GOD.
HEH.
HEE HEE.
HA HA
ARE YOU ALL RIGHT?
HA HA HA
HA HA
I'M GREAT.

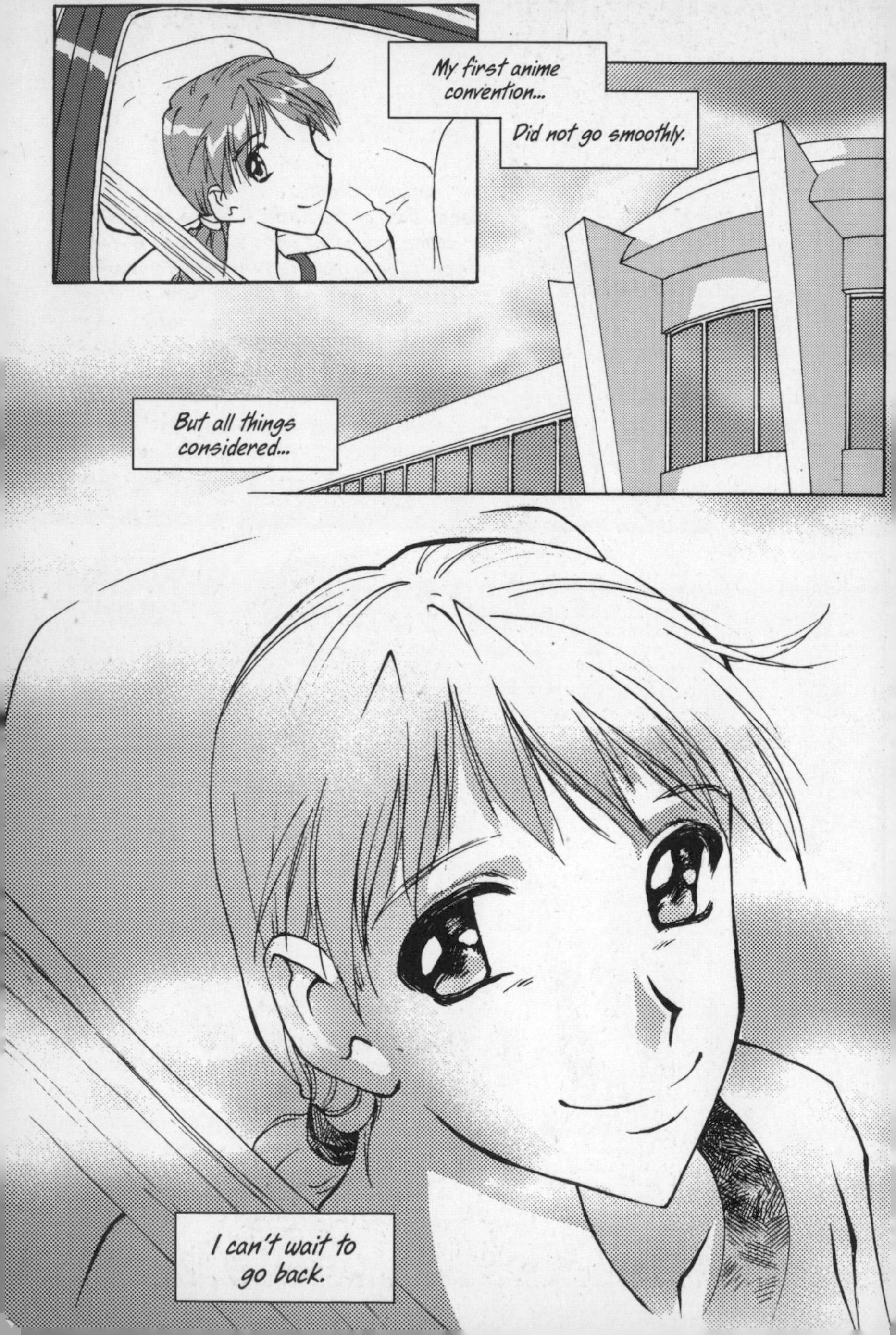
My first anime convention...
Did not go smoothly.
But all things considered...
I can't wait to go back.

IN THE NEXT VOLUME OF...

Svetlana Chmakova's

DRAMACON

One year later, Christie is a year older and a year wiser. Back at the Lakeside Anime Convention, but with a new artist and a new online venture, she can't wait to reunite with Matt. Unfortunately, it seems that Matt has brought someone along to the con, too: a new girlfriend. Fighting their feelings for each other, which are as strong as ever, in spite of the distance, Matt and Christie do their best to keep their relationship from getting too complicated and chaotic. But nothing is more chaotic than a fan convention, and what the head says is not always what's best for the heart! Read on in Dramacon Vol. 2!

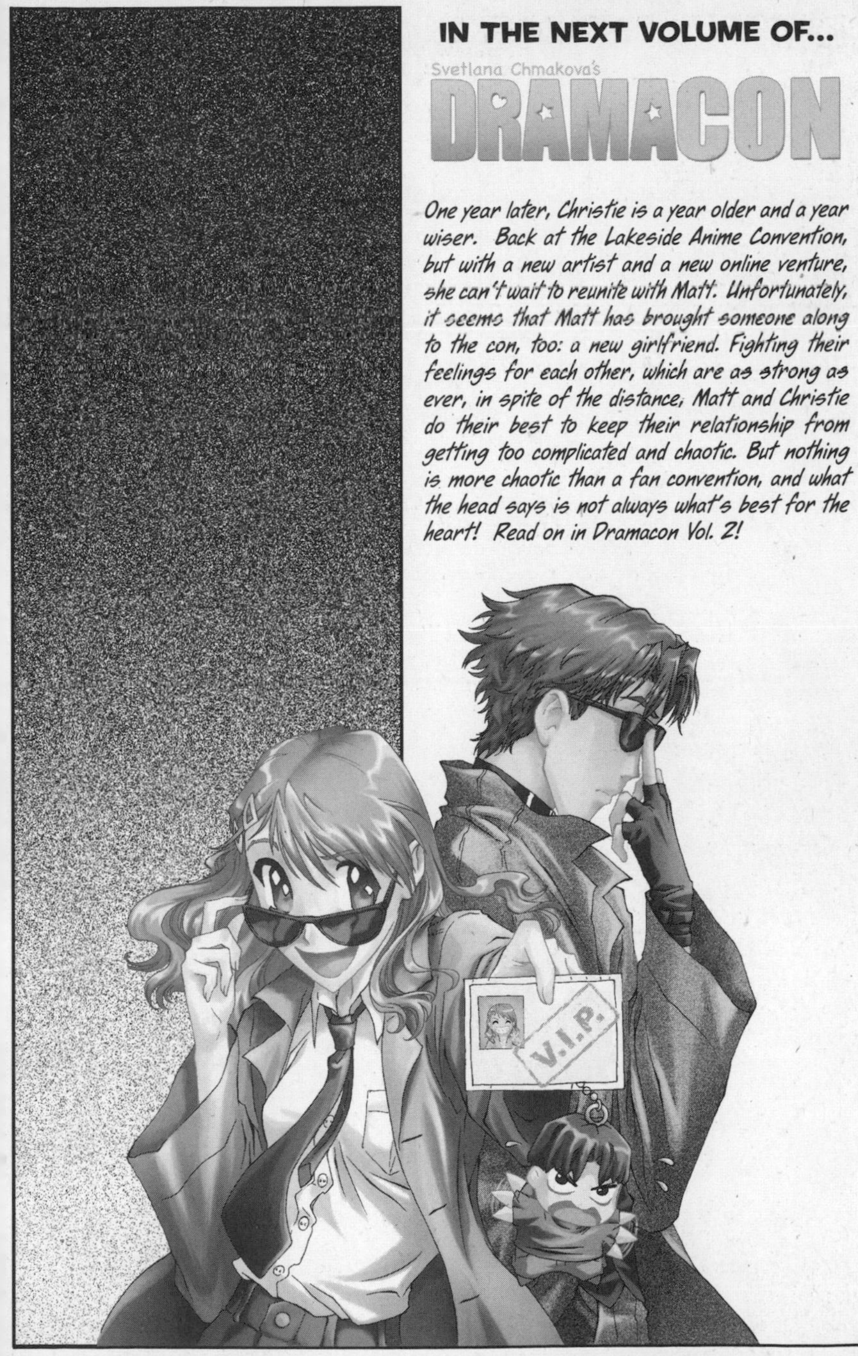
V.I.P.

♡ ~THANQ's~ ♡

Man oh man, where do I even START. I just know I'm going to forget someone >< But here goes, in no particular order:

Lillian — bestest editor ever. Thank you for the kind words, the encouragement and the kicks in the bum when I needed them ♥

Wirepop and GAM — for being so understanding and giving me the time to finish this book.

My ♥**FANS**♥ — for all your kind comments and the assurances that I do NOT suck. Those really make a difference on bad days. Also — forever thanks for reading my stuff.

My friends — for not giving up on me as I holed up in my room for half a year with this.

My sister — for laughing at all my jokes and always asking for more.

My Mom — for making sure I don't forget to eat

My Dad — for making sure my computer works

(My family and friends are awesome, did I mention that yet? 'Cause they are.) ♪♪

And a special thanks to **Alexis** and **Dee** for helping me with the toning. I AM NOT WORTHY OF SUCH FRIENDS ♥ Especially Dee, who sacrificed work and sleep to help me in the final dash ♡

...Aaaand I'm running out of page space. Thank you, everyone who helped and bought this book.!!!

Luv, Svet. ♡

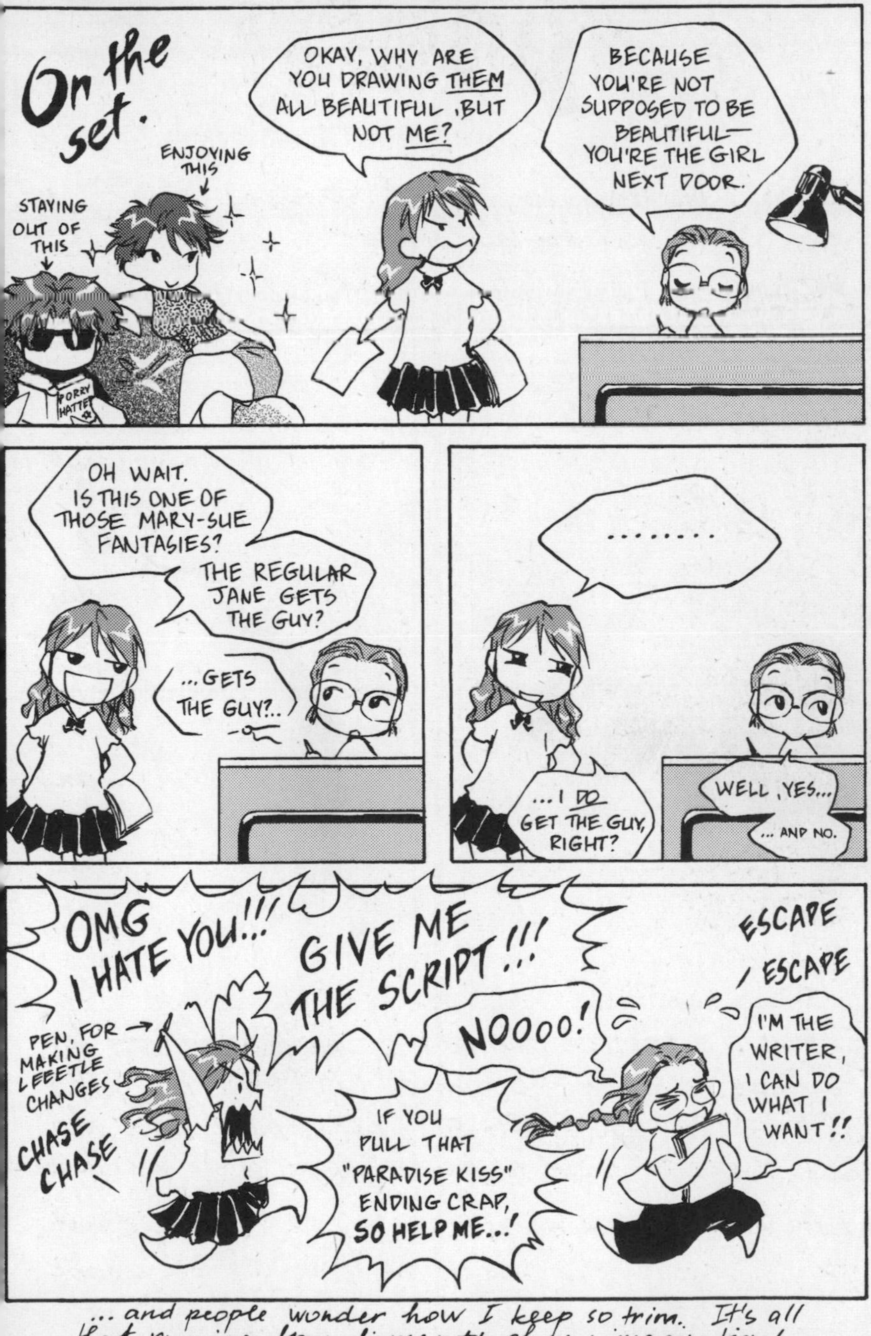
On the set.
OKAY, WHY ARE YOU DRAWING THEM ALL BEAUTIFUL, BUT NOT ME?
BECAUSE YOU'RE NOT SUPPOSED TO BE BEAUTIFUL— YOU'RE THE GIRL NEXT DOOR.
ENJOYING THIS
STAYING OUT OF THIS
PORRY HATTE
OH WAIT. IS THIS ONE OF THOSE MARY-SUE FANTASIES?
THE REGULAR JANE GETS THE GUY?
...GETS THE GUY?...
....
...I DO GET THE GUY, RIGHT?
WELL, YES...
...AND NO.
OMG I HATE YOU!!!
GIVE ME THE SCRIPT!!!
ESCAPE
ESCAPE
NOOOO!
I'M THE WRITER, I CAN DO WHAT I WANT!!
PEN, FOR MAKING LEEETLE CHANGES
CHASE CHASE
IF YOU PULL THAT "PARADISE KISS" ENDING CRAP, SO HELP ME...!

... and people wonder how I keep so trim. It's all that running from figments of my imagination!

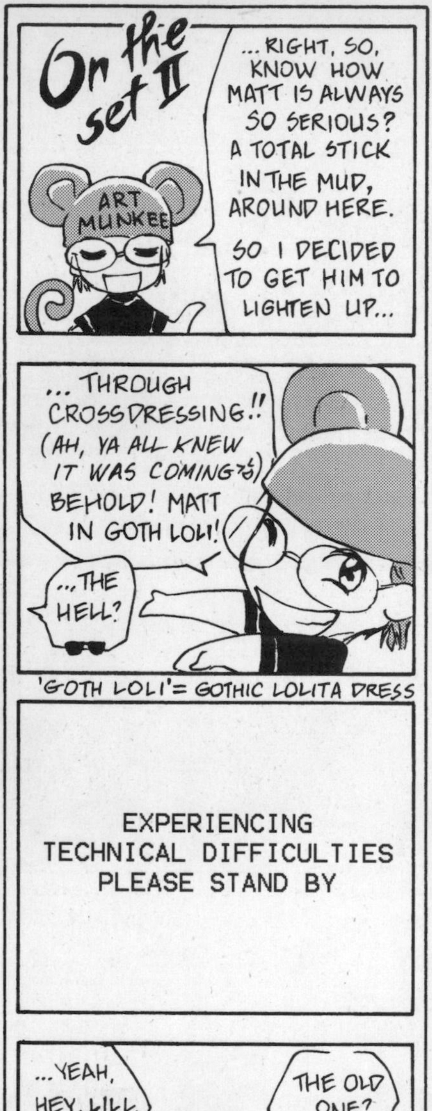
On the set II
...RIGHT, SO, KNOW HOW MATT IS ALWAYS SO SERIOUS? A TOTAL STICK IN THE MUD, AROUND HERE.
SO I DECIDED TO GET HIM TO LIGHTEN UP...
ART MUNKEE
...THROUGH CROSSDRESSING!! (AH, YA ALL KNEW IT WAS COMING) BEHOLD! MATT IN GOTH LOLI!
...THE HELL?
'GOTH LOLI'= GOTHIC LOLITA DRESS
EXPERIENCING TECHNICAL DIFFICULTIES PLEASE STAND BY
...YEAH, HEY, LILL.
THIS BOOK NEEDS A NEW WRITER.
THE OLD ONE?
SHE, UH... ACCIDENTALLY FELL OFF A CLIFF.
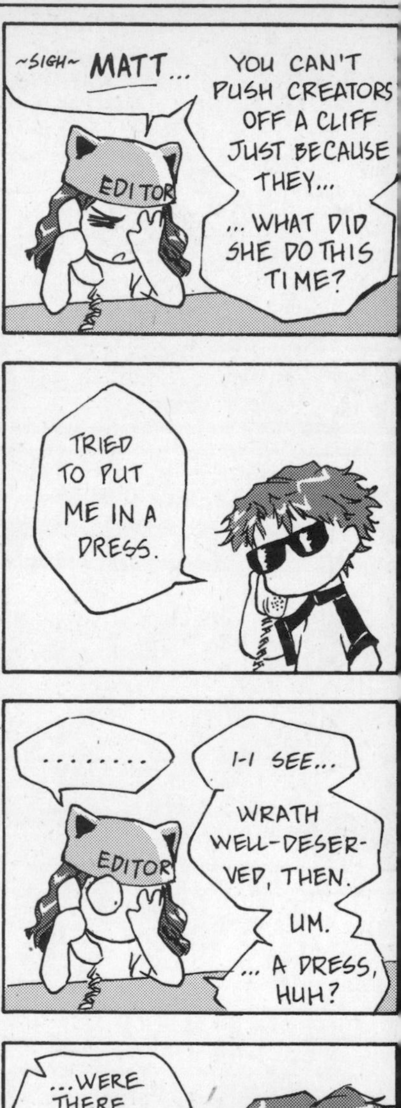
~SIGH~ MATT... YOU CAN'T PUSH CREATORS OFF A CLIFF JUST BECAUSE THEY...
... WHAT DID SHE DO THIS TIME?
EDITOR
TRIED TO PUT ME IN A DRESS.
....
I-I SEE...
WRATH WELL-DESERVED, THEN.
UM.
... A DRESS, HUH?
EDITOR
...WERE THERE PICTURES?
....
CRUSH-

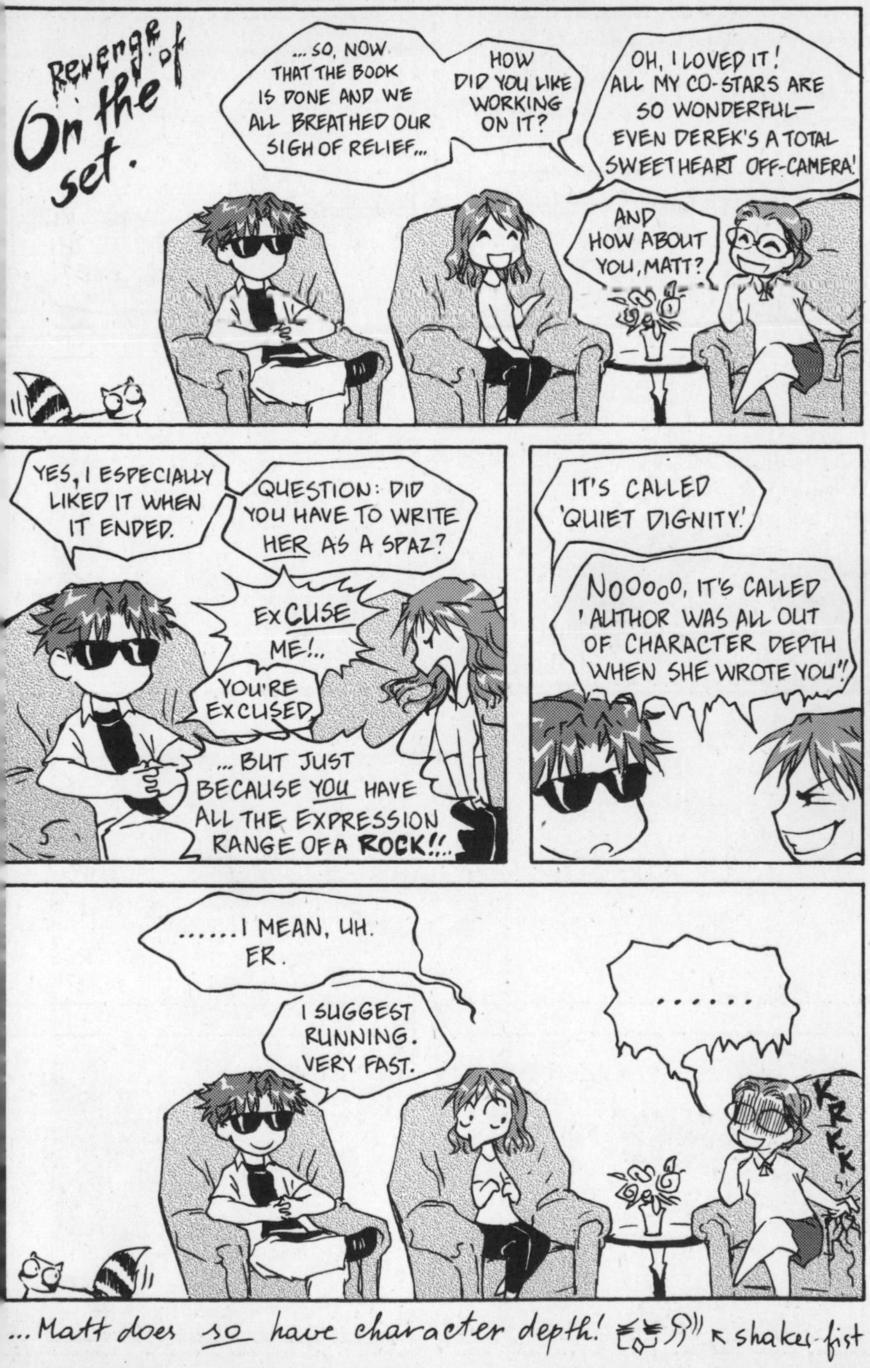
Revenge of On the set.
...SO, NOW THAT THE BOOK IS DONE AND WE ALL BREATHED OUR SIGH OF RELIEF...
HOW DID YOU LIKE WORKING ON IT?
OH, I LOVED IT! ALL MY CO-STARS ARE SO WONDERFUL— EVEN DEREK'S A TOTAL SWEETHEART OFF-CAMERA!
AND HOW ABOUT YOU, MATT?
YES, I ESPECIALLY LIKED IT WHEN IT ENDED.
QUESTION: DID YOU HAVE TO WRITE HER AS A SPAZ?
EXCUSE ME!..
YOU'RE EXCUSED.
...BUT JUST BECAUSE YOU HAVE ALL THE EXPRESSION RANGE OF A ROCK!!..
IT'S CALLED 'QUIET DIGNITY.'
NOOOOO, IT'S CALLED 'AUTHOR WAS ALL OUT OF CHARACTER DEPTH WHEN SHE WROTE YOU'!
......I MEAN, UH. ER.
I SUGGEST RUNNING. VERY FAST.
......
KRKK

...Matt does so have character depth! ↖ shakes-fist

Svetlana Chmakova's

DRAMACON

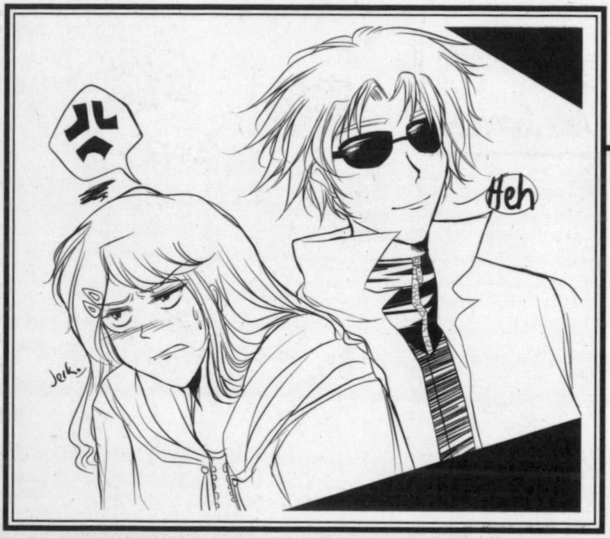
Jerk..
Heh

"BEST INKS!"

Yasmin Saaka (Shady)

OHIO

"BEST MASCOT!"

Andre Richard

CANADA

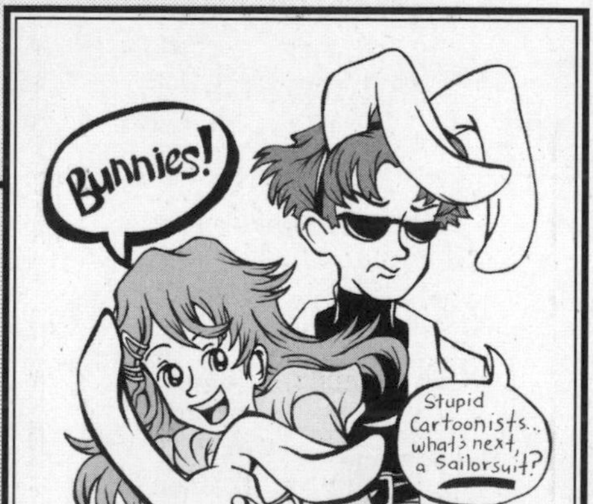
Bunnies!
Stupid Cartoonists.. what's next, a Sailorsuit?
umm.... I just wanted you to sign my book
Drama Con

"BEST EXPRESSIONS!"

Amy Capobres

IDAHO

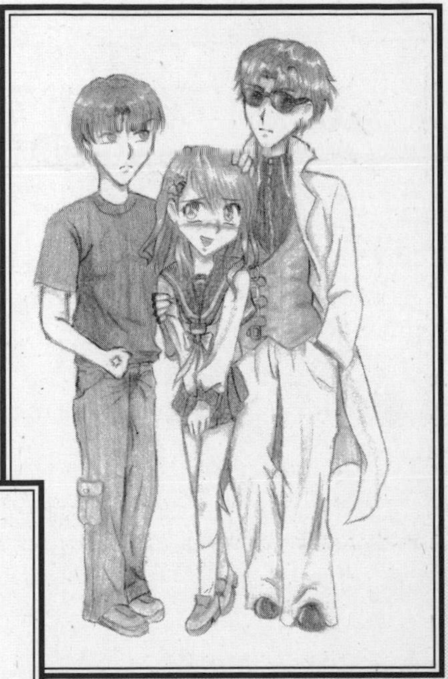

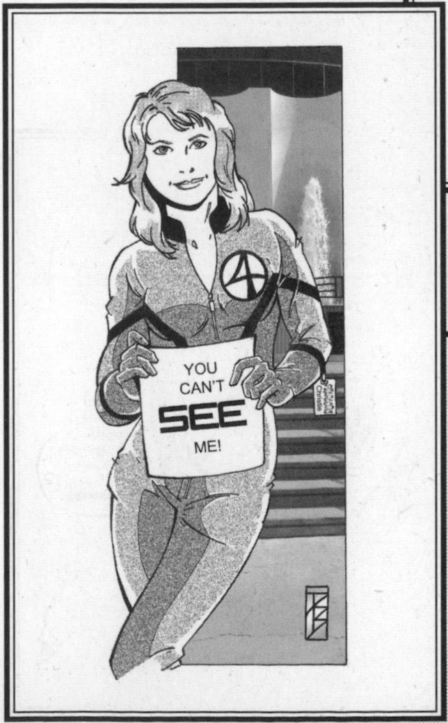
YOU
CAN'T
SEE
ME!

"BEST COSTUME!"

Duanne Barbour

VIRGINIA

"BEST PLUSHIE!"

Roxanne Tran

CALIFORNIA

MATT
DRAMACON
Fall 2005
Fan Art by Dee
You rawk, Svet!!

"BEST BADASS!"

J. Dee Du Puy

MASSACHUSETTS

"BEST EXAMPLE OF WHY EDITORS DON'T DRAW!!"

Lillian Diaz-Przybyl

CALIFORNIA

Tokyopop
vs.
Mangapop!
(Round 1, FIGHT!)

FAN ART

"BEST PUFFY SHIRT!"

Nichol Ashworth

MASSACHUSETTS

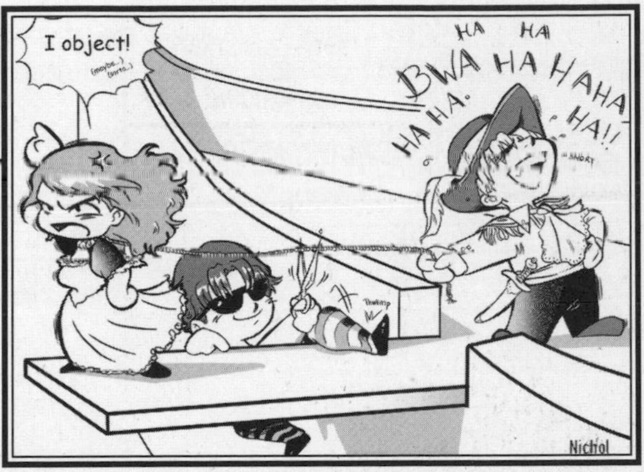
I object!
HA HA
BWA HA HA HAHA HA HA. HA!!
SNORT
Nichol

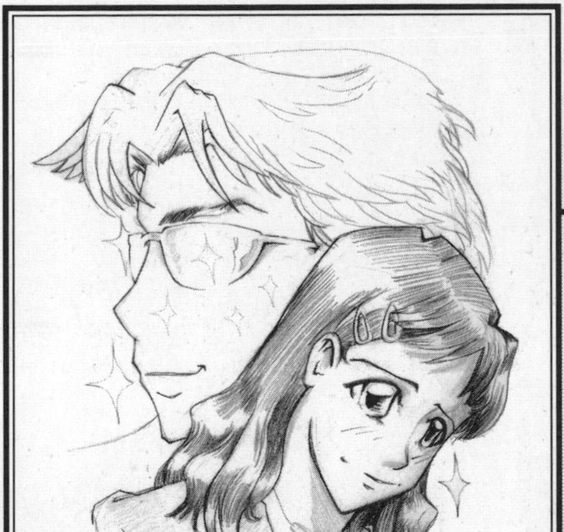

"BEST SHOJO SPRINKLES!"

Hope Donovan

CALIFORNIA

Svetlana Chmakova's

DRAMACON

HI-HO, YA'LL! YOUR FRIENDLY NEIGHBORHOOD EDITOR IS HERE TO PRESENT HOW SVET PUTS US ALL TO SHAME BY BEING TOTALLY AWESOME. THIS IS ONE OF MY FAVORITE PAGES FROM THE BOOK, SO I THOUGHT I'D SHOW IT FROM INITIAL THUMBNAIL TO FINAL FINISHED PAGE.

SHUUUT UP!
FOOOOM
MEN!
YOU!
FLINCH
COUGH COUGH
GRUMBLE
DRAG DRAG

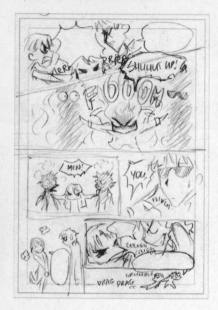

THUMBNAILS:

ANYONE IN EDITORIAL CAN VOUCH THAT GIVEN THE CHANCE, I TEND TO GUSH ABOUT HOW EVEN WITH EMPTY WORD-BALLOONS, SVET'S WORK CAN MAKE ME LAUGH OUT LOUD (OR GET ALL MISTY-EYED), AND THIS PAGE FROM CHAPTER 3 IS A STELLAR EXAMPLE OF THAT. THIS BOOK HAS A LOT OF COMIC MOMENTS, BUT CHRISTIE SPONTANEOUSLY COMBUSTING (AND SINGED DEREK'S WHEEZY REACTION) REALLY CRACKED ME UP. EVEN IN A ROUGH SKETCH, THE ENERGY OF THE SCENE IS RENDERED WITH SKILL AND ENERGY.

FOOOOM
JAB
FLINCH
COUGH COUGH
GRUMBLE
DRAG DRAG

PENCILS:

SINCE THE LAYOUT OF THE PANELS AND POSITIONING OF THE CHARACTERS IS ESTABLISHED IN THE THUMBNAILS STAGE, THE PENCILS MOSTLY INVOLVE CLEANING UP LINES AND RENDERING THE IMAGES WITH MORE DETAIL. NOT THAT IT'S EASY, MIND YOU, AND IF THERE IS SOMETHING IN THE IMAGE THAT LOOKS WONKY (LIKE THE PERSPECTIVE, OR SOME PART OF THE ANATOMY), THE PENCIL STAGE IS WHERE THE EDITOR SHOULD POINT IT OUT SO IT CAN BE FIXED WITHOUT HAVING TO REDO LATER STEPS.

SVETLANA MAKES A MANGA!

GRR
RRR
JAB
FLINCH
COUGH COUGH
GRUMBLE
DRAG DRAG

INKS:

INKING IS AN ART THAT IS UNDERAPPRECIATED BY MANY CASUAL READERS. ESPECIALLY IN MANGA, WHICH IS PRIMARILY IN BLACK AND WHITE, GOOD INKING ADDS A LOT OF THE VOLUME AND DEPTH TO THE IMAGE. I LIKE HIGH-CONTRAST ART, SO I ALWAYS ENJOY SEEING WHERE SVET ADDS IN HEAVY BLACKS, TOO. IT'S FUN TO SEE EVERYTHING STARTING TO LOOK SO POLISHED AND DRAMATIC!

TONES:

FINALLY, DIGITAL TONES ARE ADDED, GIVING THE ART ITS FINISHED LOOK, AND CREATING BOTH REPRESENTATIONS OF COLOR AND, MORE IMPORTANTLY, TEXTURE. EMOTIONAL EFFECTS LIKE THE LIGHTNING BOLTS OR THE LITTLE SHOJO SPARKLES ARE USUALLY DONE THROUGH TONES. PRETTY NEAT, HUH? BEST THING ABOUT BEING AN EDITOR IS THAT INSTEAD OF HAVING TO LEARN HOW TO DRAW YOURSELF, YOU GET TO WATCH OTHER PEOPLE DO IT, AND DO IT SO WELL!

SIGNING OFF!
-LDP

(SEE YOU IN BOOK 2!)

GRR
RRR
FOOOM
JAB
FLINCH
COUGH COUGH
DRAG DRAG
GRUMBLE

TAKUHAI 宅配
WANNA DO TAKUHAI?
THE NEW SIZZLING HOT MANGA MAGAZINE
SIGN UP FOR FREE
WWW.TOKYOPOP.com
Ai from *Princess Ai*
Princess Ai © & TM TOKYOPOP Inc. and Kitty Radio, Inc.

Written by Keith Giffen, comic book pro and English language adapter of *Battle Royale* and *Battle Vixens*.

Join the misadventures of a group of particularly disturbing trick-or-treaters as they go about their macabre business on Halloween night. Blaming the apples they got from the first house of the evening for the bad candy they've been receiving all night, the kids plot revenge on the old bag who handed out the funky fruit. Riotously funny and always wickedly shocking— who doesn't *love* Halloween?

OT
OLDER TEEN
AGE 16+

Preview the manga at:
www.TOKYOPOP.com/iluvhalloween

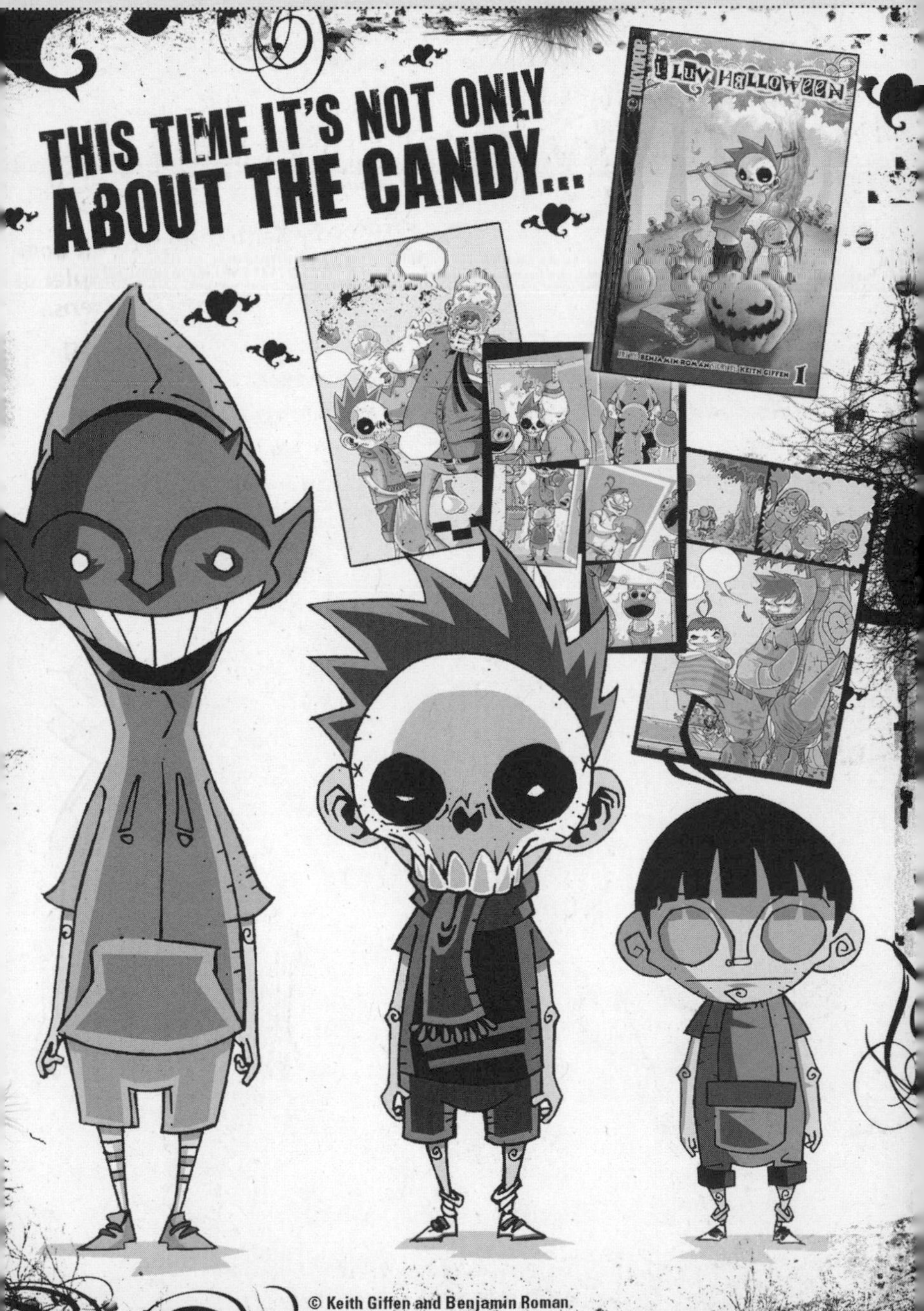
THIS TIME IT'S NOT ONLY
ABOUT THE CANDY...
I LUV HALLOWEEN
BENJAMIN ROMAN
KEITH GIFFEN
1

SAMURAI CHAMPLOO

BY MASARU GOTSUBO AND MANGLOBE

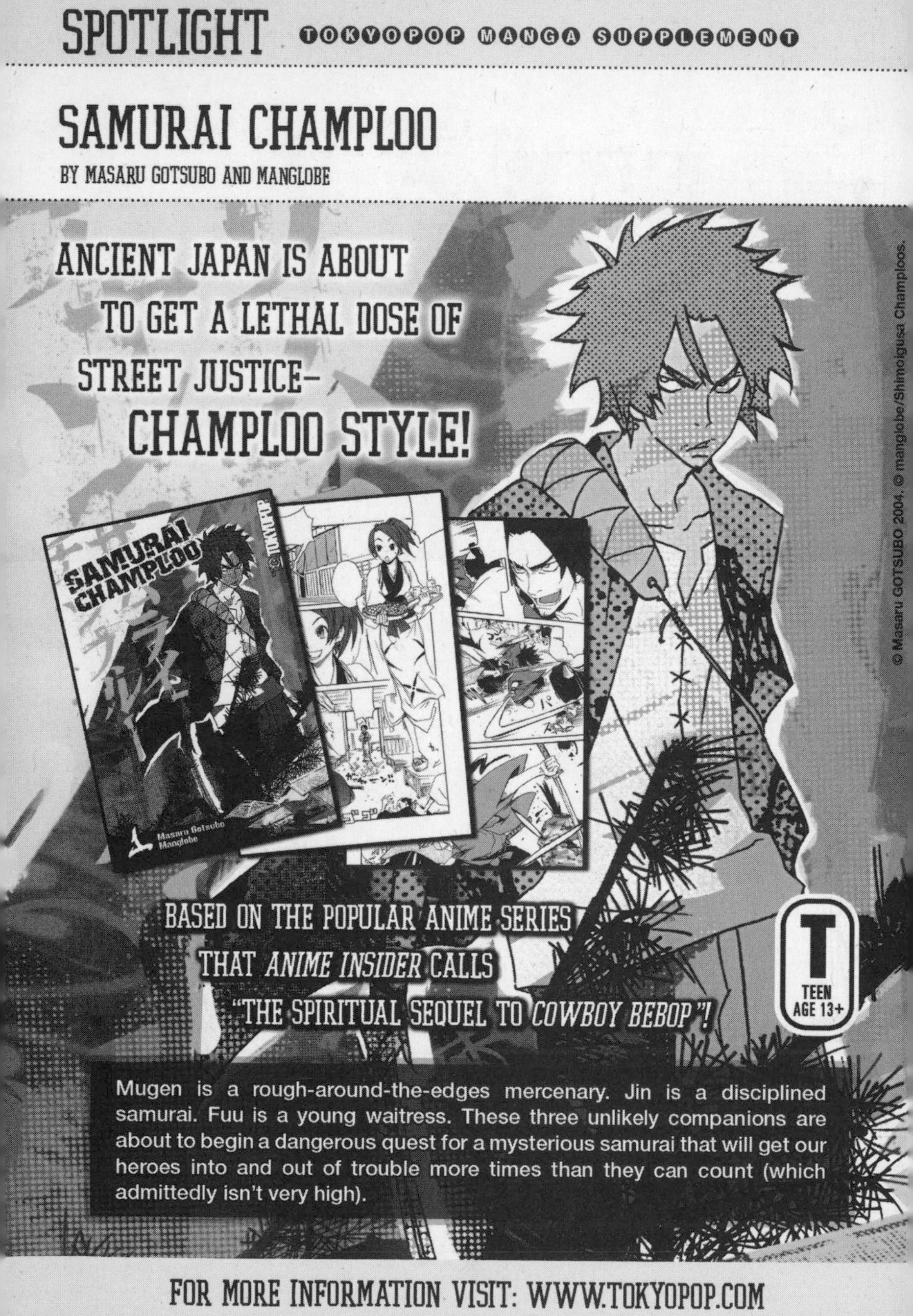
ANCIENT JAPAN IS ABOUT TO GET A LETHAL DOSE OF STREET JUSTICE— CHAMPLOO STYLE!
SAMURAI CHAMPLOO
TOKYOPOP
Masaru Gotsubo
Manglobe
BASED ON THE POPULAR ANIME SERIES THAT *ANIME INSIDER* CALLS "THE SPIRITUAL SEQUEL TO *COWBOY BEBOP*"!
T
TEEN AGE 13+
© Masaru GOTSUBO 2004. © manglobe/Shimoigusa Champloos.
Mugen is a rough-around-the-edges mercenary. Jin is a disciplined samurai. Fuu is a young waitress. These three unlikely companions are about to begin a dangerous quest for a mysterious samurai that will get our heroes into and out of trouble more times than they can count (which admittedly isn't very high).

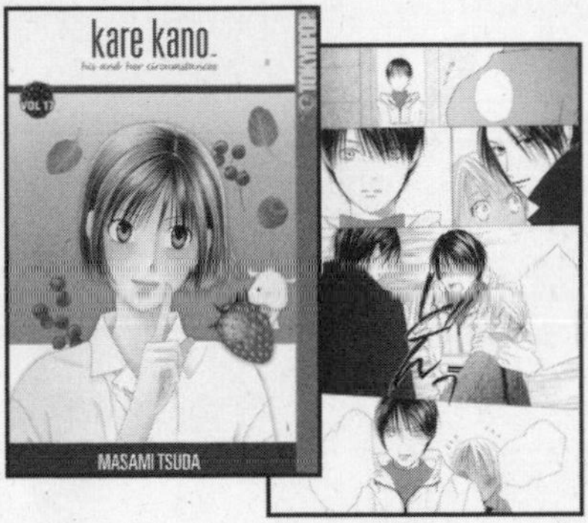
kare kano.
his and her circumstances
VOL 17
MASAMI TSUDA

BY MASAMI TSUDA

KARE KANO

Kare Kano has a fan following for a reason: believable, well-developed characters. Of course, the art is phenomenal, ranging from sugary sweet to lightning-bolt powerful. But above all, Masami Tsuda's refreshing concept—a high school king and queen decide once and for all to be honest with each other (and more importantly, themselves)—succeeds because Tsuda-sensei allows us to know her characters as well as she does. Far from being your typical high school shojo, *Kare Kano* delves deep into the psychology of what would normally just be protagonists, antagonists and supporting cast to create a satisfying journey that is far more than the sum of its parts.

~Carol Fox, Editor

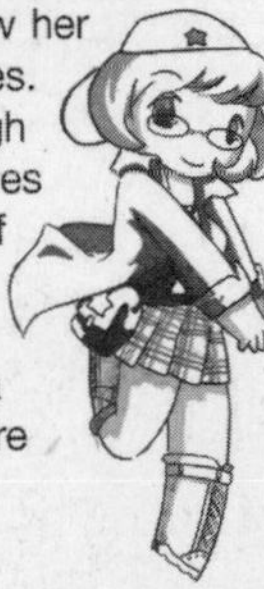

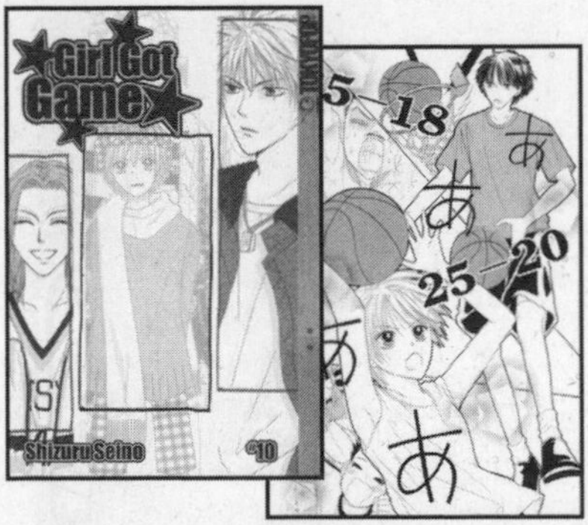
Girl Got Game
Shizuru Seino
#10

BY SHIZURU SEINO

GIRL GOT GAME

There's a fair amount of cross-dressing shojo sports manga out there (no, really), but *Girl Got Game* really sets itself apart by having an unusually charming and very funny story. The art style is light and fun, and Kyo spazzing out always cracks me up. The author throws in a lot of great plot twists, and the great side characters help to make the story just that much more special. Sadly, we're coming up on the final volume, but I give this series credit for not letting the romance drag out unnecessarily or endlessly revisiting the same dilemmas. I'm really looking forward to seeing how the series wraps up!

~Lillian M. Diaz-Przybyl, Jr. Editor

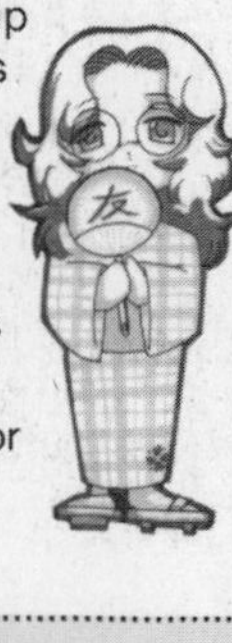

REBIRTH

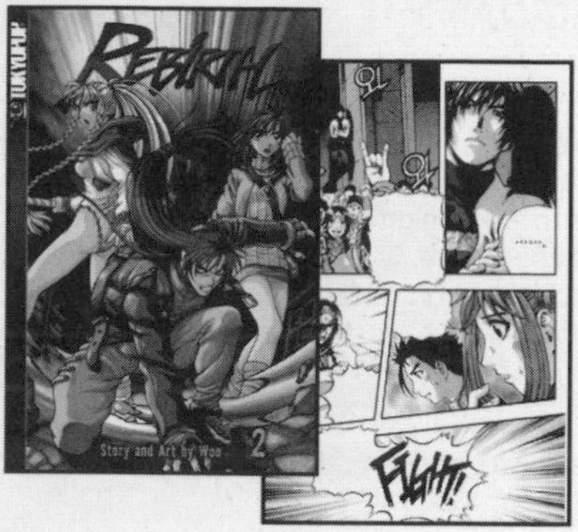
REBIRTH
TOKYOPOP
Story and Art by Woo
2
FIGHT!

BY WOO

Every manga fan has their "first love." For me, that book is *Rebirth*. I've worked on this series in one fashion or another since its debut, and this epic, action-packed vampire tale has never yet let me down. *Rebirth* is a book that defies expectations as well as first impressions. Yes, it's got the dark, brooding vampire antihero. And, sure, there's lots of bloodshed and tight-bodied maidens in peril. But creator Woo has interwoven an enthralling tale of revenge and redemption that, at its heart, is a truly heartbreaking tragedy. Were you a fan of TV's *Angel*? Do you read Anne Rice? Well, my friend, *Rebirth* is for you!

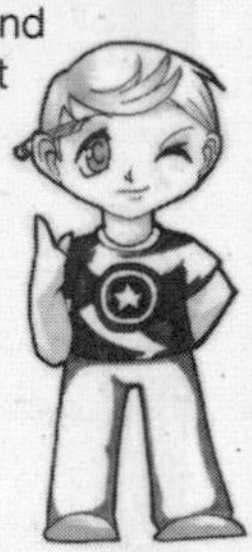

~Bryce P. Coleman, Editor

TRAMPS LIKE US

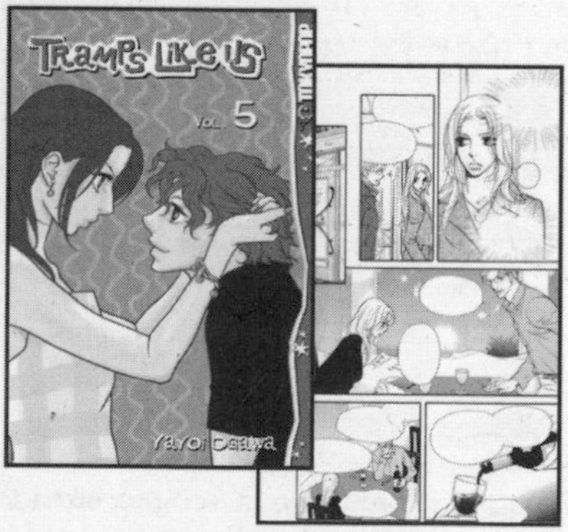
Tramps Like Us
VOL. 5
TOKYOPOP
Yayoi Ogawa

BY YAYOI OGAWA

Thrillingly erotic but relentlessly realistic, *Tramps Like Us* turns gender stereotypes on their head. Sumire Iwaya, a beautiful and busy news exec, is disappointed by the men in her life. So she takes in a gorgeous young boy and makes him her pet. As a man, am I offended? Not really. Actually, I find it really sweet. Sumire is no wide-eyed, skirted, young manga vixen. She's tall, womanly, with a wide mouth and serious, appraising eyes. Momo is cute as a puppy one minute, graceful and petite the next. But the book only indulges the fantasy aspect partway. The abnormal situation gets awkward and even burdensome. I love it. And the tone Carol Fox sets in the English adaptation is one of the best around.

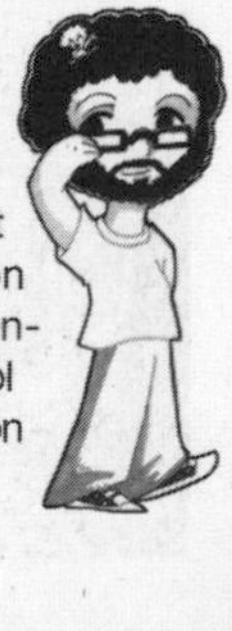

~Luis Reyes, Editor